The FRENCH COLLECTOR

Journal and Letters of Théodore Leschenault,
Botanist of the Baudin Expedition

The Charles and Joy Staples South West Region Publications Fund was established in 1984 on the basis of a generous donation to The University of Western Australia by Charles and Joy Staples.

The purpose of the Fund is to highlight all aspects of the South West region of Western Australia, a geographical area much loved by Charles and Joy Staples, so as to assist the people of the South West region and those in government and private organisations concerned with South West projects to appreciate the needs and possibilities of the region in the widest possible historical perspective. The fund is administered by a committee whose aims are to make possible the publication by UWA Publishing of research and writing in any discipline relevant to the South West region.

Charles and Joy Staples South West Region Publications Fund titles

1987
A Tribute to the Group Settlers
Philip E. M. Blond

1992
For Their Own Good: Aborigines and Government in the Southwest of Western Australia, 1900–1940
Anna Haebich

1993
Portraits of the South West
B. K. de Garis

A Guide to Sources for the History of South Western Australia
Compiled by Ronald Richards

1994
Jardee: The Mill That Cheated Time
Doreen Owens

1995
Dearest Isabella: Life and Letters of Isabella Ferguson, 1819–1910
Prue Joske

Blacklegs: The Scottish Colliery Strike of 1911 Bill Latter

1997
Barefoot in the Creek: A Group Settlement Childhood in Margaret River L. C. Burton

Ritualist on a Tricycle: Frederick Goldsmith, Church, Nationalism and Society in Western Australia
Colin Holden

Western Australia as it is Today, 1906 Leopoldo Zunini, Royal Consul of Italy, edited and translated by Richard Bosworth and Margot Melia

2002
The South West from Dawn till Dusk Rob Olver

2003
Contested Country: A History of the Northcliffe Area, Western Australia
Patricia Crawford and Ian Crawford

2004
Orchard and Mill: The Story of Bill Lee, South-West Pioneer
Lyn Adams

2005
Richard Spencer: Napoleonic War Naval Hero and Australian Pioneer
Gwen Chessell

2006
A Story to Tell (reprinted 2012)
Laurel Nannup

2008
Alexander Collie: Colonial Surgeon, Naturalist and Explorer
Gwen Chessell

The Zealous Conservator: A Life of Charles Lane Poole
John Dargavel

2009
"It's Still in My Heart, This is My Country": The Single Noongar Claim History South West Aboriginal Land and Sea Council, John Host with Chris Owen

Shaking Hands on the Fringe: Negotiating the Aboriginal World at King George's Sound
Tiffany Shellam

2011
Noongar Mambara Bakitj and *Mamang*
Kim Scott and Wirlomin Noongar Language and Stories Project

Guy Grey-Smith: Life Force
Andrew Gaynor

2013
Dwoort Baal Kaat and *Yira Boornak Nyininy*
Kim Scott and Wirlomin Noongar Language and Stories Project

2014
A Boy's Short Life: The Story of Warren Braedon/Louis Johnson
Anna Haebich and Steve Mickler

Plant Life on the Sandplains: A Global Biodiversity Hotspot
Hans Lambers

Fire and Hearth (revised facsimile edition) Sylvia Hallam

2015
Running Out? Water in Western Australia Ruth Morgan

A Journey Travelled: Aboriginal–European Relations at Albany and Surrounding Regions from First Colonial Contact to 1926
Murray Arnold

The Southwest: Australia's Biodiversity Hotspot
Victoria Laurie

Invisible Country: South-West Australia: Understanding a Landscape Bill Bunbury

2016
Noongar Bush Medicine: Medicinal Plants of the South-West of Western Australia
Vivienne Hansen and John Horsfall

2017
Never Again: Reflections on Environmental Responsibility After Roe 8
Edited by Andrea Gaynor, Peter Newman and Philip Jennings

Ngaawily Nop and *Noorn*
Kim Scott and Wirlomin Noongar Language and Stories Project

2018
Dancing in Shadows: Histories of Nyungar Performance
Anna Haebich

2019
Refuge Richard Rossiter

That Was My Home: Voices from the Noongar Camps in Fremantle and the Western Suburbs
Denise Cook

The FRENCH COLLECTOR

Journal and Letters of Théodore Leschenault,
Botanist of the Baudin Expedition

Translated with an
Introduction and
Notes by

Paul Gibbard

UWA PUBLISHING

First published in 2023 by
UWA Publishing
Crawley, Western Australia 6009
www.uwap.uwa.edu.au

UWAP is an imprint of UWA Publishing
a division of The University of Western Australia

This book is copyright. Apart from any fair dealing for the purpose of private study, research, criticism or review, as permitted under the *Copyright Act 1968*, no part may be reproduced by any process without written permission. Enquiries should be made to the publisher.

Copyright © Paul Gibbard 2023

The moral right of the author has been asserted.

ISBN: 978-1-76080-216-5

 A catalogue record for this book is available from the National Library of Australia

Cover design by Sarah Warren
Typeset in 12 point Bembo Book
Printed by Lightning Source

 uwapublishing

For my parents

Contents

Acknowledgements	ix
Introduction	1
A Lost Manuscript	1
An Unexpected Posting	4
Early Life and Family	9
Revolution and Imprisonment	15
The Expedition to Australia	21
The Journal	29
Legacy	41
Translator's Note	47
A Chronology of Théodore Leschenault	49
A Chronology of the Baudin Expedition	57
Leschenault's Shipmates Mentioned in the Journal	63
Map of Leschenault's Travels, May 1801 – April 1802	72–73
Journal of Théodore Leschenault, 1800–1802	75
Chapter 1: Le Havre to Tenerife	77
Chapter 2: Tenerife to the Isle of France	97
Chapter 3: South-west New Holland to Timor	133
Chapter 4: Timor	155
Chapter 5: Van Diemen's Land and Western Port	199
Appendix: A Note on the Macpas, a Tribe from the Interior of Africa; Information about Madagascar	231
Portrait of Théodore Leschenault by Charles-Alexandre Lesueur	237

Contents

Selected Letters — 239

  Introduction — 241

  1. Théodore Leschenault probably to Antoine-Laurent de Jussieu, undated (before mid-September 1800) — 242

  2. Pierre-Alexandre-Laurent Forfait to Théodore Leschenault, 27 Fructidor, Year VIII [14 September 1800] — 246

  3. Théodore Leschenault to Antoine-Laurent de Jussieu, 5 Vendémiaire, Year IX [27 September 1800] — 248

  4. Théodore Leschenault to Antoine-Laurent de Jussieu, undated (c. 16 October 1800) — 249

  5. Théodore Leschenault to Robert Brown, undated (c. 17 May 1802) — 251

  6. Théodore Leschenault to Antoine-Laurent de Jussieu, 20 Brumaire, Year XI [11 November 1802] — 253

  7. Samuel Leschenault to Antoine-Laurent de Jussieu, 4 Messidor, Year XI [23 June 1803] — 259

  8. Théodore Leschenault to Antoine-Laurent de Jussieu, 17 July 1807 — 261

  9. Théodore Leschenault to the directors of the Muséum d'histoire naturelle, 4 November 1807 — 264

  10. Théodore Leschenault to Jean-Pierre Bachasson, comte de Montalivet, 7 November 1813 — 266

  11. Théodore Leschenault to Robert Brown, 11 July 1814 — 268

Notes — 273

Bibliography — 307

Index of Scientific Names — 321

General Index — 325

Acknowledgements

This book was begun as part of the Baudin Legacy Project funded by an Australian Research Council (ARC) Discovery Project grant. I am very grateful to the directors of that project, Jean Fornasiero, Margaret Sankey and John West-Sooby, for inviting me to translate Leschenault's journal.

I would also like to thank François-Henri and Odile d'Hotelans Leschenault du Villard for giving me generous access to family materials relating to Théodore Leschenault in Paris and Chalon-sur-Saône, and for their hospitality. I would also like to acknowledge the late Henry Leschenault du Villard (1915–2017), with whom I spoke briefly and who did much to preserve the botanist's legacy.

I was in Paris in early March 2020 when the Covid-19 outbreak cut short a research trip I was taking and I am extremely grateful to Brigitte Schmausch, conservator at the Archives nationales in Paris, who supplied me with a copy of the recently acquired holograph manuscript of the Leschenault journal, along with additional information. I am also indebted to Michel Jangoux for sharing his knowledge about Leschenault over the years and for his hospitality in Brussels. I am grateful to Sarah Warren for designing the cover of this book and drawing the map of Leschenault's travels and would like to thank the following people for the help and advice they have given me: Jean-Marc Argentin, Gabrielle Baglione, Roz Bluett, Sylvie Brassard, Paul Doughty, Claude Elly, Andrew Endrey, Jean-Renaud Geoffroy, Rosemary Gibbard, Yasmin Haskell, Stephen Hopper, Brenda Larsen, David Mabberley, Ibirahim Njoya, Erica Persak and Gillian Pink.

I am grateful to Terri-ann White, former director of University of Western Australia Publishing, for commissioning this book, to Kate Pickard, its publishing manager, for her help in getting this book to press, and to Melanie Dankel for copy-editing the text.

I would also like to express my thanks to staff at the following institutions: the Archives nationales de France, the Bibliothèque nationale de France, the Bibliothèque centrale at the Muséum national d'histoire

ACKNOWLEDGEMENTS

naturelle, the Bibliothèque Mazarine, the Bibliothèque de l'Institut de France, all in Paris; the Muséum d'histoire naturelle, Le Havre; the Archives municipales, Chalon-sur-Saône; the Archives départementales de Saône-et-Loire, Mâcon; the British Library; the Natural History Museum, London; the Reid Library at the University of Western Australia; the State Library of Western Australia; and the State Library of New South Wales.

I would also like to thank the ARC for supporting my initial translation work on the journal, the ARC Centre of Excellence for the History of Emotions for funding some of my research travel, and the University of Western Australia for granting me study leave to work on this book.

Introduction

A Lost Manuscript

On 3 December 2016, a manuscript written over two centuries earlier – and long thought lost – was put up for sale by the auction house of Geoffroy-Bequet in the town of Royan on the French Atlantic coast. The auctioneers indicated a guide price of €4000 to €6000 euros for this 'exceptional' handwritten account by the botanist Théodore Leschenault of his journey to Australia with the expedition of Nicolas Baudin in the years 1800 to 1802.[1] The slim notebook, which had the words *Journal particulier* (Private journal) inked on its fragile covers and contained 132 pages of neat handwriting, attracted interest from around the world. Once the auction got under way, the price rose quickly beyond the estimate in the catalogue and the bidding developed into a contest between just two parties. It came to a close at €110,000 – but the journal was never delivered to the winning bidder. The French government took the view that, although the manuscript had been in private hands for over 200 years, it was a public document. According to the *Code du patrimoine* (Heritage Law) of France, all papers that 'originate in the activities of the State' are classed as belonging inalienably to the public archive.[2] The government could classify Leschenault's journal as just such a document for two reasons: firstly, Leschenault had travelled on the expedition as a salaried employee of the Ministry for the Navy and Colonies; and, secondly, Pierre Forfait, the head of the ministry, had stipulated that all journals written by the naturalists during the voyage were to remain government property.

He had made this point explicitly in the instructions he gave Baudin in September 1800:

> Before you leave, advise these people [the naturalists] on my behalf that it is expressly forbidden for them [...] to pass on to others the journals they keep [...]. The Republic is paying all the expedition's expenses, and it is she alone who must reap the rewards [...]. Inform them that anyone who infringes this reasonable injunction will be dealt with harshly and advise them that nobody is permitted [...] to send back to Europe any account that may deprive the government of its property rights over the products of the voyage. In accordance with these orders, I instruct you, when you are on the point of re-entering our ports, to collect all the journals written aboard the two corvettes and to allow no one to go ashore before you are certain that each has fulfilled his duty in this respect.[3]

On previous government expeditions, naturalists had sometimes tried to claim their journals and collections as their own private property; Forfait wished to avoid a repetition of any such disputes. When Leschenault's journal came up for auction in 2016, the government asserted that it ought to have been deposited with the Ministry for the Navy and Colonies after the expedition's return to France and should never have passed into private hands. The government entered into negotiations with the auction house and in mid-2018 the journal was lodged with the Archives nationales de France (National Archives of France) in Paris.

Where had the journal been in the intervening 200 years? As the final page of the manuscript indicates, Leschenault finished writing up his journal in Sydney on 2 September 1802 (he gives the date as '15 Fructidor, Year X', using the French republican calendar). The journal was sent from New South Wales to France aboard one of the ships of the expedition, the *Naturaliste*, which left Port Jackson in November 1802, and arrived in Le Havre nearly seven months later, in June 1803. Leschenault requested that the journal be sent on to Antoine-Laurent de Jussieu, a professor of botany at the Muséum d'histoire naturelle (Natural History Museum) in Paris.[4] It was Jussieu, one of France's leading botanists, who had helped Leschenault to obtain his position on the Baudin expedition. After the professor had finished reading it, Leschenault asked that it be forwarded to his mother, Marguerite, who lived in Chalon-sur-Saône, the middle-sized Burgundian town and river port where he and his siblings had grown up.[5] After the journal reached the family in Chalon, it seems that Leschenault's younger brother, Samuel, made a copy of chapters 3 to 5, which dealt with the Australian and Timorese sections of the journey, and sent this partial copy to the Ministry for the Navy and Colonies in Paris. Presumably the brothers felt that by supplying the ministry with the text of this section of the journal they were fulfilling the spirit of Forfait's official instructions. This copy was eventually deposited in the Archives nationales, along with many other documents relating to the expedition. For decades this copy of the journal was the only version known to historians.

The exact path taken by the original journal from Chalon in around 1803 to the auction house in Royan in 2016 remains something of a mystery. The journal may have been returned by Marguerite and Samuel to Théodore after his arrival back in France in 1807 – he would certainly have found it useful to refer to while writing up his article, 'Note on the Vegetation of New Holland', which was published in 1811. Did the journal pass through the hands of François Péron, who quoted from it in the first volume of the official account of the voyage, published in 1807?[6] In fact, it seems more likely that Péron was lent Samuel's copy by the ministry. When Théodore died childless in Paris in 1826 at the age of 52, a victim of 'apoplexy' (or stroke), having only recently retired as a government naturalist, the original journal perhaps passed to Samuel, the chief beneficiary of his will. Samuel died in Paris in 1854, his only known child Stéphanie (1811–1830) having pre-deceased him. The journal might subsequently have found its way to the brothers' first cousin once removed, Jean-Baptiste-Antoine Leschenault (1775–1859), at whose château, Le Villard, north-west of Chalon, various other items from Théodore's travels finished up during the nineteenth century. We do not know how long the journal remained in the hands of the Leschenaults: whether it was privately sold or given as a gift outside the family or whether it remained for a period in the possession of the Leschenault du Villard family, the last of whom, Henry, great-grandson of Jean-Baptiste-Antoine, died in Tarbes in 2017 at the age of 102.[7]

The present translation makes the complete text of Leschenault's journal available to readers for the first time. Its first two chapters, which were previously unknown to historians, record Leschenault's thoughts and observations as he travels from Paris to Le Havre and on to Tenerife and the Isle of France (modern-day Mauritius) between October 1800 and April 1801. These are followed by the three chapters, already known from Samuel's copy, that relate his experiences in New Holland (western Australia), Timor, Van Diemen's Land and southern New South Wales (present-day Victoria) between May 1801 and September 1802. Translations of eleven letters from the period 1800 to 1814 are also provided, offering additional perspectives on Leschenault's involvement in the expedition.

An Unexpected Posting

When Théodore Leschenault applied to join the Baudin expedition as a botanist in 1800, he could not have felt any great certainty that he would be selected. He was then aged 26 and had no experience of professional collecting. Three other candidates in contention had more impressive qualifications. André Michaux, who was then 54, had already undertaken a long plant-collecting trip to the Middle East and had worked for over a decade as a French government botanist based in the United States. Antoine Ledru, aged 39, had botanised on Baudin's previous expedition to the West Indies on the *Belle Angélique*. Jacques Delisse, aged 27, had experience working as a pharmacist and had studied botany under René

Louiche Desfontaines and chemistry under the comte de Fourcroy in Paris. In his application letter, Leschenault was quite frank about his deficiencies, admitting that his knowledge of botany was only 'modest'. Nevertheless, he explained at length how he would go about examining and describing any new plant he encountered and pointed out that he had some skill in drawing and was a fluent writer. He also offered the confident assertion: 'I [...] have an honest nature, the composure and courage to endure the trials of a long and difficult voyage, and a burning desire to learn.'[8] Jussieu, who was the president of the commission established by the Institut national de France to organise the scientific side of the expedition, offered a measured assessment of the candidate:

> Citizen Leschenault, a student of the Museum, has developed an interest in botany these past few years and has sufficient expertise to name a certain number of plants without having recourse to books and can identify most of the genera that he does not know with the help of books. He has also acquired the ability to dry plants properly and draw them quite accurately and everything seems to indicate that he is the product of a good upbringing.[9]

Leschenault would have hoped at best to obtain the position of assistant botanist on the voyage. However, after Ledru resigned from the expedition, Leschenault received a letter in September 1800 from the Ministry for the Navy and Colonies appointing him to the position of senior botanist. Preferred ahead of Delisse, he was awarded the same rank as the much more experienced Michaux. Leschenault wrote to thank Jussieu, describing the 'great surprise' he felt on learning that he was 'to be classed as a head [botanist] rather than an assistant'. And in a letter written in Sydney two years later, he acknowledged to Jussieu how lucky he felt to have been selected for the voyage: 'I am highly conscious of the obligation I owe you for placing your trust in me and selecting me ahead of several others.'[10]

Leschenault received his appointment six years after being released from prison in 1794. He had spent more than six months incarcerated with his father and elder brother in a former convent in Chalon during the Terror, after they had been identified as 'enemies of freedom' by the local Committee of Surveillance. His family had close ties to the local nobility, which made them suspect at a time when the revolutionary government was fighting enemies within and outside France.

It is not entirely clear how Leschenault spent the years between 1794 and 1800 and made the transition from prisoner of the Revolution to government botanist. At some point after his release from prison, Leschenault found work in the transportation industry. When he married in April 1796, he was working at a staging post in Saint-Léger-sur-Dheune, a town of around 900 inhabitants located 15 kilometres to the north-west of Chalon on the main coach road between Paris and Lyon. Leschenault may have worked in both civilian and military logistics: he later suggested that during the 'stormy years of the Revolution' he worked in 'different branches of administration',[11] while his nephew Eugène Deschamps reported that his uncle had worked in the 'administration of military transportation'.[12] There was no shortage of work in organising army transport and supply chains in the mid-1790s as the French fought on multiple fronts against the Austrians, Prussians, British and Spanish in the War of the First Coalition. According to Deschamps, Leschenault filled all his spare moments outside work with the study of natural history. At the time of his marriage to Marguerite Bonin, who was the 16-year-old daughter of a Chalon merchant, he was financially very well-off: according to a departmental marriage register, his property was valued at nearly 80,000 francs.[13] The Leschenault family had evidently managed to retain most of their property holdings during the most radical period of the Revolution.

Théodore's name apparently features on the list of students who enrolled at the École centrale de santé (Central School of Health) in Paris in 1796.[14] Whether he took up this position as a medical student is unclear. His marriage did not endure, and he moved to Paris without his wife at some point in the next few years. Deschamps suggests that he only travelled to the capital later, in June 1799, in order to sort out some family matters that had arisen after his father Claude-Théodore died, in Paris, at the end of 1798. (In fact Claude-Théodore died on 30 August 1797.) It was on this trip, according to Deschamps, that his uncle 'made contact with several distinguished savants'.[15] All we know with certainty is that by mid-1800, Leschenault was living in Paris and had come to the attention of Jussieu at the Muséum d'histoire naturelle. He may have been introduced to Jussieu by two of his cousins from Chalon, Marc-Antoine-Joseph and Pierre-Jacques Leschenault, who certainly did study medicine in Paris in the late-1790s. First-year students took the subject *materia medica,* in which they learned about the medicinal properties of plants from museum staff. Alternatively, Leschenault may have introduced himself to Jussieu by letter or encountered him at public lectures or the regular public plant-collecting trips that Jussieu led to places such as the Bois de Boulogne as part of the museum's educational programme.[16]

There are obvious reasons why the expedition to Australia might have appealed to Leschenault, with the opportunity it offered to travel the world and study plants little known to Europeans. However, Abel Jeandet, a distant relative of the botanist, offers an alternative explanation in a biographical sketch published in 1883: he reports a rumour that Leschenault sailed across the oceans in order to 'escape from storms at home'.[17] By the time Leschenault set out from Le Havre aboard the *Géographe* though, his marriage had in fact been dissolved. The revolutionary government had legalised divorce by a decree of 20 September 1792; it enabled spouses to separate either by mutual consent or if one spouse alleged an 'incompatibility of temperament and character'. Marguerite took the latter course, registering her petition on 31 August 1799; she did not have to produce evidence of incompatibility, but was required to convene three meetings of their close family members (after one, three and six months) in an attempt to bring about a reconciliation.[18] Théodore did not appear at any of these meetings and the divorce was finalised on 8 October 1800. Leschenault makes no mention of Marguerite in his journal. In fact, she seems far from his thoughts: on 16 October 1800, for example, he records how some 'very pretty women' came aboard the *Géographe* in port and observes:

> I would have been greatly delighted if one of the ladies who came into my cabin had decided to remain for the entire voyage. Sixteen years of age, large black eyes; with such a girl I might banish any periods of tedium. (p. 79)

In a letter copied into the early pages of his journal, Leschenault offers some thoughts on why he wished to participate in the expedition:

> I hope to gain some credit from it and prepare the ground for all the satisfactions of heart and mind in later life – those supreme delights that are independent of the events that occur in life. (p. 80)

He saw the voyage as an opportunity to enhance his reputation, refine his sensibility and develop his intellect. And it did indeed lay the grounds for his later professional advancement. Thanks to the experience he gained in the Antipodes, he was able to make a career for himself as a government botanist in an era when such positions were extremely rare. He had to scramble around for work in the years immediately following his return to France from the southern hemisphere,[19] but his prospects improved with the restoration of the monarchy, and in 1816 he was sent to the newly recovered French colony of Pondicherry as *naturaliste du roi* (naturalist to the new king Louis XVIII). After his return from India, he set out on a government mission to Brazil, French Guiana and Surinam in 1823. Through his travels and writings, his collecting work and collaborations, he became well known in European scientific circles. To make his career, however, he had had to leave behind his family and his provincial home.

INTRODUCTION

Early Life and Family

Leschenault was born in Chalon at quarter past midnight on 13 November 1773, as the baptismal register of the parish of Saint-Vincent records. He was given a mouthful of Christian names: 'Jean Baptiste Louis Claude Théodore', with the first two names added in the margin of the register, perhaps as a priestly correction or a parental afterthought. The names 'Claude Théodore' were those by which his father went, 'Louis' was the name of the reigning king, while 'Jean Baptiste' may have been intended to honour his absent godfather (a well-placed tax official in Paris)[20] along with several forebears (and the biblical prophet John the Baptist).

Naming carried a significance within the Leschenault family that was allied to its ambition. Théodore's father, Claude-Théodore Leschenault, who descended from a line of Burgundian surgeons, was intent on raising his family from its position in the middle class into the nobility. With this goal in mind, he had gone about acquiring several marks of noble standing. In 1764, he had married a daughter of the nobility, Dame Marguerite Gauthier, whose father Pierre was designated an *écuyer* (squire), a title denoting the lowest rung on the ladder of French nobility. As a result of his alliance with the Gauthier family, who owned the noble estates of Tournelle and Bays in Savigny-en-Revermont (around 50 kilometres south-east of Chalon), Claude-Théodore began to call himself the *conseigneur* (or 'joint lord') of those estates.[21] He also acquired a noble estate of his own; in 1768 he bought the small fief of Rupt,[22] which gave him the right to call himself the *seigneur de Rupt* (lord of that manor). During the Middle Ages, the purchase of a nobleman's land had elevated the buyer directly into the nobility, but this practice had been brought to an end by Henri III in 1579. For any man aspiring to join the nobility in the seventeenth or eighteenth century, it was still a useful step to acquire the trappings of a fiefdom. In Théodore's baptismal entry, his father's name has an aristocratic sound, *seigneur de Rupt, conseigneur de La Tournelle et des Bays*, although he had not, in fact, been officially admitted to the aristocracy. A Leschenault coat of arms did already exist by this time; it had been registered in 1696 by Claude Leschenault, a lawyer at the Dijon *parlement*, who belonged to a different branch of the family. The heraldic symbols on his shield made reference to a possible origin of the surname, the oak tree or *chêne*: in the upper section of the escutcheon were two green oak trees against a silver background; in the lower, a silver tower against a blue background.[23]

If the Leschenaults of Chalon were to make the leap into the nobility, it would first be necessary for Claude-Théodore to obtain a particular legal position. Since the mid-seventeenth century, it had been possible for lawyers to purchase certain offices from the Crown that could lead to the ennoblement of their family. Service in some offices conferred nobility after 20 years (or death in office); others required two generations of a family to serve for 20 years each. Families ennobled in this way joined the *noblesse de robe* (nobles of the robe), or legal nobility, an additional class of hereditary nobles alongside the *noblesse d'épée* (nobles of the sword), whose rank was associated with military service, and the *noblesse de sang* (nobility of the blood). This social ascent had become possible when Théodore's grandfather changed his profession. All the males in Théodore's direct paternal line, prior to his father, had been surgeons by profession, stretching back four generations into the sixteenth century. His grandfather Jacques Leschenault, born in around 1696, had worked as a surgeon in Saint-Jean-de-Vaux for more than 20 years before moving the short distance to Chalon, where he took up the position of alderman on the town council in 1744. Five years later, Jacques entered the legal ranks, acquiring the position of *procureur du roi* (a judicial officer who represented the king) in the office of the *eaux et forêts* in Chalon (the special court that oversaw rights of usage in the waterways and forests). The role of this court was to resolve disputes that might arise over hunting in the royal forests; the harvesting of wood, nuts, fruits or honey; the use of their soils, rocks and pasturages; and fishing and navigation of the waterways.[24]

Jacques's son, Claude-Théodore, followed him into the law. Born at Saint-Jean-de-Vaux in 1730, Claude-Théodore acquired the position of *procureur du roi* in the courts of Chalon in 1761.[25] He did not work in his father's field of *eaux et forêts*, but rather in the combined institutions of the *châtellenie*, the *bailliage*, the *présidial* and the *chancellerie*. These offices had somewhat different functions. The *châtellenie* and the *bailliage* were both lower courts, with the latter having a broader jurisdiction, while the *présidial* was an appeal court. The *chancellerie* was concerned with preparing documents that derived from royal authority and managed the sales of various rights, privileges and official positions.[26] After working across these offices for a number of years, in 1777 he purchased the position of *secrétaire du roi* (secretary to the king) in the chancellery attached to the *parlement* of Dijon. A *parlement* was a type of superior court rather than a legislative parliament along British lines. The Dijon *parlement* stood above the *bailliage* and *présidial* in the judicial hierarchy. The position of *secrétaire du roi* did not come cheaply: the purchase price for such a position in the provinces was in the order of 70,000 livres.[27] (By way of comparison, the house in central Chalon that Claude-Théodore bought at around this time cost 28,000 livres.) The office of *secrétaire du roi* was highly prized as it conferred nobility in the 'first degree': that is, the family of the office-holder would be ennobled if he served 20 years or died in office. And so, if all went to plan, Claude-Théodore would have expected to join the nobility in 20 years' time, in 1797... Many such office-holders on the path to ennoblement began to use noble titles before they had officially acquired them. It is not surprising then to see Claude-Théodore's name followed by the noble title *écuyer* in the baptismal entry for his daughter Eugénie in 1785.

Théodore therefore spent his early years at the heart of a large, well-connected and ambitious middle-class family. His father owned several large houses in central Chalon, including one at 51 Grande-Rue, purchased in January 1774. Théodore was the fifth child of nine, four of whom died in infancy. At this time Chalon was an affluent town with a population of close to 10,000 people. As the main port above Lyon on the river Saône, it was an important entrepôt for goods such as wine, wheat, hay, wood, sand, stone and iron along the route between northern and south-eastern France. It was also a major legal, administrative and religious centre. Théodore gained useful connections with other wealthy families in the town and, in later years in Paris, drew on support from two of the most celebrated former sons of Chalon: Dominique Vivant-Denon, director of the Louvre, and the inventor Nicéphore Niépce.

Théodore may well have been educated at home by a private tutor, since his father had been a stern critic of the local school. This had formerly been run by the Jesuits, but after the closure of their colleges in 1763, a man named Nicolas Bizouard from Dijon had taken over as the school's principal. In 1770, Claude-Théodore joined the mayor and council in denouncing Bizouard as 'incompetent, ignorant, cantankerous, quarrelsome, deceitful, proud [and] resistant to every decision of the authorities'; the students in the school, they suggested, 'not only learn nothing' but have been 'depraved to the extent that oaths are common in the mouths of all students, even the youngest'.[28] Whether from tutor or schoolmaster, Théodore seems to have acquired a good understanding of Latin during his early years; it is not clear whether his interest in botany also developed at this time.

Most of our information about Théodore's relations with his family derives from a handful of documents written between 1800 and 1825, which all postdate the death of his father in Paris in 1797. They contain many expressions of fondness for his mother and siblings. While feeling homesick in Timor, Théodore wrote in his journal:

> Mother, my brothers, my friends, those of you for whom I primarily write this account: while I am so far away, you are no doubt deeply concerned about what has become of me. But please set your minds at rest. Five thousand leagues from my homeland, I can still feel the warmth of your unwavering affection... Mother...! At this word my soul flies across the intervening distance and I enclose you in a fond embrace. (p. 189)

Soon after his arrival back in France in 1807, he travelled from Paris to Chalon to see his mother. She died two years later in June 1809.

The siblings to whom Théodore seems to have been closest were his younger brother Samuel (born in 1776) and sister Eugénie (born in 1785). Samuel initially made his career in Burgundy, becoming mayor of Saint-Vallerin in 1809 and working as a banker in La Clayette, before moving to Paris. Eugénie married Jacques-Charles Deschamps in Chalon in 1809 and afterwards went to live with her husband in Lyon; it was her son Eugène (born in 1813) who wrote an entry on Théodore for the *Nouvelle Biographie générale* in 1859. Théodore frequently expressed his affections for his siblings in his letters; for instance, as Eugénie's marriage approached in 1809, Théodore made preparations to return to Chalon and asked his brother Samuel to 'embrace her for me and tell her that I love her with all my heart'.[29] Théodore's enduring fondness for Samuel and Eugénie was reflected in the will he wrote in October 1825, some six months before his death, in which he left his estate to Samuel, from which a bequest of 20,000 francs was to be drawn for Eugénie.[30]

Théodore's relations with his eldest brother, Louis-François (born in 1768), and youngest brother, Théodore-César (born in 1779), seem to have been complicated by the financial problems in which these two embroiled themselves. In July 1801, Louis-François, who had been a lay canon in the cathedral chapter of Saint-Vincent before the Revolution, sold the family house in the Grande-Rue for 25,000 livres on behalf of Théodore and himself; at that time Théodore was travelling along the western coast of New Holland. In a letter written to a cousin in 1807, Théodore refers despairingly to his brother's financial problems and mental state:

> I greatly wish that my brother's unfortunate affairs were brought to a close. The only cause of anguish to me on returning to France was to see him in a state I was far from anticipating, as nothing seemed to predict such a disaster when I left. [...] He seems to have given in to despair and is unable to take his own interests in hand. I currently have hopes of finding a position for him, but

if this doesn't eventuate I really don't know what will become of him, as the life he is now leading is very sad and desperate. The sacrifices I am making are the only ones my present position allows.³¹

Louis-François's wife, Marie-Pierrette Coudery (born in 1776), also seems to have caused Théodore anguish when she refused to repay him money he had lent her from his government pension. He was so upset by her behaviour that he declared:

I swear I'll make no further sacrifices for her. I would have made any sacrifices for her to the extent that my circumstances allowed, but she has opened my eyes to the sort of gratitude I should expect.³²

Théodore's youngest sibling, Théodore-César, served in his early twenties as a quartermaster sergeant with the 32nd demi-brigade of the French infantry, a regiment that fought in the Egyptian and Syrian campaign of 1798–1801. In June 1802, Théodore-César sold his half-share in another of the family houses, but also apparently ran into financial difficulties. Théodore reported of him in 1807:

I've seen my youngest brother; he seems happy, content and more sensible. I will also do what I can to be of help to him when I have sorted out my own affairs.³³

Théodore's aunt, Anne Leschenault (1736–1822), was, by contrast, a model of probity. Having joined the Congregation of the Hospitaller Sisters of St Martha in 1756, a religious order that ran the hospital for the poor and sick on the Île Saint-Laurent in Chalon, she was appointed to the position of mother superior in 1787. She managed the hospital during the Revolution, when the sisters were obliged to wear secular clothing, and was still in charge when Théodore returned to France. He referred to her admiringly as *notre bonne tante de l'hôpital* (our worthy aunt at the hospital).³⁴

INTRODUCTION

Revolution and Imprisonment

Théodore was fifteen years old when revolution broke out in the summer of 1789. It would lead to a profound alteration in the fortunes of the Leschenault family, shattering their dream of ennoblement and throwing Claude-Théodore out of his job. The Chalon region, like other parts of France, had experienced economic problems in the preceding years: there had been poor grain harvests, livestock shortages and an overproduction of wine, while trade in iron and textiles along the Saône had declined and taxes had increased. There had also been political turmoil, with the establishment divided by Louis XVI's aborted attempt to reform the *parlements*.[35]

When the king convened a meeting of the Estates-General in Paris to resolve an impasse over new taxes, the three estates (the clergy, the nobility and the commoners) of the *bailliage* of Chalon gathered, as did the other districts of France, to compile their *cahiers de doléances* (lists of grievances) and to elect their representatives. The divisions within Théodore's extended family were clear: Claude-Théodore, as a property owner, was eligible to vote with the commoners; his wife's cousin and his *conseigneur*, Gabriel Gauthier de la Tournelle, was invited to vote with the nobility. As it turned out, the four deputies elected by the commoners all came from the legal fraternity, one being Jean-Joseph Petiot, Claude-Théodore's successor as *procureur du roi* in Chalon.[36]

The meeting of the Estates-General in Paris did not go as planned for the king. When a stalemate developed around voting procedures, the Third Estate broke away from the nobility and the clergy, and on 17 June 1789, declared itself to be the National Assembly, seizing for itself, as William Doyle puts it, 'sovereign power in the name of the nation of France'.[37] As troops gathered around Paris, posing a threat to the continued existence of the Assembly, protesters attempted to seize arms and grain stores, and on 14 July, with the help of deserting soldiers, stormed the Bastille. A new municipal administration took control of Paris, protected by a civil militia. News of the uprising soon reached Chalon and, on 17 July, a volunteer militia formed there and the general council swore loyalty to the National Assembly.

The Leschenaults, whose fortunes were closely bound up with the structures of the *Ancien Régime*, must have viewed these developments with great apprehension. During the Great Fear of late July, rumours spread of armed bands roaming the countryside. Peasants armed themselves, fearing a violent backlash from the nobility, and in some regions launched attacks against manor houses and châteaux. To calm this rural ferment, the National Assembly decided during an all-night sitting on 4 August to abolish feudalism and to scrap noble privileges and the sale of legal offices. Further decrees, damaging to the Leschenaults' interests, followed: in November 1789, the *parlements* were placed on vacation; in June 1790, hereditary nobility and honorific titles were done away with; in August 1790, the *parlements* were abolished all together; and, finally, in July 1793, all feudal dues and rights were annulled, with feudal title deeds to be burned.[38]

The town of Chalon avoided, for the most part, the civil strife that engulfed Paris and western and southern France over the next few years. Until April 1793, the town council was presided over by merchants and lawyers with moderate political leanings who generally managed to maintain food supplies and control public order as war raged, the Republic was declared, and the king was executed. Counter-revolutionary elements in Chalon largely avoided open confrontation. A handful of young aristocrats emigrated to join foreign armies; the main source of opposition lay in the priesthood, who mostly refused to swear the required oath of loyalty to the constitution. Several of Théodore's relatives played minor roles in events affecting the town. His aunt Anne was called as a witness in proceedings held against the reactionary bishop of Chalon, Jean-Baptiste du Chilleau.[39] And, when the Assembly carved up France into 83 new administrative regions or *départements*, one of Théodore's cousins, Marc-Antoine-Joseph Leschenault (father of the doctors), was sent to Paris to lobby the deputies to have Chalon named the *chef-lieu* (capital) of Saône-et-Loire.[40]

The worsening crisis in France during 1793 was to produce serious repercussions for the Leschenault family. Faced by royalist insurrection in the Vendée and foreign invasion, the National Convention, dominated by the radical Montagnard faction, gave extensive powers to the emergency Committee of Public Safety and purged the legislature of the more moderate Girondins. Southern cities, including Bordeaux, Toulouse, Marseille and nearby Lyon, rebelled against Parisian rule over the summer. Chalon, however, with its council controlled by radicals after the local elections in April, sided with the central government. A first phase of arrests of opponents of the Revolution took place in Chalon over spring and summer 1793: around 30 men, mainly clergy and the relatives of *émigrés* (those who left the country for political reasons), were imprisoned. A second phase began after the Convention issued the Law of Suspects on 17 September 1793 – a sweeping decree that enabled committees to imprison people they deemed to be 'supporters of tyranny' or 'enemies of freedom', along with the relatives of *émigrés* and 'former nobles [...] who have failed to display their commitment to the Revolution at all times'. Over the next twelve months, the Committee of Surveillance for the Chalon district sent some 165 men and 130 women to prison.[41] The criminal tribunal of the *département*, sitting in Chalon, ordered six men to be executed in this period, a very small proportion of the roughly 16,000 people guillotined in France during the Terror.[42] Claude Javogues, the 'deputy on mission', sent by the Convention to combat insurrection in Saône-et-Loire, was highly critical of the leniency that prevailed in Chalon.[43] Officials also made symbolic changes in the town: some street names were changed, with the place des Carmes, for example, becoming the place de la Révolution. And they ordered a day of revolutionary festivities in November: liberty caps were worn, a tree celebrating the Montagnards was planted, and cartloads of feudal papers were burned.[44]

Towards the end of 1793, the Leschenault family were targeted by the Committee of Surveillance. Members of the National Guard called on the family on 24 November and placed Claude-Théodore and his two eldest sons under arrest. The three men appeared before the committee several days later. Claude-Théodore was identified as an *aristocrate très prononcé* (firm believer in noble privilege) and was found guilty of displaying a lack of commitment to the Revolution and an absence of patriotism. His eldest son, Louis-François, labelled a *muscadin* (or royalist dandy), the term deriving from the musk perfume worn by the fashionable, was considered suspect for the same reasons, and the two were incarcerated in the Convent of the Cordeliers on 2 December 1793. The records do not indicate that Théodore was convicted on the same date as his father and brother; a list sent to the Committee of General Safety in Paris on 11 December 1793 alludes to the arrest of only the elder of the two brothers. Théodore's nephew, Eugène Deschamps, however, believed that his uncle had been 'imprisoned with his family in 1793', so it may be that Théodore joined his father and brother in the convent that same month.[45] He was certainly in prison by 2 April 1794, according to another list, which labelled him a *muscadin* lacking commitment to the public cause.[46] At the time of their incarceration, Claude-Théodore was 63 years old, Louis-François was 25 and Théodore just twenty.

Established by the monastic order of the Cordeliers in the fifteenth century, the convent stood on the southern side of the Île Saint-Laurent in Chalon and overlooked a branch of the Saône river called the Genise. After fires and flooding, the buildings had largely been reconstructed in 1730.[47] In the wake of the Assembly's decree of January 1790 abolishing religious orders, the monks moved out and the buildings were stripped of their fittings. The prison consisted of three main buildings: the former chapel formed the northern side of the complex, while two residential wings ran south from either end of it. These three structures enclosed a cloister and quadrangle and a wall on the fourth side stood parallel to the Genise.

The prisoners occupied the two wings of the former convent and were permitted by the Law of Suspects to fit out their rooms with their own basic items of furniture. According to a diagram drawn up on 8 July 1794 by one of the inmates, the surveyor André Violet, the different rooms of the convent held between one and nine prisoners.[48] Théodore slept in bed number 48, which was located in the former sacristy on the ground floor in the left wing of the convent. He shared the room with five other inmates. He was listed as being an 'ex-noble', while two of the others in his room were local officials and three were merchants. On the floor above Théodore, his father and brother had a cell to themselves overlooking the courtyard. They occupied beds 77 and 78 and were also described as being former noblemen.[49] This label must have provoked a bitter feeling in the Leschenaults: the family had leapt from being commoners to ex-nobles without ever having enjoyed the status of nobility. They had for company a genuine aristocrat from their extended family: Théodore's mother's cousin Gabriel Gauthier de la Tournelle was there, as was his uncle Louis-François-Anne Gauthier. Both had been convicted of failing to display any interest in the affairs of the Republic, with his uncle in particular singled out as a man who 'lived only for pleasure'.[50] Another of Théodore's uncles, Joseph Magnien, a senior legal figure in the town, also occupied a cell, having been imprisoned for having an *émigré* son. The backgrounds of the other inmates varied widely: they included aristocrats, army officers, priests and monks, lawyers, engineers, surveyors and local officials, merchants, shopkeepers and artisans, clerks, servants, farm labourers and a beggar.

Conditions in the prison were not overly harsh.[51] Inmates were allowed to converse and walk in the courtyard when they wished. They were sometimes allowed to leave the prison temporarily to attend to personal matters, although had to pay for an accompanying guard. For a small bribe, the guard might allow the prisoner to stop for a drink at the tavern. Prisoners had to pay for their meals: soup and boiled meat at midday and, in the evening, roast meat or a stew and salad. Wealthier inmates were required to subsidise the cost of food for their poorer companions. Prisoners lodged occasional complaints, on one occasion requesting better quality bread, drinkable wine (two bottles per ten-day week from their families) and also a cook. Several incidents upset the relative tranquillity of the prison. On 16 December 1793, eleven inmates, including 'the two Leschenaults' (probably Théodore's father and brother), were transferred to the ordinary criminal prison for several days for disturbing the peace. An investigation was ordered when notes containing derisive comments about the government were thrown over the wall from the prison. One prisoner escaped in December 1793, but was soon recaptured. And in April 1794, a temporary prisoner, an engineer named Jean-Louis Pouilly de la Tour, died by suicide in one of the cells.

The elder two Leschenaults spent nearly ten months imprisoned in the convent, while Théodore seems to have spent between six and ten months there. After the fall of Maximilien Robespierre and other leading Montagnards in July 1794, many prisoners in Paris and the provinces were released. The three Leschenaults were set free on 26 September 1794 and that same day the town council granted them a Certificate of Probity, confirming that it had 'never been made aware of any complaint about their integrity'.[52] The end of the Terror was followed by a period in which moderate bourgeois republican rulers sought to stabilise the Revolution. The unsold properties of individuals condemned for reasons other than emigration were restored to their families by a decree of May 1795. Earlier radical measures relating to social welfare and universal education were abandoned and churches were allowed to reopen.

The Leschenault family's aspiration to join the nobility, however, appeared to have reached an end; Théodore went out and got a job working in the transportation industry. It would only be later, after Napoléon Bonaparte crowned himself emperor of the French in 1804, that the Leschenaults' aristocratic aspirations revived. Théodore then began to sign himself with the noble-sounding flourish 'Leschenault de la Tour', perhaps in allusion to the *tour* (tower) that features on the Leschenault coat of arms, or perhaps as an aggrandisement of

'Tournelle' (small tower), the name of one of the estates over which his father had claimed joint lordship. His brother Samuel, drawing on the name of the fiefdom bought by their father, styled himself 'Leschenault de Rupt'.

Théodore's experience of the Revolution doubtless shaped his later political views. Discussing slavery on the Isle of France in his journal, he condemns the practice as 'an outrage against nature', but refuses to endorse its immediate abolition on the grounds that '[i]f we destroy the established order of things, we must be careful not to allow chaos to ensue – a chaos [...] worse than the previous compact' (p. 105). The memory of his spell in prison remained painful for many years. After returning from the southern hemisphere, he confided to Samuel that he had no desire to move back and rejoin his family in their home town. 'I dread living in Chalon', he wrote. 'Although I take delight in being with you all, many other things summon up sad and unpleasant thoughts.'[53]

The Expedition to Australia

When news spread across Europe in 1798 that the French government was planning to sponsor a voyage of exploration to Chile, Tahiti and New Holland, it attracted the interest of many naturalists. The voyage had been proposed by Nicolas Baudin, a captain who had served in the French navy and merchant marine and had recently led an expedition to the West Indies for the purpose of collecting plants and animals. The professors at the Muséum in Paris, who had benefited from his collections, placed their support behind his new proposal and it was soon approved by the Directory. Due to a shortage of funds in this time of war, however, the voyage was postponed. Two years later Baudin contacted the Institut national, a leading academic body, in an effort to revive the idea.[54] A commission of eight members of the Institut reviewed Baudin's plan and proposed a more limited itinerary: they recommended exploring the uncharted sections of the southern, western and northern coastlines of New Holland, and the straits between New Holland and New Guinea in the north and between Van Diemen's Land and New Holland in the south.[55] On 28 April 1800, this plan was placed before the First Consul, Napoléon Bonaparte, who gave his approval, emphasising that, alongside its charting and exploring duties, the expedition must also 'bring back interesting objects from the three kingdoms, especially animals and plants that could be naturalised in our region'.[56] Bonaparte's motives for endorsing the expedition were probably quite varied, since it was a project that could, as John Dunmore puts it, 'advance science, shed some glory on his administration, embarrass his enemies, and bring back reliable information about British plans in the western Pacific'.[57] Although the voyage was primarily framed as one of scientific discovery, the naturalists who travelled to New South Wales implicitly understood its strategic objectives and offered assessments of the British settlement at Sydney and the potential for French colonisation in these parts.[58]

This 'voyage of discovery to the southern lands', as Péron's account was entitled, took its place in a long tradition of European exploration in the region. It had been suggested in ancient times that a vast unknown southern land mass (*terra australis incognita*) must exist to balance the lands of the north. A French navigator, Binot Paulmier de Gonneville, claimed to have discovered this land after storms drove him east from the Cape of Good Hope in 1504. In the seventeenth century, the Dutch encountered a landmass to the south of New Guinea and gave it the name New Holland, but after Abel Tasman sailed eastwards in the Roaring Forties winds, sighting Van Diemen's Land in 1642, it became clear that New Holland could not be the *terra australis* of legend, which was thought to extend further to the south. The outlines of the landmass below New Guinea became clearer after James Cook mapped sections of its eastern coastline in 1770, calling this region New South Wales. It was not known with certainty, however, whether New South Wales was directly connected to New Holland in the west and Van Diemen's Land in the south or separated from them by straits.

INTRODUCTION

A wave of French explorers visited the region between the 1760s and 1790s. The routes sailed by Louis-Antoine de Bougainville in 1768 and Jean-François-Marie de Surville in 1769 brought them near to the eastern side of Australia, but it was only in 1772 that French navigators made landfall: Marc-Joseph Marion du Fresne in southeastern Van Diemen's Land and François de Saint-Allouarn at Shark Bay in New Holland. In early 1788, La Pérouse's scientific expedition spent six weeks at Port Jackson with the newly arrived British First Fleet before vanishing in the Pacific. Antoine Bruni d'Entrecasteaux was sent out to look for La Pérouse and explored south-western New Holland and D'Entrecasteaux Channel in Van Diemen's Land in 1792 and 1793. The question of whether there existed a great southern landmass distinct from New Holland, New South Wales and Van Diemen's Land had still not been resolved when the Baudin expedition set out in 1800. Matthew Flinders, who formed the view that no such land existed, transferred the name *terra australis* to the continent he charted – unaware that Antarctica lay further to the south.[59] The Baudin expedition travelled with an extensive collection of charts and books compiled by earlier explorers, and in his journal Leschenault makes particular reference to the works of Cook and Jacques-Julien Houtou de Labillardière, botanist on d'Entrecasteaux's expedition. Plunged into melancholy as he sailed for Van Diemen's Land, Leschenault could not help recalling all the European navigators and naturalists who had perished in these regions for their 'love of science' (p. 201).

The instructions that Forfait provided to Baudin for the expedition set out an itinerary and a timetable for the charting work to be done in the 'southern lands'.[60] He did not spell out guidelines for all aspects of the voyage; instead, he asked Baudin to refer to several parts of the instructions drawn up for La Pérouse's expedition – in particular, those relating to scientific activities, conduct towards Indigenous peoples, and the health of the sailors. The instructions concerned with natural history were quite general and simply urged the explorer to:

examine the nature of the soil and the plants of different regions, and everything that is related to the physics of the globe. He will collect natural, terrestrial and marine curiosities; he will classify them by order and will draw up a detailed description of each species in which he will record the places where they have been found, the use that the local natives make of them, and, where plants are concerned, the properties that the natives attribute to them.[61]

Another document supplied to Baudin directed the botanists to focus on commercially valuable plants, posing the basic questions:

What are the main, dominant or rare species of tree which make up the forests? Are any types of fruit traded? What use do the natives make of the trees. What other uses can be made of the wood and fruits. *Idem* for shrubs and fruits.[62]

It was intended that more specific instructions for the scientists would come from experts in their fields. Leschenault, for example, was given 'a note on experiments to be performed on monocotyledons' by Augustin Pyramus de Candolle, a Swiss botanist whom he had met in Paris.[63] He presumably received advice also from Jussieu and it might have been expected that the more experienced Michaux would offer him guidance as the voyage unfolded.

When the two vessels of the expedition, the corvette *Géographe* and its slower consort, the former supply ship the *Naturaliste*, left Le Havre on 19 October 1800, they carried 22 naturalists and artists among the 256 people who figured on the crew and passenger lists.[64] Leschenault had been assigned to the *Géographe* and was allotted the seventh cabin on the port side. The fact that this expedition was travelling in a time of war was brought home vividly to all when, within a few hours of setting out, the ships were stopped by a British frigate and the expedition's passports were checked. The expedition arrived at its first port of call, Santa Cruz, Tenerife, on 2 November, where, while Baudin was delayed in obtaining wine and fresh provisions, the naturalists had the chance to explore the nearby hills and towns and meet the local inhabitants. From Tenerife, it took the expedition four months to complete the passage round the Cape of Good Hope to Port Louis on the Isle of France. The naturalists suffered boredom and discomfort in the doldrums, but found some distraction in catching and examining marine creatures, from tiny salps to sharks, and studying atmospheric phenomena and sea temperatures.

The expedition suffered several setbacks on the Isle of France. Feigning illness, numerous members of the expedition defected: in total, ten of the artists and naturalists (including the senior botanist Michaux), four officers and around forty crew remained behind on the Isle of France. Baudin also had trouble obtaining credit and provisions and the ships remained in port for forty days instead of the planned fifteen. When the expedition finally left the Isle of France on 25 April 1801, it was ten weeks behind schedule.

The expedition first sighted New Holland near Cape Leeuwin on 27 May. Baudin figured that, with the southern winter approaching, it made sense to defer the plan to head to Van Diemen's Land, and the expedition sailed northwards instead, reconnoitring the coastline. They soon came across a noteworthy geographical feature, unknown to Europeans, which they named Geographe Bay. The naturalists went ashore on the continent for the first time, collected their first specimens, and had their long-awaited first encounter with its Indigenous inhabitants. When stormy weather rolled through the bay, Leschenault found himself stranded ashore with a small group of shipmates for three miserable nights. The foul weather continued after he returned aboard ship and the *Géographe* lost contact with the *Naturaliste* while manoeuvring to leave the bay. The vessels made their way northwards separately, missing each other at various rendezvous points. Leschenault fell seriously ill but recovered by the time the *Géographe* entered Shark Bay. During the two weeks the *Géographe* spent in the bay, Leschenault was able to go ashore and make collections on Bernier Island. The vessel spent the following month charting the north-west coast of New

Holland, before heading to the Dutch-controlled port of Kupang in south-west Timor in order to resupply. The *Naturaliste* came into port a month after the *Géographe*, having waited for its consort at Rottnest Island and Shark Bay. It was a troubled stopover: sailors and scientists contracted dysentery and fever, head gardener Anselme Riedlé fatally so; disputes occurred between officers; and there was even a duel. Leschenault spent his time ashore studying plants and animals, Timorese customs, and the Malay language. He was granted permission by Baudin to transfer to the *Naturaliste* for the next leg of the voyage, as that vessel had no botanist or gardener aboard.

The ships sailed for Van Diemen's Land in November and spent a month of the summer in D'Entrecasteaux Channel, where the naturalists made large collections of specimens and had numerous meetings with the local Indigenous people. From there the ships sailed northwards along the east coast, stopping at Maria Island, and then became separated once more. The *Naturaliste* continued into southern Bass Strait, where Leschenault was able to explore several of the Furneaux Islands, before crossing to the mainland, where he was one of a party that charted and explored Western Port. From there the *Naturaliste* sailed to Port Jackson. While in port, its captain, Emmanuel Hamelin, took the decision to return to France, and in mid-May the *Naturaliste* left Port Jackson with the aim of sailing first to the Isle of France. Contrary winds off Van Diemen's Land halted the vessel's progress and it was forced to turn around and go back to Port Jackson. There it was reunited with the *Géographe*, which had arrived a week earlier, having sailed westwards along the uncharted southern coastline as far as the Nuyts Archipelago, encountering Matthew Flinders' *Investigator* along the way.

During the stopover in Sydney, Leschenault botanised with 'tireless enthusiasm', according to Péron.[65] He explored the Blue Mountains and the Hawkesbury and Parramatta rivers with Colonel William Paterson, lieutenant governor of New South Wales, and went collecting with several other botanists, Robert Brown and Peter Good from the *Investigator*, and George Caley, who was based in Parramatta and worked for Sir Joseph Banks.⁶⁶ Brown formed a favourable view of Leschenault, describing him as an 'acute observer', and the two men exchanged Australian plant samples after they returned to Europe.⁶⁷ While in Sydney, Leschenault also had the opportunity to observe the local Eora people. Baudin, meanwhile, ordered the construction of a new vessel, the schooner *Casuarina*; it would be able to sail closer to shore than the *Géographe*, permitting more precise survey work to be done. Having decided to send the *Naturaliste* back to France with the collections made so far, Baudin convinced Leschenault to transfer once more to the *Géographe* in order to continue his botanical work in New Holland.

The three ships sailed out of Port Jackson on 18 November 1802 and made first for King Island in Bass Strait. There they were caught by a British vessel carrying an unexpected letter from Philip Gidley King, governor of New South Wales, reminding the French that the British claim on Van Diemen's Land pre-empted any that they might wish to make. Leschenault and Péron went ashore on King Island and were obliged to take shelter in a sealers' camp when bad weather trapped them there for ten days. After the naturalists had been collected, the *Géographe* and *Casuarina* sailed for Kangaroo Island. Leschenault and Péron made extensive collections ashore during the three weeks that the *Géographe* was at anchorage at Eastern Cove. The *Casuarina* meanwhile charted Spencer Gulf and Gulf St Vincent, but on its return missed the planned rendezvous with the *Géographe*.

As the *Géographe* sailed for the Nuyts Archipelago with its haul of live kangaroos and emus from the island, Baudin recorded in his journal a quarrel that he had had with Leschenault. Although he had on one occasion praised the botanist's 'kind and sociable nature and [...] very calm temperament',⁶⁸ Leschenault, along with the other naturalists, had often irritated him by their habit of returning late from trips ashore and their reluctance to inform him of their discoveries. When Baudin evicted Leschenault from his cabin in order to provide shelter for the kangaroos, the botanist's vaunted equanimity vanished:

> [...] in order to find them [a] suitable place [Baudin wrote] I had to create [...] at least one [malcontent], for he showed his displeasure in no uncertain way, saying reproachfully that if he was still aboard, it was well and truly my fault, since I had not allowed him to leave on the *Naturaliste*.[69]

After failing to find one another in the Nuyts Archipelago, the *Géographe* and *Casuarina* made contact again in King George Sound in February 1803. There Baudin once more found fault with Leschenault. He was unhappy that the botanist and Péron had gone to visit friends from the smaller vessel while the assistant gardener Antoine Guichenot had been left to collect specimens and prepare pots of plants. 'This was work and not wit', wrote Baudin. All Péron and Leschenault would have to show, by contrast, was their verbosity: 'they will have composed 60 pages of writing [...] which will be all wit and no work'. Nevertheless, Leschenault was able to report to Baudin that he had collected 200 new species of plant in King George Sound.[70] After leaving this anchorage, the expedition continued its survey work up the west coast of New Holland, revisiting Shark Bay and charting the north-west coast for a further month before crossing to Timor in May. Leschenault's name does not appear on any of the labels of the plants collected after King George Sound, which may indicate that he fell sick during this second journey along the western coastline. Illness forced him to abandon the expedition at Kupang and he remained behind when the ships left port on 3 June. By July he was well enough to travel and took passage first to Batavia (present-day Jakarta) and then to Semarang, where he found lodgings with a congenial host, Nicolaus Engelhard, governor of the North-East Coast of Java. Using Semarang as his base, Leschenault explored central and eastern Java, Madura and Bali over the next three years. He finally returned to France in July 1807, after nearly seven years away, and carried with him the large collections of natural history he had made in the Dutch East Indies. This was more than four years after the *Naturaliste* and three years after the *Géographe* had arrived back in port to a lukewarm reception from a government preoccupied by war with Britain. Leschenault was awarded a modest pension of 1800 francs by the administration in November 1807 but struggled with the large debts he had acquired during his travels. He had to engage in sustained lobbying of Emmanuel Crétet, minister of the interior, and Denis Decrès, who had replaced Forfait as minister for the navy, before he was awarded a one-off payment of 10,000 francs in August 1808 as compensation for the illness he had suffered during the Baudin expedition and for the collections he had donated to the Muséum.

The Journal

The Baudin expedition generated a welter of paper records, ranging from logbooks, tables, catalogues, journals, labels, letters and reports through to drawings, paintings, learned articles and books. The government in this period required all naval officers to keep a personal journal of their voyages. Some of those kept by the officers of the Baudin expedition are dispassionate in tone, recording details of wind direction, sail arrangements, bearings and distances travelled; others, such as those of Baudin, Pierre Milius and Jacques de Saint-Cricq, offer more in the way of personal reflection and commentary. The naturalists of the expedition were also expected to keep journals, although they do not appear to have received specific advice about the form that these should take. For Baudin's previous expedition to the West Indies, Jussieu had compiled explicit instructions:

> [The naturalists] will keep a journal in which each object is described. Separately from this journal, they are asked to make another in which they daily record all events and the story of their voyage, including observations of any type which they are inclined to make.[71]

Leschenault kept two such types of record during his travels: what he calls his 'botanical journal' and his 'private journal'. He sent his botanical journal back to Jussieu in two parcels: one parcel, containing four notebooks with Latin descriptions of 40 plants and drawings of 38 of these, was shipped from Sydney on the *Naturaliste* and reached Jussieu at the Muséum; a second parcel, comprising some 800 descriptions and 250 drawings, was given to Baudin during the second stopover in Timor but was later apparently lost.[72] While Leschenault intended these for an expert readership, he seems to have written his 'history' of the voyage with others in mind – not just botanists and naval officials, but also his family and friends – and its tone varies accordingly.

Leschenault's private journal covers the period from 2 October 1800 to 25 April 1802, that is, the 19 months from his departure from Paris to the *Naturaliste*'s first arrival in Sydney. It also includes a short section on the weather that the *Naturaliste* encountered later off Van Diemen's Land in June 1802 during its brief excursion from Port Jackson. According to the final page of the manuscript, Leschenault completed the journal on 2 September 1802, during his second stay in Sydney (although he did add at least one marginal note after this date). As some crossed-out titles indicate, he initially intended to include a description of Port Jackson and its inhabitants in the fifth chapter of the journal. It is not clear whether he continued his account during the next section of the campaign, from Sydney to Timor, as no such journal appears to have survived. In any case, Leschenault had struggled to keep his narrative up-to-date after sailing out of D'Entrecasteaux Channel in February 1802. In a letter to Jussieu, he apologised for the gaps in the journal, explaining that he had initially been busy classifying plant samples and had then fallen ill in Sydney.[73]

The manuscript of the journal appears to be a fair copy produced by Leschenault on the basis of notes he had made earlier. Although he writes in a neat hand and weighs his ideas carefully, he warns Jussieu of his account's shortcomings:

> [O]ften, later observations made me aware that I was mistaken in my conjectures, and so you will find a great many crossings-out and added notes in my journal. There would have been a great many more if I had had the time to reread it closely and to muse on each of the sensations I felt in the act of observing. I ask you to forgive my style and spelling. An account written hastily in a ship tossed constantly by the waves and intended only for a beloved mother and forgiving friends cannot be as accurate as one written in the solitude of a study. In any case, on a voyage of this sort, events occur in such rapid succession that the mind is constantly distracted by new objects and cannot perceive them from all the perspectives they offer.[74]

While the journal indeed contains crossed-out words, inserted lines and notes, and even several pages of text pasted in at a later point, Leschenault exaggerates the spontaneous character of his narrative. Various factors, such as the many chronological leaps backwards and forwards, indicate that his text is not a simple first draft but is based, at least in part, on earlier notes. For example, in the midst of his day-to-day account of the *Géographe*'s slow passage through equatorial calms in the Atlantic, he alludes to the fact that his friend François-André Baudin 'was forced by ill health to remain behind at the Isle of France' (p. 98) – a development that occurred months later. At times he makes careful choices about where to include information, placing a table of measurements from the Atlantic crossing after his description of the Isle of France to prevent the figures from 'interrupting the narrative' (p. 115). Leschenault appears to have been concerned that even this more polished version of the journal would not live up to the expectations of his famous mentor Jussieu; by claiming that it was written hastily and in difficult conditions, he no doubt sought to deflect potential criticism.

Leschenault structures his journal quite loosely. While it is, for the most part, a day-to-day record of events, it resembles a sort of patchwork of different types of document. Leschenault inserts transcriptions of personal letters and official letters, catalogues of plants and marine animals, and tables of data measuring temperatures and humidity at sea. He also includes descriptions of places he has not visited: an account of life in a west African village, based on a conversation with Michaux's assistant, the former slave Bognam-nonen-derega; and a description of Madagascar, based on an interview with a French naval officer. Leschenault organises some sections thematically rather than chronologically: observations made over a period of months while in port in Kupang appear under headings such as 'Natural History', 'Morals, Dress and Customs of the Wealthy Malays' and 'Reflections on the Malay Language'. He also provides short essays in which he attempts to explain different phenomena, with titles that include 'The Phosphorescence of the Sea' and 'On Atmospheric Humidity'.

The tone that Leschenault adopts in his journal varies according to his subject matter and intended readership. If some parts of his journal were composed for his mother and friends (as he suggested in his letter to Jussieu), others were intended for fellow botanists and officials at the Ministry for the Navy and Colonies. The register he uses ranges from the dry and impersonal, in the empirical observation of nature, through to highly emotive outbursts. The passages in which he expresses homesickness, obligation, melancholy or apprehension are mostly intended for his family and friends; he even addresses his mother directly during his stay in Timor. He records debts of gratitude to his hosts on the Isle of France and Timor and to friends on the expedition, noting the care with which the medical officer François-Étienne Lharidon de Créménec tended him during bouts of illness. Friendship is as worthy of recording as new plants: Leschenault provides a list of his closest friends aboard the *Géographe* (pp. 193–94). It is probably no coincidence that four of the five friends had aristocratic associations: of them, only Péron did not. Leschenault does not, however, record any animosity towards his shipmates in the journal: the furthest that he goes is in suggesting that Baudin could have displayed greater consideration towards naturalists who were unused to sea travel. The language of sensibility, common to certain types of eighteenth-century novel and private correspondence, appears in different places in the journal. Leschenault employs it in the letters to an unnamed friend, which he transcribes at the start of the journal. On arriving at the Normandy coast, he describes his feelings in these terms:

> As I watched the ocean's restless waves break on the shore, I was seized by a feeling of terror. This, *this* will be my home for several years! I cried. And tears welled up in my eyes; I thought about my mother, my precious family, the friends I admire. I am leaving all behind! A painful feeling, which was tempered only by the pleasant conviction that I would sometimes feature in their thoughts and on my return I would clasp them to my breast and never leave them again! Oh, misery is the condition of man! Why must we always suffer in our search for happiness? (p. 78)

This sort of sentimental language features in the journal alongside more impersonal forms of expression, used when Leschenault writes for his fellow botanists at the Muséum. In his description of a *Xanthorrhoea* spear observed at Geographe Bay, he supplies precise detail using technical language:

> From the centre of the clump emerges a single scape 8- to 10-feet tall, which is woody in consistency and bears a spike thickly covered with capsules that have three valves and three locules. (p. 136)

In a letter written to Jussieu in Sydney, Leschenault reflected on the way in which he recorded his observations in his journal: 'I have avoided the systematic mentality which I believe to be detrimental to observation', he explained, 'and have supplied only an account of phenomena'.[75] He wished to convey that he was working as an unbiased observer, recording his observations freely, and not attempting to make them conform with any pre-existing system. This was a way of indicating to Jussieu that he was following his mentor's 'natural method' in relation to plant classification rather than Linnaeus's 'artificial system'. Linnaeus had categorised plants according to a small number of predetermined features, taking account mainly of their pistils and stamens, whereas Jussieu had proposed that plants be arranged into groups by considering a much wider range of features, including a plant's root, stem, cotyledons, flower, fruit and so on, according to relationships that appeared to be self-evident in nature.[76] In his journal, Leschenault comments on the scientific methodology he uses in another area – when trying to account for changes in atmospheric humidity at sea. He records the difficulty he experienced in moving from data to general theories:

> So many specific and local factors produce variations [...] that it is very difficult to establish a general theory. One may readily formulate conjectures, but as soon as one tries to fit them to the data, they are often contradicted, or even demolished, by the results. (p. 120)

As a relatively inexperienced naturalist, Leschenault seems eager to emphasise, for the professors at the Muséum, that although he may struggle to provide explanations for what he observes, he nevertheless approaches each question using the correct method.

As Leschenault travelled further from France, his journal reveals his changing attitude towards his plant-collecting activities. On Tenerife, he climbed into the hills and dutifully listed all the plants he came across, even though these were already well known to European botanists. He enjoyed a moment of discovery when he found a new species of fungus growing on the laurel trees. On the Isle of France, he chose not to spend time classifying specimens or visiting herbaria, but instead concentrated on familiarising himself with tropical plants growing in the wild. On Timor, although most of the plants he came across had already been classified by Europeans, he was able to study at close quarters the ways in which local people used them. In Australia, however, the situation changed dramatically: he was regularly confronted by plants no

European had described before. As he explained to Jussieu, this was an intoxicating feeling:

> It is only with difficulty that I may describe for you the sensations I felt the first time I went ashore on an unknown coast. I felt a confused pleasure which filled my mind, everything kindled my interest, pebbles, shells washed up on the beach, plants. I collected everything with incomparable eagerness but was soon obliged to abandon a portion of these riches I had recklessly amassed.[77]

After landing at Geographe Bay, he drew up a list of the plants he had collected. He made efforts to identify them, referring to recently published books by British and French botanists, and named the first new species he found in honour of Baudin. For each new location that he visited, he offered a summary of the plant life he encountered. Although the vegetation he observed at Shark Bay was low and dreary, many new species were to be found there. At Western Port, the plants were 'strong and vigorous' and grew on a thick layer of compost; the soil, he speculated, would be 'highly suited to all our European crops' (p. 229). At Geographe Bay, the soil was:

> more suitable for herbaceous plants than for tall trees; the former grow there with astonishing vigour, though smothered by their own profusion. If the land were cleared, the soil would quickly lose its fertility. The trees, it is true, grow to an extraordinary size, but they do not have the straight and slender trunks which we so commonly observe in our European forests. Several of the herbaceous plants are suitable for human consumption, but none of the trees appeared to bear edible fruit. (pp. 146–47)

In D'Entrecasteaux Channel, his optimistic first impressions were disappointed:

A student of nature might hope to discover a vast field for his observations behind this curtain of greenery, but going ashore he finds only a sandy soil which reluctantly supports a scattering of scraggy plants. [...] [F]rom time to time one comes across spots where a regular covering of shade creates perpetually damp conditions [...]. But the naturalist faces another obstacle to his enquiries here: the vegetation is so densely tangled that he cannot penetrate into the thickets, which, in any case, do not possess a great variety of plant life. The most numerous plants along the channel are undoubtedly those of the Compositae and myrtle families: its covering of vegetation is, as it were, parcelled out between them. (p. 216)

The journal does not contain an overview of Australian plant life as a whole; had the journal continued beyond Sydney, perhaps it might have done so. Several years after returning to France, Leschenault did publish a summary of the continent's flora in his 'Note on the Vegetation of New Holland'. There he suggested that, although the plants of Australia did not seem useful for food, they might reveal valuable medicinal or commercial properties in the future. He characterised the vegetation as generally 'dreary and sombre',[78] the fruit woody and the leaves tough due to the poor soil and dry climate; however, its plants were of the greatest interest to naturalists. Most plants belonged to new genera or, if they did not, the species were mostly new. Plant life was grouped into a small number of families, mainly Proteaceae, heathers, Compositae, Leguminosae and Myrtaceae (the latter containing the genus *Eucalyptus*, to which most of the large trees in Australia belonged); overall, the large number of different species appearing in similar soils and climatic conditions confirmed, as Leschenault saw it, Jussieu's conception of 'natural families'.[79]

Leschenault's journal does not just record the natural history of the places he visited: he was also a keen observer of the different peoples he encountered. Before departure, the expedition had received instructions about how to pursue anthropological research from several members of the newly established Society of the Observers of Man in Paris. Joseph-Marie Degérando had emphasised the importance of learning the languages of Indigenous peoples so that the observer would be able to study not just their physical appearance but all aspects of their social, cultural, political and religious lives. Louis-François Jauffret, secretary of the society, and Georges Cuvier, the comparative anatomist, also offered macabre advice about obtaining skulls and skeletons, if necessary by boiling down corpses with caustic potash.[80]

The first anthropological observations made by Leschenault relate not to any foreign peoples but to the Norman peasants he encounters on his journey from Paris to Le Havre. Before the ships leave port, he also writes a description of the 'Macpa' (or Makpa) people of west Africa, recording their physical characteristics, social organisation, religion, music, clothing, animals and hunting practices, deriving all his information from a 'very intelligent' Makpa youth, Michaux's assistant Bognam-nonen-derega (p. 233). Leschenault also reports how Makpa children are abducted by a neighbouring people and sold as slaves to English traders – his first allusion to the slave trade, which was to resurface as a theme in the Isle of France and in Timor.

On Tenerife, Leschenault takes an interest both in the Spanish-speaking islanders and in its former Indigenous inhabitants. If he offers unflattering portraits of the modern Tinerfeños, complaining of the island's 'horribly dirty and persistent' beggars and prostitutes (p. 93), he shows more sympathy towards the Guanches – a people who arrived in the Canary Islands during the first millennium BCE and are thought to be related to the pre-Islamic Berbers of north Africa.[81] In a survey of the island's history, Leschenault praises the courage that the Guanches displayed in resisting the Castilian conquest of the island during the fifteenth century and discusses their funerary customs. The Guanches, as he explains, carefully embalmed the remains of their relatives and placed these in wooden chests in remote recesses within caves. He is critical, however, of the way in which these graves sites have been treated in recent times:

> The difficulty involved in reaching these simple and respectful memorials could not protect them from European curiosity. The sanctuary of the dead has been violated; more of these sepulchral caves are discovered every day. (p. 94)

The Baudin expedition was presented with several of these mummies; Leschenault received a thigh bone, which was subsequently stolen from him. As he sailed from Tenerife towards southern waters, he ruminated on the Spaniards' genocide of the Guanches and on the fate that might await the Indigenous peoples of Australia. In the Canaries, fierce strangers had confronted a happy and independent people with terrible new weapons:

> Those centuries are not long past; oppression and despair drove this people to extinction. None of them survives... We are setting out to visit unknown peoples; perhaps the moment of their discovery will be the start of their misfortune. (p. 96)

But then, reflecting on the evolution that has occurred in Western institutions, he has a change of mind: 'But no, that can't be true, today governments are more enlightened, they will be just...' He concludes the chapter with a direct address to the Indigenous peoples he is about to encounter in the southern hemisphere, taking his inspiration perhaps from Degérando's instructions. The anthropologist had drawn a contrast between brutal Spanish conquistadores and members of the Baudin expedition, who would arrive on new shores as 'peace-bringers and friends'.[82] Leschenault offers this assurance:

> Inhabitants of the South Seas: we are prepared to brave dangers for the glory of our nation and the advancement of science and navigation, but we will not come onto your lands as destroyers. Your manners, customs and beliefs will be respected. We bring you tools that will make work easier and plants and animals that will diminish your privations and enhance your enjoyment of life.

In exchange for all these benefits, we request simply the welcome and hospitality that are due to any man. (p. 96)

In his journal, Leschenault records encounters with Indigenous Australians at Geographe Bay, D'Entrecasteaux Channel, Maria Island and Western Port, and offers additional observations about the Eora of Sydney in a letter to Jussieu. The first encounter, at the Vasse-Wonnerup Estuary in the south-west of the continent, lasted just an hour: the Noongar men gestured at the French party to retreat back towards the sea. Leschenault was able to record only a small number of details about them: their physical appearance, clothing, weapons and a few words of their language. Despite Degérando's caution against making hasty judgements, Leschenault concluded that this people dwelt 'as far from a state of civilisation as it is possible to be' (p. 144). They displayed no curiosity, only animal-like fear, and, though they did construct skilful fish-traps, they did not seem to have boats or bows and arrows. His encounters in other regions did little to alter this negative impression.

Labillardière, in his *Relation du voyage à la recherche de La Pérouse* (Account of the Voyage in Search of La Pérouse), had described a series of amicable exchanges between the French and the Indigenous people of D'Entrecasteaux Channel in early 1793.[83] These stories created favourable expectations among members of the Baudin expedition, which were initially fulfilled when they landed there in January 1802. They had a number of friendly meetings with the Bruny Islanders and Péron spoke of the 'inexpressible pleasure' he felt on seeing the way in which the lives of the local people matched 'the sparkling descriptions of the happiness and simplicity of the state of nature' that he had often enjoying reading about.[84] In addition to Labillardière's writings, Péron might have had in mind those of Cook on the Tahitians and Rousseau's account of pre-social man in his *Discourse on the Origin and Basis of Inequality among Men* (1755). However, on two subsequent occasions, the locals launched seemingly unprovoked attacks against the French as they were leaving in their boats. On one occasion, a spear thrown from the edge of a beach injured a midshipman in the shoulder; on another, a stone struck Baudin on the hip. Members of the expedition felt compelled to revise their views on 'natural man', with Leschenault observing:

> I admit that I am surprised, after so many instances of cruelty and betrayal reported in all the voyages of exploration, to hear sensible people say that men in their natural state are not in the least part malicious, and that they can be trusted and will only strike when roused to vengeance. (p. 208)

These ideas perhaps influenced the way he interpreted the behaviour of the Indigenous people that he encountered in Western Port: he formed the impression that they were trying to lure his colleague Pierre Milius into the bush in order to attack him. In Sydney, he took a forlorn view of the Eora way of life under the British: if they had 'not been civilised' and preferred to keep 'their old customs', this was in no way due to 'national pride' but rather to 'dull-witted apathy'. They seemed fond of tobacco and spirits and he witnessed them begging and fighting among themselves. And yet, even as he expressed these views, he felt some scruples about the judgements he was making, perhaps casting his mind back to Degérando's instruction that observers should make every effort to gain a comprehensive view of their subjects. Perhaps the real problem, Leschenault speculated, was that European knowledge of the Indigenous inhabitants of New South Wales was far too limited:

> In a century in which civilisation is pushing [...] into all corners of the globe, it is interesting to try and grasp everything that may shed light on natural man, but, although there are some learned and observant men in this colony, the metaphysical history of the indigenous peoples remains almost unknown. Is it really the case that these men of nature resemble a society of badly behaved children who, in all that they do, perform only a series of horrific, unreflecting actions?[85]

INTRODUCTION

In his studies of the Timorese of Kupang or slaves on the Isle of France, Leschenault had had the opportunity to observe his subjects at close quarters over many weeks, but his interactions with Indigenous Australians had been relatively brief, even while in Sydney, and hampered by language difficulties. Here, at least momentarily, he sounds a note of caution about the conclusions he had earlier reached in relation to the first Australians and considers reserving judgement until more can be learned.

Legacy

When he finally returned to France in 1807, Leschenault was carrying with him a collection of around 900 plant specimens and 400 animal specimens; none of these, however, was from Australia. Rather, they were the result of three years of private collecting in the Dutch East Indies, supplemented by some specimens he had obtained in Cayenne and Philadelphia during his journey back from Batavia to France. The scientific harvest of the Baudin expedition had returned aboard the *Naturaliste* and the *Géographe* several years earlier, in 1803 and 1804 respectively. On the botanical side, the *Naturaliste* carried fourteen cases of dried specimens and seeds, along with 69 half barrels of living plants. To the despair of André Thouin, a botanist who came down from the Muséum to manage the transportation of the Baudin expedition's specimens from Le Havre to Paris, of the 800 live plants (comprising 250 species), only around a dozen looked healthy, a further 20 were clinging to life, and the rest appeared dead.[86] This result was not entirely surprising as there were no botanists or gardeners left aboard the *Naturaliste* to tend the plants during the return journey and rats had eaten the new buds that appeared during the Atlantic passage. The *Géographe* carried a further six cases of dried plants along with a thousand living specimens looked after by the assistant gardener Antoine Guichenot. The survival rate on the *Géographe* was better; around 25 percent of specimens made it to France alive. A large collection of seeds and living plants was sent to Joséphine Bonaparte at the Château de Malmaison, including a packet containing the seeds of 130 species of plant addressed to her by Leschenault.[87] Joséphine succeeded in growing a number of Australian plants in her gardens and a dozen of these, including acacias, a melaleuca and a eucalypt, were illustrated by Pierre-Joseph Redouté for Aimé Bonpland's book *Description des plantes rares cultivées à Malmaison et à Navarre* (A Description of the Rare Plants Grown at Malmaison and Navarre, 1813).

The plants received by the Muséum were placed at the disposal of the botanist Labillardière, who referred to them in compiling his *Novae Hollandiae plantarum specimen* (Plant Specimens of New Holland, 1804–1806).[88] It was thought by some historians that these botanical collections were incorporated by Labillardière into his private herbarium and later sold. In 1814, however, Leschenault wrote to Robert Brown indicating that the Australian plants collected by the Baudin expedition were still housed in the Muséum.[89] In recent years, specialists such as Michel Jangoux have searched through the Muséum's store rooms and come to the conclusion that specimens from the Baudin expedition lost their identity as a collection when they were incorporated into the general herbarium of the Muséum by René Desfontaines in 1808. Jangoux has identified 2466 specimens collected by the expedition that remain in the Muséum, some of which bear Leschenault's original labels.[90]

Leschenault has been criticised by some modern commentators for failing to publish descriptions of the plants he collected in Australia.[91] He himself was well aware at an early stage that he had not met the expectations of his fellow botanists. Robert Brown, in his *Prodromus florae Novae Hollandiae et Insulae Van Diemen* (Introduction to the Flora of New Holland and Van Diemen's Land) of 1810, had suggested that Leschenault's illustrations of plants from the west coast of New Holland and Java were 'eagerly awaited'.[92] Writing to Brown in 1814, the Frenchman justified his inaction in these terms:

> I have been deterred from undertaking the publications I might have done by the loss of my botanical journal which contained

nearly 800 descriptions and 250 drawings. I gave the journal and drawings to Monsieur Baudin when I left the expedition at Timor. On my return to France, I heard nothing about these papers that were of such importance to me. I would have had to work solely from dried plants. In any case, your fine work left me little to do.[93]

It was not possible for Leschenault to trace the location of these papers since Baudin had died on the Isle of France in 1803. And Brown's *Prodromus* was, in any case, a comprehensive work, containing descriptions of more than two thousand Australian plant species, including over one thousand that were new to science. The sole article Leschenault published on the plant life of Australia was his 'Note on the Vegetation of New Holland'; it appeared in 1811 in the *Annales du Muséum d'histoire naturelle* and was republished, in slightly modified form, in 1816, in the *Voyage de découvertes aux terres australes* (Voyage of Discovery to the Southern Lands).[94] He wrote more extensively about his travels in the Dutch East Indies, publishing five articles between 1807 and 1811. Several of these were also published in English translation and one in particular, on the subject of poison trees, was widely discussed in scientific journals.[95] Leschenault was, however, keen to play a role in writing the history of the Australian expedition. After Péron died in 1810, having published only one volume of the *Voyage de découvertes*, Leschenault made it known that he wished to take over Péron's position as official historian of the voyage. A friend of Péron's (whose name is not known) wrote to Montalivet, the minister of the interior, in 1811 to dissuade him from offering the job to Leschenault. The writer of the letter suggested that Péron, fearful of certain colleagues who were 'jealous of his fame' and who might try and 'appropriate his many treasures', had explicitly stated that Leschenault was not suitable for the task.[96] Leschenault applied to Montalivet for the position in 1813,[97] but without success: the minister, whether influenced by Péron's friend or not, allocated it instead to Louis Freycinet. The reason why Péron turned against Leschenault in his final years is not clear; the two men had been friends during their Australian travels. Leschenault's struggle for money after his return to France undoubtedly hindered his ability to pursue a botanical career. To make ends meet, he was obliged to take up work as a government inspector of merino sheep and between 1811 and 1813 rode around remote departments of France inspecting their flocks. With his appointment in 1816 to the position of government naturalist, based in Pondicherry, India, he was once again able to collect exotic plants and published several articles on these. But publications were never the main focus of his career: during his postings to India and, later, South America, he was more preoccupied with collecting specimens for colonial botanical gardens and for the Muséum and with pursuing the French government's strategic goals.

Although Leschenault was highly regarded as a collector in European scientific circles, in the decades following his death in Paris in 1826, his name started to slip into obscurity. Several efforts were made by his descendants in the second half of the nineteenth century to commemorate his work. His nephew Eugène Deschamps published an article about him in the *Nouvelle Biographie générale* in 1859, while a distant cousin by marriage, Abel Jeandet, an archivist in Mâcon, published a longer survey of his life and writings in 1883. After much lobbying, Jeandet also succeeded in convincing the mayor of Chalon to rename one of the streets of the town 'rue Leschenault de la Tour' in 1889.

Leschenault's name is much more widely known today in Australia than in France. This is chiefly due to Robert Brown's decision to name a genus of Australian wildflower from the Goodeniaceae family for a man he described as his 'esteemed friend Lechenault, a famous traveller and accomplished botanist'.[98] Mistakenly omitting the 's' from the Frenchman's name, he spelled the genus *Lechenaultia*, which has since been a cause of confusion. These plants (for which the correct spelling is *Leschenaultia*) are to be found mostly in Western Australia and include species whose brilliant flowers range from the reds of *L. formosa* and blues of *L. biloba* to the pinkish-yellow wreaths of *L. macrantha*. Later botanists and zoologists paid tribute to Leschenault in a host of specific names ranging from starflowers through to bats, plovers and lizards. The French also named three geographical features on the west coast of Australia for Leschenault: an island in Shark Bay, a headland located between modern-day Perth and Lancelin, and an estuary to the north of Bunbury. The French name for the island was never adopted by the British: instead, it is called 'Salutation Island', a name given to it by the Royal Navy surveyor Henry Mangles Denham in 1858. The name 'Leschenault Estuary' did, however, gain currency in the Colony of Western Australia, and the botanist's name spread to other places nearby. The peninsula between the estuary and the sea is occupied by the Leschenault Conservation Park and the name is also attached to an outer suburb of Bunbury flanking the inlet, a caravan park, a primary school and a medical centre. When a settlement developed near Cape Leschenault, to the north of Perth, the state government's naming committee recommended against using the botanist's name there, since it was already employed elsewhere, and instead suggested 'Chalon', in honour of his home town. The townsfolk disliked this name and discarded it in 1968 in favour of the name 'Seabird', taken from a local shipwreck and pastoral lease.[99] The previous name is still present there in 'Chalon Street'. In Western Australia, Leschenault is also commemorated in the names of several streets in Perth, Bunbury and Albany. The Australian locations all use the simple early form of his surname, 'Leschenault', by which he was known at the time of the Baudin expedition, rather than the later embellished form, 'Leschenault de la Tour', which appears on that single French street sign. During his lifetime, Leschenault experienced sudden successes and abrupt reversals of fortune; as an historical figure, he has faded and flashed in Franco-Australian memory in a similarly erratic way. With the rediscovery of the original manuscript journal of his voyage to Australia, his reputation may be due for reassessment.

Translator's Note

The manuscript journal of Théodore Leschenault's voyage to Australia was thought lost for many years until it was put up for auction in 2016 in Royan (Charente-Maritime); it was acquired by the French nation and is housed at the Archives nationales de France, Paris, shelfmark: MAR/5JJ/56/B. I am grateful to the conservators at the Archives for giving me permission to use this manuscript as the basis for my translation. The manuscript is stored there alongside a copy made by Théodore's younger brother, Samuel, of chapters 3 to 5 (shelfmark: MAR/5JJ/56). This copy has served as a useful supplement to the original: a note glued into the original by Théodore has apparently become detached and been lost, but the text of the note has been preserved in Samuel's copy and has been used in the present translation.

Théodore Leschenault's manuscript journal is written in a cloth-bound notebook featuring the words *Journal particulier* (Private journal) on the cover. It contains 132 numbered pages of text and spans a period of 18½ months, from 10 Vendémiaire, Year IX (2 October 1800) to 27 Germinal, Year X (17 April 1802). This notebook seems to represent a fair copy based, at least in part, on earlier writings. It also contains a number of marginal notes. Where the content of these notes could be seamlessly incorporated into the main text of my translation, I have done so; otherwise these notes appear as endnotes. Leschenault records that he completed the journal on 15 Fructidor, Year X (2 September 1802) in Port Jackson. A marginal note about the sinking of the schooner *Entreprise*, which occurred on 27 October 1802, was obviously added later. As some crossed-out titles at the start of Chapter 5 (page 98 of the manuscript) indicate, Leschenault intended to continue the journal and describe Port Jackson and its inhabitants. The most significant editorial intervention I have made is to move two passages, a 'Note on the Macpas' of west Africa and a description of Madagascar, into an appendix, as these short texts do not relate directly to the expedition.

Some terms that Leschenault uses to describe the Indigenous peoples of Australia and Africa, such as *sauvage*, *naturel*, and *nègre*, and their English equivalents, 'savage', 'native', and 'negro', are considered offensive today, but were commonly in use at the time he wrote and have been retained to preserve the tone of the original. Leschenault also deploys a number of negative ethnic or racial stereotypes that were often used by western Europeans at the time about various other peoples.

Leschenault writes in a generally clear hand; I have indicated the small number of places where I found the text illegible. Occasionally he leaves a blank space where he intended to insert a date at a later moment and I have also indicated these gaps. His spellings of people's names and the scientific names of plants and animals are not always consistent or accurate and I have replaced these where necessary with accepted spellings (e.g. replacing the place name 'Point Chiquel' with 'Point Gicquel', or the former plant genus *Maxeutoxeron* with *Mazeutoxeron*). Leschenault often places commas or semi-colons between clauses where modern usage requires a full stop; I have modernised his punctuation accordingly.

Leschenault generally cites dates according to the French republican calendar, which was in use in France between 1793 and 1805. This calendar places the start of the republican era on 22 September 1792, the day on which the French Republic was proclaimed; this was the beginning of Year I. The twelve months were renamed, with the year starting with the autumn month of Vendémiaire (derived from the Latin term for the grape harvest). The months consisted of three ten-day weeks, or *décades*. The five or six additional days required to make up the solar year were called 'complementary days'.

A Chronology of Théodore Leschenault

1773   (13 November) Born at quarter past midnight in Chalon-sur-Saône, Burgundy, fifth child of Claude-Théodore Leschenault, *procureur du roi* (judicial officer), and Marguerite Gauthier.

(14 November) Baptised Jean Baptiste Louis Claude Théodore in the parish of Saint-Vincent, Chalon-sur-Saône.

1793   (December) Father and elder brother Louis-François imprisoned in the former Convent of the Cordeliers on the Île Saint-Laurent, Chalon-sur-Saône, under the Law of Suspects; Théodore soon joins them in prison.

1794   (26 September) The Leschenaults are released from prison.

1796   (19 April) Leschenault marries Marguerite Bonin in Chalon-sur-Saône. He works at this time at a staging post in Saint-Léger-sur-Dheune.

1797   (30 August) Death of father in Paris.

1800   (14 September) Appointed as botanist to the Baudin expedition.

(8 October) Wife Marguerite divorces him due to the 'incompatibility of their temperaments and characters'.

(19 October) He sails from Le Havre on *Géographe*.

(2–14 November) Expedition is at Tenerife.

1801   (16 March – 25 April) Isle of France (Mauritius).

(27 May) West coast of New Holland sighted.

(2–6 June) Leschenault collects plants at Geographe Bay; encounter with Noongar people at Vasse-Wonnerup Estuary; stranded ashore.

(27 June – 14 July) Shark Bay; goes ashore on Bernier Island.

(22 August – 13 November) Kupang, Timor; transfers to *Naturaliste*.

1802   (13 January – 16 February) D'Entrecasteaux Channel, Van Diemen's Land; encounters Indigenous people.

(18–27 February) At Maria Island; finds tombs.

(10–19 March) In Banks Strait; explores Waterhouse Island and southern Furneaux Islands; stranded on Clarke Island and Preservation Island by storms.

(9–18 April) Explores Western Port.

(25 April – 18 May) In Port Jackson; botanises with Robert Brown and Peter Good.

(28 June – 18 November) Port Jackson again after *Naturaliste*'s abortive attempt to sail to the Isle of France. Transfers to *Géographe*.

(2 September) Completes his journal.

(18 November) Sails out of Port Jackson in *Géographe*; *Naturaliste* leaves on the same day, bound for France,

carrying his journal and many drawings and plant specimens.

(10–24 December) Goes ashore on King Island with Péron and others; stranded by a storm.

1803 (January) Botanises on Kangaroo Island.

(4 February) Ordered by Baudin to relinquish his cabin on *Géographe* to kangaroos.

(10 February) Lands on St Peter's Island, Nuyts Archipelago.

(17 February – 1 March) King George Sound.

(16–23 March) Shark Bay again.

(31 May) Abandons the expedition at Timor due to illness, leaving many papers with Baudin (now thought lost).

(July) Sails to Batavia (present-day Jakarta).

(August–October) Explores the coast eastward of Batavia.

(3 October) Arrives in Semarang, where he receives the patronage of Nicolaus Engelhard, governor of the North-East Coast of Java.

(24 October) Sets out on a journey to Surakarta and Yogyakarta.

1804 After falling ill in Yogyakarta, he is carried back to Semarang by porters.

(February–October) Convalesces in Semarang.

(October–December) Travels east along northern coast of Java.

1805 (January–July) Continues his travels as far as Pasuaran; crosses the island of Madura from west to east.

(July–September) In Banyuwangi; studies a poison plant found nearby.

(18–22 September) Climbs Mt Ijen to assess the acidity of the water in its crater lake. Explores the coast of Bali.

(4–7 November) Climbs Mt Bromo from Pasuaran. Visits Malang.

1806 (February) In Surabaya.

(August) Returns to Semarang.

(October) Leaves Semarang for Batavia.

(27 November) Sails from Batavia in steerage on American brig *Sally and Hetty* bound for Cayenne and Philadelphia.

1807 (April–June) Collects in Philadelphia and its environs.

(16 July) Arrives in Saint-Nazaire.

(3 November) Awarded a government pension of 1800 francs.

Publishes articles on travels in Java.

1808 (28 August) Awarded 10,000 francs from the government as compensation for collections he deposited with the Muséum d'histoire naturelle and for illness suffered during the Baudin expedition.

1809 (May–June) Stays in the countryside at former abbey of Vaux de Cernay.

(17 June) Mother dies in Chalon.

1810 (13 October) Joins the Knights Templar in Chalon.

Publishes a celebrated article on two poisonous tropical plants, 'Memoir on the *Strichnos tieute* and *Antiaris toxicaria*', in *Annales du Muséum d'histoire naturelle*.

1811 Works on a Malay grammar and dictionary under contract to the Imprimerie impériale.

(22 July) Appointed government inspector of merino sheep; travels in rural France over the next two years.

Publishes four articles on his travels in New Holland and the East Indies.

1813 Publishes a pamphlet entitled 'Note on the Epidemic which in 1812 Afflicted Sheep Flocks in the Southern Departments of France'.

1814 (6 April) Abdication of Napoléon.

(14 April) Leschenault joins a deputation from Chalon that swears allegiance to the restored monarch Louis XVIII.

(June) Obtains a post writing reports for the Department of Agriculture.

(November) Waits in vain in Rochefort for British approval to travel to Pondicherry.

1815 (22 June) Second abdication of Napoléon after the Hundred Days.

1816 (17 May) Sails from Ile-d'Aix on the *Licorne* with other officials to take repossession of Pondicherry from the British under the Treaty of Paris; his position is *naturaliste du roi* (naturalist of the king).

(26 September) Arrives in Pondicherry.

1817	(October) Visits Karikal.
1818	Travels to Salem.
	(October) Travels to Coimbetore with the aim of exploring the Western Ghats, but his trip is curtailed when he contracts yellow fever.
1819	(April–June) Travels again to Coimbetore and to the Nilgiri mountains in the Western Ghats.
	(September 1819–January 1820) Travels to Bengal, stays at the botanical garden in Calcutta.
1820	(April–June) Travels in southern India.
	(July) Sails from Tuticorin to Colombo, explores Ceylon, collects cinnamon plants.
	Publishes four articles in *Mémoires du Muséum d'histoire naturelle* about his work in India.
1821	(February) Ill with dysentery, he returns from Ceylon to Pondicherry.
	(24 August) Leaves Pondicherry on the *Sylphe* bound for the Isle of Bourbon (Réunion) carrying cinnamon trees from Ceylon.
	(20 September) Arrives at the Isle of Bourbon.
1822	(5 February) Leaves the Isle of Bourbon on the *Régulus*.
	(27 May) Arrives in Nantes.
	(17 August) Appointed a chevalier of the Legion of Honour by Louis XVIII.
	Publishes three articles on his travels and botanical work in India and Ceylon.

1823 (11 June) Departs Brest on the *Rhône* with naturalist Adolphe Doumerc on a government mission to French Guiana and Surinam.

(July–October) Rio de Janeiro and Bahia, Brazil.

(November–December) In Cayenne and Nouvelle-Angoulême, French Guiana.

(11 December) Completes a report on conditions at the French settlement in Nouvelle-Angoulême.

(mid-December) Leaves for the Dutch colony of Surinam; spends three months there.

1824 (April) Returns to Cayenne; publishes a pamphlet entitled 'Extract from a Voyage to Surinam' analysing how Dutch methods of government in Surinam could be applied in French Guiana.

(31 August) Abandons his mission due to illness and leaves for France on the *Bayonnaise*.

(November) Arrives in Paris.

1825 (3 October) Writes his will in which he leaves the bulk of his property to his brother Samuel, 20,000 francs to his sister Eugénie, and a smaller sum to his housekeeper.

1826 (1 January) Retires from government service.

(14 March) Dies at home, 367 rue Saint-Honoré, Paris.

(16 March) A funeral service is held by his family at the Madeleine Church; he is buried in Père Lachaise Cemetery.

A Chronology of the Baudin Expedition

1798　(July–August) Nicolas Baudin proposes a plan for a scientific voyage of discovery around the world; receives endorsement from the Muséum d'histoire naturelle and the Ministry for the Navy and Colonies.

1800　(March–April) A new plan, shaped by scientists from the Institut de France, refocuses the voyage on New Holland and Van Diemen's Land. The First Consul, Napoléon Bonaparte, approves it.

(19 October) *Géographe* and *Naturaliste* depart Le Havre carrying 256 people, including 22 naturalists and artists.

(2 November) Arrive Santa Cruz, Tenerife, where Baudin encounters delays in obtaining wine and fresh provisions.

(14 November) Depart Santa Cruz.

1801　(16 March) Arrive in Port Louis, Isle of France (Mauritius), where numerous scientists and crew abandon the expedition.

(25 April) Depart the Isle of France.

(27 May) West coast of New Holland sighted.

(30 May – 10 June) Exploration of Geographe Bay and interior. *Géographe* is separated from *Naturaliste* in a storm.

(14–28 June) *Naturaliste* is at Rottnest Island; its crew explore the island and the Swan River.

(27 June – 14 July) *Géographe* is at Shark Bay.

(15 July – 19 August) *Géographe* explores the north-west coast of New Holland.

(16 July – 5 September) *Naturaliste* is at Shark Bay.

(22 August) *Géographe* arrives in Kupang, Timor.

(21 September) *Naturaliste* arrives in Kupang.

(21 October) Death of the head gardener Anselme Riedlé in Timor.

(13 November) The expedition leaves Kupang for Van Diemen's Land.

1802 (13 January – 16 February) D'Entrecasteaux Channel, Van Diemen's Land.

(18–27 February) Maria Island.

(8 March) *Géographe* and *Naturaliste* are separated again.

(10 March) *Naturaliste* enters Banks Strait.

(17 March) *Géographe* enters Banks Strait.

(19 March – 18 April) *Naturaliste* explores the islands of Banks Strait, Port Dalrymple (Van Diemen's Land) and Western Port (in present-day Victoria).

(28 March) *Géographe* sails westward from Wilson's Promontory charting the 'unknown' southern coast.

(8 April) *Géographe* meets Matthew Flinders' *Investigator* in Encounter Bay.

(8 April – 8 May) *Géographe* explores the northern coast of Kangaroo Island, Gulf Saint-Vincent, Spencer Gulf and the coastline of New Holland as far as Nuyts Archipelago.

(25 April) *Naturaliste* arrives in Port Jackson.

(18 May) *Naturaliste* leaves Port Jackson on its first attempt to sail to the Isle of France.

(20–21 May) *Géographe* at anchor off Bruny Island.

(22 May – 4 June) *Géographe* charts eastern Van Diemen's Land despite illness among crew.

(20 June) *Géographe* arrives in Port Jackson.

(28 June) *Naturaliste* returns to Port Jackson.

(18 November) *Géographe*, *Naturaliste* and newly built *Casuarina* leave Port Jackson.

(6 December) Anchor off King Island, Bass Strait.

(7–28 December) *Géographe* and *Casuarina* explore King Island and the Hunter Islands.

(8–9 December) Schooner *Cumberland*, sent from Port Jackson by Governor King, finds *Naturaliste* and *Géographe* at King Island; Emmanuel Hamelin and Baudin are reminded of British intentions to establish a southern settlement.

(9 December) *Naturaliste* sails for the Isle of France.

1803 (2 January – 10 January) *Géographe* and *Casuarina* at Kangaroo Island.

(11 January – 31 January) *Casuarina* explores Gulf St Vincent, Spencer Gulf and Port Lincoln; *Géographe* remains at Kangaroo Island.

(1 February) *Casuarina* and *Géographe* sight one another off Kangaroo Island but separate without making contact.

(3–7 February) *Casuarina* in Nuyts Archipelago awaiting rendezvous.

(6–11 February) *Géographe* in Nuyts Archipelago; the two ships miss one another.

(13 February) *Casuarina* arrives in King George Sound.

(17 February) *Géographe* arrives in King George Sound.

(1 March) *Géographe* and *Casuarina* leave King George Sound.

(9–13 March) Survey coast from Cape Leeuwen to Rottnest Island.

(16–23 March) Shark Bay.

(23 March – 29 April) Explore north-west coast of New Holland as far as Cassini Island.

(6 May – 3 June) In Kupang, Timor.

(3 June) Depart Timor with the aim of surveying the coast of New Holland as far as the Gulf of Carpentaria.

(7 June) *Naturaliste* arrives in Le Havre.

(8–27 June) *Géographe* and *Casuarina* survey sections of the New Holland coast as far as the Tiwi Islands.

(7 July) In the Arafura Sea, with winds contrary and animals unwell, Baudin orders *Géographe* and *Casuarina* to sail for the Isle of France.

(7 August) *Géographe* arrives in the Isle of France.

(19 August) *Casuarina* arrives in the Isle of France.

(29 August) *Casuarina* decommissioned; its crew transfer to the *Géographe*.

(16 September) Baudin dies on the Isle of France.

(16 December) *Géographe* departs the Isle of France under its new commander Pierre Milius.

1804   (3–24 January) Stopover at the Cape of Good Hope.

(25 March) *Géographe* arrives in Lorient.

1807   First volume of François Péron's official account of the voyage, *Voyage de découvertes aux terres australes* (Voyage of Discovery to the Southern Lands), is published.

1810   (14 December) Péron dies in Cérilly.

1816   Final volume of the official account, written by Louis Freycinet, is published.

1824   Second edition of the *Voyage de découvertes* is published.

Leschenault's Shipmates Mentioned in the Journal

BAILLY, CHARLES-JOSEPH (1777–1844), mineralogist on the *Naturaliste*, transferred to the *Géographe* at Port Jackson on 3 November 1802. He studied geology while at the École polytechnique (a military academy in Paris) between 1796 and 1800; after the Baudin expedition he joined the navy's hydrographic service, where he worked from 1806 until his retirement in 1840.

BAUDIN, FRANÇOIS-ANDRÉ (1774–1842), lieutenant on the *Géographe*, left the expedition under the pretext of illness at the Isle of France on 25 April 1801. He sailed from there to the United States and arrived back in France in December 1801. During the Napoleonic Wars he saw action in the Caribbean as captain of the frigate *Topaze* in 1805, was promoted to rear admiral in 1808, and commanded a division and squadrons in the Atlantic, Mediterranean and North Sea theatres.

BAUDIN, NICOLAS-THOMAS (1754–1803), commander of the expedition and captain of the *Géographe*. After serving in the French navy and the merchant marine, Baudin had been recruited by the Austrian government to lead scientific expeditions to Asia and India in 1788 and to southern Africa and New Holland in 1792, but both voyages were curtailed by shipwreck. Baudin subsequently commanded a voyage to the West Indies on the *Belle Angélique* to collect specimens on behalf of the Muséum d'histoire naturelle between 1796 and 1798. The success of the voyage prompted him to propose a new expedition to the Pacific and Southern Lands. He died on the Isle of France on 16 September 1803.

BELLEFIN, JÉRÔME-JEAN-CLAUDE (1764–1835), surgeon second class on the *Naturaliste*.

BONNEFOI DE MONTBAZIN, LOUIS-CHARLES-GASPARD (1778–?), midshipman first class on the *Géographe*, made acting sub-lieutenant at Timor on 20 October 1801 and promoted to sub-lieutenant on 24 April 1802. He had been an apprentice on the *Belle Angélique* on Baudin's voyage to the West Indies.

BOUGAINVILLE, HYACINTHE-YVES-PHILIPPE-FLORENTIN DE (1781–1846), midshipman second class on the *Géographe*, was made acting midshipman first class at Timor on 20 October 1801 and transferred to the *Naturaliste* at Port Jackson on 3 November 1802. He was the son of the famous explorer Louis-Antoine de Bougainville (1729–1811), who circumnavigated the globe between 1766 and 1769. Hyacinthe had studied at the École polytechnique before joining the Baudin expedition. On his return to France, he took part in preparations for the planned invasion of England and saw action in the English Channel and off Greenland. He was promoted to commander in 1811, made baron of the Empire in 1812, and was captured by the British in the *Cérès* off Rio de Janeiro in 1814. Under the Restoration, he was promoted to captain (1821) and between 1824 and 1826 circumnavigated the globe on the frigate *Thétis* on a diplomatic mission for the government. He was promoted to rear admiral in 1838.

DELISSE, JACQUES (1773–1856), assistant botanist on the *Géographe*, left the expedition at the Isle of France on 25 April 1801 due to illness. He remained on the island where he set up a pharmacy, helped found several learned societies, and became a director of the Banque de Maurice, only returning to France in 1848 after the death of his wife.

DEPUCH DE MONBRETON, LOUIS-ALEXANDRE (1774–1803), mineralogist on the *Géographe*, transferred to the *Naturaliste* on 3 November 1802 and abandoned the expedition at the Isle of France on 3 February 1803 due to illness. He was the son of Alexandre-Jean Puch de Monbreton (1744–?), a cavalry officer who had attended the Estates-General in 1789 as a deputy for the nobility. Louis had studied at the École des mines before joining the expedition. He died on the Isle of France in February 1803.

FAURE, PIERRE-ANGE-FRANÇOIS-XAVIER (1777–1855), geographer on the *Naturaliste*, transferred to the *Géographe* at Port Jackson on 3 November 1802. He left the expedition on 15 December 1803 at the Isle of France, where he settled. He married in Port Louis in 1807 and taught mathematics at the Lycée colonial. He had studied at the École polytechnique in Paris between 1796 and 1799.

FREYCINET, LOUIS-CLAUDE DE SAULCES DE (LOUIS FREYCINET) (1779–1842), sub-lieutenant on the *Naturaliste*, made acting lieutenant on 20 March 1801 and promoted to lieutenant in March 1803. After entering the navy as a midshipman in 1793, he fought alongside his elder brother Henri in battles against the Royal Navy off Genoa and the Hyères Islands in 1795, and then served under him as sub-lieutenant on the schooner *Biche*. During the Baudin expedition, he was given command of the *Casuarina*. After his return to France, he worked at the Dépôt général de la Marine (the navy's hydrographical office), where he completed the official narrative of the voyage, begun by Péron, and also published its navigational volumes. He was also promoted in 1811 to *capitaine de frégate* (commander). In 1817 he was given command of the corvette *Uranie* and set out (with his wife Rose hidden in his cabin) on a new scientific expedition to Brazil, Africa, Australia and the Pacific. Although the *Uranie* sank off the Falkland Islands in 1820, Freycinet managed to shepherd the expedition home on a new ship. An account of the journey, *Voyage autour du monde* (Voyage around the World), written by Freycinet and others, was published between 1824 and 1844.

FREYCINET, LOUIS-HENRI DE SAULCES DE (HENRI FREYCINET) (1777–1840), sub-lieutenant on the *Géographe*, made acting lieutenant at Timor on 20 October 1801, and promoted to lieutenant on 5 March 1803. He entered the navy as a midshipman in 1793 with his brother Louis, saw combat in the Mediterranean, and obtained command of the schooner *Biche* at a young age. He had charge of the *Géographe* during Baudin's bouts of illness and was disappointed when, after the captain's death on the Isle of France, Pierre Milius was named commander. After his return to France, Freycinet was given command of the brig *Phaéton* and lost his right arm and shattered a leg during encounters with British warships in the Caribbean Sea. In 1809 he was promoted to *capitaine de frégate* (commander) but remained blockaded in French ports for the remainder of the war. Under the Restoration, he served as governor of the Isle of Bourbon (present-day Réunion) (1821–1825), French Guiana (1827–1828) and Martinique (1829–1830). He was promoted to the rank of rear admiral in 1828 and was appointed major general of Toulon in 1830 and maritime prefect of Rochefort in 1834.

HAMELIN, JACQUES-FÉLIX-EMMANUEL (1768–1839), captain of the *Naturaliste* with rank of *capitaine de frégate* (commander). After spending his early years on the staff of slave ships, he joined the navy in 1792 and fought in the Atlantic and Mediterranean theatres, receiving promotion to the rank of commander. After his return from the Baudin expedition, he helped organise the Boulogne fleet for Napoléon's planned invasion of England and was given command of the frigate *Vénus*. Escaping the Channel blockade in 1808, he sailed for the Indian Ocean and harassed British interests in the Bay of Bengal and Sumatra. He was captured during the battle for the Isle of France in 1810 and, after his release, was promoted to rear admiral and given command of the squadron at Brest. He was later appointed major general of Toulon in 1818, commander of Mediterranean naval forces in 1822, inspector of naval personnel in 1832 and director of the Dépôt général de la Marine in 1833.

LESCHENAULT'S SHIPMATES MENTIONED IN THE JOURNAL

HEIRISSON, FRANÇOIS-ANTOINE-BONIFACE (1776–1834), sub-lieutenant on the *Naturaliste*.

LE BAS DE SAINTE-CROIX, ALEXANDRE (1759–1828), second-in-command on the *Géographe* with rank of *capitaine de frégate* (commander). He was dismissed from the expedition in Timor after displaying insubordination to Baudin and duelling with François-Michel Ronsard; his departure on 2 November 1801 was officially attributed to illness.

LESUEUR, CHARLES-ALEXANDRE (1778–1846), joined the *Géographe* as an assistant gunner, fourth class, on the understanding that he would serve as Baudin's personal artist; after defections at the Isle of France, he was appointed as one of the expedition's official artists. Prior to the expedition, he attended school in Le Havre, joined a cadet battalion at the age of fifteen, served in the national guard between 1797 and 1799, and spent a year as a conscript aboard a naval cutter. He may possibly have acquired drawing skills at the school for hydrography. Alongside his work as an artist on the Baudin expedition, he also collected specimens of natural history with François Péron. On his return to France, Lesueur worked closely with the zoologist in preparing the official account of the voyage, compiling the first volume of the atlas, but was resentful when Louis Freycinet was allotted the task of continuing the work after Péron's death. In 1815 he was engaged by the Scottish geologist William Maclure (1763–1840) to travel with him to the West Indies and the north-eastern United States as a draughtsman and naturalist. After this arrangement ended, Lesueur supported himself by teaching art in Philadelphia. He also continued his research in natural history, with a focus on ichthyology, and in 1826 joined Robert Owen's short-lived utopian community at New Harmony, Indiana. After his return to France in 1837, he continued to work as a naturalist and artist. In 1845 he was appointed director of the new natural history museum in Le Havre but died before its inauguration.

LEVILLAIN, STANISLAS (1774–1801), assistant zoologist on the *Géographe*, transferred to the *Naturaliste* at the Isle of France on 22 April 1801 and died at sea on 29 December 1801 from dysentery and fever contracted in Timor. He had previously accompanied Baudin on his voyage to the West Indies on the *Belle Angélique*.

LHARIDON DE CRÉMÉNEC, FRANÇOIS-ÉTIENNE (1768–1807), medical officer second class on the *Géographe*, upgraded to first class on 13 October 1801 just prior to the expedition's departure. Three years after his return to France he drowned himself in a river in Brittany.

MAUGÉ, RENÉ (b. between 1756 and 1758, d. 1802), zoologist on the *Géographe*, died during the stopover at Maria Island on 21 February 1802 from dysentery contracted in Timor. He had joined the Muséum d'histoire naturelle as an assistant naturalist in mid-1795 before embarking on Baudin's expedition to the West Indies on the *Belle Angélique*.

MAUROUARD, JEAN-MARIE-TOUSSAINT (1772–?), assistant helmsman first class on the *Géographe*, was promoted to acting midshipman first class in Timor on 20 October 1801 and transferred to the *Naturaliste* in Port Jackson on 3 November 1802. He studied at the École polytechnique alongside Pierre Faure and Charles-Pierre Boullanger (1772–1813) before joining the expedition.

MERLOT (b. *c.* 1784, d. after 1803), originally called Bognam-nonenderega, was a Makpa youth who had been abducted as a child from what is now eastern Nigeria and sold into slavery (see Leschenault's 'A Note on the Macpas', p. 232). After perhaps living for a time in Saint-Domingue, he was bought by André Michaux in the United States and taken to France in 1796. Michaux obtained a post for him as assistant gardener on the *Naturaliste*; his age was recorded as fourteen on the crew list, although that may not be accurate. Michaux and Merlot left the expedition at the Isle of France on 20 April 1801 and travelled on to Madagascar, where they established a commercial garden. After Michaux's death in 1802, Merlot worked for a time in the gardens of the local nobility in Foulpointe (Mahavelona) before being sold again into slavery.

MICHAUX, ANDRÉ (1746–1802), botanist on the *Naturaliste*, left the expedition at the Isle of France on 20 April 1801. Michaux had grown up on Satory farm, a royal domain near Versailles, and studied at the Trianon gardens and Jardin du roi under botanists such as Claude Richard, Louis-Guillaume Le Monnier, the Jussieus and André Thouin. He made collecting trips to England, the Auvergne and Spain, and botanised in the Middle East between 1782 and 1785. On his return, he was sent on a government mission to the United States to identify trees suitable for shipbuilding that could be naturalised in France. During his eleven years in America, he established nurseries, made journeys of exploration, and sent thousands of seeds and saplings back to France. After leaving the Baudin expedition, he went with his companion Merlot to Madagascar and established a garden at Toamasina, but died of a fever there on 11 October 1802. He published his *Histoire des chênes de l'Amérique* (History of American Oak Trees) in 1801 and his *Flora boreali-americana* (Plants of North America) appeared posthumously in 1803.

MILIUS, PIERRE-BERNARD (1773–1829), lieutenant and second-in-command on the *Naturaliste*, promoted to *capitaine de frégate* (commander) at Timor on 20 October 1801, left the expedition due to illness at Port Jackson on 18 May 1802. He then sailed to Canton (Guangzhou), where he stayed for several months before returning to the Isle of France. He took command of the *Géographe* at Port Louis on 28 September 1803 after Baudin's death. During the Revolutionary Wars, he saw action in the Atlantic campaign and at the Battle of Groix and was captured while supporting the Irish Rebellion. After the Baudin expedition, he took command of the frigate *Didon* but was captured once more in an engagement off north-west Spain in 1805. Under the Restoration, he held the posts of governor of the Isle of Bourbon (1818–1821) and governor of French Guiana (1823–1825), and corresponded with Leschenault about public health in those colonies and the spice trade.

PÉRON, FRANÇOIS (1775–1810), assistant zoologist on the *Géographe*. He volunteered for the revolutionary army in 1792 and fought for two years against the Prussians on the Rhine. Captured at Kaiserslautern, he was imprisoned, losing an eye due to disease or injury, and was repatriated after several months. He enrolled in medical school in Paris in 1797 and over the next three years also pursued his interest in natural history and studied at the museum. On his return from the Baudin expedition, he published a number of papers, mainly on marine animals, and was commissioned to write the official account of the voyage, but died of tuberculosis before he could complete the second volume.

PETIT, NICOLAS-MARTIN (1777–1804), joined the *Géographe* as an assistant gunner, fourth class, on the understanding that he (like Lesueur) would serve as a personal artist to Baudin; after defections at the Isle of France, he was appointed one of the expedition's official artists. The son of a Parisian fan-maker, Petit may have trained in the newly founded national school for graphic arts in the mid-1790s before joining Jacques-Louis David's studio at the Louvre. After his return to France in March 1804, he was granted a year's leave by the Ministry for the Navy and Colonies to recover his health and complete his drawings from the expedition. However, while trying to dodge a carriage in a Paris street, he fell and injured his knee, developed gangrene, and died a few days later, on 21 October 1804.

RIEDLÉ, ANSELME (1768–1801), gardener on the *Géographe*, died of dysentery at Timor on 21 October 1801. A native of Augsburg in Bavaria, Riedlé was working at the Muséum d'histoire naturelle by 1795. He collected plants for Baudin on the voyage of the *Belle Angélique* to the West Indies and was awarded a medal by the Société d'agriculture in Paris for his work.

RONSARD, FRANÇOIS-MICHEL (1769–1836), sub-engineer first class on the *Géographe*, given the functions of sub-lieutenant on 29 September 1801 and then lieutenant on 20 October 1801 during the stopover in Timor.

SAINT-CRICQ, JACQUES DE (1781–1819), sub-lieutenant on the *Naturaliste*, was made acting lieutenant in Timor on 20 October 1801. During his service in the Napoleonic Wars, he experienced both triumph and disgrace. As captain of the frigate *Clorinde*, he captured HMS *Junon* in an action off Guadeloupe in December 1809. After the Battle of Tamatave, however, which was fought off Madagascar in May 1811 and ended in defeat for the French, he was found guilty at a court-martial of having abandoned his commodore during combat and was imprisoned for three years.

VASSE, TIMOTHÉE-THOMAS-JOSEPH-AMBROISE (1774–c. 1801), helmsman second class on the *Naturaliste*, originally from Dieppe, was lost in the waves while attempting to get on board a dinghy in Geographe Bay on 8 June 1801. It was generally assumed that he had drowned although a rumour grew up in subsequent years that he made his way back to Europe aboard a whaling vessel. In 1838 Wardandi Noongar people recounted to the colonist George Fletcher Moore that Vasse had made it to shore and had survived in the region for a number of years – an episode that endures in Wardandi oral history.

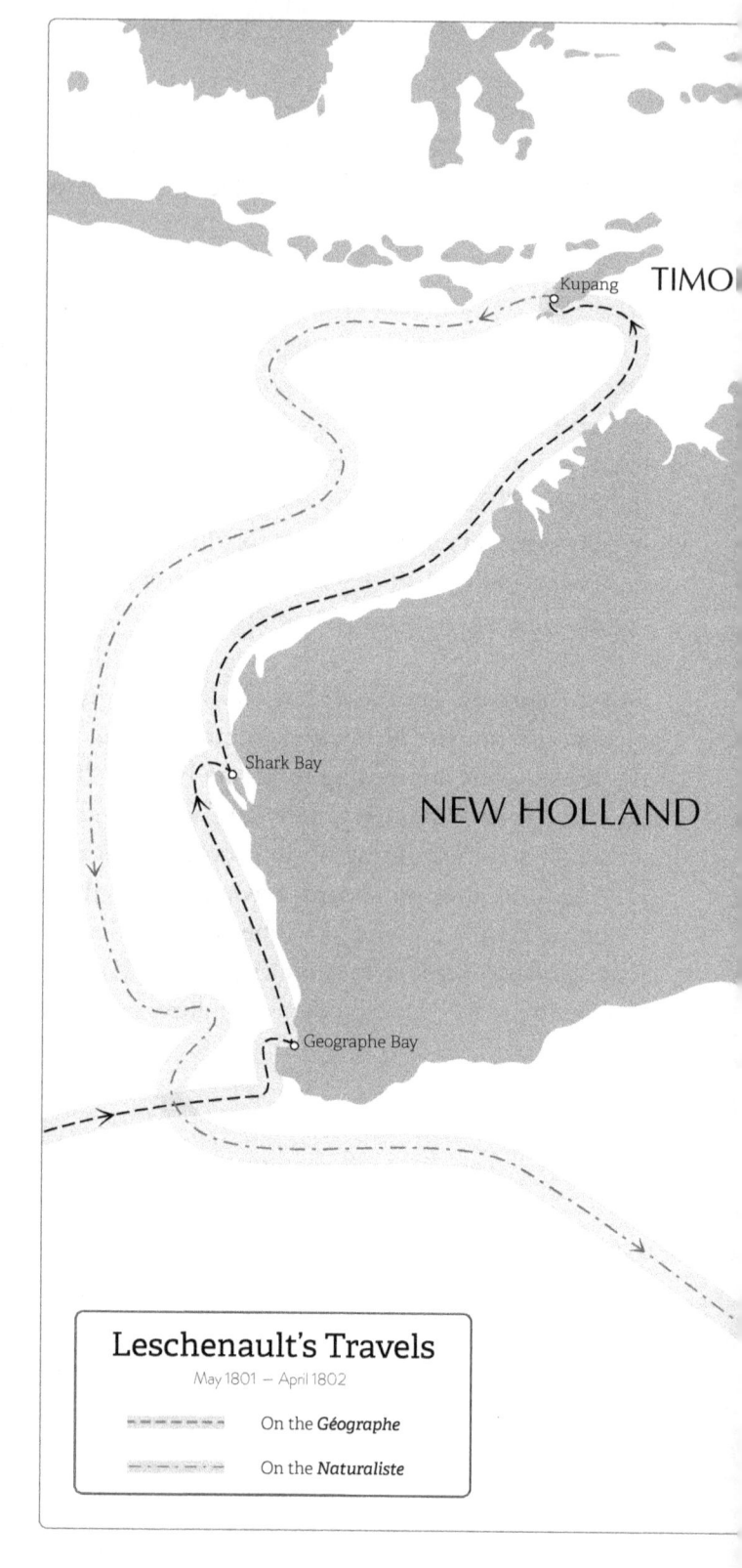

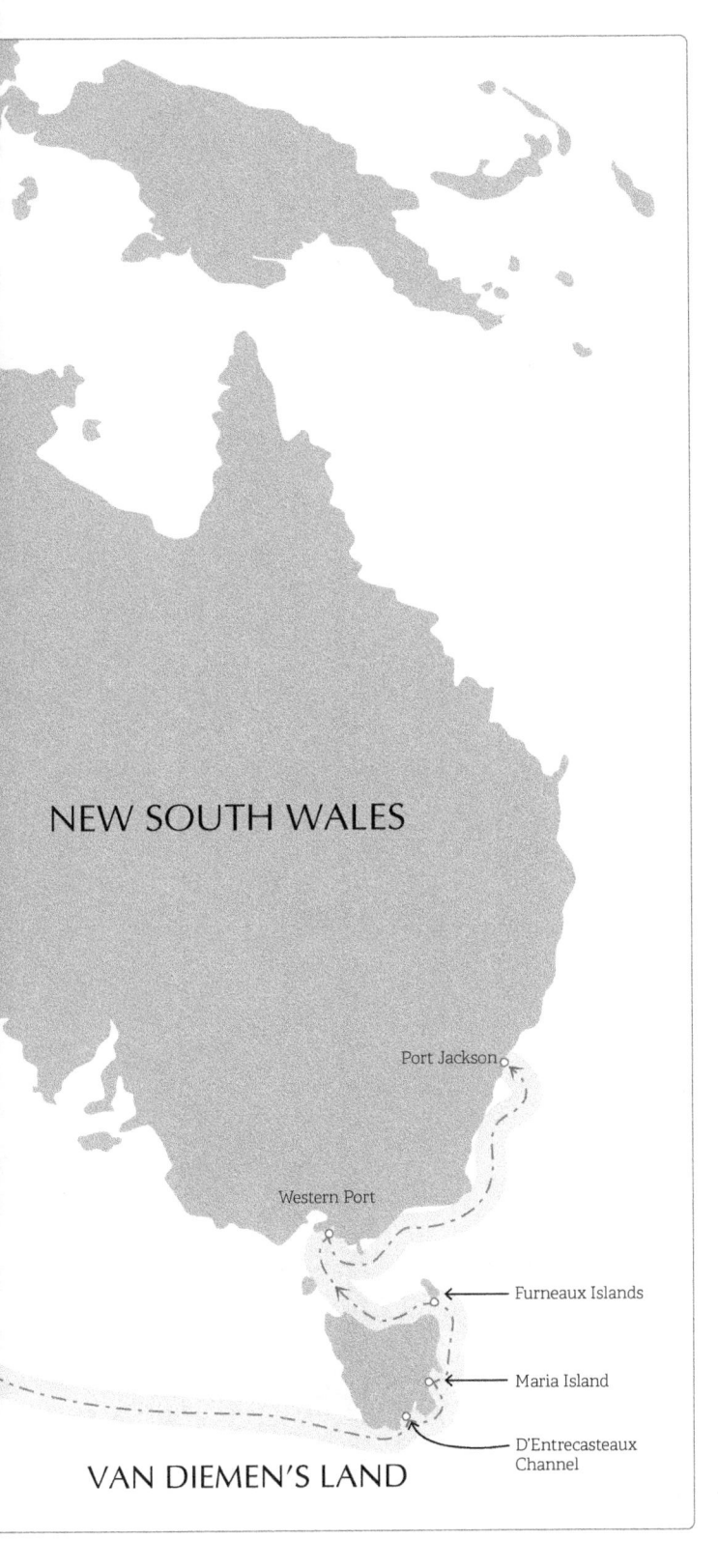

JOURNAL OF THÉODORE LESCHENAULT, 1800–1802

Chapter 1

Stay in Le Havre; Arrival in Tenerife; Stay on that Island

First Letter, Le Havre, 10 Vendémiaire, Year IX [2 October 1800][1]

I arrived yesterday after a two-day journey in a rather shabby coach. The constant jolting I experienced was made up for by the sight of the Pays de Caux.[2] The houses are set apart in such a way that even in this flat country they take on a varied and romantic appearance. One might wish for such an arrangement to be adopted across a large part of France.

Each farm stands alone, with its yards, gardens and fields encircled by a grassy embankment planted with a hedge, the lovely foliage of which creates a cooling effect while the roots support the mound it grows on. One is surprised to see a farmhouse with a thatched roof appear at the end of a charming avenue. These dwellings are all very clean and tidy. The peasants seem prosperous and well-dressed. In general, the women have fresh complexions and regular features, but their appearance is spoiled by their strange headgear. They wear huge sugarloaf bonnets, which are usually decorated with gold or silver embroidery and topped with strips of pleated muslin that fall down behind the head. They draw their hair up into a large chignon that is concealed from the front and extends down to the shoulder. This headwear stands so tall that a small woman's face makes up only half the total height.

There are magnificent views over Le Havre from Ingouville hill, which is where the town's merchants have their country houses.

I have already made several excursions along the sea shore and found *Fucus* and *Ulva*, marine plants that figure in Linnaeus's *Cryptogamia*.[3]

As I watched the ocean's restless waves break on the shore, I was seized by a feeling of terror. This, *this* will be my home for several years! I cried. And tears welled up in my eyes; I thought about my mother, my precious family, the friends I admire. I am leaving all behind! A painful feeling, which was tempered only by the pleasant conviction that I would sometimes feature in their thoughts and on my return clasp them to my breast and never leave them again! Oh, misery is the condition of man! Why must we always suffer in our search for happiness?[4]

★ ★ ★

Second Letter, 20 Vendémiaire [12 October 1800]

Yesterday I went to dine, just half a league away, at the country house of Citizen Germain, a wealthy resident of Le Havre. He has a very fine garden in which he grows exotic plants. He invited the expedition's botanists to call and he treated us with the utmost consideration.

His country house is located on Ingouville hill, which I spoke of in my last letter. Its position is utterly delightful.

The garden is arranged in terraces and above these there is a charming wood in which several exotic shrubs grow. Citizen Riedlé, the expedition's head gardener, identified several plants whose names were not known to Citizen Germain.

I have fallen in love with the countryside around Le Havre and when I return I plan to spend several months in this delightful region. You will come and visit me and your charms will brighten up this retreat of mine. You will be far from the rowdy delights of the capital, but you will be with a true friend. This idea greatly appeals to me, though it may only be a far distant pleasure. I am grateful for the power of my imagination, which offers me a foretaste of the pleasures I shall enjoy on my return.

We should have set off already. We tried to leave this morning, but one of the ships touched bottom and we had to turn back. A huge bank of pebbles is blocking the entrance to the harbour and it grows bigger every day. If something isn't done about it, soon no vessel will be able to tie up in this great port.

★ ★ ★

Third Letter, 24 Vendémiaire [16 October 1800], to Citizen J

You no doubt imagine that I am already a long way from France and yet it is from Le Havre that I write to you. We have been kept in port by perpetual adverse winds and we do not know if we shall leave for several days.

This time has not been wasted. We have used it to get to know one another. Sailors and naturalists get along perfectly. These encouraging ties of friendship have been strengthened each day by meals given and received.

The sailors had feared that we would be unbearably conceited due to our status on board as 'men of science'. For our part, we had expected them to be rough, uncultivated men. We were fortunate to have been completely mistaken. All the officers are extremely well-mannered and we have nothing but praise for the way they have treated us. There is every indication that this will continue.

Yesterday the commander held a lunch aboard for the prefect of the department, the maritime prefect, several high-ranking officers, and some very pretty women.[5] The ship was decked with flags and music played as the prefect was welcomed aboard. The ladies toured the ship and visited our tiny cells, which they thought charming. I would have been greatly delighted if one of the ladies who came into my cabin had decided to remain for the entire voyage. Sixteen years of age, large black eyes; with such a girl I might banish any periods of tedium.

The ladies lunched in the commander's cabin; other tables were laid for the men. After lunch, the commander presented the prefect of the department with one of the medals struck to commemorate the expedition.

My enthusiasm for the voyage has not waned in the slightest; in fact it has only grown, and if my intuitions are in any way accurate, my journey will be a happy one. In any case, I hope to gain some credit from it and prepare the ground for all the satisfactions of heart and mind in later life – those supreme delights that are independent of the events that occur in life.

Adieu, my friend, I will send you news from Tenerife and the Isle of France.

P.S. I've just this minute heard that we may leave tomorrow. I shall sleep aboard tonight, my little compartment is completely ready. It measures 6 feet square. It has a bed, which sailors call a 'berth', a small desk, a few cupboards, and a chair – such is my furniture. The light enters through a porthole measuring 16 inches square. Despite the lack of space, I have stowed all my belongings in such a way that I can easily get to them. It's only on a ship that you learn how to organise things properly.

For three years this small cabin will be my refuge: in all that time, how often my thoughts will fly to you.

★ ★ ★

Fourth Letter, 27 Vendémiaire [19 October 1800]

The ship is casting off, the gates of the dock are open, the *Naturaliste* is already unfurling her sails, huge crowds line the pier... All the faces are naturally lined with worry to see men setting out to encounter great dangers... I can see mothers, wives and lovers; their gazes cling to men they adore... Perhaps they will never see them again!!... Tears run down their cheeks... When will I see tears of joy flow on our return?!...

CHAPTER 1: LE HAVRE TO TENERIFE

I can hear music of farewell from the heights of the harbour, a thousand hats wave, it's the final adieu... The officers' speaking-trumpets and the boatswains' whistles signal that we are about to get under way; sailors perched on the yards untie the ropes furling in the sails... The swaying motion of the ship increases... I'm off!!... Farewell, my friend... farewell for a very long time, perhaps... Just think, at some future moment, a sentient being will be thinking of you in the middle of the New Holland deserts... farewell... farewell.

Nota. I'll give this final letter to the pilot who has stayed on board our ship to see us under sail.

★ ★ ★

Journal

On 26 Vendémiaire, Year IX of the Republic [18 October 1800], an American corvette, the *Portsmouth*, carrying plenipotentiary envoys who had come to conclude the peace between the French Republic and the United States,[6] tried to leave at the same time as our ships; however, when the *Naturaliste* touched bottom, all three corvettes were forced to return to port.

On the 27th [19 October] we were more fortunate. A huge crowd lined the pier as we left port at ten in the morning. The town farewelled us with music. We got under way in fine weather with winds from the south-east.

The American ship was saluted with 13 cannon. It returned the same salute and moved away from us as we headed north-west. The *Géographe* did not put on full sail as the *Naturaliste* was not moving as fast.

At midday, an enormous number of scoters.

At 2 o'clock we met an English frigate that was cruising around 4 leagues off Le Havre. We were flying the flag of truce. When we were abeam of it, within pistol-shot, an officer hailed us in French, threatening to fire his broadside unless we struck our colours at once.

Commander Baudin hastily launched his longboat and went across to present the passport that the English government had granted the expedition. He was received very warmly by the English captain, who afterwards came on board our ship. He was accompanied by a young officer (the son of Admiral Gardner),[7] who, a few days earlier, had been sent to Le Havre as a negotiator. They left after inspecting the ship. The frigate was the *Proselyte*, which Dutch royalists had seized and sailed to England.[8]

We continued on our way; by evening the coast of France was lost to sight.

On the 28th [20 October] the winds shifted from south-south-west to south. The sea was calm all day. On the horizon we made out ten to twelve merchant ships bearing westward.

On the 29th [21 October] the wind blew strongly and shifted from west-north-west to north-north-east; the sea was stormy. At 6 o'clock in the morning we were in sight of the English coast. We tacked; at midday we sighted the Casquets, on which the English keep a light, and the small island of Alderney, which is theirs, close to the French coast. At 5 o'clock the winds turned favourable and and we headed westward. That day we saw a great many porpoises. Most of the naturalists and several officers suffered badly from sea-sickness; I was one of those who suffered least.

On the 30th [22 October] the winds shifted from north-north-west to north-north-east; we sighted Lizard Point (on the English coast). In the evening we left the Channel behind.

On 1 Brumaire [23 October], winds from east-north-east to south-south-east, clear skies, a calm sea.

On the 2nd [24 October], winds south-south-east and south. Fog.

On the 3rd [25 October], the winds shifted from south-south-east to north-eastward. There was a heavy sea. In the morning we saw a small whale 50 feet from the ship. At midday we caught sight of a vessel heading westward. At 4 o'clock the wind rose sharply; the sea was very heavy. We saw two halcyons, or storm birds, following the ships. It is said that this bird is the herald of storms;

this bird of ill omen is the size of a large swallow and resembles it also in its flight and form. When it grows tired it rests on the waves, raising its wings like sails. It is found a very long way from land. It is the *Procellaria pelagica* of Linnaeus. At night the weather worsened and it rained heavily. A brig was sighted nearby; we lost sight of the *Naturaliste* in the bad weather.

On the 4th [26 October] the *Naturaliste* drew back into view at 8 o'clock in the morning. The wind varied from north-west to north-north-west, the weather was fine, and a heavy sea was running.

On the 5th [27 October] the sea was still very rough, with winds from the north-east, and cloudless skies. We rounded Cape Finisterre (on the Spanish coast). We perceived very clearly that we were entering warmer regions. My thermometer, which in Le Havre reached 10° on the Réaumur scale,⁹ was now showing 16°.

On the 6th, 7th and 8th [28, 29 and 30 October] the wind blew constantly from the north-east, with clear skies and a calm sea.

On the 9th [31 October] there was no change in the wind and weather. At 5 o'clock we sighted an approaching English privateer. It confirmed its hostile intention by firing a cannon shot. The commander hove to and waited for it, but it turned away. It followed us at a distance all through the night.

On the morning of the 10th [1 November] the English privateer seemed intent on approaching us. When the commander ordered the cannons run out, the privateer turned away and did not reappear. At five o'clock in the evening we sighted the Pico de Tenerife poking through the clouds and, below, the nearer shore of the island. The sailors estimated that we were 18 leagues from the former and 8 leagues from the latter.

★ ★ ★

Our Stay on Tenerife

As it was too late on the 10th to come into port, we plied to windward by short boards all through the night and in the morning resumed our way.

We soon had a clear sight of the black rocks that rise steeply on the eastern point of the island of Tenerife, which is part of the archipelago known to the Ancients as the Fortunate Isles – although its appearance does not offer the slightest justification for this pleasing name. I would call it 'The Desolate Land Forsaken by Nature' instead.

If you try to imagine vast precipitous mountains of rock, reddish or black in colour, composed of lava and volcanic ash, and deep ravines carved out by torrents, you will have a good idea of these rocky slopes, to which I can think of nothing comparable in Europe. Noxious *Euphorbia* and good-for-nothing *Cacalia* grow abundantly on the parched summits, their pale green forms standing out against the brown earth.

As you round a solitary basalt outcrop jutting into the sea, you catch sight of Santa Cruz, which is on the southern flank of the island. There are a few fields of crops; it is quite a pleasant-looking town. All the houses are neatly whitewashed and roofed with hollow tiles. It is quite similar in appearance to a number of small towns in Provence.

On 11 Brumaire [2 November], a Sunday, we anchored at half past nine in the morning and at two in the afternoon we went ashore.

We were immediately set on by a mob of hideous old crones begging for alms. As we spoke no Spanish and had no *maravedí*, the small coin of the country, we were unable to get rid of them. The more irate we became, the more doggedly they pursued us, and some of our group had their unpleasant company for most of the day.

The centre of the town appears deserted. The doors are all closed, as are the windows; the latter are covered with large shutters fitted with a sort of flap, around 1 square foot in size, which those inside can raise up in order to spy on passers-by. There are no goods on display outside the shops; you have to go inside to see what is for sale.

While some stern moralists complain that our elegant Parisian ladies exhibit their charms rather too frankly, the excessive modesty affected by Spanish ladies will undoubtedly exasperate admirers of the fair sex. They fasten their clothing all the way up to the collar and attach at their waist a sort of hood which they draw over their head and pull so far down that the only part of their body visible is the eyes. They look rather like our own peasant women when they are caught in the rain and pull a skirt over their head in order to keep themselves dry.

In general, the women are very swarthy and unattractive. I did, however, see two or three dressed in very flattering clothes. When they are convinced of their own beauty, they take every opportunity to uncover their faces. Coquetry is common to all countries.

It is customary for women of the lower classes to wear light-coloured clothing and felt hats; wealthy women wear black silk with lace-fringed hoods.

Men wear a large thick cloak over rather loose-fitting clothes. While this may seem quite a strange thing to do in a hot country, usage teaches that the lighter a cloak's colour, the more effective it is at blocking the sun's rays.

After exploring part of the town, we decided that it was time to dine. It was exceptionally difficult to find an inn, and when we managed to do so, exceptionally difficult to make ourselves understood. We were eventually served a very poor dinner for which we were asked to pay a very high price.

After dinner we went to pay a visit to His Excellency the Governor General of the Canary Islands, Don Perlasca.[10] We were entertained very courteously.

The houses of the least well-off members of our provincial middle class are more lavishly appointed than those of the richest Spaniards of Tenerife. They have large, sparsely funished rooms with white-washed walls that are hung with crude colour engravings of male and female saints of every different order. Light enters through large sash windows. I believe that these large unfurnished rooms and broad sash windows are useful in a hot country because they enable air to circulate more freely and deny hiding places to the vast numbers of insects that rapidly swarm over everything.

On the 14th [5 November] two artists, the second lieutenant of the *Géographe*,[11] and I decided to visit Laguna, a town a league and a half from Santa Cruz. The road that leads there is in a terrible state and we stumbled over loose stones and our shoes were torn by sharp rocks. These minor inconveniences were all forgotten when we reached a high point overlooking the town. The most beautiful scene spread out below us: Santa Cruz was at our feet, there were rocky hills to our left, and fishing boats sailed serenely on an unruffled sea with the island of Gran Canaria bounding the horizon.

I studied the vegetation along the way. I saw many plants which are extremely difficult to grow in our greenhouses, but which are so abundant here that they become a nuisance. These include several species of *Euphorbia*, the *Periplocas*, the *Cacalias*, the *Agaves*, etc., etc.

The town of Laguna is just like Santa Cruz. One sees the same shutter-flaps, the same houses and the same hoods, though the streets are even emptier, and the inns even worse and more expensive. A squalid tavern is the only place in which to eat, and we were served an old hen, or an old cock, seasoned with saffron, a truly disgusting dish for those who are not used to it. They threw in a few eggs and figs and charged us five *gordos* (French francs) for the lot.

We returned by a different path and I somewhat made my peace with Tenerife's stone hills. They offered at once the most monstruous and dramatic scenery. We risked breaking our necks as we negotiated them. We descended into an extremely deep ravine. It was the most sublimely terrifying place one can imagine. In the rainy season the water funnels down this natural channel, which empties into a vast basin; before that, though, the water passes along an aqueduct that powers a mill. This aqueduct is very sturdily built and stands around 30 feet above the basin. We had to walk along it for quite a long way, even though we ran the risk of tumbling over the edge – something all the more likely as the rockface juts over it in several places. We did not lose heart, however, and made it to the end of the aqueduct. A new difficulty arose: a wooden trough sloped down at its end, offering us just as great a chance of smashing ourselves to pieces if it broke or we lost our balance. We stopped to confer. The sun had sunk below the horizon and we could not turn back. It would have taken us two hours to negotiate rocky slopes that were treacherous even in full daylight. We decided to tackle this descent and we all made it down safe and sound.

We were returning to town around the base of the hills, cheerfully discussing our day's adventures, when, passing by a deep recess, we heard a pitiful voice call out, begging for our help. We went towards it. Stones had been piled up to form an enclosure, the entrance to which was hung with a filthy mat. In the dim light of dusk we could make out a man lying completely naked on the damp ground. As soon as he saw us, he hauled himself onto his knees, joined his hands together and spoke again in his mournful voice. The sight of this poor wretch melted out hearts. We emptied our pockets for him. He had never before perhaps received such a large sum of alms – and never before had I given alms with such a glad heart. Any man who is well enough off to enjoy the comforts of life, and yet still feels sorry for himself, ought to contemplate that man of the Tenerife rocks!

On the 15th [6 November] I returned to Laguna[12] once more, and the country around it offered me a more favourable impression of the island. Setting out from Laguna in the opposite direction from Santa Cruz, you see fields, herds of animals, and grazing land. The soil is deep and fertile, formed from thick black volcanic ash. I was told that farmers have three harvests a year. Even after an eleven-month drought and in this advanced season, I came across green vegetation. The *Euphorbias*, which are so plentiful on the rocky hills of Santz Cruz, do not grow at all in this part of the island. The locals cultivate a large amount of Caribbean cabbage (*Arum esculentum*) in low damp places.

A league from Laguna there is a beautiful laurel wood where the trees are as broad and tall as our European oaks. A stream runs through it, charming ferns spread their lovely serrated leaves, and the slender branches of shrubs twine together in delicate shades of green. An admirer of Apollo, dreaming in the shade of his sacred tree, would doubtless have been inspired by this enchanting place.

★ ★ ★

Condition of the Plant Life on the Island of Tenerife in the Middle of the Month of Brumaire or November (Early Days of November 1800)

At this time all the plants in Europe have lost their leaves; nature begins to slumber.

When we arrived on Tenerife, it had been in the grip of a drought for eleven months and, according to the inhabitants, the previous summer had been excessively hot. During the twelve days that we were on the island, the thermometer rose to 22° and 23° (Réaumur scale).

I observed that nearly all the annual plants had withered away. The leaves of the fig trees and vines were starting to fall. *Datura stramonium*, which is very common in the region, displayed all the different stages of plant growth – that is, from corollas still enclosed in the calyx to open and withered capsules. I observed the two extremes of development in the cotton tree, *Sida indica* and *Periploca*. The laurels were in flower and in fruit, but the fruits were more numerous, and were mostly ripe.

The land around Santa Cruz is barren. The Spaniards' natural indolence poses an insurmountable obstacle to its cultivation. And so the fields, which are covered with enormous volcanic boulders, appear more like bare, burnt ground than farmland. It would take a more industrious people to exploit it properly. (I think that vines could be grown there sucessfully, and yet scarcely any are found around Santa Cruz.) To protect the soil, which on these hillsides would be carried away by rains in the wet season, they have taken the precaution of building small dry stone walls, which form terraces that are wider or narrower according to the slope of the ground.

The valley stretching from Laguna to the laurel wood I mentioned above is fertile, but I was surprised to see that it is completely bare of vegetation. It seems to me that plantations of fruit trees such as figs, oranges or bananas would draw in moisture more powerfully, moderate the extreme heat of the climate, and create a pleasant haven for the farmer.

The region around La Orotava (from what I have been told) is the most productive on the island; it boasts large plantations of vines, banana trees and orange trees. There are also a great many apple trees, but the fruit, while rather fine in appearance, has a bitter and unpleasant taste.

Sugarcane is grown at the village of Adex [Adeje].

A small amount of flax is also grown, and it is used pure or else mixed with flax imported in large quantites from Holland or the Baltic countries.

They also grow, if only in small amounts, all the crops found in northern and southern Europe, due to the fact that a range of temperatures occur across this mountainous island.

A List of some Plants I Saw around Santa Cruz and Laguna

Fig trees
Banana trees
Vines
Cotton trees   I saw few of these.
Laurus indica
Laurus nobilis   The wood from these is used for building.
Visnea mocanera   The *Visnea mocanera* has 16 stamens.
Erica arborea   This tree sometimes grows to a height of 25 feet.
Parietaria arborea
Hypericum androsaemum   This plant also grows in the countries of southern Europe.

Cineraria populifolia
Euphorbia canariensis ⎫ From which commercial
Euphorbia quadrangularis ⎭ euphorbium resin is derived.
Periploca ...
Cacalia ficoides
Eranthemum salsoloides
Convolvulus floridus   This has an aromatic wood.
Convolvulus canariensis   Creeper.
Achyranthes aspera
Cactus opuntia   The insect from which cochineal is derived lives on this particular plant; however, this insect is not found on Tenerife.
Agave americana
Sida indica
Oxalis minuta
Illecebrum paronychia
Ornithogalum longibracteatum   This bulbous plant grows plentifully in the cracks of rocks; it is found in Europe.
Datura stramonium   A very dangerous narcotic plant.
Arum esculentum   Its root is used as food.
Several species of fern and *Asplenium*.

In the Laguna woods I found a *Fungus*, which must belong to the genus *Clavaria*, growing in abundance on the trunks of the laurel trees. On the inside it consists of a soft green substance which smells like laurel. Its exterior is greyish brown. This *Clavaria* is mamellated; it looks quite similar to a piece of cauliflower heart. As it grows it lengthens and develops fissures and divides into several parts, which curl back on themselves. It then takes on a woody consistency; its exterior turns a deeper brown. It does not lose its laurel smell. I named it *Clavaria lauri*.[13]

Citizen Broussonet, a distinguished botanist and the French government consul in Tenerife, devotes himself to studying the botany of the Canary Islands with the utmost zeal.[14]

CHAPTER 1: LE HAVRE TO TENERIFE

*General Observations on the Island of Tenerife
and Other Islands of the Canaries*

The Santa Cruz roads are not very safe and the winds from east-south-east are sometimes fierce. These have sunk several ships at anchor. Small vessels have difficulty approaching the mole, against which the waves break violently. When the sea becomes even a little choppy, rocks just below the surface at the corner of the mole increase the danger. According to sailors, it is flawed in its construction. The Santa Cruz roads are, however, the safest and most commonly used in all the Canaries.

The Spanish move water considerable distances and at low cost by means of wooden conduits that run up and down on light, flimsy supports. Some of these aqueducts are 3 or 4 leagues long. This ingenious method is in widespread use across the island.

There are very few birds in the countryside around Santa Cruz and Laguna. I attribute their scarcity to a lack of cover and the large number of birds of prey which live on the cliffs. Since they are generally left in peace, they know little fear; it would thus be very easy to reduce their numbers. Among these birds, I observed the common sparrowhawk, which is known by the common name 'tercel' in France; it is very widespread.

The white vulture; the same bird is found in Egypt and along the southern coast of Spain.

The flycatcher seems to be the same as that found in France; its plumage is slightly less golden.

There are neither hares nor foxes, but a great many rabbits.

A large species of red partridge; the same as that found in Africa.

There are no reptiles.

All trade is conducted through the ports of Santa Cruz and La Orotava. The former has special rights. All ships sailing to the Americas must leave from this port and ships arriving from the Americas must land their cargo at Santa Cruz. It also enjoys the advantage of conducting the trade of all seven islands that make up the archipelago; in any case, all ships that resupply in the Canaries call at this port. The supplies available are cattle and sheep, which are small, along with black pigs, all sorts of poultry, excellent oranges and wine.

Vidonia wine is Tenerife's main article of trade; there is also a little Malvasia wine.[15] In peace time the English ship out the former and, in war time, it's the Anglo-Americans and the neutrals who do so.

Brandy is exported to America, to Havana, Cuba and the province of Venezuela. Over there it is preferred to Spanish brandy. But this product does not come from Tenerife alone; it is sent in large quantities from other islands of the Canaries to merchants in Santa Cruz, who ship it on from there.

A small amount of silk is harvested, some of which is exported to Europe; the rest is worked up on the island and the finished products are sent to the Americas.

The other products traded include small amounts of soda, saffron and orchil (Linnaeus's *Lichen roccella*). After it has been processed with human urine and lime, this plant supplies a purple dye that is used in our European factories. It is difficult, and even dangerous, to collect this plant, as it grows on steep cliffs overlooking the sea. It was once one of Tenerife's main articles of trade, but much less of it has been gathered in recent years.

The oars used in Tenerife are vastly superior to our own due to their light weight and flexibility. They are made from *Laurus indica*.

Santa Cruz has 12,000 inhabitants and the island as a whole 90,000. The basic necessities are extremely expensive and scarce. This problem would be even more acute if French privateers cruising in these parts in recent years had not captured a considerable number of prizes, which they have brought in and sold. There is a garrison of three regiments which has swelled the population and increased consumption. The Spanish government was forced to send these troops to protect the colony from attack by the English, who carried out a raid several years ago under the command of Admiral Nelson. They were vigorously repelled and the admiral lost an arm and an eye.[16]

The monasteries and churches of Santa Cruz are all built in the same simple style, but their interiors are smothered with decorations and gilding, heaped on in the most bizarre Gothic manner.

There are two rather beautiful fountains, one of which is in marble. This was built in honour of the Virgin. When the Spanish captured Tenerife, the Guanches worshipped a goddess who they said had appeared 400 years earlier in the exact same place where the fountain stands today. Superstitious Spaniards claim that this goddess was the Virgin, who had wished to reveal herself to men floundering in the darkness of superstition and idolatry, and so they erected the monument.[17] In this way, one error was replaced by another.

On the right as you enter the town is a tree-lined esplanade, built on the orders of the marquis of Branciforte,[18] who was governor of the Canaries before the previous one.[19] Its entrance looks like the gate to a monastery.

The inhabitants of Tenerife have very dark complexions; their faces betray only laziness and taciturnity. Squatting in the streets, hordes of beggars pluck lice from one another and harass passers-by with their persistent pleas – offering up a picture of direst penury and inveterate idleness. In a trading town a traveller ought to be diverted from such a repulsive scene by the lively sight of throngs of citizens going about their business. But the Spanish misanthrope almost always prefers to remain shut in at home. Should we attribute such dreary behaviour and profound poverty to the current war, which interferes with all commercial undertakings, or to an inept administration, or to the influence of the monks?

There is an excessive number of streetwalkers. Like the beggars, they are horribly dirty and persistent.

The country houses around Santa Cruz appear as dismal as those in the town. They are squat and plain and have no trees around them to cast the cooling shade that is so necessary in a hot climate.

The Canary Islands remained independent until 1344, when a Spaniard named Luis de la Cerda, who belonged to the royal family of Castile, assumed the title 'Prince of the Fortunate Isles'.[20] In 1402 the islands came under the control of Jean, baron de Béthencourt, who took the title of 'king'.[21] His descendants still live on Tenerife, penniless and obscure. The islands were then ceded to Dom

Henrique, the Portuguese infante. They now belong to Spain.[22] Tenerife is the seat of government.

The seat of the Inquisition is on Gran Canaria.

It is also the most fertile of all the islands. But little is done to encourage farming; it has some olive trees. The habitants go fishing off the coast of Africa, where they salt their catch.

Sugar and a few masts are produced on the island of Palma, and silk on Gomera. Remarkably, this is the only one of the Canary Islands on which deer are found. A sugar mill has recently been built there. Hierro is the most barren of the islands; its inhabitants collect large quantities of figs, from which they make brandy.

Lanzarote and Fuerteventura conduct a large trade in soda; 45,373 quintals[23] were exported from Lanzarote in 1798.

In times when marvels were eagerly welcomed and accepted, a thousand outlandish tales were told and written about the Guanches, the ancient inhabitants of the island of Tenerife, and today it would be very difficult to separate the true history of these people from the welter of nonsense. Not a single one of their descendants is alive today.

The Guanches displayed their courage in their resistance to the Spanish. They had great respect for the dead. After embalming the venerated remains of their friends and relatives, they carried them into caves which are accessible today only by means of ropes and ladders. They placed them reverently in wooden chests raised up on daises. The difficulty involved in reaching these simple and respectful memorials could not protect them from European curiosity. The sanctuary of the dead has been violated; more of these sepulchral caves are discovered every day. The dessicated bodies, each one wrapped in seven goatskins, are removed. We were given several of these mummies. (I had a thigh bone from one of these mummies; it was somehow stolen from me.)

While at Monsieur de Cumberland's house I saw small cylindrical pieces of baked red earth, with a hole down the middle, which this ancient people probably used for making calculations. I also saw a hook that had been fashioned rather crudely from horn. These objects had been found in a tomb.

CHAPTER 1: LE HAVRE TO TENERIFE

A resonant lava is found on the island of Tenerife; it was used by the Guanches in the way that we use an alarm bell.

I greatly wished to visit the fertile region around La Orotava and see the aftermath of the volcanic eruption that occurred near the peak on 9 June 1798.[24] I also wanted to climb the peak, the summit of which is one of the highest points in our hemisphere, but our stopover did not last long enough and I was not able to satisfy my curiosity.

The island of Tenerife is, of course, a child of the volcanoes, which belched it up from the ocean depths. It formed part of the archipelago which the Ancients called the 'Fortunate Isles'. Today the region around Santa Cruz in no way offers either a charming retreat or a smiling expanse of nature. But has it always been such a barren place? Were the rocky hills, which are now so arid, once covered in rich humus, which would have been especially fertile in a climate so conducive to plant growth? Several observations support such ideas. The ravines run in the same direction as the hills standing between them — that is, they run down towards the sea. The torrents which shaped these ravines must have carried away the humus and deposited it on the sea floor. The bay of Santa Cruz provides evidence for my claim. Its bed consists of silty sand, which was undoubtedly carried down by the action of the streams. There are strong grounds for believing that such aridity is simply the work of time, which delights in destroying all that it creates — a truth that offers much material to naturalists and philosophers in their deliberations and theorisings.

We stayed on Tenerife for eleven days. My health suffered slightly from the change of climate. I had several bouts of fever, but the attentions I received from Citizen Lharidon, surgeon, soon mended this minor ailment. By the time we departed, I was in the best of health.

I left the island of Tenerife with no regrets. We had been made welcome, it is true, but what a difference there is between the cold courtesy of the Spanish and the simple heartfelt congeniality which is a mark of the French everywhere.

On 22 Brumaire [13 November], at 3 o'clock in the afternoon, we weighed anchor. Propelled by a moderate breeze from the northeast, we sailed along the southern coast of the island. This coast is a little less steep and less barren than the rocky hills around Santa Cruz. Pine trees growing among the rocks and a few isolated houses inform the traveller that man inhabits this wild region.

The weather was fine. The calm sea bore a reflection of the coastline disappearing behind us. Sitting on the poop deck of the ship, I stared back at the land we were leaving behind. Here, I said to myself, lived an independent people, unknown to Europeans. They were happy, for the astonishing fables of the Ancients were not entirely without foundation. With a more fertile soil, the people were doubtless able to fulfil all their needs and their desires were as innocent and simple as their ways. Devoid of ambition, they possessed all the virtues that make for man's happiness in society.

Fierce strangers, driven by greed and avarice, entered this untroubled land. In vain a farming people took up arms to defend their homes. The strangers bore new and terrible weapons, which brought terror and death from afar. They conquered without glory and acquired a new homeland... Those centuries are not long past; oppression and despair drove this people to extinction. None of them survives... We are setting out to visit unknown peoples; perhaps the moment of their discovery will be the start of their misfortune. But no, that can't be true, today governments are more enlightened, they will be just...

Inhabitants of the South Seas: we are prepared to brave dangers for the glory of our nation and the advancement of science and navigation, but we will not come onto your lands as destroyers. Your manners, customs and beliefs will be respected. We bring you tools that will make work easier and plants and animals that will diminish your privations and enhance your enjoyment of life. In exchange for all these benefits, we request simply the welcome and hospitality that are due to any man.

While I was occupied with these solemn, weighty thoughts, the island faded in the dusk and soon disappeared.

Chapter 2

Passage from Tenerife to the Isle of France;
Stay on this Island; Meteorological Observations;
Descriptions of the Animals

On 24 Brumaire [15 November] we crossed the Tropic of Cancer at the 22nd degree of west longitude.

The weather remained fine and the winds favourable until 1 Frimaire [22 November]. During this period we saw a great many flying fish and several mats of a seaweed commonly called 'grapes of the tropics'. It is known to the Portuguese as 'sargasso' and is Linnaeus's *Fucus natans*.

On 1 Frimaire, while in the 8th degree of north latitude, we entered a calm which lasted until the 19th [10 December]. It was interspersed with 'flaws' (in maritime terminology a 'flaw' is a brief storm), several of which were quite violent. During this time we experienced the hottest weather of our passage from Tenerife to the Isle of France, although the thermometer did not rise above 26° Réaumur scale.

During this calm we caught four young sharks and a porpoise; we saw several dolphinfish but did not catch any.

Following a storm on the 13th [4 December], the sea, while still very rough, was covered with large numbers of luminous zoophytes, which I have described below in the section 'Phosphorescence of the sea'. The spectacle they created on the ocean was magnificent.

During our short passage from Le Havre to Tenerife, we had all behaved politely and considerately towards one another, but no especially close bonds had formed. Each man was absorbed with thoughts arising from the prospect of such a long voyage. But after we left Tenerife, friendship grew between us as we found more common ground in our temperaments and tastes. Such friendship could only enhance the perfect harmony that always reigned between naturalists and sailors. My closest friends were Citizens Depuch, mineralogist, Péron, responsible for all physical and meteorological observations, Baudin,[25] lieutenant, who was forced by ill health to remain behind at the Isle of France, and Bougainville, midshipman, son of the famous navigator of the same name. My new friends' conversation, as informative as it was entertaining, made the days pass more quickly for me perhaps than they had done several months earlier when I was surrounded by the many delights that Paris has to offer.

The twenty days of calm that we experienced were, however, wearisome and seemed to everyone to last an age. We were in the 'torrid zone', it was very hot, and the flaws of rain that fell on us daily forced us to close the gratings, scuttles and portholes for part of the day. Warm damp fumes rose from the hold but, even after we had opened up, the outside air was too sluggish to cleanse the ship, being unable to circulate quickly enough to remove the putrid vapours.

We were all struck by a general feeling of malaise. We sweated constantly and profusely and were gripped by an unquenchable thirst which grew keener the more we tried to assuage it. (We were rationed one and a quarter pints of water per day, but some among us had their own supplies.) Citizen Sainte-Croix Le Bas, commander, who was responsible for maintaining cleanliness aboard ship, oversaw its regular fumigation. These measures, along with the attentions of Citizen Lharidon, surgeon, ensured that no serious illnesses resulted from the extreme heat.

The soul of a man at sea is like the element that bears him up: the soul too has its calms, its storms and its days of serenity.

CHAPTER 2: TENERIFE TO THE ISLE OF FRANCE

A dead calm always left me shattered, both physically and mentally. I preferred stormy weather even though the rolling of the ship was very wearing.

During the time we spent in the tropics, the sun set each evening in such brilliant displays that it seemed to be trying to make up for all the suffering inflicted by its perpendicular rays during the day. Each evening I took fresh delight in admiring the spectacle of the multicoloured clouds, which each day assumed new shapes. The azure sky often took on a greenish tinge as it was bathed with orange, while thin clouds billowed below in a blaze of brilliant pinks, crimsons, violets and purples. The daystar sank into this haze of vivid hues, which were reflected across the surface of the sea. A clear night soon followed and we gratefully inhaled the cool air that soothed our dry lungs.

There is undoubtedly nothing more majestic than the night-time spectacle of a calm sea and a clear sky. It elevates the soul and enlarges the mind. It is astonishing to see for the first time. Once you become accustomed to this unchanging sight, however, you grow weary of its monotony and long for the more varied, though more limited, views and perspectives offered by woods, mountains and valleys, their dim outlines fading into darkness. Ah, those lovely cool nights beside the Seine, so soothing and so inspiring, back in my own country! Now a more majestic scene appears before my eager gaze, but, 4000 leagues from family and friends, I wander over the bottomless depths…

The calm finally broke on the 19th [10 December]. A moderate breeze rose from the south-east, we were then in the 2nd degree of north latitude. These south-easterly winds, which sailors call 'general winds', are usually only encountered in the southern hemisphere. The north-easterly winds that prevail between the Equator and the Tropic of Cancer are called 'trade winds'.

On the 21st [12 December] we crossed the line of the equator at the 25th degree of west longitude. It was a day of festivities for the sailors and they performed the baptism ceremony. This idiotic and very ancient ceremony is practised by sailors of all nations. All who have never crossed the line before are doused in sea water. You can buy yourself out of this drenching by giving a little money to the crew. As there were a large number of us who had never sailed before, the sailors made quite a substantial sum out of us and spent the rest of the day making a merry racket.

A few days after crossing the line we saw several albatrosses (*Diomedea exulans*, Linn.), which sailors call 'Cape sheep'. It was long thought that this bird was only to be found in the southern hemisphere, but several navigators confirm having encountered large numbers of them in high northern latitudes.

On 14 Pluviôse [3 February 1801], at 8 o'clock in the morning, we sighted the Cape of Good Hope. It was around 8 to 10 leagues distant. In the finest weather imaginable we rounded this famous cape, which struck fear into the sailors of bygone days – who called it the 'Cape of Storms' due to the foul weather that almost always prevails in these regions. A short time before rounding the Cape of Good Hope we saw several floating clumps of *Fucus pyriferus*.

The Cape of Good Hope is renowned for its wines and produce. All the plants of Europe and the Indies grow there equally well. This fertile region with its mild, salubrious climate is a delightful place to stop. It is the most convenient port of call on the trade route between Europe and the East Indies. The Dutch established a settlement there in the middle of the seventeenth century. The English captured this colony, one of the most prosperous in the world, during the current war.[26]

This southernmost point of Africa, reputedly known to the Ancients, was sighted in 1487 by the Portuguese navigator Bartolomeu Dias.[27] Vasco da Gama rounded the cape ten years later and was the first navigator to take this route to the East Indies.[28] Manuel, king of Portugal, changed the name from the 'Cape of Storms' to the 'Cape of Good Hope'.[29]

We had left Tenerife almost three months earlier. This was the first land we had seen. We would have been delighted to stop over in a place praised so highly by all sailors, but we were aware that it did not feature as a port of call on our route. The weather was fine and we hoped to arrive in the Isle of France within a month, and so this mild fancy of ours faded as that fertile land was lost to sight.

The slow pace of the *Naturaliste* delayed us a great deal. Our passage from the Cape of Good Hope to the Isle of France took 40 days, although ordinarily this journey is done in around 20 to 25 days.

On the morning of 28 Pluviôse [17 February] we saw several blowers[30] playing in the water. The ship passed quite close to them. The waves broke over their massive forms as though breaking over rocks. Water spurted so powerfully from their blowholes that it spread in the air in a thick mist. At times they launched their huge bodies 12 to 15 feet out of the water and then fell back down with a great thump, the water churning with froth and continuing to heave for a long time afterwards. Any boat nearby would have run the risk of being swamped.

The naturalist will find a subject worthy of reflection and admiration in the way that nature links, by fine and almost imperceptible gradations, these gigantic children of the ocean depths with those microscopic creatures which in part endue the sea with the brilliant phosphorescence that observers admire in the dark of night.

On 12 Ventôse [3 March] we were caught in a strong gale which lasted 30 hours. All that time we ran under fore-sail and main stay-sail; the main top-sail tore while the sailors were trying to brail it up. The rolling was so violent that everything was thrown about. Several of us (including myself) were injured by falls, which occurred whenever we tried to move about. After thirty miserable, exhausting hours, the weather turned fine. The *Naturaliste*, which vanished from sight during the storm, reappeared on the 14th [5 March]. Finally, on 23 Ventôse [14 March], at half past four in the afternoon, we sighted the coast of the Isle of France on the horizon.

As we neared land we saw several strands of Linnaeus's *Fucus granulatus*. We also saw a great many 'straw-tails', a bird so named for the two very long feathers that extend from its short tail. It is also called the 'tropic-bird' because it is almost always found in the torrid zone.

We had been at sea for more than four months. Our fresh provisions had run out and, although there were no cases of illness on board, the crew still needed to recover their strength. Sailors know only extreme emotions, exposed as they are to danger on all sides. A few hours of fine weather very quickly cause them to forget a terrifying storm which threatened to sink their ship just a short while before. They are worn out by hard work and privation, they have often been short of healthy food: the sheer joy they feel on sighting a port that offers rest and plenty cannot be properly understood by those who have never known the hardship of a long sea journey. Each man gazed eagerly at this promised land.

We plied to windward by short boards all through the night. Early in the morning of the 24th [15 March], we turned north-west and ran with the wind astern, propelled at 5 or 6 knots (around 2 marine leagues[31] an hour) by a moderate breeze for the whole morning. Large numbers of boobies and strawtails flew around the ship.

We could soon make out the houses in the districts of Poudre d'Or, Rivière du Rempart and Pamplemousses. It was the season in which plant growth is most vigorous and the countryside was covered with a rich carpet of greenery. Leaning on the ship's handrail, I admired the magnificent scene offered to my sight by these vast fields of rice, corn and sugarcane interspersed with dense woods and crowned, in the south, with the high mountains of Black River, and, in the west, with those of Pieter Both and Le Pouce. We rounded a little islet named Gunners' Quoin and left behind on our starboard quarter Flat Island, Round Island and Serpent Island. None of these small islands has any fresh water; they are uncultivated and uninhabited. It is not easy to reach them, even in a small boat, due to the encircling reefs. They serve as a haven for a great many birds.

As we approached land, Cannonier Point on the north of the island saluted our French ensign with a cannon shot and lowered its flag three times. We returned the fort's salute.

The commander, under the impression that we had been recognised as French, fired two cannon shots to summon the pilots, but they did not come. The wind fell away, and as we could not enter the harbour that evening, we dropped anchor in 19 fathoms, on a bottom of coral, opposite Tombeau Bay. The *Naturaliste*, which had stood further off, anchored at the entrance to the harbour.

The clear sky was mirrored in a perfectly smooth sea. I remained on deck for part of the night and the silence was broken only by the solemn muffled roar of waves breaking on the reef that runs almost the whole way around the island. A light breeze carried to us the lovely scent of lemon trees and orange trees and all the other fragrant plants that grow so plentifully in its fertile soil. I eagerly inhaled this delightful aroma. As a beautiful morning dawned, this splendid tableau of nature began to fill with life and movement.

In Paris I had been given a great many letters of introduction for the leading residents and so felt sure that I would have a pleasant time exploring the colony. I was impatient to go ashore.

We weighed anchor early in the morning. The wind was very light and we made slow progress towards the harbour. The pilots at last came on board. They informed us that the appearance of our two ships had greatly alarmed the colonists. As we hadn't given the signals of the day, it had been generally assumed that we were English. The distance between our ships after we rounded Gunners' Quoin had lent weight to this error. The signal had been given that we were the enemy and a small vessel sailing from the Isle of Bourbon had stood close in to shore to avoid us, at the risk of foundering on the reef. It had not been reassured by our flag of truce, as the English often cruise in these waters flying the same flag. The whole colony was under arms, ready to repel any incursion by an enemy known for its brazen duplicity. In the evening, however, seeing us anchor under the forts, those who had taken us for the enemy were somewhat reassured. A debate had nevertheless taken place about whether to open fire on us.

The colonists on the island seem to feel a genuine loyalty to France. However, as the French government has long embraced philanthropic principles, they are wary of all ships arriving from Europe. Their fortunes and their lives hinge on any small changes that might be made to the old regulations governing the colonies. They hold up the disastrous events on Guadeloupe and Saint-Domingue as justification for opposing government orders that would abolish age-old laws.[32] It is only due to their firm resolve that France has managed to retain a colony that offers French ships a valuable port of call on the passage to India.

After we had anchored in the harbour, several commissioners[33] came on board. Once they had established that we were not charged with any mission that might undermine order in the colony, and that the crew were not suffering from any contagious diseases, we were allowed to go ashore. The welcome we received could not have been warmer had it come from our own relatives and friends.

For my part, I am extremely grateful to Citizens Choteau, notary, Besnard, Gallet and Leblanc. The first of these prevailed on me to stay with him in the port and I spent a large part of my visit to the Isle of France in the homes of the other three. These kind hosts lavished on me care, affection and all manner of delights; I shall always count the days I spent with them very happy ones.

My Stay on the Isle of France

Some time before coming to the Isle of France I had read Bernardin de Saint-Pierre's *Voyage* to this island.[34] Either the governance of the colony must have changed a great deal, or Bernardin's book offers a tissue of falsehoods in relation to how things are now (if I rely on what I have seen) and how things were before (if I rely on what I have heard *here on the spot*). In describing the torture and suffering of the black slaves, he allows his imagination to run wild. The picture he paints has its origin in profound compassion, but such a sensation, which arises only in the virtuous heart, cannot take precedence over truth – which must always be the historian's primary concern. If Bernardin does not precisely follow the topography of this region in his engaging novel *Paul and Virginie*, people will not, for that reason, read it with any less curiosity or delight. But the colonists of the

Isle of France will not easily forgive him for representing them as cruel and immoral torturers. Did he think that the truth could never cross 4000 leagues to refute his claims?

I will certainly never be an apologist for slavery. I will never say to men: 'Take other men from their countries, treat them as your property, force them to serve your needs, compel them to obey your whims.' It is an outrage against nature, which condemns it. But should governments view such practices from a philosophical perspective? If we destroy the established order of things, we must be careful not to allow chaos to ensue – a chaos no doubt worse than the previous compact, however imperfect. The whole matter can be summed up in the following question, which is perhaps difficult to resolve: Can a government preserve its colonies to some advantage if it *immediately* abolishes slavery for men of colour?

I toured a number of properties, some of which were very large. Everywhere I went, I saw negroes who were well-treated and well-fed and not overburdened with work. Indeed, putting aside human sentiment for a moment, slaves cost a considerable amount of money, and so a master, simply out of self-interest, that prime mover of men's actions, will make sure that his property is well-looked after and not ruined by regular mistreatment. I am aware that there are some exceptions: there have been cases of vicious and tyrannical masters. But not only is such behaviour abhorrent to the other colonists, if such misdeeds are frequent and come to their attention, then brutal owners are forced to sell their blacks.

The Isle of France was discovered at the end of the sixteenth century. Several navigators, who claimed that the island was known to the Ancients, named it Cerne, using the name that Pliny had given to an island in this region.[35] Some historiographers believe that he was referring to Madagascar. The Dutch established a settlement here in the seventeenth century and called the island 'Mauritius'. But once they had their colony at the Cape of Good Hope, this port was no longer of any commercial use and they soon abandoned it.

At the start of this century the French established a settlement here and gave the island the name that it has kept. The colony soon grew rich and prosperous as an entrepôt between India and the metropole.

It is the entrepôt trade that sustains the Isle of France, since its export trade, consisting of coffee from the Isle of Bourbon, sugar, arrack, a small quantity of cloves and a little indigo (which is scarcely grown any more), is not profitable. Cotton cloth, leather and rice are brought in from India, livestock from Madagascar, coconut oil from the Seychelles; wine, woollen cloth and other goods are shipped to the island by European merchants.

Since the current war began, all imported goods have become extremely expensive. The colony is supplied only by neutral vessels and privateers, and has very limited communications with France.

If the colony were captured, it would soon be ruined. It was abandoned by the Dutch; the English would soon do the same, as the Cape of Good Hope serves all their needs. It is even possible that they would fill in the harbour so as to be rid of the problem the island poses them once and for all. And hence the colonists, who are loyal to the metropole out of self-interest as much as sentiment, are prepared to repel any invasion, even though it would long be over by the time the French government could send help.

At the time of its discovery, the Isle of France was uninhabited and covered with forests. It had no quadrupeds or reptiles but was home to countless birds. Fish and turtles were plentiful along its coast. The turtles have now disappeared and the birds are less numerous. Fish are still plentiful and make up a large part of the inhabitants' diet. The island has often been ravaged by terrible hurricanes. The Europeans who settled here saw their crops destroyed every year and their houses demolished. Large-scale land clearance has reduced the frequency of this destructive scourge, which no longer has a fixed season. The hurricane of 1789, however, was one of the most violent, and all the ships in the harbour were driven ashore, and some sank. All crops were ruined and several men died in this natural cataclysm.

The harbour is capacious, bounded on one side by the harbour hill and on the other by little Tonneliers Island, which is connected to the mainland by a well-constructed roadway around a mile long.

The town lies in a valley that runs from the harbour to the foot of the mountains of Pieter Both and Le Pouce. The valley must extend back around a mile and a half. The houses are mostly constructed of timber and are usually just a single storey high, with a courtyard and a garden on either side. Although unpaved, the streets are broad and lined with shade trees, in single, double or quadruple rows; these belong to the genus *Mimosa* and are called 'blackwoods' by the locals. The trees secrete a yellow gum which is highly soluble in water and might be used instead of gum arabic. The streets have wide footpaths on either side. The layout of the houses is cleverly suited to the hot climate. Each dwelling consists of a number of separate pavilions. Their many windows create a constant draught of air, which keeps them cool. The interiors are tastefully decorated and their inhabitants do not lead lives greatly different from ours in France, apart from the fact that they must sleep for an hour or two during the day due to the intense heat.

We arrived in the Isle of France in the season when plant growth is most vigorous. I was impatient to explore the lush countryside I had seen from a distance. I received warm invitations from several people for whom I had letters of introduction.

The day after my arrival I had the pleasure of meeting Citizen du Petit Thouars, a distinguished botanist,[36] who, by virtue of his long stay on the Isle of France and his passion for botany, has acquired a comprehensive knowledge not only of the plants of this colony, but also of those of Bourbon and Madagascar. He has been exploring these islands for eight years. He was kind enough to show me part of his herbarium and gave me to understand that he would shortly publish a description of the new plants he had collected: the reputation of its author will ensure that this work is eagerly received.

After staying in the port for two days, I visited the country house of Citizen Gallet, a former naval officer. He lost no time in introducing me to his neighbours and I spent a large part of my stay on the island in the most delightful company. I was fortunate enough to make the acquaintance of Captain Lhermite. In Europe, this mariner enjoys an exalted reputation for his bravery and naval acumen.[37] His warlike talents are matched only by his modesty and congeniality. He extended me the offer of his friendship. He even invited me to stay with him in town but, having already yielded to the warm entreaties of Citizen Choteau on the day of my arrival, I could not take up the captain's kind proposal.

Early each morning I would go for walks in the countryside. I was presented with the wonderful new sight of alleys of double roses running along the edge of woods in which orange, lemon and pineapple trees grew in great abundance. (Oranges on the Isle of France are not good.) I felt as though I had been transported to the fabled garden of Armida.[38] It was always hard for me to leave these enchanted groves in which such delightful varieties of foliage were displayed by so many trees unknown in our regions, all of them remarkable for their fragrance and exquisite flowers.

Although nature everywhere offered me abundant opportunities for collecting, I gathered just a small number of plants. We were staying only a short time on the Isle of France. It was more beneficial for me to take frequent walks and so gain a deeper understanding of warm-climate plants than can be acquired from hothouses and herbaria. Any time I might have spent classifying plant specimens would have encroached on my botanical walks. In any case, we were due to stop here for a lengthy period on our return journey, and I resolved to put all that I should have learnt on my travels to good use during that stay.

I went to visit Citizen Céré,[39] director of the botanical gardens. I was received by this worthy citizen with his characteristic warmth and kindness. He showed me around the gardens, which he has set out in an admirably neat and ordered fashion and maintains with just the limited funds that the government can provide in the current circumstances. I saw several nutmeg trees, which were flourishing, and two breadfruit trees, which were in fruit. I also observed two very fine *sambles*, or funeral trees of Madagascar.[40] It is a species of dioecious palm tree and is remarkably beautiful in appearance. These gardens contain a wide variety of large trees, which are generally well looked after, but I saw almost no herbaceous plants or undershrubs. Having so few gardeners at his disposal, Citizen Céré has not perhaps been able to cultivate these sorts of plants — something that would be extremely useful since the gardens, which are vast, could host the greatest collection of useful plants from the hot countries.

Cinnamon, cloves and nutmeg acclimatise perfectly on the Isle of France. Large plantations of these have already been established by several private citizens. I saw more than 20,000 clove trees on a property belonging to Citizen Besnard and a large section of these were already productive. The cultivation of such crops here will completely undermine the measures taken by the Dutch to confine these precious plants to the Moluccas.[41]

Raspberry bushes have spread so rapidly that they have become a nuisance, even in the forests. These raspberries do not have the same taste as those found in Europe.

Justicia betonica is widely grown here; it is used to make lovely garden borders. This pretty undershrub has the advantage of growing astonishingly quickly and can be pruned in any way without being harmed. It can be grown from cuttings.

The brother of Citizen Baudin, our commander, brought a plant named *Ayapana* over from the Americas;[42] according to Citizen du Petit Thouars, it is a type of *Eupatorium*.[43] The leaves of this plant closely resemble those of *Justicia betonica*; they have a very aromatic flavour and are somewhat styptic. People here consider them a universal panacea and tell stories of the almost miraculous cures they have brought about, but such extravagant praise must be treated with caution. Several of these plants have been sent to Paris.

The soil on the Isle of France is very fertile but landowners demand too much of it. They sow two or sometimes three crops a year, which quickly exhausts the soil. Newly cleared land yields up to sixty to one, while land that has been worked for a certain number of years only brings in from ten to twelve.[44] Some landowners have started manuring their land, which has produced good results. To rest the soil, they plant camanioc or sweet cassava; the root of this plant is eaten by the blacks. It is only harvested after 18 months to two years. During this time, leaf and stem debris enriches the soil, readying it for wheat, which is sown there next. Rice is usually grown on newly cleared land; it is the dry rice of Cochinchina.[45]

Note on the Plants We Brought out from Europe

We placed the trees – apple, pear, fig, plum, apricot, peach and vines etc., etc. – between decks, arranged beneath the gratings so that they would receive light from above and fresh air. They were planted very close together in buckets and half barrels.

When they were brought on board, they had all their leaves, which they only dropped ten or eleven days after our departure.

Three or four days later they put on new leaves, but not in the usual way. The upper buds were the only ones that developed; the lower ones mostly remained dormant. Just a few of these grew, at different stages, much later on.

In most cases, all shoots, from the upper and the lower buds alike, wilted, the leaves curled up, and the sickly young saplings soon took on a withered appearance.

I removed several pieces of bark and observed that the sap was not abundant, as it is in spring. Instead of being easy to remove, the bark stuck to the wood as it does in winter. The wounds I made dried. No swellings formed. Several fruit set but quickly dropped off.

Should we ascribe the plants' general sickliness to their being set too close together in the buckets? Or should we rather ascribe it to their position between decks? But some walnuts and chestnuts that were planted in their shells in these buckets sprouted very healthy saplings and did not seem to suffer any harm. In fact, air circulated freely between decks and the trees were often in the sun.

I think that the growth of the plants was halted by exhaustion. After fulfilling all nature's demands in their own country, these plants were suddenly moved into new temperatures that commanded immediate fresh growth when rest was needed, and they became worn out. As a result, the upper buds were the only ones that developed, although the temperature and humidity ought to have favoured general growth.

In temperate countries, which have well-defined seasons, sap never completely stops circulating. In winter, this circulation slows and the nutritive sap grows more concentrated; how far then is this slowing of the sap necessary to the vigorous growth that must follow?

From these different observations, I have come to the conclusion that the most favourable season for transporting living plants from a temperate climate to a warmer one would be spring. The sap vessels, filled with nutritive sap, would be able to support vigorous growth, rather than producing abortive shoots that harm the trees, as I observed. And if the young saplings had not been pruned, they would undoubtedly have died. Despite this precaution, several of them did, in fact, die.

Observations on an Albino Woman

In Citizen Maillard's house on the Isle of France I saw an albino woman, or white negress. She was the daughter of a native father and mother from the African coast. She was 17 and of normal height and proportions for a girl of that age. Her hair was woolly and dull blond; she kept it completely covered with a headscarf at all times and was ashamed to reveal it. She had drab white skin and her face was covered with brown spots. She had blue-grey eyes and sparse pale eyelashes and eyebrows. Her features, which were characteristic of her race, were quite regular but her colouring was repulsive. The skin on her arms was scaly, with a light down of hair. Her feet were pretty in shape and size. She was short-sighted and could not easily bear strong light. She was quite strong and worked at the sugar mill feeding cane into the rollers. She ate the same food as the other negroes. She was very shy. When I tried to examine her, she lowered her head, and I was obliged to use force to raise it up again. She had firm breasts which were of a size normal for her age. I was told that she has the menstrual discharges peculiar to her sex, and that, despite several requests, she has declined all intimate liaisons with men – something that is put down to a defect in her temperament. Her father and mother together produced children who were alternately white and black.

Notes on a Negress's Lying-in

Citizen Besnard informed me of quite an interesting occurrence. If the account that he was given is accurate, one of his negresses gave birth on the same day to two children: one was black and the other had evidently been fathered by a white man. The latter child (the white one) came into the world second. Citizen Besnard questioned the woman who told him that, on the same day, she had had congress in the morning with a black man and in the evening with a white man; and she had no doubt that her pregnancy dated from that day because the interval matched up perfectly. And, in any case, she had not had congress with any man for a long time before that and a long time afterwards, and the children had consequently been born in the order of their conception. I leave it to physiologists to avail themselves of this observation which was relayed to me and vouched for by a man in whom one may place the utmost confidence.

Notes on some Animals of the Isle of France

White ants, or termites, cause great damage to the houses. They destroy house timbers and furniture. They also devour tree trunks. In the woods I frequently came across trees of which nothing remained but the bark; this had not been attacked, but it broke very easily, and within I found only a dust that was as black as compost.

Snails that were brought out to the Isle of France a short time ago have multiplied so rapidly that they have become the scourge of the farmers. They are very large and have elongated spiral shells.

The martin,[46] a bird belonging to the jay family, is the snail's enemy; but this bird also causes a lot of damage to the rice crop.

The cardinal and the bengali[47] are two very attractive birds. The first is a species of sparrow with red plumage. The second is much smaller and has varied plumage. Sometimes they destroy the wheat and rice crops entirely. There are blacks on the farms whose job it is to collect the snails and chase away these destructive birds with slings.

The tanrec is a quadruped recently brought over from Madagascar. It is the size of a rabbit and makes a burrow like a mole. They proliferate remarkably. I was told that the female gives birth to up to thirty young. The blacks eat this animal.

A small grey lizard is found in abundance in the houses. It is not at all harmful; in fact, it eats mosquitoes and other insects, which are present here, as in all hot countries, in vast numbers.

The mason fly makes its nest in houses, constructing it, rather like the swallow, using damp earth. Inside this, it fashions several oblong cylindrical cells in which it lays an egg; it places dead insects beside this. When the grub hatches, it finds nearby all the food it requires until it changes into a nymph. It only leaves the nest when it is an adult.

The green fly is very unusual and feeds on large cockroaches, which on the Isle of France are called *cancrelas*. As soon as it locates one of these, it goes up and touches it. It seems to possess some irresistible power that paralyses all the physical faculties of the cockroach, for as soon as it is touched it ceases all movement, as though it were dead. The fly then looks for a hole into which to drag its prey, returns and seizes one of the cockroach's antennae with its claws and drags it into the hole, where it devours it. If, while the fly is away, someone touches the cockroach, the spell is broken, and it flees. The trance in which it had been held a moment before does not seem to cause it any harm.

These two flies are similar in size and appearance to wasps in our own country.

A large species of spider is very common and its gold-coloured silk is so strong that it could be used as thread. This spider, which is not at all poisonous, sets its web between two trees. This is strong enough to stop the largest insects.

In the flat stones of the mango one almost always finds a beetle resembling a cockchafer, black and about the size of a broad bean. I very carefully examined some pieces of fruit containing the beetle; I examined the stones with the same care. Neither the fruit nor the stones had been perforated. When removed, the insect is in a deep sleep; it must be warmed up before it will start to move. I was told that, wrapped in a piece of paper, it could live for more than six further months without air or any form of food.

Sequel of My Stay on the Isle of France

When we arrived on the Isle of France, the colonists were still deeply affected by the death of Governor Malartic.[48] This respected administrator had enjoyed the trust of all the colonists. He had managed to maintain order and peace during the most difficult of times. His funeral prompted an outpouring of sorrow. During our stay, a memorial in his honour was being erected at the end of the Champ de Mars, which lies behind the town. Citizen Malartic was succeeded by Citizen Magallon.[49] This professional soldier works tirelessly to supply the colony's essential needs and to keep it safe from harm. He anticipates an attack by the English and makes preparations for such a contingency.

We were unable to obtain all the help we had hoped for from the government of the Isle of France. There was no money available and this dearth was felt acutely in the officers' mess during the passage to Timor.

Several officers and naturalists who had fallen gravely ill were unable to continue the voyage. For my part, I was sorry to lose the company of Citizen Michaux, associate member of the Institut national and head botanist of the *Naturaliste*, and Citizen Delisse, junior botanist on the same ship. The expedition was deprived of two learned men: Citizen Michaux, in particular, who had already travelled extensively and whose reputation far outshines any words of praise I might offer, was an irreparable loss. The responsibility for this splendid realm of natural history then fell to just Citizen Riedlé and me, but we could not hope by our efforts to make up for Citizen Michaux's store of knowledge. Citizen Riedlé was also lost to the expedition later in an unfortunate incident: against all the advice of his friends, he did not rein in his overly zealous exertions and so consigned himself to an early grave.[50] He had previously undertaken a voyage to the Americas with Citizen Baudin, commander, who was profoundly affected by his death.

★ ★ ★

The following meteorological observations should have appeared before the account of my stay on the Isle of France, as they were made during the passage from Tenerife; I have swapped the order to avoid interrupting the narrative.

★

Table showing longitude and latitude; the temperature of the air and the sea, according to Réaumur's thermometer; the humidity of the air, according to Saussure's hygrometer;[51] observed from 1 to 9 Brumaire [23 to 31 October 1800] and until 9 Nivôse following [30 December 1800], the day on which the sun was at our zenith. These inform the reflections I offer on meteorology, below.

Date	Longi-tude west	Latitude north	Midday			Midnight		
			Thermo-meter	Hygro-meter	Sea	Thermo-meter	Hygro-meter	Sea
1 Brumaire[52]	9.44	48.15	8.5	82	11	9	84	–
2	10.58	47.2	10	82	11.5	11	90	–
3	13.3	46.54	10.5	85	12	11	90	–
4	14.6	45.18	11	90	12	11.5	89	–
5	14.39	42.48	10	86	12.4	11	84	–
6	15.3	39.44	13.5	90	15	13	90	–
7	14.59	36.18	14.5	89	16.5	15	88	–
8	15.29	33.19	15	83	16.5	15.5	82	17
9	16.43	31.2	16	81	17	16.5	79	–
10	17.52	28.48	16.5	78	–	–	–	–
23[53]	19.59	26.3	18.7	91.5	–	–	–	–
24	21.37	23.21	18.7	91.5	–	–	–	–
25	22.23	20.4	20.7	93	19.7	–	–	–
26	22.21	16.57	21	94	21.5	–	–	–
27	22.7	14.24	20.5	96	22.3	–	–	–
28	21.29	12.8	22.7	88	23	–	–	–
29	20.19	10.4	23	86	–	–	–	–
30	19.29	8.57	25.3	80	–	–	–	–
1 Frimaire	19.26	8.5	26	86	24	23	84	24
2	19.2	7.35	24.5	89	24.5	23.6	95	23
3	19.1	7.44	25	92	24	23.6	90	24
4	18.49	7.29	24.3	90	24	23	94	23.5
5	18.3	6.55	22	99	23	21.8	100	21.8
6	18.31	6.57	23	94	24.8	21.5	96	21.5
7	18.27	6.46	25	90	23.8	21.8	98	22.7
8	18.32	6.41	24	91	22.8	21.7	96	21.7
9	18.18	6.22	20	105	21.7	21.5	93	22.3
10	18.14	5.11	19.5	102	21.7	20.8	100	21.7
11	18.48	4.26	24	95	22.3	21.3	96	22.3
12	19.36	3.42	23	94	21.4	20	96	22.5

CHAPTER 2: TENERIFE TO THE ISLE OF FRANCE

13	19.59	3.8	22	95	21.2	19.3	101	21.2
14	19.32	2.49	22.5	92	22	19	102	20.8
15	20.12	2.29	22	94	21	20	97	20.6
16	20.5	1.59	21	89	20.8	19	95	21.6
17	22.2	2.12	24	89	19	19	95	21.6
18	22.6	2.24	19.8	99	20.8	18	98	21.2
19	22.5	1.46	21.8	93	21.8	19.8	97	21.3
20	23.26	1.18	24	92	21.4	20.2	95	20.2
21	24.51	0.22	22.8	97	21.6	20.2	95	20.2
22	25.42	1.1 south	22.3	92	20.2	19.2	98	20.4
23	26.33	2.13	23.6	88	21.7	20.5	95	21.2
24	27.31	3	24.2	90	22	20.6	97	22.8
25	28.39	3.54	22.4	90	22	21	97	21.5
26	29.12	5.2	21.7	96	20.7	20	92	20.3
27	29.43	6.31	21.7	90	20.7	19.2	97	20.3
28	30.3	8.3	21.6	95	20.3	19.8	95	20.8
29	30.26	9.35	21.3	90	20.5	20.6	93	20.6
30	30.27	11.1	21	91	20.5	20.2	91	19.8
1 Nivôse	30.14	12.44	20.7	91	20.3	20	92	20.5
2	30.2	14.19	20.2	88	19.8	19.6	92	20.3
3	28.32	15.4	19.9	88	19.8	19.8	88	20.2
4	27.39	17.26	21.2	90	19.9	17.8	98	20.2
5	26.18	18.56	21.7	85	19.9	16.8	99	19.9
6	25.27	20.5	21.4	89	20.2	18.5	92	20.3
7	24.53	21.4	21.8	85	19.9	18.5	85	19.9
8	24.31	21.58	20.3	90	20	17.8	85	19.7
9	24.28	23.1	23	84	20.7	–	–	–

This table has been copied from that which Citizen Péron, zoologist aboard the *Géographe*, kept very carefully – and which he still maintains.[54]

★ ★ ★

The following conjectures cannot be anything other than partial. Having observed just a few general phenomena, I have tried to offer an explanation for them. But Citizens Depuch, mineralogist, and Péron, zoologist, who apply themselves with the utmost diligence and acuity to understanding both particular and general phenomena, will be able to offer a more valuable analysis of these complex observations.

On the Heat Encountered Between 1 Brumaire [23 October] and 9 Nivôse [30 December], and on the 9th [30 December], When the Sun Was at Our Zenith

Phenomena

Between 1 and 27 Brumaire [23 October and 18 November] the heat rose in increments.

28 Brumaire to 13 Frimaire [19 November to 4 December] was the period in which we experienced the hottest weather.

13 Frimaire to 9 Nivôse [4 December to 30 December]: although we were nearing a region in which the rays of the sun have a stronger effect, it was much less hot than between 28 Brumaire and 13 Frimaire [19 November and 4 December].

Conjectures

During the second period, we were only around 50 to 60 leagues from the coast of Africa. The north-easterly winds came out of the vast stretches of burning sand that fringe the land in that part of the world. As they did not have to travel far to reach us, they did not have the chance to cool. Our proximity to the coast and the direction of the wind were, in my view, the reasons for the hotter weather that we experienced. The heat would have been even greater if not for the fierce rain-bearing flaws we encountered each day. The fine variations in the thermometer that can be observed in the preceding table for 9 and 10 Frimaire [30 November and 1 December] are due to these downpours. On the 8th [29 November] the mercury rose to 24°. On the 9th [30 November] it went down to 20° and on the 10th [1 December] to 19.5°. On these two days, the rain saturated the air with so much moisture that the hygrometer rose abruptly from the 91° that it showed on the 8th [29 November] to 105° and 102° on the 9th [30 November] and 10th [1 December].

From 13 Frimaire [4 December], the heat declined appreciably, although, for the first few days, we were only moving very slowly away from the coast. The initial changes in temperature must have been due to the continuing calm weather and rains; the searing African air could only travel slowly towards us through an atmosphere that was repeatedly subject to cooling.

But when the winds shifted from north-east to south-west, the change in temperature was due to our distance from the coast. Indeed, the thermometer regularly showed 23° to 26° near the coast of Africa but rose no higher than 20° to 22° between 24° and 30° of longitude, a difference all the more notable as we were moving towards the sun's perpendicular.

On 8 Nivôse [29 December] we were in latitude 21° 58' south and the thermometer rose to only 20.3°. And on 9 Nivôse [30 December], when we were in latitude 23° 10' south and the sun was at our zenith, the thermometer rose to just 23°, quite a moderate temperature when compared with the 26° we experienced on 1 Frimaire [22 November] in latitude 8° 5' north when we were still around 24 degrees (or 480 sea leagues) away from the sun's perpendicular. But on 9 Nivôse [30 December] we were far distant from the coast, with the wind blowing from the direction in which the coast lay; on 1 Frimaire [22 November] we were very near the land and the wind was blowing from the same region.

These remarks may be compared against the preceding table, which I shall also draw on in what I shall say shortly about atmospheric humidity and the temperature of the sea.

★

On Atmospheric Humidity

Humidity does not attain equilibrium in the atmosphere in the same way that heat does. So many specific and local factors produce variations in humidity that it is very difficult to establish a general theory. One may readily formulate conjectures, but as soon as one tries to fit them to the data, they are often contradicted, or even demolished, by the results.

It is accepted that heat holds water in a state of evaporation and thus produces more or less humidity in the atmosphere. In accordance with this principle, it would be reasonable to assume that a specific temperature acting on a regular body of water must cause the humidity it produces to reach a state of equilibrium and must maintain it in this state. Let us consider the results obtained from our experiments.

In the preceding table, I looked for a sequence of days in which the temperature did not vary greatly. I found that between 26 Frimaire and 7 Nivôse [17 and 28 December], there were nine days in which the air temperature varied by only seven-tenths of a degree and the sea temperature by nine-tenths of a degree (temperatures measured at midday). These variations are not great and yet the hygrometer varied by 11 degrees.

From this I conclude that to establish a *general theory* it would be necessary to study the history of each sort of measurement, so to speak, and properly understand the *specific causes of the variations*, separating these from the *general causes*; then one might *actually* understand the effects produced by the latter causes.

However, I believe that I can observe two distinct periods in the results obtained up until now. The first extends to 10 Brumaire [1 November]. During those ten days the humidity was generally greater at midday than at midnight, but the temperature did not rise above 16°. The heat was not great enough to evaporate a large amount of water and the water vapour it did produce rose only to a moderate height. When the sun sank below the horizon this vapour quickly condensed and, as it fell, the atmosphere grew clearer.

The second period takes in the observations made between 23 Brumaire and 9 Nivôse [14 November and 30 December]. There are two things worth noting in this period: firstly, the humidity was generally lower at midday than at midnight; and, secondly, the hygrometric figures display no relation to temperature, and, hence, to the amount of water vapour or humidity in the atmosphere.

The cause of the first phenomenon lies in the fact that hotter temperatures hold water in a state of evaporation closer to dissolution; as a result, the molecules, which are spread further apart, have a weaker influence on the hygrometer. But at night these molecules draw closer together, since the upper vapours do not tend to rise as they do during the daytime, and yet they are still too dispersed to descend completely; hence they exert a stronger influence on the hygrometer, which accordingly registers greater humidity at midnight than at midday.

If one did not seek to understand the causes of the second phenomenon and simply examined the hygrometric readings, one might initially believe that the humidity varied little in comparison with the range of temperatures that we encountered in different latitudes. However, several facts prove the contrary.

(1) The iron and steel items on board the ship remained shiny as far as Tenerife but became covered in a thick layer of rust as we progressed through the torrid zone. This rusting offers undoubted evidence of very high levels of humidity.

(2) Between the tropics, the atmosphere is almost always laden with vapours that turn the sky and horizon hazy.

(3) These vapours are present in such large quantities that they cause the temperature measured in the sun to vary markedly from the temperature measured in the shade.

Example

The thermometer showed	in the sun	in the shade
23 Frimaire [14 December]	33°	23.6°
24 *idem* [15 December]	36°	24.2°
2 Nivôse [23 December]	41.5°	20.2°
3 *idem* [24 December]	42°	19.9°

When it is very hot, water molecules held in a vaporous state are spread out more widely and have a constant tendency to rise. This, as I explained above, is the reason why they have a weaker influence on the hygrometer. But these vapours, which are constantly replenishing through a strong force of attraction, move vertically, causing them to envelop, so to speak, each of the sun's rays. And although they deprive the sunrays of their expansive influence, these rays continue to exert their direct influence. This is the cause, I believe, of the enormous difference between temperatures measured in the sun and in the shade.

On the Temperature of the Sea

Between 1 and 10 Brumaire [23 October and 1 November], the sea temperature was higher than the air temperature.

From 10 Brumaire to 9 Nivôse [1 November to 30 December], the air temperature was higher than the sea temperature.

Winds and storms, the ebb and flow of tides, and currents constantly stir up the sea; great volumes of sea water are shifted about by these unceasing forces. The heat of the water readily reaches equilibrium. This is the reason why the temperatures of the sea offer such a contrast with those of the atmosphere. Might one not conclude that, at a certain depth, the temperature of sea water must be the same in every climate? We did not have the instruments to verify this. Only one experiment was performed, using a device invented by Citizens Péron and Depuch,[55] and although this experiment was not entirely successful, the result suggested a difference of 11 degrees between the temperature of the surface water, which was 24°, and the temperature measured at a depth of roughly 80 fathoms, which was only 13°.

The water collected at 80 fathoms seemed to me to have as salty and as bitter a taste as the water at the surface. This water was yellow but transparent; did it just happen to be this colour, or is it always so?

★ ★ ★

The Phosphorescence of the Sea[56]

The causes of this phosphorescence are very well known. Several learned observers have described the animalcules which cause it,[57] but I was surprised by the variations in the phenomenon. And, in my view, it is difficult to explain these causes satisfactorily, since phosphorescence can be seen to increase and decrease in the same location without any noticeable change in the atmosphere.[58]

On 18 Brumaire [9 November], the sea in the Santa Cruz road was highly luminous. At 8 o'clock in the evening, as I was returning aboard the *Géographe*, the wake of our boat blazed and the oars seemed to plunge into molten metal, as each time they slapped against the water there was a flaring of the phosphoric flames, which, the day before and the day after, were scarcely noticeable, even though the air temperature and the condition of the sea changed very little.

On 11 Nivôse [1 January], between 24° and 25° of south latitude and 25° and 26° of west longitude, when the sea was very still and brightly lit by the moon, there was a great deal of phosphorescence at 10 o'clock in the evening and none at all at 11 o'clock, even though the ship remained motionless in the dead calm then prevailing.

However, phosphorescence is generally more prevalent and more frequent near the coast, as I observed in the Channel and along the coast of Tenerife. We scarcely encountered it at all between 16° and 24° of south latitude and 30° and 25° of west longitude.

I believe that the marine flames observed by Dr Bajon[59] during his passage from France to Cayenne, flames which he said formed in the water at a depth of 2 to 3 feet and which he encountered very frequently towards the 12th, 10th and 8th degrees of north latitude (observed also by Monsieur de la Coudrenière),[60] are due to a species of zoophyte,[61] which we found in great numbers after a storm between 2° and 3° of north latitude.

The sea was brightly lit by luminous, motionless forms, which I initially thought due to a large amount of phosphoric material that had combined and condensed. The sight of this watery fire that created no heat was magnificent. At a depth of several feet, the zoophyte in question appears as a large cloud of light, blurry and uneven in outline. But when it drifts on the surface of the water, its shape appears distinctly in the darkness. We were all struck by how regular the bodies of these creatures appeared and we caught several in a small net. We realised then that this phenomenon was caused by a zoophyte which is more or less cylindrical in shape, 4 to 5 inches long, and 1 inch in diameter.

This creature, which has a fishy smell, is phosphorescent in every part. It drifts on the waves and has no apparent power of motion. It is formed of a semi-transparent, jelly-like substance, with faint dirty-yellow markings, and is covered with an irregular scattering of large tubercles. It is rather tough in consistency. It has a hollow interior, regular along its whole length, which contains sea water.

The phosphorescence ceases when the creature is still but it glows brightly when it is squeezed or shaken about. Citizen Péron preserved one in vinegar. One of my colleagues claimed to have observed a movement of contraction and dilation, which I did not see. In any case, it has no apparent circulation, and can only have a very obscure sense of life.[62]

... The picture done for Commander Baudin does not seem to me at all accurate. An attempt was made to show it in its luminous state, and so it was painted a bluish-green colour, which is nothing like the colouring it has in its resting state. This is its more usual state and the one in which it ought to have been depicted.

I dried one of these creatures in an effort to preserve it, but its body, which must have been 1 line in thickness,[63] grew as thin as parchment. As it dried it lost all its tubercles and became covered in a layer of sea salt, which sparkled brightly and had an acrid smell.

The phosphorescence appears from small luminous spots inside its body, which are somewhat elongated and very close together. When the phosphorescence ceases, these spots appear less transparent than the rest of its body.

Descriptions of Several Animals which I Observed during the Passage from Le Havre to the Isle of France

Small black petrel, *Procellaria pelagica* (Linn.); common name: storm bird

This bird is found in almost all seas. It travels a great distance from land. When it finds itself caught in a storm, or anticipates one, it will follow in a ship's wake, hoping no doubt to take refuge on it. It flies fast with a motion resembling that of the swallow. It often sets its webbed feet on the waves, raising up its wings. As it follows ships more commonly – and more obstinately – in stormy weather, it has been called the 'storm bird'. One was found dead on the deck after a violent squall. It had probably been killed by the shaking of the rigging.

Albatross; *Diomedea exulans* (Linn.); Cape sheep

During our passage from Tenerife to the Isle of France five albatrosses were killed. They were stuffed by Citizen Maugé. Citizen Péron put together the skeleton of the fifth. These birds have a wingspan of 9½ to 10 feet and measure 4 feet from the tip of the beak to the end of the tail.

Albatrosses have white beaks and white feet, but after death the blood extravasates and coagulates, turning them brown.

Of the five killed, two were russet-coloured and the other three had white breasts and backs. Does this variation in colour indicate different species, or different sexes, or just a difference in age? They all have exactly the same body shape, they behave in the same way, and both sexes are found among individuals of the same colour; all this leads me to believe that age alone is the reason for this variation. These birds live together despite their different colouring; a white one and a reddish one were killed alongside one another.

The down of these animals is as beautiful as that of the swan. When the albatross sits on the water, it displays no fear on being approached. It can be found very far away from the coast; its strength and the speed of its flight mean that it never encounters strong adversaries on the seas it roams. More tyrant than victim, it knows no danger; the length of its wings perhaps prevents it from taking off easily.

One of the albatrosses was killed on the wing; its stomach was empty. The other four were killed while resting on the waves. They had filled their stomachs so recently that the food inside had not spoiled. The sailors made good use of the enormous octopus tentacles that were 2½ inches in diameter and had suckers the size of hazelnuts. In one of the albatrosses we found a tapeworm that was 50 feet long. The flesh of this bird has an unpleasant taste.

Sharks; *Squalus carcharias* (Linn.)

We caught several juvenile sharks. The flesh of this fish is very white, friable, and has a bland taste. The flesh of old sharks must be very tough; this fish does not swim on its back, as several naturalists have suggested. I only saw one turn a little on its side to take a bait it was thrown.

Remora; *Echeneis remora* (Linn.)

The remora attaches itself to the shark by means of 18 plates on the top of its head; it is never more than 6 or 7 inches in length. The remora should not be confused with the suckerfish *Echeneis naucrates* (Linn.). The latter differs from the remora in having 24 plates rather than 18. In any case, the suckerfish does not have a forked tail and can grow up to 2 feet long. Sharks are commonly followed by another fish, called the pilot fish, *Gates ductor*[64] (Linn.). It does not attach itself to the shark but rather follows it. It can grow up to 2½ feet in length. It has alternate black and white bands which encircle its body.

The pilot fish I observed swam near the flanks or the dorsal fins of the shark, which these different fish probably follow because they find a reliable source of food in the scraps of its prey or in its faeces. There is also perhaps an instinct among the weak to shelter from danger by staying close to a strong and invincible creature; they are able to evade its voracious appetite by closely watching its movements, which is quite easy for them as they are extremely agile. I never witnessed a pilot fish 'scout and inspect' the bait thrown to a shark.[65]

It would be a mistake to think that remora, suckerfish and pilot fish follow only sharks. The first two species sometimes attach themselves in great numbers to the hulls of ships. The Ancients believed that just one of these small fish could halt a vessel's progress. Pilot fish also follow ships; the Dutch call them 'muck fish'.[66]

We caught a porpoise, *Delphinus phocoena* (Linn.). It was 6 feet long. The flesh of this fish is black, and, in my opinion, has a taste somewhat similar to hare. The sailors greedily drank the warm blood of this porpoise; they claim that it has the power to prevent what they call 'land sickness'. This is a swelling that is sometimes experienced as one approaches land after a long passage. We found in this fish's body a large number of vesicular worms (*Hydatis hydatigena*, Linn.).

Diodon? ... This fish has the remarkable ability to inflate its body at will. If you ignore its tail, which is very short, and its fins, it looks just like a spiny globe or ball. When it is not inflated, it is around 5 inches long, and tapers towards the tail. It has a flat head, around 1½ inches long, which makes up around a third of its total length. Its mouth is angular and only slightly protrusive and it has large eyes; its jaws are bony and sharp. Inside its mouth there are four bulges, two in the upper part and two in the lower. The animal probably uses them to crush the shellfish it feeds on. Its whole body bristles with sharp spines, which are triangular at the base, set in the skin by means of three bony roots, like a caltrop in shape. Its belly is milky white with a few black markings; its back is ultramarine blue with more numerous markings. When its skin is dried, the blue colour turns brown.

Inflation occurs by means of a pouch that the animal fills by sucking in air and water. This pouch[67] is inside it and lies over the intestines.

This fish feeds on a shellfish that I shall discuss below. I found fragments of this shellfish in its intestinal canal, which is around 3 feet long. This fish was always semi-inflated when I saw it, moving around a foot below the surface of the water.

It makes no movement to avoid being caught. Its only defence is to inflate rapidly; its sharp spines would undoubtedly cause injury if it were not handled with care.

I kept one of these fish for some time and was careful to change the water frequently. I noticed that each time I replaced the water, it sucked in a large volume, kept it inside for some time, and then expelled it. After doing this it seemed livelier and more agile.

We found large numbers of this fish in 30° south latitude.

On 2 Pluviôse [22 January 1801], in 34° south latitude, we found great quantities of a small univalve shellfish, which has a very unusual shape. It roughly resembles a small turtle to which an appendage has been attached at the front.[68] When the creature advances its foreparts out of its shell, it is on this appendage that it rests its tiny head, and its large mantle, which is divided into two sections, serves as a pair of fins. A portion of this mantle even spills out of the side openings in the shell, which is around 4 lines wide and 6 lines long. The shell is transparent; its upper side is reddish-brown and its underside is clear. Its rear end is rounded and armed with three very sharp spines. The creature's mantle is a reddish-grey colour with a fringe of white.

This shellfish floats on the waves and is preyed on by the *Diodon*. In all the *Diodons* that were dissected I found a great many pieces of this shellfish, unmixed with any other sort; from which it seems reasonable to conclude that it serves as an important food in this fish's diet. However, where we found the one, we never found the other.

In the same waters we found a great many of a species of mollusc that must be placed in Citizen Cuvier's class of cephalopod molluscs.[69] The foreparts of this animal's body are free; it can withdraw them when it wishes into a sort of sac, which forms, as is the case with cuttlefish, the rear part, and half the total length, of its body. It has two small retractable tentacles on its head; these do not protrude very far. Its head is crowned with eight crests and a sort of hood which extends as far as the mantle or sac. When it wishes, the animal can fold back the two large fins which are attached on the sides of the forepart of its body under the hood. On the left side of its forepart there is a yellowish spot the size and shape of a small grain of barley. Soft in consistency and located inside the body, it presses against the animal's mantle without being attached to it.

This mollusc is around 1 inch long, swims with great agility, and is grey in colour. Some portions of its body are a very dark grey.

Salpa (Linn.); mollusc with the common name: organ pipe
(not to be confused with the madrepore called organ pipe)

It has been given this name due to its cylindrical shape. It opens at either end, with each end having two lips which contract and dilate. It is by means of these contractions and dilations that the animal is able to move. It has a jelly-like consistency and is perfectly transparent. On the inside of the pipe there is a sort of membrane, which is transparent also, and which in the case of larger individuals bears transversal striations. This membrane is connected to a spherical sac which is firm and a very dark yellow in colour. When I squeezed this sac, a yellow material came out: could this be the animal's stomach?

Salps usually travel several together, joined in a regular line somewhat resembling the arrangement of pipes on a bird-organ.

I observed several different species. Some were 3 inches long and 4 lines in diameter and had a slightly yellowish hue. Others were around 6 inches long and half an inch in diameter; they were as clear as the finest crystal. Another species had a very long horn at each of its ends and this was of the same substance as the rest of its body. And one final species was 10 inches long and 5 inches in diameter. The spherical sac, which I believe to be the stomach, varied according to the size of the animal.

South of the equator we very often encountered the medusa described by Monsieur de la Martinière in the *Voyage of Monsieur de La Pérouse* and depicted in figures 13 and 14.[70] I would add to his description that the large tail of the medusa turns in a spiral form, just like the tracheas of plants, and that the animal can extend it and draw it in as it pleases.

In the same latitudes, we also found the sea lizard[71] that Monsieur de la Martinière observed in the Bashee Islands, and which is described in the *Voyage of La Pérouse* and drawn in figures 15 and 16.[72] I observed that the four small tentacles on the animal's head are retractable, and are not arranged in parallel, as the image appears to show, but that two are on its upper side and two on the lower.

The number of branches in the legs and the appendages of the tail varies according to the size of the animal. There is a perceptible opening on the left side of the body, which dilates and contracts. I believe that this opening allows passage for the generative organs and secretions, as is the case with snails. I saw a white viscous substance come out of it, which I think must be faeces.

CHAPTER 2: TENERIFE TO THE ISLE OF FRANCE

The coloured illustration done for Commander Baudin shows its shape and colouring very accurately.

This animal always stays on the surface of the water.

Citizen Baudin informed me that the interior mechanism by which it breathes could be seen with a magnifying glass: the air, appearing as so many small beads, first by process of inhalation crept along to the far end of the tail and then, by exhalation, came out again in the same manner. I realised that Citizen Baudin had been misled by the small silver band which runs lengthways along the animal's back, a slight creasing in which gave back a reflection of the light; but as Citizen Baudin seemed attached to his idea, I didn't insist further.

After rounding the Cape of Good Hope we came across a snail floating on the waves, which was around the same size as a vine snail. Its shell is turbinate and purple in colour; its mouth, which lacks a bourrelet, is angular with rounded corners. The animal floats on the water by means of an elongated operculum, containing a network of vesicles, which resembles a mound of transparent froth. There are two forked tentacles on the back of the animal's head. Its mantle is short.

I saw this animal release a liquid which was a very beautiful shade of violet.

When the animal is removed from its shell, its head, which is very elongated, resembles the genitals of a male monkey.

One of the ones we caught was covered in a very attractive sea foam; Citizen Baudin had it painted in that state.

It is *Helix janthina*. Monsieur Hawkesworth, who edited the first *Voyage* of Monsieur Cook, believes that this shell may well be the *purpura* of the Ancients. Monsieur Forster is not of the same opinion.[73] I placed some of the liquid secreted by this animal onto a piece of paper. Its colour faded markedly as it dried.

We found several other species of mollusc; all are transparent, gelatinous and remarkable for their brilliance, colouring and elegant forms. If I were to try and describe them, I could only offer a very crude picture of them, as their features are unlike those of any other creature. The visible organs common to all other animals are not found on these – or are, at least, invisible to the eye of an untrained observer. It is only in their more or less vigorous movements of contraction or dilation that they in fact reveal they are living creatures. Citizen Petit's colour pictures offer a much more accurate idea of what they are like than I could give.[74]

However, I cannot refrain from offering a description of one of these animals. I was struck by its beauty: a skilled craftsman could not fashion a piece of jewellery with a more delightful or more regular form. I do not believe nature can create anything more perfect.

This mollusc resembles a flower, 2½ inches in diameter, turned upside down in full bloom. The peduncle is around 2 inches long. It is very bulbous and is made up of tubes which sit one on top of the other and are attached in parallel, each one having an external opening that dilates and contracts. This peduncle is kept in a vertical position by a robust oval-shaped air chamber, which sits at the top and holds the flower upside down.

The petals of this moving flower are cylindrical and are about the size of the shaft of a small feather. They can bend in any direction just like an earthworm and have pointed ends. These petals are flesh-coloured; at their base is a bead of the same colour, the size of a pea. The disk of the flower is made of a large number of capillary filaments, which are pink in colour with black spots.

This animal swims with great agility. It was caught by Citizen Maugé, zoologist, in 34° south latitude and 5° east longitude.

Travellers on the open sea should take care to examine the objects that drift past their vessels. If this were done, I am convinced that the realm of natural history would be enriched with a great many animals unknown along the coast. This activity mostly dispelled the tedium that arose during our extremely long passage from Tenerife to the Isle of France. Every day we found fresh objects to observe and describe; a purse net attached to the end of a pole is the only device required for this absorbing form of fishing.

Chapter 3

Arrival on the Coast of New Holland; Discovery of Géographe Bay; an Encounter with the Natives; Wreck of our Longboat; a Gale; Stay in Shark Bay; Passage to Timor

We left the Isle of France on 5 Floréal [25 April 1801] and had a very favourable passage to New Holland, enduring no discomfort apart from that occasioned by the absence of our friends who had remained in the Isle of France.

During this passage we saw a great many Cape petrel. Several of them were caught on lines baited with small pieces of meat. They are voracious birds and can be found several hundred leagues from land. They have a remarkable capacity to disgorge an enormous amount of fat which cools to the consistency and colour of congealed olive oil. The fat has a strong and unpleasant odour. Does the petrel use it to attract the fish that it feeds on? Or does it use the fat to calm the turbulence of the waves when resting on them? Or does it simply use it to make its feathers impervious to water?

On 7 Prairial [27 May] we sighted Cape Leeuwin, which, according to the observations of Citizen Saint-Cricq, sub-lieutenant, lies in latitude 34° 7' 50" south and longitude 112° 26' east. In the evening we hove to and the commander had the dredge lowered. Among several zoophytes, sponges and eschara brought up by the dredge, I observed a very pretty green-fronded lithophyte. I kept one as a specimen. (*Nota*. The dredge also brought up a species of sponge which was bright red in colour and stained the fingers of those who touched it. Citizen Depuch, mineralogist, was wearing nankeen trousers which were stained with this colour and these stains resisted several attempts at washing.) During the night the currents drove us far to the west. On the 8th [28 May] we drew near land again.

On the 9th [29 May] we ran very close in along the coast that stretches from Cape Leeuwin to a headland behind which a bay opens to the south with an entrance around 13 leagues across. As it did not appear on the charts, Citizen Baudin named it Géographe Bay. According to Citizen Saint-Cricq's observations, the southern headland of the bay lies in latitude 33° 52' and longitude 112° 22', while the northern headland lies in latitude 33° 17' and longitude 111° 50'. A rock which is thought to have been sighted between the two headlands, but outside the bay, lies probably in latitude 33° 20' and longitude 111° 49'.

Until this point we had visited countries which, it is true, had different climates, crops and animals from those we were familiar with in Europe, but whose inhabitants had more or less the same morals, customs, passions and needs as ourselves. Now the scene was set to change: we were to observe a country that was still a child of nature and which had not yet been despoiled by the enterprises of a sophisticated people. Here we would be able to judge whether civilisation, by multiplying our pleasures, has not diminished our happiness.

There was nothing appealing in our first sight of New Holland: in the foreground of the Leeuwin coast a white, sandy scarp slopes evenly down to the shoreline, apart from where a white lagoon, barren and featureless, extends about a mile in length. The scarp is completely covered with small bushes, the dark foliage of which is interrupted only by a number of landslides. The ridge is crowned with tall trees. I suspect that the sand here contains large amounts of marl[75] and lime, which is what I think makes it so fertile. The sounding line, which repeatedly showed a bottom of sand mixed with fragments of shell and madrepore, and several large beds of bluish clay which I sighted along the beach, have given me grounds for a conjecture: I believe that the fertility of the soil would increase the further inland one went. Wherever the scarp had crumbled away, allowing us to see into the interior, we could make out that the land was covered with tall trees. Along this coast the sounding line always showed between 30 and 60 fathoms. During the day we did not see any natives, but in the evening several fires indicated that this barren coast was not without inhabitants.

On the 10th [30 May] we entered the bay; that evening we anchored about 3 miles from land.

On the 11th [31 May] Citizen Freycinet,[76] sub-lieutenant, took a dinghy with Citizens Depuch, mineralogist, and Riedlé, head gardener, to the southern side of the bay.

In the short amount of time they spent on land they were not able to go very far from the shore. They did not find any fertile soil in the ground they covered. They saw only a few bushes or undershrubs, tough grasses and rushes. The vegetation here was not very vigorous, but they observed that the interior of the country was much more thickly wooded.

According to Citizen Depuch, the humus, or vegetable soil, along this part of the coast contains a mixture of ochre, clay and mica and lies on a granite base. He brought back several samples of this granite and the soil that lies on top of it. Although we saw several fires inland, close to where they made their landing, they, however, did not see any natives.

Citizen Riedlé brought back quite a large number of plants, though only a few were in flower or fruit. The advanced season gave us little hope that our collecting would be any more successful. (The month of Prairial in the southern hemisphere corresponds to the month of Frimaire in our climate,[77] an unproductive period for plants in almost all European countries.)

I described several of the plants which had characteristics distinct enough for them to be classified.

I observed:

A species of *Scirpus* which could prove quite useful. Its long leaves are so tough that Citizen Riedlé wasn't able to break a single one. This grass has the benefit of being able to flourish in a soil which, according to the two above-mentioned observers, is poor.

The gum plant mentioned by Vancouver, and which Phillip observed on the east coast of New Holland.[78]

The trunk of this tree grows to 7 or 8 feet in height and often bifurcates; from the top of each part issues a thick clump of very brittle leaves, filled with pith and resembling a clump of grass. These leaves have the form of quadrangular prisms, diamond-shaped and broadening markedly towards their base.

The bark, which resembles a mosaic of small diamonds all perfectly joined together, is made up of strips an inch and a half long stacked one on top of the other, all of exactly the same size. These are the vestiges of leaves.

Gum oozes out in great profusion between these strips or leaf remnants – a dark reddish-brown resin that solidifies into tears, which are sometimes as large as an egg. From the centre of the clump emerges a single scape 8- to 10-feet tall, which is woody in consistency and bears a spike thickly covered with capsules that have three valves and three locules. Citizen Riedlé never saw it in flower and only found capsules that were open and without seeds. Phillip asserts that the gum of this tree is an excellent remedy for dysentery. (Like Labillardière, I believe that this tree is a species of *Dracaena*.[79] I saw one of these trees in flower in Port Jackson and learnt that it belonged to a new genus named *Xanthorrhoea* by the English.)[80]

I also observed the *Banksia nivea*. It was not in flower or in fruit.

A species of *Glycine* to which I gave the specific name *ilicifolia* because its tough leaves are prickly and serrated like those of the holly.

A small bulbous plant and, lastly, a very pretty undershrub with beautiful red flowers which, as I believed that it had not yet been described, I named *Baudinia* after Commander Baudin.[81] (This plant features among the drawings and descriptions of plants I have sent back.)

Nobody went ashore on the 12th [1 June] but the commander sent a dinghy to inspect the far end of the bay. The midshipman in charge of it reported that the whole stretch he explored was covered with very fine trees nearly down to the shoreline. He did not see any natives.

On the 13th [2 June], Citizen Péron and I landed on the eastern side of the bay. A very fine, white sand, possessing, I believe, the same vegetative elements as that found along the Leeuwin coast, forms a scarp 40 to 50 feet high and nearly twice that in width. The slope which faces the sea is quite steep and the plants there are not very vigorous.

A species of creeping *Mesembryanthemum* with white flowers and thick triangular leaves grows there. Might it be *edule*? Several species of undershrub are also found there. I observed one from the orach family – it's an *Atriplex* with a very downy stem and leaves and a salty taste.

When I reached the top of the scarp I gazed admiringly across a flat country which is covered with very large trees forming a magnificent forest. A gentle slope leads down to the plain. The far side of the scarp, which also consists of sand, possesses a fertility that is lacking on the seaward side. Bushes around 12- to 15-feet tall cover part of the land. A beautiful species of *Genista* with dense, reddish wood grows there.

A *Leptospermum*, which resembles the weeping willow in shape.

There are a great many crab holes in the sand but we did not see any crabs.

I found fertile soil at the foot of the scarp, a thick blackish compost, several feet deep, formed by the debris of the plants which grow there in great profusion. These plants have much in common with our European ones.

I came across celery in abundance; a plant I judged, after inspecting its leaves, to be burnet; parsley; several species of sow thistle, geranium and plantain; and a very lovely species of *Gnaphalium* with white flowers.

The trees of the forest are very big. I saw several which were 30 to 40 feet in circumference. They belonged to the genus *Eucalyptus*.

I also observed a large tree of the genus *Melaleuca* which has a very thick, soft, pliable bark that is easily removed. As one advances inland, the vegetation grows denser and it becomes difficult to make any progress due to the large number of herbaceous plants.

I killed a gannet and a very beautiful red-bellied parrot. We saw several other small birds but none was noteworthy for its song or the beauty of its plumage.

We came across the footsteps of a man and a child freshly imprinted on the sandy shore, trees burnt around their base, and trampled grass, leaving us in no doubt that this coast was inhabited. Citizen Péron wandered a short distance away from us and found traces of a recent fire around which lay scraps of fish and shellfish. With so many signs of the natives all around, we were surprised not to see a single one of them.

We set off in the boat at noon to return to the ship. Scarcely had we put to sea when we saw a thick cloud of smoke rise into the air close by, or so it seemed. We turned about and landed a second time, hoping we might have our desired encounter. But when we reached the top of the scarp we realised that the smoke was more than 2 miles away. If we had set off into the dense vegetation we would have run the risk of never finding our way back again. In any case, the ship was anchored 3 leagues from shore and the winds were contrary. We returned on board.

When we got back we learnt that the commander had gone ashore with several other naturalists. They had seen a number of huts and one native. But they had offered him different gifts in vain; he wouldn't take anything. His refusals were accompanied by threatening gestures and he fled as soon as they tried to approach.

Several officers from the *Naturaliste* had also been ashore, further to the south of us. On their return they reported that they had found a river,[82] and that it looked to be navigable for a small boat, but they hadn't seen the mouth. They added that it was lovely country and the banks of the river teemed with black swans and pelicans.

Citizen Baudin gave the order to Citizen Le Bas, commander, to take the longboat the following morning and explore this river.

The *Naturaliste*'s small dinghy was ordered to accompany it. It was to follow the coastline until it found the mouth of the river and then travel upstream as far as possible.

We left at 3 o'clock the next morning and were set ashore at 6 o'clock. Citizen Hamelin and the two officers who had reported their discovery the previous day were in charge of the *Naturaliste*'s small dinghy. We met and it was decided that they would look for the river mouth by sea and that we would follow the course of the river until we reached it. We began walking along the shore and covered around a league in a southerly direction. We came to the head of a salt lake which lay immediately behind the scarp which, as it were, walls in all this country. Beyond a hillock holding back the waters of the lake, we could make out the river around 200 yards away. In these parts its banks are marshy and covered with samphire. We walked parallel to its course for an hour, until we could go no further, as the river joined the lake at that point. We had our breakfast while we waited for the dinghy, filled with high spirits by this little expedition. Across the river lay pleasant country and swans and many other aquatic birds flew over the water in great profusion.

Some time later the dinghy arrived. Up to this point it had met with a considerable depth of water. We got aboard and the dinghy continued upstream against a very slight current, which may even have been caused by the ebb of the tide. After we had gone about a league, the water became so shallow that the dinghy kept touching the bottom. We tried to gain the left bank of the river, where there appeared to be more water, but as the dinghy grounded again we had to turn about. The salinity of the water had decreased only slightly up to this point. Large tree trunks lay in the middle of the river, having apparently been carried there by the water – which suggests that flooding occurs in the rainy season. Could this river simply be an area of low ground into which a lake empties in the rainy season?

We encountered a great many birds but they did not allow us to approach near enough to shoot at them. The left bank is densely wooded and has a pleasant aspect; the other, by contrast, is marshy along its entire length.

As we were returning we saw a great quantity of smoke rising above the trees on the left bank, appearing to come from five or six different fires situated close together. We tried again to steer the dinghy towards that side but in vain. The bed of the river grew shallow and we had to continue on our way. When we judged that we were opposite the spot where the longboat lay, we were landed on the right bank so that we could walk over to the seashore. But scarcely had we stepped from the dinghy when we heard shouting and saw five or six natives standing on the opposite bank making what were undoubtedly threatening gestures towards us. We got in again and made a third attempt to bring the dinghy to their side. The bed of the river again grew shallow, but we did not want to miss this opportunity to meet the natives, so Citizens Freycinet[83] and Heirisson, officers, and Lharidon, surgeon, Depuch, mineralogist, and I all entered the water. The natives sat down and watched us for some time; but when we came within gunshot of them they fled, calling out the word *vélou, vélou*, over and over.[84] They were entirely naked except for a sort of mantle of fur-covered skin which hung down behind from the shoulders to the middle of the back. Two of them carried long sticks. A russet dog of the fox-dog breed followed them. By the time we reached the bank they had disappeared into the woods. They continued to cry out *vélou, vélou*, and the dog howled in a similar way to them, the howl of a dog that has been shut in and held back against its will. We moved up to the edge of the wood but had no wish to enter. Our guns were loaded only with small shot and we could not easily have defended ourselves in this dense woodland against men whose numbers were unknown to us and who had behaved towards us in a hostile manner. In any case, it was going to get dark soon and we had a long way to go to reach our longboat. It seemed unwise to begin a course of action which might have disastrous consequences. On several branches we hung glass necklaces, a small mirror and a knife — with which we made several notches in the branches to show the savages how it is used. The shouting and howling had died down and we assumed that they had withdrawn inland. We noticed a well-trodden path running alongside the river, which made us think that this area was ordinarily inhabited. We were quietly withdrawing when we became aware that the savages were creeping silently through the brush, 20 paces behind us, doubtless with the aim of surprising us. They had removed that sort of mantle which covered their shoulders and had armed themselves with long spears and a type of dagger, a foot and a half in length, shaped like a spearhead. This weapon was so highly polished that several of us thought at first that it was made of iron. We immediately turned and aimed our guns at them. They began shouting at us again and spoke heatedly amongst themselves as they brandished their spears and daggers at us – these being made not of iron but of very dark, highly polished wood.

The spears they waved in their left hands had shafts 6 or 7 feet long. We could not make out the material used for their tips. A piece of wood 1 foot long and 2 inches wide is attached to its upper part. This piece of wood is no doubt used to propel the spear with greater force. When throwing the spear they shake this piece of wood very rapidly. Realising that these savages had made up their minds to attack us, we continued to face them as we gradually withdrew. Their gestures became more and more threatening. We entered the water and began to cross to the far side. The water came up around our waists and we repeatedly sank into the mud. It had been agreed when we left the dinghy that we would return on foot to the longboat, so we assumed that the dinghy must already have set off. If this had been the case, and the savages more numerous, our position would have been very serious. As our guns were not fully loaded, they would not have created a terrifying enough effect to make the savages flee.

But Citizens Hamelin and Le Bas had watched them retreat at the start and had remained there to see how our encounter would end. When they saw that we were being followed they came immediately to our aid with the boat crew.

At this spot the river divides into two branches. Citizens Hamelin and Le Bas had got out onto the point formed between these branches. When we caught sight of them we retreated in their direction. Seeing that there were more of us now, the savages halted but kept on making their threats and often repeated the word *mouille*[85] as they pointed at the two sides of the river.

Once we reached the others, we made various gestures towards them to let them know that we were not their enemies. Citizen Depuch took a green branch and advanced into the middle of the river alone and unarmed, but as they continued to brandish their spears, he withdrew. When he had rejoined us, one of the natives then walked out, still bearing his weapons, to the middle of the river. He made no attempt to cross to our side, so I untied my neckerchief and I placed it on a branch. We then moved back around 15 paces and motioned to him to come and collect the present we were offering. We noticed that he mimicked very precisely and with great ease the words that he heard us utter. He came forward, looked at the neckerchief, and put it back in the same place. Then he turned towards the savages who were on the other bank and said something to them. We wanted to approach him but he immediately renewed his threats. Citizen Hamelin threw him a red snuffbox which bore the image of a negro's head. He picked it up and gave a cry of delight as he showed it to his companions. Then he cast it onto the ground. I threw him a small mirror. He looked into the glass and started with surprise. He looked behind it, doubtless trying to find the figure who had startled him, and then threw it down again. Three more natives made up their minds to come over to him. They always remained 15 paces away from us and each time we tried to approach them they resumed their threatening gestures. The sun had gone down and so we were obliged to withdraw. They made no attempt to follow us. They turned back the way they had come but did not take away any of the items we had given them.

If we had had enough time, perhaps we might have managed to meet them at close quarters; but the entire scene that I have just related took only an hour – too short a time for us to gain the confidence of men who were ill-disposed towards us.

There were five of these savages. Two more then came to join them and perhaps still more remained hidden in the brush. They were of average height and were pleasantly proportioned. Five were black, but two had red skin, which I consider to be an effect of concoctions they use, because their skin and their hair, which is long and straight, were of the same colour. The others wore their hair cut short but it did not seem to be woolly. Two or three of them had a tuft of beard on the lower part of the chin. They had very white teeth and none seemed to be missing any, as far as I could judge at that distance. (We remained always at a distance of about 15 paces from them.) I say this because Dampier states that the savages from the western part of New Holland are in the custom of pulling out their two front teeth.

It seems that they live in small groups, with each group having its own territory and defending its borders. They might perhaps have thought that we were a wandering band of men who were looking to settle there and so took up arms to defend their land. Indeed, the word *mouille* that they repeated as they pointed to different sides of the river was undoubtedly meant to indicate a separate territory where we could remain without disturbing them. When we withdrew, they did not follow us; their intention was not to attack us but simply to rid themselves of strangers whom they mistrusted. It does, however, seem that they have their wars, as their spears and that dagger-like weapon seem more suited for fighting against men than for killing animals for food.

When we saw them initially, they were unarmed and were wearing their mantles, which they removed when they took up their weapons. Their dwellings must therefore have been nearby. It is unfortunate that they were so suspicious of us, as this denied us the chance to observe their domestic life.

During our absence, Citizen Ronsard, sub-lieutenant, encountered a man and a woman on the shore. The man ran off but the woman, stricken no doubt by fear, collapsed on the sand. Citizen Ronsard went up to her but was unable to allay her terror. She crouched there, completely naked except for one of those mantles of which I have spoken. It served as a sort of bag and contained several roots which were fibrous and black and as big as hazelnuts.[86]

Citizen Ronsard took these roots and replaced them with glass beads, knives and small mirrors. At a moment when she thought she was no longer being observed, she crept behind a bush. She was allowed to go. She was around 20 years old and was heavily pregnant, very ugly and very dirty. Her breasts hung down to her thighs.

Others who explored the area found several huts but all were abandoned. They left behind our glass beads, knives and mirrors. These huts are built in the crudest fashion possible and are at most 4 feet high and could barely provide shelter for two men.[87] They consist of sticks pushed a short way into the ground and covered over with the bark of the *Melaleuca*, which I discussed above. The same type of bark is also spread across the ground inside the huts and doubtless serves as bedding.

These people strike me as being as far from a state of civilisation as it is possible to be. They do not display the slightest curiosity – curiosity being the mark of a desire to learn. Their fear is like that which one sees in wild beasts. Without risk of error, we may pass judgement on the level of enterprise and enlightenment displayed by a people who have neither clothing, nor boats, nor even the bow and arrow – a weapon which has until now been found in almost all societies.[88] New Holland is flanked by the Moluccas, New Guinea, the Friendly Islands and New Zealand and yet the customs of its people differ strikingly from those of all its neighbours.[89] Is it possible that the inhabitants of this vast land have their own separate origin? It will be up to those who study the migration of different peoples to resolve this question.

The winds were contrary. As the longboat lay far downwind of our ships, Citizen Le Bas ordered the coxswain to beat across and anchor in a spot he indicated. We walked there in the meantime and lit a large fire. We were all very hungry and impatiently awaited the arrival of the longboat, which was carrying the supplies for our supper. But at this point we were told that the longboat had foundered a league further up the shore; it was only with difficulty that some food had been saved – and even this had been spoiled by sea water. We went immediately to the scene of the wreck. There

CHAPTER 3: SOUTH-WEST NEW HOLLAND TO TIMOR

was a very heavy swell and the longboat had already filled with sand. The sailors waited until the following day to try and refloat it. Using wet sails, masts and oars we built a small tent under which we spent a very unpleasant night, each of us taking a turn on watch so that the natives couldn't surprise us if they decided to come and cause us trouble.

Citizen Hamelin left that same evening in the dinghy to inform the commander of this disaster and organise help to bring us away.

The dinghy did not return the following day. To make matters worse, all our food had been spoiled by the sea and our water had been lost or drunk. When nobody came, we grew extremely worried about Citizen Hamelin, particularly as the weather had been foul during the night and we had found a stocking on the shoreline belonging to one of the officers who had gone with him, along with an oar blade from the dinghy. We were visited by several birds that day, including a red-billed oyster catcher, a small turtledove, a grey swift and a quail similar to our European ones. We went to look for water. Some distance from our camp we found a hollow in the sand containing brackish water. We were driven by necessity to drink it but it did not have any harmful effect on us. It appears that we should have sought around here in vain for better water, for the earth was trampled flat all around the hole and several pipes made out of celery stalks were scattered around it. The natives undoubtedly used them to suck up the water when they were thirsty and they would not have bothered to come here if they had found better water elsewhere. We did not stray far from our camp as we were of a mind to stay together in case the order should come to embark immediately.

We spent the second night in a state of profound apprehension. The following day, Citizens Depuch, Péron, a helmsman and I walked around 2 leagues along the shore until we reached a place abeam of the ships where we could try and signal them.[90] The only provisions we carried for the four of us were one bottle of water and two ship's biscuits. We lit a large fire and fixed a boat hook to the crown of a tree with our handkerchiefs fluttering from its tip. A few moments later the ship began to move towards shore and a boat was sent out in the direction of our camp. We too headed towards our camp and learnt when we got there that the delay had been caused by the bad weather of the night before last, which had driven Citizen Hamelin's dinghy into the open sea. He had only got on board his ship, hungry and exhausted, after battling the sea for 24 hours. We were sent supplies and equipment for righting the longboat, in case this were possible, but, unable to do so, we returned on board ship the next day, having spent three days and three nights ashore. Our small boats had great difficulty reaching the ships and, as soon as we were on board, a very strong gale blew up and we barely had time to get under way.

The *Naturaliste*'s dinghy landed that same day. The swell was very heavy and a sailor named Vasse was swept away by the waves as he tried to get on board and was drowned.

General Reflections on Géographe Bay

All the low, flat country we have recently explored appears never to have been convulsed by the great destructive forces which have transformed the surface of the globe in other regions. No peaks rise greatly above the general level of the land, nor are there any major bays or abrupt breaks in the coastline: it is all quite uniform.

The mountains whose rounded summits we could make out in the distance are perhaps very ancient and form the backbone of the continent. However, all the country which we explored near the coast appeared to consist of alluvial soil lying on low rock and covered over in varying degrees by vegetable detritus, which has accumulated there over time in particularly large quantities due to the fact that a sandy scarp which almost entirely encloses this region prevents it from being carried away by the rains. The soil is very fertile but is much more suitable for herbaceous plants than for tall trees; the former grow there with astonishing vigour, though smothered by their own profusion. If the land were cleared, the soil would quickly lose its fertility. The trees, it is true, grow to an extraordinary size, but they do not have the straight and slender trunks which we so commonly observe in our European forests. Several of the herbaceous plants are suitable for human consumption but none of the trees appeared to bear edible fruit.

The land lies in a latitude that augurs a climate of the mildest sort. Even though we were there in its winter season, the days were very warm. Its climate is comparable with that of the Cape of Good Hope but it seems to enjoy a further advantage in that it is never visited by hurricanes. Indeed, one never comes across ravines scoured out by torrents or trees toppled by storms.

It would be particularly easy to cultivate crops in this region as the ground is not stony, the slopes are not steep, and the soil requires only a light turning. The land is especially suited for grazing. It is only a pity that water is not plentiful, as this will halt any incursion of European enterprise. In any case, further investigation is required before a judgement can be made. A person who knew nothing about France would form a very false impression if he evaluated the country solely on the basis of a trip through the heathland of Bordeaux or along the coast of Brittany. The rains which fall on the high mountains visible in the interior of New Holland must go somewhere: if there is no river, is it not reasonable to assume that these waters form vast lakes? (*Nota.* Having acquired greater experience in evaluating coastlines *from afar*, I am of the view that the entrance to a harbour, or at least to a sizeable inlet, may lie to the north of the bay. I base this view on a sketch map of the coast.)

We saw few insects and no quadrupeds apart from the dog that was following the natives we met. Citizen Levillain, zoologist on the *Naturaliste*, lost his wire-haired hunting dog in New Holland.

Fish are not plentiful in the bay. We caught very few and those were small in size.

On the morning that we left the land, we killed on the shore an amphibious quadruped which had the head of a cat. It bore a strong resemblance to the sea otter which appears in plate 43 of Cook's *Third Voyage*.[91] But the animal had no tail, perhaps as a result of an accident. Two days beforehand, I had wounded another, but it had had the strength to drag itself into the sea, where I watched it struggle for more than a quarter of an hour in the water, until it died and was carried away by the waves.

Passage to Shark Bay; Stay on the Smaller Dorre Island, or Barren Island; Passage to the Island of Timor

When we weighed anchor on 19 Prairial [8 June], we were at the head of the bay and the wind was blowing from the open sea. We were forced to tack and the ship made slow progress into the wind. For a moment during the night, as we rounded the southern headland, we were in very great danger. We were separated from the *Naturaliste* by this gale, which lasted for three days. She did not rejoin us when the winds abated and we were filled with grave fears for her. The *Géographe* had struggled to escape the head of the bay and she worked to windward much better than the *Naturaliste*. What fate then had befallen our friends? Our minds were racked by the gloomiest thoughts.

After tacking for a time at the entrance to the bay, we headed north. The meeting places, in case of separation, were, firstly, Swan River, then Shark Bay, and finally Timor. The wind, or some other factor best understood by sailors, prevented the commander from going to the first rendezvous. After passing within sight of Rottnest Island, which is only a short distance from the Swan River, we went directly to the second rendezvous.

We were accompanied the whole way by Cape petrel. From time to time we glimpsed the coast, though only, it's true, from a very great distance. It had the same appearance as Leeuwin's Land, though in a few places it seemed a little steeper.

I was gravely ill at this time but, as my friends tended me with great care and I have a strong constitution, I was quickly restored to health.

CHAPTER 3: SOUTH-WEST NEW HOLLAND TO TIMOR

Shark Bay is bounded on its eastern side by the mainland of New Holland, and on its western side by Dirk Hartog Island and the two Dorre Islands, or Barren Islands.[92] There are two entrances, one between Dirk Hartog Island and the larger of the Dorre Islands; the other between the smaller of these islands and the mainland. It was by the latter, northern, entrance that we came into the bay.

The point on the mainland is very broken, as the tide, running in against the rock, has caused many cave-ins. The brow of the land appears to be covered in dry grass. We anchored first opposite the smaller of the Dorre Islands. The next day we went ashore and gathered objects of natural history. Then we sailed to the top of the bay, to a strip of land called Middle Island on the charts. A survey by officers of the *Naturaliste* has established, however, that this so-called island is in fact attached to the mainland. The commander anchored off this peninsula but was driven away by bad weather before he had the opportunity to explore it. And so we returned to the anchorage off the smaller Barren Island and again went on shore. Two tents were set up: one for the commander and another for the naturalists.

The name Barren Island aptly describes the island's appearance. As we came in to land, we passed several lone rocks, some of which are connected to the island at low tide. Coming closer, we saw the same unusual formation that we observed in Leeuwin's Land and in Géographe Bay: that is to say, a scarp shutting off the hinterland – although in this case it was composed solely of loose sand which appears to shift about in the passing storms. Low-growing plants and large clumps of tough, brittle grass of the genera *Cyperus* and *Spinifex* grow across the tops of the small mounds that take shape among the shifting sands. On the far side of the scarp, the terrain rises almost imperceptibly towards the centre of the island, which is around 2 or 3 miles across. The ground is composed entirely of sand, which in several places has developed a hard crust. There isn't a single tree on the island that is 8 feet high or taller. It is completely covered with small bushes which sport a dreary-looking foliage. They belong to many different varieties and most of these seem to be new. I came across an abundance of *Dammara* (a species of

Melaleuca), which is illustrated in volume 4 of Dampier's *Voyage*,[93] along with the plant shown in figure 3 of the same plate.[94]

I had still not recovered completely from my illness and every evening my legs swelled tremendously. I took moderate exercise during this period and was restored to full health.

An enormous number of kangaroos live on the island. Far away from men, they live in undoubted peace. They have no enemies to fear apart from a few sea-eagles; by taking shelter under the impenetrable bushes, they defy these voracious birds. We came bringing strife and terror to their refuge and killed a great many of them.

This creature is around the size of a large rabbit and is reddish-grey in colour.[95] Its tail is covered with short hair and resembles that of a rat. Its hind legs are very long and are bigger than the forelegs. The hind legs have three toes and one of these has two claws. The forelegs are short and slender and have five short digits. The female has a pouch on the underside of her large belly,[96] inside which there is a long teat. In this pouch, which opens and closes by dilation and contraction, she provides refuge for a single young one. During the first two days we killed only females. In the following days we killed a number of males as well – but always a greater number of females, all of which were carrying a young one in the pouch. No doubt this additional weight made it more difficult for them to escape. This creature ordinarily remains beneath the dense foliage of a species of *Mimosa* bush, the spreading branches of which tightly intertwine and form an impenetrable shelter. We had to beat the bushes very vigorously to drive out the kangaroos and then fire at them swiftly, as they leapt out from one bush and under another almost before we could take aim.

Each mother's pouch holds a single small kangaroo, which made me think that she does not carry her young for very long. The young were not all the same age: we found some which had no fur and had not opened their eyes; others, however, were very big and fled when the hunter came to collect his kill. One of the young ones, which was slower than the others in leaving its place of refuge, was captured, and, rather than appearing frightened, licked the man who had just killed its mother and ate the food that it was offered. The commander kept the creature for several months, until it died by accident in Timor. It grew perfectly tame and was affectionate and easy to feed. It ate bread and was very fond of sugar water.

One day while out botanising I came upon a lizard resting on a piece of vegetation. It was 4 to 5 inches long (including the tail) and was dirty grey in colour. It had a broad head and great bulging yellow eyes which were cold and sinister. Its rather stubby tail was about an inch and a half long and covered with tubercles. There were tubercles also at the ends of its toes. I approached it and, rather than hurrying away, it stared back at me. Conscious that some lizards can be venomous, I wrapped the skirts of my cloth coat around my hand and seized it. It made no movement to escape but instead raised its tail and sprayed from all the tubercles along this a viscous liquid that was almost black in colour.[97] I was very glad then that I had acted with such caution.

When I grasped the lizard its tail broke off; as happens with all lizard tails, it kept on twitching despite that fact that it was no longer attached to the trunk. I preserved the creature in spirits. No mark could be seen on the dark-brown cloth of my coat.

We also came across two very large lizards. One was blackish in colour, with a short, truncated tail and broad scales, and moved slowly.[98] The other was very agile and had beautiful green skin and a very long, slender tail. It belongs to the genus *Gouanaea*.[99]

There are also a great many land snails but we found only their empty shells. There are two species of snail: one is half an inch long and has a pointed whorl; the other, however, has a flattened whorl and is about half an inch in diameter.

A great number of shellfish live along the shoreline: a species of oyster which clings to the rocks in great colonies (the same as is found on the Isle of France); the Ethiopian Crown; a species of small clam; a species of trochus with an unattractive colouring (it was still covered by its epidermis), Citizen Maugé, zoologist, believes it to be a new species; a species of large worm-shell.

Fish are plentiful in the bay. We caught great quantities of a large red fish, the flesh of which has a very nice taste. Two thick bumps swell from its highly elongated occipital bone, giving it a 'hunchback' appearance (this was the nickname the sailors immediately gave it).

We also saw an enormous number of whales. I observed that they always swam in pairs, which suggested that it was their mating season. (*Nota.* These whales were not of the type that supplies spermaceti. That species can be identified by the way in which it blows water through its spout at an oblique angle. The whales we saw in Shark Bay blew water directly upwards.)

Sea snakes are also very common in the bay.

The currents bring a great amount of driftwood to Dorre Island from nearby land. There is no fresh water. I observed that the dew was very heavy.

On [blank][100] we finally brought our dreary stay on Dorre Island to an end and sailed out of the bay. We continued on our way northward and encountered nothing of interest during our passage to Timor. We could occasionally glimpse the land, but from so great a distance that we were unable to make out even its most general features.

On [blank][101] we rounded the westernmost point of New Holland. It is here that Willem's River[102] flows into the sea; its water is salty.

Several days later we sailed to within 5 or 6 leagues of an island, and the commander sent Citizen Ronsard, sub-lieutenant, to reconnoitre it. He was not accompanied by any of the naturalists. He reported that the island was composed of bare reddish rocks. He found three freshwater streams; it was easy to get ashore. The island lies 3 leagues at most from the mainland of New Holland. Citizen Ronsard collected several plants and I have classified some of them. He also found some beautiful shells: the most remarkable of these are the huge spirulas, which curve in regular spirals, and admirals. Due to the presence of this beautiful shell, the commander decided to name the island Admiral Island.[103] Someone else had proposed naming it Three Springs Island. This name would have signalled to navigators that fresh water was to be found there, a vital resource along a coast which until now had yielded no fresh water. Citizen Ronsard also caught sight of a scrawny dog which had probably been left behind by visitors from the mainland.

We continued exploring the north-west coast for some time and passed within sight of an extensive archipelago. It seemed to me that it would be highly valuable to undertake a detailed reconnaissance of these islands, as such work may well cause the New Holland mainland to be redrawn far to the south of where it has so far appeared on the charts. I leave it to navigators and geographers to judge the significance of an observation of this kind.

One of these islands was remarkable in its shape and looked like an upturned bowl.

We saw a great many fires as we sailed along a considerable stretch of coast which is thought to form part of the mainland. We were further struck by the sight of one area burning with astonishing intensity. We were of the view that this conflagration must have begun when the natives left one of their fires untended and it had spread to surrounding trees.[104]

On [blank],[105] the commander set our course to the north. Several men on board were suffering from scurvy and we had a general need for fresh provisions. We had no idea that our stay in port, to which we greatly looked forward, would prove to be so deadly.

Chapter 4

Arrival in Timor; a Note on the Political Organisation of Kupang and its Trade; Morals and Customs of the Wealthy Malays of Kupang; Morals and Customs of the Ordinary Malays; Natural History; a Note on the Malay Language

We sighted the southern coast of Timor on 3 Fructidor [21 August 1801]. The coast is mountainous and tall trees grow right up to the summits.

On the 4th [22 August] we entered the strait which lies between the island of Semau and the western tip of Timor and dropped anchor there. The commander sent a boat to Kupang to inform the Dutch governor of our arrival and to request the services of a pilot.

The strait is at most a league across and has everywhere a considerable depth. It is highly picturesque: both shores are covered with trees and appeared all the more pleasant to us because our gaze had for a long period traversed only the barren, sandy beaches of New Holland. On the Timor shore we could make out several fishermen at work and small craft. A boat was sent out and made contact with the natives.

On the 5th [23 August] the boat which had set out on the previous day returned with two pilots, one Malay, the other French. The latter had served with the Dutch East India Company for seven years as master gunner at the fort. That evening we dropped anchor in Kupang roads, around a mile from land.

On the 6th [24 August] the commander went ashore. He went to call on the governor and dined with him. He asked the governor for three houses: one for himself, one for the naturalists and the officers, and a hospital for the sick. Monsieur Lofsteth (this was the governor's name)[106] granted the request. The house allocated to the commander belonged to Madame van Este, widow of the governor before last – it was he who received the unfortunate Bligh with every consideration after the *Bounty* had been commandeered.[107] The house allocated to the naturalists belonged to Monsieur Gabriel Wentz, a Malay of mixed race who was the civil lieutenant of Kupang. The governor's former house was allocated to serve as a hospital. It had been reduced to a ruin four years previously when Malays from the island's interior came down to drive away the English who had seized the Dutch trading post, with the Malays slaughtering a number of the English in the process.[108] As the building had no roof, we soon fashioned one out of fronds of the latanier.[109]

On the 7th [25 August] our belongings were taken ashore and we moved into lodgings on dry land.

The Kupang roadstead is very extensive and has three entrances. One is very narrow and runs from south to north: this is the one we entered by. A broader one lies to the west of Kupang, between Semau and the small island of Kera, which is low, sandy and uninhabited, and is around a quarter of a league in diameter and covered with trees. The final channel lies between the island of Kera and Timor and is little used.

The low-lying country around Kupang is lush and attractive. Vegetation crowds right down to the shoreline and there are several groves of coconut trees whose majestic crests sway gently in the breeze and shade the modest dwellings.

The town is in the north-west of Timor. A fort situated on a rocky eminence overlooks the town and a small stream flows around the foot of the rock. When the tide is high, small craft and even Chinese junks can enter the stream, making loading and unloading very easy. With minor expenditure, it could be made into a port which would be suitable and safe for small ships.

The river divides the town into two parts, which are linked by a wooden bridge. The fort and the governor's house are on one side; the Chinese quarter runs along the shoreline on the other side. Malays occupy the rest of the town.

The town has a pleasing appearance. Its main streets are shaded by mango trees and banyan fig trees (*Ficus indica*), known also as spreading figs because of the way their branches send down roots towards the ground, which would be capable of starting new trees if care were not taken to cut them back. These extraordinary trees are the same size as walnut trees and produce great quantities of figs that are mainly eaten by a large species of bat (which is Valmont de Bomare's roussette).[110] The trunks of these trees have many crevices which shelter a large species of lizard which has light grey skin with red markings. It has a very harsh cry which could be rendered as the word *oukou* produced loudly in the throat. Is it a gecko?

The houses lining the main streets are simple and regular in design and are occupied by the wealthiest townsfolk.

When they captured the Dutch fort four years ago, the English, through the indignities they inflicted on the populace and their general lack of restraint, prompted several families to flee, some to Batavia, and others to the island's interior. The families appealed for help to the Malays of the interior, and they came down and slaughtered a number of the Englishmen and sent the rest rushing back to their ships. However, as any people may, after wreaking revenge for their compatriots, the Malays turned riotous; they looted and tore down the houses of the rich, and some of these have still not been rebuilt. As a result of these events, the inhabitants of Kupang grow anxious whenever they glimpse a European ship. They immediately take up arms and prepare to offer the sternest possible resistance. Our behaviour has taught them that not all Europeans are like the English. They hate the latter in the same degree that they appear disposed to love the French.

We were witness to the hatred that the Malays bear the English nation. During our stay an English frigate cruising the Timor coast was alerted that two French ships lay at anchor in Kupang roads.

They came by to ascertain our identity and if possible seize our vessels. As they approached, armed Malays assembled, apparently full of wild rage. Several of the Malays said that if they were lucky enough to kill any Englishmen they would 'eat their heads'. We sent one of our boats across to the English frigate and showed them the passports which their government had granted our expedition. The frigate departed and harmony was restored.

This frigate was the *Virginie*, which had been captured from the French during the current war.[111]

The Malay is distrustful, courageous and strongly attached to his customs. He would have difficulty accepting a master who interfered with his traditional practices or oppressed him too strongly. However, being lazy and unambitious, he has all too readily grown accustomed to the Dutch yoke, as the Dutch demand neither direct taxes nor labour. Only when there are special works to be done, which exceed the capability of the slaves at the fort, do the tributary kings supply the Company with the men that it requires – and for each man the kings receive an amount of rice and arrack. But do the kings then pass this on to the men who do the work? I suspect not. When, at the governor's order, a group of Malays went with our carpenters to fetch the wood we needed to build our longboat, they carried no provisions with them, and the French sergeant who went with them told me that they are not usually given any and have to supply their own.

On Timor and its dependent islands there are five greater kings and fifteen lesser kings who pay tribute to the Company.

The first group is composed of: the raja Amari, who lives one league from Kupang; the emperor or *keizer* Amarasi, one day's journey from Kupang (a great many sandalwood trees grow in his kingdom); the raja of Solor, who is Moslem; the raja of Savu; and the raja of Kupang. The latter does not live in Kupang, but resides for part of the year on Semau, the small island of which he is also the sovereign, and for the remainder of it in a dwelling around half a league from Kupang. The government, which is the true ruler, summons the rajas from time to time to perform a few ceremonial duties, by which they retain the vestiges of their former power – but the rajas are careful not to oppose the Dutch commander in anything.

As a mark of their office, the five greater rajas all possess a cane with a gold knob on which is engraved the company symbol ℣. The Malays call these *raja rotan mas*. The lesser rajas instead have a cane with a silver knob bearing the company symbol. These rajas generally possess only limited authority, which the governor constrains as he sees fit. In his dealings with these minor potentates, the governor always adopts a dignified manner, which greatly impresses them.

The Malays seem very attached to their kings but do not accord them the same marks of respect which other peoples of the Indies so readily offer theirs. I visited several kings and saw them always surrounded by their subjects and seated in the middle. They seemed more like friends to their people than their masters. They are only to be distinguished from their people by the calico gowns they wear. When they leave their dwellings with their retinue, they travel on foot, but their bags of betel and weapons are carried for them and a Chinese parasol is held open above their head.

Each year the tributary rajas are required to offer the Company certain amounts of sandalwood and wax, and a certain number of slaves and horses, in the form of gifts. These gifts are transported to Concordia Fort with great ceremony. The kings travel with them and their subjects walk ahead and behind performing dances and battles in time to loud cries and deafening music. In return, the Company gives them a few guns and a very small amount of powder, as well as knives, sabres and various European trinkets. It has to be said that this exchange is greatly to the advantage of the Dutch. Each year a brig transports these gifts to Batavia where the sandalwood is sold to the Chinese, who extract from it an essential oil which they value highly. They also make idols and furniture from this wood and burn it in their temples.

Sandalwood is harvested principally along the southern coast. Its price varies according to size: in Timor it ranges from 7 piastres up to 25 or 30 piastres per picul (125 pounds *poids de marc*), and I am told that what sells here for 20 piastres would fetch 50 piastres in Canton.[112]

Trade is not solely the preserve of the Company. Several Chinese junks come to Timor at the end of the western monsoon to buy a range of commodities from private traders: wax, slaves, sandalwood, birds' nests, trepangs, sharks' fins and horses.

The wax is of high quality and is obtained from the forests in the interior of the island.

Slaves are worth 20 to 40 piastres each; the ones from Roti are the most sought after.

The nests are those of the swiftlet *Hirundo esculenta*. There are two different types of these: one is made entirely from mucilaginous material and is eaten by the Chinese; the other is made from grass and has no use.

The trepang is a species of *Mentula* which is fished on the Sahul Bank.

The horses are small and closely resemble those from the department of Nièvre.

Birds' nests, trepangs and sharks' fins are considered powerful aphrodisiacs. The Chinese make them into jellies which are regarded as a delicacy as well as a kind of panacea.

The Company imposes duties of 4 percent on exported goods and 6 percent on imported goods. In addition, it levies a departure duty on each ship that leaves the roadstead. It also reserves the right to grant private citizens authorisation to sell at retail arrack, meat and candles, and to run gambling houses. It sells special licences, almost all of which are purchased by the Chinese.

The Malays are exempt from all personal taxes but each Chinese aged more than 12 years must pay a charge. Together these different taxes provide the Company with an annual revenue of 7000 to 8000 piastres, which it uses to pay its employees and maintain the garrison. When the Dutch wish to construct public buildings, they invite wealthy individuals to make a contribution – a voluntary payment imposed only to the extent of the giver's generosity.

The most profitable items to import into Kupang are iron, rope, boats' grapnels, long fine-bladed knives, sabre blades, guns, necklaces of small glass beads and an assortment of all the metal items we make in Europe.

All Malays who have a little money engage in trade and do so skilfully. They have no doubt learnt from the Dutch and have turned this knowledge to their advantage.

When we arrived in Timor only a very small number of whites were working for the Company. The garrison is made up of Malays from Java. I don't know why these soldiers should have such poor physiques but they did not appear very daunting to me. I don't know whether they possess a nimbleness that makes up for their lack of strength.

The Company has two stations which are run by white men. One of the stations lies in the interior of the island of Timor, the other on the island of Savu – the largest and most remote island in the Dutch dependency. This station is headed by a Frenchman who has worked for the Company for 32 years. These positions require little effort and are respectable retirement posts for long-serving employees. These men spend their time settling disputes between kings, administering justice and looking after the interests of the Company, but their decisions may be appealed, and the governor of Kupang may either overturn or ratify them.

Theft is punished by strokes of the rattan or by enslavement.

A number of Malays are Christian and at the fort there is a church served by a Malay minister.

Until now, the island of Timor has been thought to be of little value. But once Europeans have established large settlements on the east coast of New Holland, any vessels travelling through Torres Strait or Endeavour Strait will call at the island, particularly as it can provide every sort of provision and it is not as unhealthy a place to stay as Batavia.

At the present time all communications with Batavia are intercepted by the English. The brig that sails from here every year has twice been forced to return to Kupang.

The great dominion that the Dutch established in the Moluccas appeared to be built on unshakeable foundations but is now on the brink of being overturned; neither the insalubrity of the climate, nor a sea bristling with reefs, nor the clever stratagems of Dutch traders can protect it against the overweening ambitions of the English.

Morals, Dress and Customs of the Wealthy Malays

Their houses have only a single storey and almost all are laid out in the same way. They usually have a tree-lined courtyard out the front. Two open galleries, their roofs supported by posts, run along the front and the rear of the houses. These galleries sometimes stand several steps off the ground and have small rooms at either end which are used for storage. Inside the houses there are three rooms, the middle one being the largest.

The front gallery serves as the main room: it is there that visitors are received, meals are taken and the family gathers. It is the most ornate part of the house, if one may count as ornaments a few cane armchairs which are varnished red, or sometimes painted gold, two pedestal tables placed either side of the entry door, and one or several lanterns hanging from the roof. Immaculate whitewashed walls and great cleanliness do instead of elegant furnishings.

Cane sofas covered with mats stand around the edges of the central room, where the midday nap is taken. The master of the house sleeps in one of the side rooms. His bed consists of a mattress 3 to 4 inches thick, stuffed with wadding, a mat, several cushions which the sleeper arranges in the way he finds most comfortable, and a muslin mosquito net.

Household tasks are carried out in the rear gallery, which gives onto a courtyard or garden. The kitchens and the slaves' huts are located here. These huts are made from bamboo and are covered in latanier fronds. The main house is built of stone up to a height of 4 feet; the rest is of timber. The roof is made from curved tiles, which are imported from Batavia along with the large baked clay tiles which are used for flooring. Tileries and potteries could be established in Timor. Citizen Depuch, mineralogist, told me that he found large amounts of clay near Kupang suitable for such industries. The tiles used in Timor have a double curve which makes the roofs lighter than French roofs (these tiles are made in the Dutch style).

Such are the dwellings of almost all the wealthy burghers of Kupang. Their lives are as simple and as uniform as the roofs under which they reside. While the master of the house attends to his commercial affairs, the mistress and their children squat on mats, surrounded by their slaves, and prepare tobacco leaves that are chewed with betel. The leaves are cut into very fine strands and then dried in the sun. A wide variety of small items are made with great skill from rice straw or latanier fronds. This sort of work requires patience but not tenacity: the heat of this country and the inherent laziness of the people incline them to avoid anything that tires them out.

They bathe two or three times a day, eat three meals, sleep in the afternoon, and all day long chew areca nuts with betel leaves, slaked lime, tobacco and gambir. (Gambir is the concentrated sap of various plants. It is brought over from Batavia. This sap looks like crumbly reddish-brown clay. It neutralizes the caustic action of the slaked lime.) They pay visits to one another in the evenings, drink tea together and only part company in the middle of the night. At these gatherings the slaves sometimes sing in choirs and accompany themselves on Malay drums or Chinese tam-tams. The Malay drum consists of a cylinder of latanier wood which has been hollowed out and covered with animal skin. These drums are struck with the hand, producing a dull and unpleasant sound. The Chinese tam-tam is made from a copper plate (which can vary in size) with a rim of 3 or 4 inches. In the centre of the plate on the outer side is a hemispherical boss which is struck with a short stick, the round head of which is wrapped in string. This instrument makes an ear-splitting sound.

At home the men wear breeches or a sarong which covers them from the waist to the knee. Over that they wear a sort of calico gown. They always oil their hair with copra and wear it either tied in a tail or loose about their shoulders. When they go out they dress in the European style and usually sport gold or silver buttons on their clothing.

The women dress in very simple clothing rather similar to the sort worn by Chinese ladies. They oil their hair with coconut and gather it behind into a chignon, winding it into a coil which they hold in place with gold pins, some of which have diamond heads, or with a comb made from tortoiseshell and decorated with gold or silver. They wear sarongs that fall from the waist to the foot, and over that a long dress which covers from the neck to the knee. The dress opens at the front and is fastened at the breast with gold pins. Over one shoulder they usually wear a red handkerchief, from the corner of which hangs a chain holding the keys for their chests. When their lips are turned red by betel-stained saliva, they wipe them with these handkerchiefs. They do not have pockets in their clothing. At home they walk about barefoot, but when they go out to parties, and when they make or receive polite visits, they wear stockings and heeled shoes. They are unused to wearing such shoes and walk in an ungainly manner; they remove this uncomfortable footwear as soon as they can.

They often decorate their chignons with the sweet-smelling flowers of *mogori*, *Uvaria cananga* and *Pergularia glabra*. When they wish to give somebody a great mark of their friendship, they will remove these flowers, which have a delightful, if somewhat overpowering, scent and offer them as a garland. On some occasions they wear garments of silk with gold brocade, or embroidered muslin, and adorn themselves with gold necklaces, bracelets, rings and earrings. They prefer fabrics which have a red lacquer base. Some of the little boxes they use for holding betel and areca nuts are finely wrought in solid silver: these precious objects come from Batavia.

Malay ladies are very reserved in public but the warmth of the climate and the languid pace of life nevertheless exert an influence on their temperaments. Here, as everywhere else, love affairs fill the hearts of pretty women and occupy their days. Their faithful slaves are their confidants and they use their huts for assignations. When they suspect that a planned tryst will be interrupted or prevented by some bore, a slave takes the lover chewed betel wrapped in a leaf, and the lover sends his mistress a similar present – which is undoubtedly little to a European's taste.

The wealthy are almost all of mixed race; their skin colour is lighter than that of other Malays and is close to that of southern European peoples. They are of medium height, their features are regular, and some of the women are even quite attractive. Usually a pair of beautiful black eyes filled with expression imparts liveliness to a face whose even brown hue is never brightened by a rosy tint. They generally appear to be younger than they really are. Their simple dress is not at all unbecoming to them. They perspire continually, which prevents them from growing stout. Their feet have a pretty shape, which is not spoiled either by the habit of wearing shoes or by a lot of walking.

As everywhere across the Indies, cooked rice (which they call *nasi*) takes the place of bread for the Malays. Their dishes consist of different types of meat browned in animal fat and seasoned with spices and pickles; these dishes have a very pleasant flavour, whetting the appetite and invigorating the stomach. They usually drink tea or fresh water. The water is good when drawn from private springs or from higher up the river. Tainted by mud, household waste, and the Malays' continual bathing, the water that is drawn too close to the river mouth is insipid, unpleasant and no doubt unhealthy.

The wealthy play ombre and fifteen, which were introduced to them by the Dutch, along with *tabla*. (I believe that the Chinese brought them this game.) The latter game is played on a small board which is divided into 48 squares and each player takes turns throwing four bamboo sticks, which are white on one side and black on the other, and then moves his small black or white counters accordingly.

Mightn't *tabla* have some connection with a game that Captain King observed among the people of the Sandwich Islands, which is played with small pebbles on a chequerboard divided into

238 squares? This remark may perhaps be of use to those who are trying to understand the migratory movements of different peoples (Cook's *Third Voyage*, volume 4, page 75).[113]

Several women are able to pluck the guitar and the harp tolerably well.

Many wealthy young people travel to Batavia, where they acquire some knowledge of commerce and arithmetic. Batavia is the Paris of the Moluccas.

When a private citizen marries or finishes building a house, each of his friends sends him a tree branch decorated with bunches of flowers and hung with presents that usually take the form of sarongs, handkerchiefs, cakes, areca nuts and betel leaves. This branch is planted in front of the house to the accompaniment of music and several different dances are performed around it. The recipient of these presents then holds a party. We witnessed one of these parties which was held by a burgher who had finished building a house. Some women came dressed in all their finery and several naturalists and officers attended; I think though that our presence made them uncomfortable and it was not a very cheerful gathering.

In any case, Madame van Este was ill. She is the only person to have sent her slave musicians to be taught in Batavia. These slaves can play a number of Dutch quadrilles, to which the Malay ladies no doubt dance very badly, hampered as they are by shoes which they are unused to wearing.

The slaves enjoy quite agreeable conditions. As it is a sign of affluence to have a great number of them working in the house, they are not overburdened with chores. Other slaves are used for outdoor tasks, such as the cultivation of rice and corn and the tending of buffalo herds.

At the time of our stay in Kupang, Madame van Este had more than 2000 slaves. Monsieur Tielman, civil captain of the town, and Monsieur Joannis, who are wealthy citizens, also had a great many.

The areas which are suitable for the cultivation of rice are held in private hands. The land must be watered by streams and not all locations are suitable. Anyone wanting to grow corn, however, can simply send his slaves out wherever he likes; the first comer sows his crop and reaps the harvest. The same piece of land is never planted twice in a row. Every year new sections of land are cleared. There are never any disputes over these tracts, as there is enough uncultivated land for each to select the land he wants. While the harvests may be plentiful, it must be said that nature does all the work: these fields, farmed by slaves who are not subject to their master's scrutiny, cannot be tended very carefully.

There are a great many Chinese, who engage almost exclusively in retail trade. They have retained their national dress and are easily recognisable by their long trousers and large jackets, and by that long plait woven from the hair that sprouts from the tip of their shaven heads. Their position here is the same as that of the Jews in Europe: they have the same love of money and use the same tricks in their commercial dealings. They are despised by the Malays, whom they cheat of their money and their goods, and by the Dutch, who make them pay all the costs of the settlement. Their faces generally have that inscrutable quality which inspires mistrust.

★

Nota. The wealthy Malays are not much concerned with having elegant houses or furniture: such outward show seems to them too impersonal a source of pleasure. But they do take to extremes what I would call a lavish taste for comfort and finery. Indeed, a Malay possessing only a small, poorly furnished house will still be followed by several slaves and will have gold buttons on his clothes. Monsieur Joannis, a very rich man, did not bother to have the ceilings of his house completed, and so some of his rooms were covered only with roof tiles. Their furniture consists simply of chests, cupboards and sofas, all of different sizes, ranged haphazardly and tastelessly along the walls, and yet while they sleep a young slave girl waves a large fan, which cools the air and keeps away mosquitoes and other insects that might disturb the sleeper. The same measure is used at meal times to drive away insects that would otherwise settle on the meat. Along with these little luxuries, the women also adore lovely scents: their beds are always perfumed with rose leaves and flowers of *mogori* and *Uvaria cananga*. When they attend gatherings, they are always careful to eat cashew nuts in order to give their breath a pleasant smell. And, even if the practice of chewing betel at first appears repulsive, it nevertheless sweetens their breath. Both sexes are sober, temperate and, as I said above, cleanly to an excessive degree.

Some believe it is attractive to let their nails grow to an extraordinary length. They have adopted this fashion, which is not widespread, from the Chinese.

Morals, Dress and Customs of the Ordinary Malays

Like the slaves, they wear their hair up, tying it back with a handkerchief that can be knotted or hitched in a variety of ways. Their clothing consists of a sarong, which falls from the waist to the knee, and another cotton garment which they wear over their shoulders and wrap around themselves when they are cold or need protection from the sun or rain. These clothes, like all the items that they wear, have a certain elegance. In addition, over their left shoulders they carry a bag fashioned from a handkerchief, the corners of which are passed though rings made from tortoiseshell, or from the base of a shell belonging to the genus *Voluta*. They put their betel in this. They wear ivory and silver bands on their arms, often a great many of them at once (I saw one man with as many as thirty-two). They sometimes walk about barefoot. Only when they have a journey to make along rocky paths do they wear a sort of sandal, which is made from fronds of the latanier, woven together and held in place on the foot by cords made from the same type of frond. Some of them carefully pluck their beards with small tweezers made from steel or bamboo.

The women have shy, gentle expressions. They wear their hair up at the back, winding it into a coil which they hold in place with a comb made out of horn or tortoiseshell. They wear sarongs that cover them from the top of the breast to midway down the leg. When they are at home they leave their breasts uncovered. They also wear bracelets and necklaces. Some wear copper bands just above the ankle. Professional dancers usually wear these latter items.

All alike grease their hair with coconut and scent it with the leaves of a species of *Pandanus,* which has a smell that Europeans find strong and unpleasant.

They wash frequently and keep their bodies very clean, as they do their huts, which are made from bamboo and roofed with straw. They sleep on simple mats which they spread across frames made from lengths of bamboo. On these they enjoy a sleep that is untroubled by pride, ambition or intrusive desires. They eat rice, poultry, pork, and pieces of buffalo meat which have been cut into strips, cured, and dried in the sun. (The Malays from the interior of Timor and from several surrounding islands eat the flesh of dogs.) Out of a single latanier frond they make buckets which hold 10 to 12 pints.

A few mats, a few bowls made out of clay or coconut shell: these are their only possessions; with these paltry riches a Malay is happy. Having no ambition, he only has to satisfy his physical needs, and these are reduced to a small number in such a mild climate and in a country where nature is so generous. If he has a small amount of rice, a few yards of cloth, a few betel leaves and a few areca nuts, he is content. He has no worries for the future. He can surrender to his chief passion – which is sleeping. It is not that their desires are never aroused – they often coveted our European trinkets – but that their desires were never strong enough to spur them to do any work for us, however heavy or light this might have been. Being so fond of repose, they always use the easiest means possible to obtain the things they want. This is the reason for the frequent thefts of which we had cause to complain. One could extend this inference to the inhabitants of all hot countries, who are generally lazy and given to thieving.

The Malays are of medium height; I never saw one as tall as 5 feet 10 inches. In general, they have good physiques, an easy bearing, and an assured gait that at times appears a little arrogant. Their features are usually pleasing and lack that uniformity which one observes among some negro peoples. A great many have a European-looking face beneath their copper skin and a cheerful, candid expression. The Malays of the interior have a more savage expression, which perhaps derives from the fact that they are little accustomed to meeting strangers. Due to their habit of not wearing shoes, their feet are highly supple and I have often seen them throw stones powerfully and to a great distance with their feet. They are able to climb trees without pressing their knees against the trunk. They cling on by their hands and the soles of their feet, without hugging the tree, and climb with surprising speed. Admittedly, the trunks of almost all the coconut trees are scored with notches, but these would be of no help to anyone wearing shoes.

I saw very few deformities among the Malays. (I don't think I saw more than three or four who were lame and they appeared to have suffered accidents.) They are highly susceptible to skin diseases, mainly to a type of whitish scurf that sometimes covers a large part of the body. (Monsieur Tielman, civil captain of the town, had this disease, which affected his leg.) They also suffer from scabies, and I saw several with deep wounds in the leg. They do not catch these diseases through a lack of cleanliness, for, as I have said before, they wash frequently. But mightn't it be the case that these diseases, which afflict the inhabitants of Timor along with a number of other peoples in hot countries, arise from the fact that their skin is constantly in contact with the air?

The Dutch doctor claimed that venereal disease did not exist in Timor, but several men learnt to their cost that prudence is more valuable than a doctor's testimony.

The Malays were generally very welcoming towards us. Perhaps they missed us after we left, but that would have been because we did not offend against their customs. They are very jealous and would look on unhappily if anyone acted too freely in public towards the women of the island. Certainly they offered women to our men, but always with an enigmatic air. Undoubtedly the men took advantage of these offers. It is very difficult for young sailors, long deprived of women, to control their desires and refrain from satisfying them, but it reflects well on all involved that these liaisons were conducted with a strain of propriety which ensured that not the slightest dispute arose.

The Malays are timid sailors[114] and clumsy fishermen. Using small, finely worked cotton nets, they are happy just to catch the small fish that are stranded by the falling tide in pools that they make with rocks along the shoreline.

They sometimes kill birds with blow-pipes and bamboo darts. I was told that they pluck the birds and preserve their bodies by stretching them out and carefully drying them, but I never managed to find out the exact process that they use.

They make very attractive items of furniture from latanier fronds and rice straw. They fashion bowls, spoons and combs from coconut, great chambered nautiluses, tortoiseshell, bamboo and buffalo horn. They make fabrics with different patterns. Using dyed thread and different weaves, they create patterns which differ from island to island. In Timor, the sarongs are usually white with a red trim made sometimes of chiné. On Savu and Roti, the sarongs have red, blue and white stripes and mottled patterning. On the island of Indé, the sarongs have narrower stripes of the same kind. On the island of Sumba, the sarongs have yellow, white and red stripes on a blue background, and white fringing. The dyes are extracted from various types of bark.

The music of the Malays is piercing and discordant and is not enhanced in the slightest by their favourite means of accompaniment, the Malay drum and the Chinese tam-tam. One can only bear listening to it from a considerable distance away. They also have a small bamboo flute which has six holes. It has a very melodious sound which is rather like that of our flageolet. They also have an instrument which is made from a piece of bamboo cut immediately after the node at either end. In the section between the two nodes, they prise up pieces of the bark and round these without detaching them from the two ends. These pieces of bark serve as the strings of the instrument. They raise them to the tone they want by sliding small pieces of wood underneath. They attach a piece of latanier leaf at either end of the instrument and form this into a suitably concave shape. Spread out like this underneath, the leaf serves to reflect its sound, which is softer than that of a guitar – but Malays prefer loud music.

Their dances are more varied. These all involve different movements of the arms and body. Some represent different activities: wars, hunts, etc., etc. They are very graceful and require a great deal of suppleness. Some are slow and others very lively. Sometimes the dancers follow the cadence of a voice and at other times that of the booming drums and tam-tams.

Description of a Celebration Held for the Malay Kings; this Celebration Takes Place Every Year

When the kings visit Kupang to make their customary gifts, they are told to come on a particular day and present a list of the European items that they would like to have. This meeting takes place in a house of one of the Dutchmen, who is responsible for receiving these requests. These gatherings are usually enlivened by various types of entertainment. Along with several others, I was present at one of these occasions.

A spacious courtyard in front of the house was illuminated by several resin torches blazing in burnished candelabra, and the Malay kings and French officers and naturalists who attended sat in chairs arranged in a semi-circle. The kings wore calico gowns and before each stood a small table bearing a box of betel and areca nuts. Behind each king's chair stood several of his subjects. The man standing directly behind the king held the cane with the gold or silver knob which is the special symbol of the alliance made with the Dutch.

Before this illustrious gathering, Malays with heads, arms and legs adorned with latanier fronds performed various dances. To my mind, the most striking was a traditional dance in which the dancers' movements followed the beat of two Malay drums. The dancers all held hands in single file. The lead dancer sang a song and the other dancers took up the chorus. He set the tempo with a bamboo stick and with this viciously caned any dancers who strayed from the rhythm. The line wound in different directions around the drums, which were at the centre. The slow steps of the dance were accompanied by strange and tortuous movements of the body and arms which were so exhausting that the dancers were soon gasping for breath and covered in sweat. The end of each dance was signalled by a shrill cry from all involved.

During the entertainment, smartly dressed young slaves offered the circle of spectators liquors and pastries of different kinds which were elegantly arranged in baskets or on gleaming platters. Before drinking the liquor offered to him, each king acknowledged his fellow rulers with a nod of his head and they responded with a similar gesture.

Each king entered the house in turn and presented a list of the items which he wanted, which would be granted to him only insofar as their value did not exceed the value of the presents which he had given the Company.

These revels lasted most of the night.

★

The Malays kiss by pressing noses together and breathing in deeply.

The inhabitants of Roti are more attractive, more shapely and lighter-skinned than those of Timor and neighbouring islands. And so the slaves from there are more expensive.

The inhabitants of Solor are cleverer and more industrious. They fashion metal articles, farm the land, and fish.

I am told that on the island of Bali, women still follow the barbarous custom of immolating themselves when their husbands die.

The Malays who are not Christian recognise the existence of a Supreme Being. They do not worship him but place great faith in spells and sorcerers. They view as such all foreigners having red hair. They ascribe to them the greatest powers, as well as to old women who dabble in creating cures from plants. I don't know if it is due to their sour tempers that old women have been associated with spells and incantations, but across all ages and among almost all peoples they have enjoyed the same sinister reputation. The tales which the Malays tell about their sorcerers are very similar to those told by European peasants.

The Malays bury their dead in the countryside, raising over the body a small rectangular mound of earth, which is enclosed by a low dry-stone wall. At opposite ends of the mound, they drive into the ground pieces of wood around 2 feet in length. A bowl containing ashes usually sits on the grave: at certain times aromatic substances are burnt in this.

The Chinese tombs are made from a type of stucco. Large and semi-circular, they are built in a very strange style. They are usually situated on the side of a hill.

The Malays from the interior wear certain necklaces which they prize very highly. They claim that such necklaces can be obtained only by exposing themselves to the gravest dangers. Spells and enchantments feature heavily in their stories but no two of these are ever consistent. There are two types of necklace: one is called *mouti sala*, the other *mouti bouha*. Both are made from a reddish substance, which is neither attractive nor valuable. I thought at first that these were pieces of fossilised coral, but the governor, Monsieur Lofsteth, told me that it was a substance which the Malays today have lost the secret of making. A necklace that is 2 spans long sells for 12 to 15 piastres. The governor gave one of these to Citizen Baudin.

★

Nota.[115] A great many Malays have fetishes or tutelary gods to which they address their prayers. The objects of such cults are usually stones or trees, as has also been observed among a number of African tribes.

CHAPTER 4: TIMOR

Some of the Malays wear a sort of amulet, which they believe will protect them from misfortune. One such piece, which I saw a Malay from the interior of the island wearing around his neck, was made from several small cords to which were attached: (1) three old pieces of cotton cloth, 2 inches square; one piece was red and the others were so dirty I could not tell what colour they were; (2) an old scrap of iron which seemed to have once been part of the latch of a casket; (3) the beaks of two parrots; (4) the beak and the feet of a bird of prey; (5) a small bone from a quadruped; (6) a small wad of hair; (7) a small cylindrical piece of wood about an inch in length. Glass beads hung from other cords. It appeared that he had been wearing this sizeable relic for a long time as it was very dirty. I asked whether he would sell it to me but although I offered him many items that he seemed to desire very much he refused to part with it. He gave me to understand that in battle it would protect him from the blows of the enemy.

*

I saw a Malay from the interior who had had a piece of gold encrusted in each of his teeth.

The offensive weapons used by the Malays are the sabre, the spear, the bow and the kris or dagger. Since meeting Europeans, they have also started using guns. To defend themselves they use shields, of which there are two types: one is large, convex and round and is made out of dried buffalo hide; the other is made out of wood and has a convex rectangular shape.

The hilts of their sabres are fashioned from buffalo horn and, though nicely carved, are strange in shape and highly impractical. These are attached to blades that are heavier at the tip, making for an unwieldly weapon. In battle, the Malays are implacable foes. Some in their fury go as far as eating the heads of their enemies. To commemorate their victories, they wear silver bracelets, around an inch and a half thick, above the elbow, one bracelet for every enemy killed.

It is with some trepidation that the Dutch summon the Malays from the interior to help them. They have reason to fear the chaos that usually ensues when a large and unruly mob gathers. The alarm signal is three cannon shots.

When a raja dies, the Malays slaughter many animals. They gather together for several days and their grief pours out in songs of lament. They perform other ceremonies which they refused to explain to me. All the raja's subjects dress in mourning clothes, which are black. The body is enclosed in a coffin and this is placed inside his house, where it sometimes remains for two to three years. During this time the wives of the dead man take turns in keeping watch over the body, until it is at last placed inside a stone tomb.

The Malays make two different types of boat: the larger sort are designed like our European craft, while the smaller ones are hollowed from a single tree trunk or made by joining several pieces of wood. These are called *corcora*.[116] They are very long with a high prow and stern and commonly have an outrigger. The paddles they use have round or oval blades. They row with great speed and sing together to coordinate their strokes. They caulk their boats with a bark similar to that of the *Melaleuca* which I saw in New Holland. This material arrives as an article of trade; it is not collected around Kupang.

The Malays of the interior hunt wild buffalo.

At Monsieur Tielman's I saw various ornaments worn by rajas from the interior of Timor: gold crescents 12 to 15 inches wide[117] which they wear on the side of the head, disks of the same metal, 8 to 10 inches in diameter, which they wear on their chests, and gold filigree snakes which they wear on chains.

We had only praise for the hospitality of the Malays. Every time I ventured inland, I would pay a visit to the rajas whose houses I passed. They always received me with the warmest displays of friendship. The rajas' houses are scarcely any grander than those of their subjects.

The Malay custom of endlessly chewing betel quickly blackens their teeth and the caustic action of the lime causes them to rot away.

It is my opinion, however, that during calls at tropical ports, sailors could greatly benefit from the practice of chewing betel and all those suffering from scurvy should be advised to use it. This gentle mastication strengthens the gums and the aromatic compounds present in areca nuts and betel must be beneficial to stomachs overloaded with fruit and drink. I speak here from experience. During the period we were in Timor, I often chewed betel and areca nut. At times it was so hot that I drank inordinate amounts of fresh water, and I also drank a lot of buffalo milk, which is considered almost fatal, but I did not suffer a single moment of ill health. On the contrary, during this stay, which proved deleterious to so many of us, my health improved and I put on weight, even though I remained on shore the whole time. A longer period of evaluation would be required to confirm the validity of my observations.

Natural History

Botany

We arrived in Timor during the dry season, when almost all the annual plants and all the grasses had been scorched by the heat. Very few trees were in flower or fruit. However, the great variety of plant life that I was still able to observe indicated that a rich, plentiful and fascinating collection of botanical specimens might be gathered during a milder season. The coast in the vicinity of Kupang is not very fertile, being of a porous, calcareous stone, generally composed of a sort of stellated madrepore, the surface of which has darkened and decomposed over time to form a shallow layer of vegetable matter, over which plant debris has accumulated. This layer is not thick enough to form a fertile base and so, with the exception of a few fig trees (*Ficus indica*), only small, spindly trees and a few lianas of the Apocynaceae family are to be seen there. The ground is thickly covered with dry grass, which suggests that the soil, while not deep enough to sustain large trees, must support an enormous variety of small annuals in the rainy season. Along the inlets and bays of the coast, where the layer of soil carried by the streams is thicker, the trees are taller. There are usually houses in these places and they are always shaded by numerous coconut trees.

Just half a league inland the country changes. Plants grow vigorously and huge fields of rice, interspersed with patches of forest, point to a soil that is uniformly rich – and lacks only skilful and methodical cultivation. The landscape varies greatly and one comes across the most delightful spots. The straight and slender stem of the areca palm, the wide, jagged leaves of the breadfruit tree, the thin pendant leaves of the bamboo and the spreading crests of the latanier form clusters of greenery which I never wearied of admiring, especially by the river where they created a contrast with the dark rocks of the banks.

Here, as in all tropical countries, there is a wide variety of delicious fruits, but a European must refrain from eating them in large quantities. When sailors who have been deprived of vegetables for several months unwisely gorge themselves on such fruit, fever and dysentery rapidly follow.

Mangoes grow plentifully here (they are better than the ones in the Isle of France), as do several types of banana (the tastiest are 7 to 8 inches long and reddish in colour), papayas, several types of eugenia, pineapples, pomegranates, grapefruit, lemons, oranges (the best is the mandarin, or Chinese orange), carambolas, bilimbis, jacks, sugar-apples, breadfruit (*rima*), coconuts, and a type of fruit called the *nam* (*Cynometra cauliflora*). A large-pipped grape, undoubtedly a type of chasselas, is picked when in season.

There are two species of latanier: one has smaller leaves (with spines on the petiole) which are used for roofing houses; the other has larger leaves which are used for making common mats, buckets, hats and various other items.

A drink called *tuak* is extracted from this tree. To obtain it, a leaf is cut off and a bowl is attached to the petiole to collect the liquid that runs out. The drink is agreeably sweet but can cause fever and dysentery. It turns sour after 24 hours. When heated on a fire, it reduces to a dark, pleasant-tasting syrup – which can be reduced by further boiling to a sugar which has the consistency of clay and tastes like barley sugar. The fruit of this latanier grows in bunches of six to eight, each around the size of a child's head. Inside are three nuts which are eaten here but have quite an unpleasant taste. These nuts sit within a fibrous husk.

The wood used for building comes from the coconut tree, the latanier, several species of fig tree, the mahogany tree, the mango tree and the tamarind tree. There are several other types of high-quality timber, but these are not found near Kupang. They are fetched from far along the coast – which is where we had to go to obtain wood suitable for building our longboat.

The wood of the latanier is very hard and difficult to work. It is not prone to rotting and insects rarely bore into it. The Malays make their drums from the trunks of these trees. They hollow out the inside and shape the wood into the form of a flower vase; the opening is then closed over with a piece of hide.

They make their boats, or *corcora*, from the large trunks of the mango tree, fashioning them out of a single piece.

They grow very little in the way of vegetables – the main ones are turnip-cabbage, lettuce, a type of white radish which has an exceptional flavour, celery, onions in very small quantities (there are two types of these: the red ones rot very quickly; the white ones are to be preferred by sailors at sea as they keep longer), shallots, garlic, sage, fennel, coriander, angelica, anise, potatoes, yams, squash, and earth-peas (*Lathyrus amphicarpos*). Not long ago, the Dutch introduced a yellow potato which is small and tasty. *Dolichos catianus* is grown in the interior, along with a species of pea which has a compressed pod with two toothed valves. This pea has a very nice flavour and is eaten green in the pod. The Malays also grow saffron, which is called *coni di negri* (false saffron), and *Canna indica*. Wild saffron is called *coni di utan*.[118]

Two species of plant from the family Apocynaceae grow plentifully here (I think they are both *Periploca*). Their roots are used for making a pleasant-tasting drink, which is considered good for the health when drunk regularly. One of these plants has broad leaves, the other, narrow; both have milky sap, a climbing stem and thick, fissured bark, which is rather soft, like cork. I did not find them in flower or in fruit.

To make this drink, which the Malays call *laru*, the root is carefully peeled and cut into pieces 3 or 4 inches long. These are placed in a bowl of water and a sufficient amount of *tuak* syrup is added (molasses or sugar may be used instead). The mixture is then left to ferment for 6 to 8 hours. The same root may be used for several months in a row. Around two handfuls are needed for a bowl of 7 or 8 pints. For the first 7 or 8 days the liquor is too strong and has a very unpleasant taste. This is usually thrown away. But it then develops a flavour which is like slightly bitter wine. The sailors preferred this drink to beer. Citizen Lharidon, surgeon of the *Géographe*, told me that it had a salutary effect on his patients. He believes that if the recipe for this drink were improved it could become highly beneficial. To preserve this root for a long period after it has been peeled, it must be placed in small packets and kept in the open air or in a very dry place. This drink could be a valuable resource for ships' crews, as I believe it to be a very good antiscorbutic. When left to ferment for more than 7 or 8 hours it turns sour.

The capsules of the cotton tree supply a down that is used for stuffing mattresses and pillows. The down from a type of *Asclepias* is put to the same use. Its milky leaves are sessile and downy, and it has large flowers that look very much like those of the *Asclepias* of Syria. The Malays call this plant *daun susu*.

On a few occasions I came across a cotton plant which, on the basis of its leaves, I believe to be *Gossypium rubrum*. It is grown in the interior of the island.

A large tree of the family Scrophularia, and related to the genus *Dodartia*, has a bark which is reputed to be very helpful for internal contusions. It has a bitter taste and is said to have the same properties as cinchona. Citizen Bellefin, surgeon of the *Naturaliste*, had quite a large amount of this collected for him.

I encountered several species of cassia: purging cassia; another with a pink flower and long black cylindrical pods which did not contain succulent pulp; and a third species, whose fruit I did not see – its flowers are magnificent, each cluster having the shape, colour and scent of a spray of gillyflowers. The tree which bears them is very tall and straight. It is an ornamental. Its wood would be suitable for building work.

Jatropha globosa, or physic nut. The Malays do not know how to extract its seed-germ. They make oil from it. It is widespread.

Aloe dichotoma. Its sap is used in place of soap.

A caper bush with large white flowers and round leaves. The Malays call it *boa api-api*.

One also finds here *Pergularia glabra*, *Uvaria cananga* and *Mogorium* (*Nyctanthes sambac*), which has sweet-smelling flowers that Malay women use to decorate their hair. They also use the flowers of the *kamuni* tree in this way; it is a small species of orange tree with a red fruit the size of a filbert nut and the aromatic smell of orange peel. There is another species of *kamuni* (I think it is a species of *Guaiac*), which does not grow in the vicinity of Kupang. In the past, the inhabitants of Timor used the wood of the *kamuni* instead of iron, I am told, when that valuable metal was unknown to them. The tree has a very hard black wood. It has a large amount of sapwood, of a yellow colour similar to box. The layers are so fine and close together that it is difficult to make them out. It would seem, from the samples I have been able to obtain, that this tree never attains a great size, and grows extremely slowly. Although slender, the trunks of these trees are often fissured and twisted.

A large tree, called the *falua* by the Malays, having a whitish bark, heart-shaped leaves and capsular fruit, secretes a tasteless white transparent gum which is highly soluble in water. It could easily be used instead of gum arabica. The Malays eat the seeds, which taste rather like hazelnuts.

Tournefortia argentea grows near the seashore. Its shiny, velvety leaves lend it a very attractive appearance. A species of *Gardenia* with sweet-smelling tubular white flowers is also found there.

Dolichos pruriens, *Dolichos curiformis*, the beautiful red-flowered poinciana, and a yellow-flowered variety, grow everywhere in great abundance, along with several species of *Phyllanthus*, *Justicia*, *Sida*, *Malva* and *Hibiscus*, and *Abrus precatorius*, *Clitoria*, *Corispermum* [*illegible word*].

And finally, from all sides, one's sense of smell is pleasantly assailed by the scent of the flowers of *Plumeria alba*, or frangipani, and one's sight by the beautiful red crowns on the tips of the branches of *Erythrina corallodendron*.

I shall refrain from providing here a longer list of the plants that I found around Kupang. Such a list would be better suited to a dedicated botanical journal.

★

Nota. Near the *negri* ruled by the raja of Amari, I saw a fig tree (*Ficus indica*) of remarkable size. Its branches covered more than an acre of ground. It grew on the side of a ravine which had a very pretty stream at the bottom. It is a very picturesque spot.

The Dutch do not permit spices to be grown on the island of Timor, but this measure, which restricts their precious crop to a small number of islands in the Moluccas, will soon prove pointless, because the trees which produce the spices acclimatise perfectly well in our colony of the Isle of France, and from there it will be possible to ship the plants to our other possessions in the Indies.

It is forbidden to grow coffee. Each citizen is permitted to keep just two plants for his own consumption.

★

Nota. I examined a small dense white stone which was round and milkily translucent. It had been found in a coconut. It was the size of a pea and had been given to Captain Hamelin by Monsieur Joannis, a burgher of Kupang. These stones are rare and are found only in coconuts which lack the three holes which provide passage for the germ. Could it be the case that the germ hardens when it cannot find an exit? This seems all the more plausible as I am told that these stones are always located in the pulp of the nut on the side where the germ should be, though around an inch from the openings.

Animals

The most remarkable birds are: the white-throated frigate; the buzzard; the sparrowhawk, which closely resembles the French tercel; the crow; a species of hornbill, which is very common; the cockatoo; several species of parrot; several species of dove, one of which has a pink head and the most beautifully coloured plumage; a quail which has a white throat patterned with close-set black spots; a starling with feathers the colour of burnished steel; several species of shrike, one of which, I noticed, has a forked tail with striking, reflexed tips; a small species of waxbill which flies in flocks of several thousand and causes considerable damage to the rice crop; several small flycatchers, some of which have very brilliant plumage; a green pigeon; a small swallow, whose mucilaginous nest is eaten by the Chinese; wild hens which have a call resembling the first notes of that of the domestic hen – it could be rendered as the word *cocrick*.

The domestic birds are: hens; cocks, some of which are huge and fearless – the Malays often set them to fight against each other and bet on them. They love these fights. Ducks are very large and expensive because they are highly sought after by the Chinese. They usually sell for a rix-dollar. (The rix-dollar is worth 48 sous).[119] Hens sell for only 5 to 6 sous. The ducks' gait is quite similar to that of the penguin.

I saw a cock which had four legs. The two extra legs were short and thin, and were attached to the base of the joint which connects the thigh to the lower leg.

The quadrupeds are: deer, which are abundant, buffalo (some are kept as livestock), horses, wild pigs, civet cats, a red monkey with a trailing tail (*Simia aygula*), a creature (a species of marmose opossum) which is the size of a marmot, grey with a large head and great bulging eyes, five digits on its forefeet and hind feet, a dangling tail, hairless from its tip to halfway along its length, carnivorous and frugivorous. Is this the cuscus mentioned by Valmont de Bomare (who draws on Christoph Barchewitz's account)?[120] Goats, sheep, several species of dog, several species of lizard, the small flying dragon, the flying fox, several species of bat, large numbers of rats. Crocodiles are very common at the river mouth.

Several species of fish are found along the coast, some of the smallest in size displaying the most brilliant colours. A great many molluscs and madrepores, remarkable for their shape and colour, also occur there.

There are a huge variety of shells and some of them struck me as being quite rare. Among those that were familiar, I observed the great chambered nautilus, which the Malays use for making spoons, the great turban shell, which supplies a very beautiful, shimmering nacre, and the pearl oyster, which has very small pearls. (This shellfish is not very common; it is not collected there.) The Polish saddle, the black hammer oyster, the lightning shell, the harlequin, the striped cone, a large striated green tusk shell, the egg cowry, the tiger cowry, the wrinkled cowry, the draught-board helmet shell and several other species of helmet shell, the clam, several of which are so large that a single valve could serve as a drinking trough for livestock. I found only two land snails: one is not at all attractive and has a flattened whorl and closely resembles the common snail of France; the other has a pointy whorl with its mouth on the left and has yellow, brown and white stripes.

I saw only three types of snake. I killed one on the seashore which was around 18 inches long and grey with black markings. I preserved it in arrack but it was spoilt by the heat. I encountered another, which was a delicate green colour, on the river bank. It was a snake of this species that bit Citizen Lesueur, artist, on the heel while he was out hunting. He was ill for several days, but alkali, administered externally and internally, neutralised the action of the venom. The third snake was around 4 feet long, dark green, and thinner than one's little finger. I was very eager to kill it but it slid away into the grass and was lost.

Mosquitoes cause a great deal of discomfort here but the real scourge is a small red ant with a very painful bite. It is the species most often found in houses. It devours everything that it comes across with astonishing speed. To keep food safe from these ants, it must be placed on tables or in cupboards which have their feet resting in bowls of water. Scorpions are small and not highly venomous: they did not seem any different from those found in the southern provinces of France.

A huge species of green mantis, about 1 foot in length, is very common.

Butterflies are common and highly diverse. Commander Baudin gathered a valuable collection of them.

When, at the end of a sweltering day, one breathes the cool evening air under the gently swaying canopy of a tamarind tree or banyan fig, one always sees Thunberg's *Lampyris japonica*[121] flitting about in the gloom. In the darkness this insect resembles a miniature wandering star.

Mineral Deposits

The vast quantities of ore washed down by streams through deep ravines that have been carved out by torrents in the rainy season suggest that rich deposits of iron are to be found in the interior of the island, near to the river – which would make it feasible and perhaps even profitable to mine them.

Gold is also found here; it is recovered mainly from a river at the head of the Kupang roads. This river flows through the territory of an emperor who no longer recognises Dutch rule. It is dangerous to travel through his lands as he is mistrustful of Europeans, even though he has adopted their customs and dress. He is said to be an educated man. He is a cause of concern to the Company; he has a great many guns but very little powder.

The gold is pale and low in grade. It is found as a dust and sometimes in grains. I saw one which was the size of a pea. The emperor keeps a careful guard over the river which is a source of wealth for him and is greedily coveted by the Europeans.

I have in my possession several pieces of jewellery which were fashioned from this gold by the inhabitants of Solor.

The island of Timor is subject to frequent earthquakes. When we arrived we saw a great many houses that had been knocked down by an earthquake a few years before. These had not yet been rebuilt.

Reflections on the Malay Language

The Malay spoken in Kupang differs very little from that spoken in Batavia. In compiling this vocabulary, which will appear at the end of my journal, I have tried to follow actual pronunciation as closely as possible. As a result, my spelling does not always match that which appears in the list given by Citizen Labillardière in the *Voyage in Search of La Pérouse*[122] – a list which is in any case much fuller than mine and extremely useful for anyone travelling in the Moluccas.[123]

The Malay language is soft and pleasant. For a Frenchman, it is very easy to pronounce. It is not punctuated by any guttural or nasal inflections of the voice. It is an easy language to learn, as there are no inversions within sentences, no conjugations or declensions, no verb tenses, participles or noun genders. With a list of words it is very easy to make oneself understood and to understand common sentences. Another helpful thing is that a great many verbs are made by combining one word which indicates the action and another which indicates how the action is performed.

Examples

to sharpen	*kria tayan*
to approach	*datan decat*

to kiss	*cassi tioum*
to remove footwear	*clouar cos*

In these examples, the words *kria* (to make), *datan* (to come), *cassi* (to give), and *clouar* (to remove), indicate the action, and the words *tayan* (sharp), *decat* (near), *tioum* (a kiss), *cos* (a stocking), indicate how the action is performed. These compound verbs, which are very common, reduce the number of words that must be learnt and ease the burden on one's memory. In addition, a single word very often expresses both the verb and its substantive.

A verb used by itself always indicates the present; but when it is preceded by the word *nanti*, which means 'wait', it indicates the future. When it is preceded by the word *souda*, which means 'enough', it indicates the past. When it is preceded by the word *bolon*, 'not yet', there is negation of an action which is still to be completed. And, finally, when it is preceded by the word *trada*, which means 'no', there is absolute negation of the action.

Examples

beta datan	I come
nanti beta datan	I shall come
beta souda datan	I came
beta bolon datan	I have not yet come
beta trada datan	I did not come, or I shall not come

The word *bole*, which means 'to be able', is used in some instances instead of the word *nanti*, and also indicates the future. The word *lebe*, 'more', used before an adjective, indicates the comparative of increase, the word *couran*, 'less', the comparative of diminution.

Elisions are frequently used in the Malay language, the most common being those of the words *trada* and *souda*.

Examples

itou tra-bagous	that is not good	instead of *trada bagous*
sou-abis	to be finished	instead of *souda abis*

Although the Malay language is used almost universally in the Indies, I do not think that it is extensive in its vocabulary or sophisticated. I am speaking here only of vulgar Malay, which differs greatly from High Malay, *Malayo bessar*, which is spoken by all educated Malays. The Bible and several prayer books have been translated into High Malay.

The Malay language has been enriched by foreign trade. Several words, which have come to them from the Chinese, Portuguese and Dutch, have since become established.

The Malays love poetry. They have songs for every activity and often improvise. A line usually contains nine or ten feet, broken after the fourth or fifth foot by a caesura. They use alternate rhymes and these are very rhythmical. The songs are a mixture of High Malay and vulgar Malay, their structure apparently governed by rules no one could explain to me.

The Malay spoken in Kupang is not the same as that spoken in the interior of Timor; that which is spoken in Kupang is, as I said above, almost the same as that of Batavia. Traditional ties and commercial relations are the reason for this conformity; however, if one travels just a league into the interior of the island, the language changes and it often happens that a Malay from Kupang will not be understood by a Malay from a neighbouring *negri*.

It is the same for the islands of Semau, Roti, Solor and Savu. All these islands, which are very close to Timor, and are dependencies of the Dutch trading post, have their own particular languages. In the *negris* which have a harbour, however, the Malay of Kupang is spoken.

Dili, a Portuguese trading post in the northern part of Timor, also has its own particular language, if I may rely on a handwritten account I read containing a short list of vocabulary. This account is in Commander Baudin's possession.[124]

Such are the observations on the language that I was able to make during my two-month stay – a language that is all the more valuable and useful to those travelling in the Indies as it is so widely spoken.

Sequel of My Stay in Timor

Mother, my brothers, my friends, those of you for whom I primarily write this account: while I am so far away, you are no doubt deeply concerned about what has become of me. But please set your minds at rest. Five thousand leagues from my homeland, I can still feel the warmth of your unwavering affection... Mother...! At this word my soul flies across the intervening distance and I enclose you in a fond embrace.

Hospitality is not offered here with that affected and artificial courtesy which, among the civilised peoples of Europe, flatters one's pride but wearies one's heart more than it gives pleasure. Here, man, being closer to nature, offers what he wishes another to have in a candid and friendly way that indifference could never imitate. When I am among you again and can relate the events of this long journey, I shall feel profound gratitude every time I mention the names of Monsieur Tielman and Monsieur Joannis, who have both overwhelmed me with their kindness. The latter, especially, insisted that I always dine with him and, whenever my work obliged me to stay away for even half a day, a succession of slaves would come to find out what was keeping me. Citizen Hamelin enjoyed this hospitality with me and when we left we were both offered food and drink of every kind. Our farewells left them in tears and I genuinely shared their sadness.

Monsieur Tielman is the captain or leader of the Kupang burghers. He is of mixed race and is the brother of Madame van Este, of whom I have already spoken. This lady was ill for almost the entire length of our stay and she met very few members of our expedition. Monsieur Tielman brought me to see her twice during the final days of our stay in Kupang and I was received with the utmost courtesy. Madame van Este is a woman aged 55; she has a very cheerful nature and is greatly loved by all around her. She is very rich and brings joy to many. She does not have any children of her own but raises several sons and daughters of her relatives in her home.

Monsieur Joannis is a wealthy citizen of mixed race. He has amassed a considerable fortune through trading. I have rarely met anyone as high-spirited as his wife. Every evening she prepared a new form of entertainment for us, helped by her two young daughters. Sometimes she had her slaves perform dances from Java or Timor, led always by the younger daughter, and sometimes she staged concerts for us, which were always, it must be said, rather discordant. The songs they sang were always about us and were often improvised.

Two or three days before we left, Monsieur Joannis held a large supper to which several of the *Naturaliste*'s officers were invited. It was a very cheerful meal and more elaborate than we had expected. More than forty carefully prepared dishes crowded the table. The master and mistress of the house did the honours with great style. At the end of the meal, Monsieur Joannis raised a farewell toast to each one of us in turn. It was through my frequent visits to this house that I was able to learn enough Malay in a short period to make myself easily understood.

Being so far removed from our way of life, the Malay does not experience the spurious desires which make it so difficult for us to achieve happiness. He is not tormented by an excessive thirst for wealth, nor does he share the dull-wittedness of the New Holland savages, who are so lacking in enterprise that they are barely able to satisfy their most pressing needs. The Malay lives in an intermediate state of civilisation and, although he cannot take pleasure in the glory, splendour and power of his nation, he at least enjoys personal and domestic happiness. What he sees around him excites in him neither pride, envy, nor ambition. A sort of degenerate child, he is readily supplied by a mild climate with all he might desire to satisfy his physical needs, and the differences in living conditions are not so great as to sap the lower orders of their self-esteem. While it is true that there are slaves, there is a great difference between the way they are treated here and the practices of our European colonies. There is no prejudice attached to skin colour because all are of the same colour. The slave feels affection for his master and hastens to anticipate his smallest desire, while the master leads a similar life to his and treats him equably.

I was also shown great kindness by Gabriel Wentz; Hendrik Tielman; Hendrik de Silva; Castor Ans Portaiaia, a wealthy citizen of Kupang; Tion Yangnan, a wealthy Chinese (張揚肯);[125] raja Amari; Amadima, raja of Savu; and Miguel Albertus, raja of Amanuban.

We had been separated from the corvette the *Naturaliste* since leaving Géographe Bay. A month had passed since our arrival in Timor. Every day we hoped to see her come into this final rendezvous. Her delay left us in almost no doubt that she had been wrecked. Our unfortunate comrades were often in our thoughts: we imagined the harrowing scene of our friends perishing among the waves or wandering a wild shoreline. These gloomy, wearying thoughts finally gave way to gladder sentiments when on the fourth complementary day [21 September] a ship appeared in the west. We held hopes that it was the *Naturaliste* and these were not disappointed. On that same day we embraced our friends after three and a half months apart and our hearts were filled to the brim with joy.

The *Naturaliste* had been to the first two rendezvous exactly as planned. The ship had called at Rottnest Island and Shark Bay in turn and had sailed much further than we had done towards the head of this bay. As Citizens Michaux and Delisse had remained behind in the Isle of France, no botanical work had been done during these two stopovers, despite the fact that conditions in these places were much more favourable for the study of natural history than those which we had encountered during our dreary stay on the smaller Barren Island. Concerned that the ships might again become separated, and taking the view that Citizen Riedlé could fulfil all necessary duties by himself on the *Géographe*, I resolved to transfer to the *Naturaliste*. I felt obliged to sacrifice certain ties of friendship for the benefits that might be gained by my serving aboard this ship. Commander Baudin was unwell. I wrote to him, setting out the reasons for my decision, and asked for his consent, which he granted me in the letter below dated 15 Vendémiaire, Year X [7 October 1801].

Copy of the Letter I Wrote to Commander Baudin[126]

Citizen,

There is no designated botanist on the corvette the *Naturaliste*. You, like myself, understand how important it is that somebody should have responsibility for this important branch of natural history. Events have shown just how necessary this is, with the ships separated for two months and two stopovers made in different places.

On the ship you command, Citizen Riedlé and I perform similar functions, which could be undertaken by one person. I therefore request, Citizen Commander, your consent to continue the expedition aboard the *Naturaliste*.

In leaving you and several of my comrades for whom I feel great friendship and admiration, I shall, it is true, be making a large sacrifice; however, if, in the smallest way, my work may prove valuable to my country and contribute to the history of the science I study, I shall feel that I have been recompensed.

Respectfully,
Th. Leschenault
Chief botanist

★

CHAPTER 4: TIMOR

Kupang
Commander-in-chief, Expedition of Discovery

To Citizen Leschenault, Botanist

My recent indisposition, of which you are aware, prevented me from replying at any earlier date to the letter which you were kind enough to send me, but I gladly take advantage of these first moments of respite from the fever that has long afflicted me to commend your decision to transfer to the *Naturaliste*.

The ship, as you well observe, having no botanist aboard, requires someone who is knowledgeable in this field so that, in the various places where we shall call during the remainder of the expedition, we may turn to good account the circumstances we encounter even if the ships are separated again. I assure you that the government will greatly appreciate the sacrifice that you are making in leaving your friends, since you do so solely with the aim of contributing to the expedition's greater success.

I shall advise Captain Hamelin of this new arrangement. You will find that he and his staff will readily supply you with all that you require for your work. And, although we shall be separated, I hope that I shall never be too far from you to render you all the services in my power.

With friendly wishes, signed: Nicolas Baudin[127]

★

The commander wrote commending me to Captain Hamelin, whom I had often met in Kupang at Monsieur Joannis's.

In transferring from the *Géographe*, I left behind a number of friends to whom I was very attached, these ties being all the stronger as they were based on great respect.

Those with whom I shared the closest bonds of friendship were:

Citizen Le Bas de Sainte-Croix, commander. This officer had already travelled a great deal in the Indies and, having also lived for a long time in Paris, possessed all the social graces, along with a very kind heart. When I fell ill as we left Géographe Bay, he looked after me like a brother. He shared all his food with me and I partly owe my recovery to his care and attention. The poor state of his health and an unfortunate affair of honour with another officer of the expedition, in which he was wounded in the left arm, forced him to remain behind in Kupang. The governor invited him to stay at his residence but he chose to stay at the fort. Before I left I was delighted to see that he was completely out of danger. I introduced him to Monsieur Joannis and I hope that he may enjoy the same hospitality that I was offered by this good and kindly gentleman.

Citizen Freycinet,[128] lieutenant, a young man who places duty above all else and combines social accomplishment with a great desire to learn.

Citizen Depuch, mining engineer, an intelligent, well-bred young man. His father was in the Constituent Assembly, a deputy for the nobility of Bordeaux.

Citizen Péron, zoologist, is far more erudite than is usual for someone aged just 25. He works every day to expand his knowledge.

Citizen de Bougainville. In future it will be counted the least of his merits that he is the son of a man who, through his courage and skill, earned the highest reputation as a navigator and geographer.

During our stay in Kupang several of our sailors were carried off by dysentery and a large number were struck down by this cruel disease when we left port. Citizen Riedlé, head gardener, was a very great loss to the expedition. He was so devoted to the study of natural history that he often braved exhaustion and discomfort in this sweltering land. He never listened to the advice of friends who warned him several times that his reckless behaviour would prove fatal. Shortly after his arrival, he experienced a violent attack of dysentery, but he did not stop working and perished as a result. Shortly before leaving Paris he had been awarded a gold medal by the Société d'agriculture. Two years previously he had gone to the Americas with Commander Baudin and during that voyage collected more than 700 living plants for the Jardin national in Paris.

An English botanist named Nelson died some years before in Kupang; he had sailed with Bligh to Tahiti and remained with him when the ship under Bligh's command, the *Bounty*, was seized by mutineers. The much lamented remains of Citizen Riedlé were placed alongside Nelson's. Over the tomb of these two men, who died far from their homelands in the service of humanity, the commander raised a small pyramid with an inscription bearing the names of those for whom this modest structure had been erected.[129]

Desertions in the Isle of France and Kupang, along with the numbers of men carried away by disease or confined to their sickbeds, left the two ships short of hands, which was a source of great concern as we set off to explore an unknown coast in the high latitudes. I hope I may be allowed here to make several observations about the deficiencies in the preparations made for this expedition. A sailor could perhaps offer more penetrating observations but I formed the following opinions.

The success of a voyage of discovery depends mainly on the health of the crew. When a ship gets into difficulties, often it is saved only by the rapid actions of its crew. For this reason, only strong, healthy men with long experience of the sea should have been recruited for our ships. Every possible measure should have been taken to preserve the health of the crew, which was not done.

Several young men from wealthy families, their curiosity aroused, hastily volunteered to join the expedition. They were accepted. But they had not considered the hardships they would face. Appalled by what their positions entailed, some remained behind in Tenerife, others in the Isle of France. By joining up, however, they had taken positions which should have been filled by expert sailors. A number of other men, who were sailors by profession at least, though weak and unhealthy, gave the impression of volunteering eagerly but did so only with the aim of collecting the six months' wages paid to the crews. They knew that they would be put ashore at the first port of call for reason of ill health. An enterprise of this magnitude should never have been undertaken at Le Havre; it is too small a port to offer a wide selection of sailors in wartime and so no real choice could be made.

I have frequently heard the surgeons of the two ships say that the medicines they obtained were poor in quality and of insufficient quantity.

The supplies of wine and flour laid in were so limited that 6 months into the expedition the officers were reduced to eating biscuit and drinking brandy. Perhaps it was thought that we could obtain provisions in the ports we were to visit. But why should anyone have placed faith in this idea, given that it is so difficult to export wine and wheat from our own ports in this time of war? As to the naturalists, the government instructed Commander Baudin that the greatest consideration should be shown towards them as *they were utterly unaccustomed to the sea* and should be given everything they needed to alleviate discomfort in their new surroundings. However, we were reduced to eating food that is difficult to stomach even after one has been sailing for a long time. It is true that we were each granted an extra 4 francs and 10 sous per day for food and drink, but as we did not receive this money in the Isle of France, we had no option other than to accept the provisions offered on board ship. For all that, I speak here simply as an observer and not as a man deceived by false promises. If we have suffered as a result of this negligent provisioning, the crews have suffered much more. Most of these men were not accustomed to very long passages; only a few had left French waters for more than several months at a time. In the tropics hard work quickly wears out a man if he is unable to restore his strength with wholesome food. He drags his weary body into these unhealthy ports of call and the climate soon exerts its malign influence. It is to such privations that I attribute the losses we suffered in Kupang.

At the present time of writing, the poor state of our crews has not yet exposed us to danger, but we are heading towards regions where the sailing will be more hazardous. Who is to say whether circumstances will remain propitious?

CHAPTER 4: TIMOR

During our stay in Timor, the commander was struck down by a virulent fever. For several days we even feared for his life. He eventually recovered.

According to the observations of Citizen Saint-Cricq, lieutenant, during the month of Vendémiaire [September–October] the thermometer on land rose during the day to between 24.4° and 25°, and during the night to between 22.5° and 23°. On one occasion only he observed it at 26.3° and 22.2°.

During this month (Vendémiaire) the sun passed through the zenith of Timor.

Nota. The rainy season, which is the season of the western monsoon, is the most unhealthy.

Chapter 5

Passage from Timor to D'Entrecasteaux Channel; Descriptions of this Channel, its Inhabitants, its Plant Life and its Soil; Maria Island, Banks Strait, Western Port[130]

On 22 Brumaire, Year X of the Republic [13 November 1801], we weighed anchor and sailed out through the channel which lies between Kera Island and Semau. We ran along very close to the latter island, which appeared to be thickly wooded.

On the 25th [16 November] we passed within sight of the island of Savu, where Captain Cook called in 1770 and which is described in volume 4 of his first voyage. The island is fertile and a great many livestock are kept there. On the same day we saw Binzoa [Raijua], an island a short distance from Savu.

On the 26th [17 November] we sailed very close in to New Savu, a small, barren, uninhabited island.

Dysentery, which had proved so deadly to both crews during our stay in Kupang, continued to ravage us. Several of those afflicted by this cruel disease perished and the remainder struggled to recover even with the close attentions of the surgeons. Aboard the *Naturaliste*, we were greatly distressed to witness the death of Citizen Levillain. He was an assistant zoologist, a man kind and gracious by nature, and a delightful companion. He had travelled as Commander Baudin's secretary on an earlier voyage to the Americas.

During that trip he had devoted himself to the study of zoology. He died on 1 Nivôse, Year X [22 December 1801], at the age of 29.

Citizen Milius, lieutenant commander, was ill for almost the entire passage. This officer had suffered from poor health since Géographe Bay. He recovered a little in Kupang but shortly after we put to sea he began to suffer as before.

During the early days of our passage the heat was considerable. The thermometer rose to 26° on the Réaumur scale, but when the wind got up from the south-west, the heat rapidly declined and in the torrid zone we encountered just the sort of temperatures we have on fine spring days in our own country. I set out here a table summarising the temperatures observed during this passage.

From 22 Brumaire [13 November 1801] to 16 Frimaire [7 December 1801] the thermometer varied between 26° and 19.3°. The usual height was from 20° to 22°.

On 17 Frimaire [8 December] it fell to 17.5°.

Until the end of Frimaire [21 December], it varied between 15° and 13°.

On 4 Nivôse [25 December], the sun being at our zenith, the thermometer rose only to 12.5°. The 5th [26 December], while still in the tropics, 12°.

On 15 Nivôse [5 January 1802] 10°.

On 18 Nivôse [8 January] it fell to 8.8°. On this day it reached its lowest point during our passage.

From the 18th it rose, with some fluctuation, to 12°.

The westerly winds hindered us for a considerable period and our passage was very long. It was only on the morning of 23 Nivôse [13 January] that we sighted the South Cape of Van Diemen's Land. We ran in very close to it.

The land around this cape is very different from the west coast of New Holland. One sees little variation there while here, on the contrary, the coast is steep and broken. Tall basalt columns, which rise in needles and in this part of the world supply the final pieces in the structure of the globe, great masses of granite, which time and the frequent storms in these parts have only gently furrowed,[131] and the remote forests that crown this region present a sight that is worthy of treatment by a skilful artist's crayon. Hushed and gloomy skies, wreaths of cloud curling through trees whose withered crowns attest to their vast age, reinforced the majesty of the scene. We were about to enter the South Seas, that stage for the great discoveries made successively over the past half-century by illustrious European navigators. In recalling the achievements of these great men, however, I am chilled to my soul as I think about the terrible and tragic ends some met!... Those immortals Cook, La Pérouse, de Langle, d'Entrecasteaux, Marion and Lamanon died far from their homelands, laid low by their own virtuous natures and their love of science!...[132]

As we approached the entrance to D'Entrecasteaux Channel, the land became flatter and appeared less rugged than at the rocky tip of the cape. On the southern headland of Recherche Bay we saw a fire, around which we could make out, with the help of our glasses, five or six natives. While we were admiring the romantic vistas that the coast presented, the lookouts cried, 'Rocks ahead'. We were running before the wind and were no more than a cable's length (120 fathoms) away from them. These are the rocks that lie to the east of Recherche Bay and barely protrude above the surface of the water. As the sea was not breaking over them, they could not be seen from a distance. We left them to port and soon entered the channel, where we ran in very close to Bruny Island. That evening we anchored in Great Bay, around a quarter of a league from Partridge Island.

I hastened to go aboard the *Géographe* to see the commander and embrace those good friends from whom I had been separated for more than two months. I was saddened to find that several were in poor health. Citizen Depuch had only recently recovered from dysentery, which had afflicted him for a very long time. Citizen Maugé, zoologist, was very ill.

On the 24th [14 January] I went ashore on little Partridge Island and walked the whole way around it. The base of this island is granitic. The soil is good and is covered with very beautiful trees which have straight, slender trunks. These trees belong to the genus

Eucalyptus. *Casuarina equisetifolia* and an undershrub of the genus *Banksia* also grow in great abundance, but this shrub was not in flower or fruit. The shoreline is covered with a parsley named *Apium prostratum* by Citizen Labillardière. It has a taste of celery mixed with European parsley. A species of orach with smooth whitish leaves also grows along the shore. I collected a great many plants in the interior of the island; the most numerous are those of the myrtle family. I found several species of *Philadelphus*, *Melaleuca* and *Leptospermum*, several aromatic plants of the family Compositae, a superb species of *Aletris* with red flowers, a species of *Xyris*, a *Clematis* and a pretty *Geranium*. Among the new genera recently named by the English botanist Smith, I observed a species of *Goodenia* with yellow flowers and several species of *Styphelia*.[133]

This small island did not appear as though it was ordinarily inhabited, but the natives visit it for short periods to collect ear shells, or ormers, which cling in great numbers to rocks along the shore. Some of these shells are up to 8 inches in diameter. I saw the charred remains of these lying in great profusion around several native shelters or huts. These shelters are at most 4 feet high and are built in a crude and flimsy fashion. A tree branch 1 or 2 inches in diameter is bent into a bow and driven into the ground at either end, forming a frame which supports several long sheets of thick bark. At their one end the sheets rest on the ground, at the other, on the bow or frame. These sheets of bark form an angle of around 45 degrees with the ground but are joined together very roughly and afford little protection against rain or strong winds to the savage sheltering beneath. In front of these huts, the openings to which somewhat resemble the mouth of an oven (these openings faced east), I always came across the ashes of old fires. The bark used to build these shelters comes from *Eucalyptus resinifera*.

As I made my way towards the point which faces Bruny Island and is only separated from it by a channel around 200 paces wide, I caught sight of savages running away in several different places on the opposite shore. I immediately rushed to the edge of the water, held up the tree branches I was carrying and shouted at the top of my lungs *gougloua*, a word meaning 'come here' in their language.¹³⁴ They returned and stood opposite me, shouting and mimicking some of my gestures. As their fear seemed to have completely dissolved, I tried to lure them towards me by showing them pieces of white paper, small mirrors and knives, while I kept on repeating the word *gougloua*. Two of them then made up their minds to cross the narrow channel at a place where the water came up only to their waists and they held their hands above their heads, no doubt to show me that they were not armed. I went up to them and presented each with a necklace of large glass beads and a small knife. Uttering cries of pleasure, they immediately displayed these to the natives who had gathered in large numbers on the opposite shore. Several more then crossed the channel in order to share in the gifts I was offering. One member of this group struck me as having a measure of authority over the others; this chief had a handsome face and a well-proportioned frame. He seemed to be around thirty years old. He came up and gave me a necklace he was wearing, which was made out of small shells of brightly shimmering mother-of-pearl threaded on a thin cord of bark or grass. He asked for a glass necklace in return, which I immediately gave him. They all received my gifts with displays of great pleasure, but when I refused to give them something that they seemed to want, they did not repeat their request. When I had nothing left to give, I walked away. Two of them came with me, although before following me they placed the presents I had given them in crevices in the rocks.

All these savages were completely naked. The one who appeared to be a chief was the only one wearing a necklace; the others wore no ornaments. Most of those I saw were young and well-proportioned; only a few were slightly built. These savages have woolly hair. The colour of their skin is not a very deep shade of black but they deliberately darken parts of their bodies, especially the upper part of the face, with ground charcoal. One young man had smeared his hair with ochre-coloured earth and arranged it into small, separate locks, so that from a distance it resembled those red oiled wigs that French ladies wore a few years ago.¹³⁵ (I apologise to the fair sex, who endow everything they touch with charm, for comparing one of their fashions with the filthy hair of this savage, but it was impossible not to be struck by the similarity and I could not find a comparison which conveyed the idea more aptly.)

The natives were not tattooed; instead all were covered with scars which had been made deliberately. By taking particular measures, they cause these to protrude by half an inch sometimes. (They reopen the lips of the wounds when these are about to close.) The parts of their bodies that they most commonly scar in this way are the shoulders, the shoulder blades, the lower back, the buttocks, stomach and chest. The scars form straight, circular or semi-circular lines.

The natives have beautiful teeth, very even and white. Just one old man was missing a tooth from his upper jaw at the front of his mouth. This was probably due to age; I don't think he had had it removed. He was the only one with a long beard, which the years had touched with white. I was accompanied by two sailors who were carrying tin boxes in which I kept my botanical specimens. One of the two men was black, and when I pointed this out to the savages they did not appear in the least surprised to see a man of their colour dressed like us and sharing our customs, but as this black man was young they wished to examine his chest, no doubt to check that he wasn't a woman.

They are extremely agile and have very keen eyesight. The two natives accompanied me only until we drew near a spot where the commander and several others happened to be. The two natives saw them first, and, terrified by the prospect of this encounter, ran away. I immediately ran after them to try and fetch them back, but within a minute they had completely disappeared.

They seem acquainted with the power of firearms.[136] When I saw a red-billed oyster catcher on the shore and conveyed to them that I could kill it with the gun I was holding, they sharply cried out the word *pegloua*, which I did not understand. As they did not appear frightened, I took aim at the bird, whereupon they immediately fled in great terror. So I slung my gun over my

CHAPTER 5: VAN DIEMEN'S LAND AND WESTERN PORT

shoulder again and called them back, assuring them that I would not shoot, and they returned.

The commander had not seen any natives when I met him but gradually they grew bolder and more approached us.

There is no water on Partridge Island, but at its southern end there is a tract of damp, low-lying ground. I am convinced that fresh water could be obtained by digging there. A great many mussels can be found along the rocks which fringe the island. I saw several quail, some very beautiful little parrots which fly in flocks, and several other birds which I refrained from shooting so as not to frighten off the natives, with whom I was eager to communicate. I also observed a species of very large black ant which has an abdomen that is equipped with a sting like a wasp's and is just as poisonous. There is a considerable depth of water around the island. Two boat-lengths from shore the water is several fathoms deep and *Fucus pyriferus* and *Fucus palmatus* grow there in great abundance.

On the 25th [15 January] I went ashore on Bruny Island at the spot where I had seen the natives gathered the day before. By the time I arrived, a boat from the *Géographe* had already landed and those who had gone ashore were warming themselves amiably around several fires with a large number of natives, who had their women and children with them that day. The natives were all clad in ragged, foul-smelling kangaroo skins, but these skins did not conceal those parts that European modesty requires should be covered with great care. In most cases the skins were tied around the natives' shoulders and the entire lower section of the bodies of both sexes was uncovered. Most of the women had shaved heads, with this done so skilfully that it appeared as though their hair had been cut with scissors. Like the men, they blackened parts of their body with ground charcoal, but some, in order to enhance their beauty, had taken it into their heads to apply a sort of red chalk to the parts of the face immediately below the cheekbone. This combination of red and black gave their faces a truly hideous appearance. Among the children I observed one who was at most eight days old. His skin was reddish and hairy and he had been wrapped in a kangaroo skin which covered both mother and child. Older children sat on their mothers' shoulders. One of the women was blind but was so used to walking in these forests that she moved just as nimbly as the others, whom she followed by the sound of their footsteps. One young girl was lame. This impairment seemed to have been caused by a dislocation of her left thigh.

There were around 60 savages, men, women and children, gathered together here. These people have the following general facial characteristics: a sunken brow, deep-set eyes, a nose which is broad but not flattened, a large mouth filled with strong teeth, and a prominent square jaw. There are a great many exceptions, however, and some of them have facial features that look almost European. The children were quite cheerful but the faces of the men were reflective of treachery and spite.

They had very few belongings: these consisted of bowls made from *Fucus palmatus*, which resemble the bags in which we keep gaming counters (they are described in the *Voyage in Search of La Pérouse*),[137] and deep baskets skilfully woven from a very strong and supple grass. These baskets usually contained one or two sharp bones, which are probably used to remove the meat from the shellfish which these people eat. Almost all of the women had a very hard cushion made out of kangaroo skin and stuffed with the fur of this creature. These oval-shaped cushions are around 10 inches across and are probably used for supporting their heads when they sleep. I obtained one in exchange for a small mirror. The woman to whom I suggested this exchange hesitated for a long time. After acquiring it I put it in my game-bag, but a short while later the cushion was stolen from me without my realising. The natives stole several other trifles from various people but, fearing that we might take retribution when we became aware of their mischief, they suddenly ran away — even though we had not displayed the slightest sign of annoyance. At first we were surprised by their sudden retreat, but realising the true reason for this, we called them back with friendly gestures, which set their minds at rest.

CHAPTER 5: VAN DIEMEN'S LAND AND WESTERN PORT

I walked inland with several others. Everywhere we found poor, sandy soil covered with ferns. I saw a great many *Eucalyptus globulus* and *Eucalyptus resinifera*, along with smaller numbers of *Casuarina equisetifolia*. In several damp places we encountered clumps of small straight shrubs of the genus *Philadelphus*. We made our way through them along several paths which led to patches of cleared, beaten earth, around which were dotted recesses of a kind under the bushes. The shape of these hideaways and the trampled grass were a clear enough indication that the natives used them as shelters. I was all the more convinced of this because I had not seen on this part of Bruny Island any of the bark shelters that I had encountered the day before on Partridge Island.

I added little to my collection that day. The same plants grow on both islands. Among the new plants that I gathered were Labillardière's *Mazeutoxeron rufum* (English botanists have given the name *Correa* to the genus *Mazeutoxeron*)[138] and a species of *Lonchitis*.

By the time we returned to our boat, the natives had disappeared, even though there hadn't been any quarrel. We went back on board ship but the *Géographe*'s dinghy remained ashore until evening.

The shoreline in this spot consists of a sandy beach where the boats cannot run close enough in that one can land without getting one's feet wet.

On the next day, the 26th [16 January], we learnt that, after we had left, the natives had returned to the beach and had remained there for some time dealing amicably with the crew from the *Géographe,* whom we had left on shore the previous day, as I mentioned before, because their boat had become grounded at low tide. While the sailors were engaged in refloating it, the natives disappeared once again. When everything had been made ready for departure and Citizen Bonnefoi, sub-lieutenant, was busy getting all his men aboard, a spear struck the shoulder of Citizen Maurouard, midshipman, who was beside him. The flesh of his shoulder was pierced right through. The spear had been thrown from behind the bank at the edge of the beach. Citizens Bonnefoi and Maurouard immediately ran over to try and find the aggressors and avenge themselves, but the natives were so well hidden that they could not be seen. So they got back into the boat, and when it was a little way out to sea they saw around ten natives armed with spears come down to the beach and hurl insults at them. The spear which wounded Citizen Maurouard had a shaft around half an inch in diameter and was 8 or 9 feet long. It was extremely sharp at one end and had a slit around half a foot long at the other end. It appears that this slit made in the upper part of the shaft allows for a light guiding device to be inserted, which separates from the spear when this is thrown.

These hostile acts were committed by the natives without our having offered them the slightest provocation. On the contrary, we had showered them with presents and none of us had done anything which might have injured them. I admit that I am surprised, after so many instances of cruelty and betrayal reported in all the voyages of exploration, to hear sensible people say that men in their natural state are not in the least part malicious, and that they can be trusted and will only strike when roused to vengeance. Unfortunately a great many travellers have fallen victim to these flawed ideas. For my part, I believe that one cannot be too wary of men whose characters have never been moderated by civilisation, and I am convinced that one should land only with great caution on coasts inhabited by such men.[139]

That day (the 26th) Captain Hamelin went to the head of the bay. He approached close enough to shore to be able to see what was happening. It seems that the events of the previous day had either made the natives apprehensive or else they planned to attack us if we landed on the shore, as the captain saw 36 natives walking along the shoreline in parties of five or six. In each party there was one man who carried a bundle of spears, and at the head of this small force a man holding a burning brand set fire at intervals to the scrub at the edge of the shore. Did they take this measure so as to be able to observe us from a distance, or was it done in order to deprive us of any means of concealing ourselves, and so surprising them?

The longboats of the two ships, having set off to Port Cygnet on the 24th to replenish our supply of water, returned without having fulfilled the aim of their mission. Those who saw the harbour declared that it was superb both with respect to the anchorage it afforded and to the fertility of the land around it.

On the 27th [17 January], we got under way with the intention of heading to North-West Port, which is at the other end of the channel, but the wind was against us and we were forced to anchor outside Isthmus Bay. (The bay was given this name because a strip of land less than 100 toises [600 feet] wide separates it from Adventure Bay.) I immediately went ashore on the mainland at a place where a rivulet of lovely fresh water falls down a steep incline. Although it is just a trickle, it would be enough to supply the two ships with all the water they needed if work were done to build a small dam (25 paces from shore), to which one could attach a tarpaulin sleeve which would carry the water as far as the longboats. Along the edge of the stream we saw paths, burnt trees and discarded shells, but none of the local inhabitants.

I walked a short distance inland, but encountered only a poor, whitish soil, which was covered with ferns. The trees there, however, grow to a considerable height. I came across several plants that were unfamiliar to me, among others, a shrub from the family Labiatae which has a straight and slender stem. The sailors wanted to cut down some of these shrubs to make shafts for boathooks and yardarms for the masts of our boats, but the wood is so brittle that a man could easily snap stems 3 inches in diameter all by himself. Being so flimsy, it was of no use at all. I collected several samples of Citizen Labillardière's *Exocarpos cupressiformis*, two other plants of the buckthorn family, another with black berries from the family Jasmineae, and a species of creeping avens.

From our anchorage we enjoyed one of those views which painters sometimes create with their imagination but which is rarely afforded by nature. At this point the channel is no more than 3 miles wide. The ranges of the mainland and the lower-lying ground of Bruny Island, rising in the east to Fluted Cape, are alike covered with magnificent trees.

On the 28th [18 January] Captain Hamelin put the large dinghy at my disposal. I went ashore first on Green Island, a small islet located in the middle of the channel. There I saw a fur seal which plunged into the waves as soon as it caught sight of me. On the shore I came across a sizeable nest which contained the broken shells of several large eggs, which I believe to be those of the largest species of pelican. This islet serves as a refuge for a great many seagulls, pelicans and gannets. I encountered an abundance of a plant of the genus *Dianella*, an undershrub of the family Rubiaceae (a species of *Pavetta* I think), and a small species of *Epilobium* which grows along the shoreline.

After little Green Island, I went ashore on Bruny Island. I walked about three-quarters of a league and the soil there was sandy and infertile. The only thing that grew beneath the tall trees covering this area was a sparse, scraggy sort of grass. I did not find any fresh water although I did come across the beds of several dried-up streams.

On a small islet just off the coast I collected a plant of the genus *Indigofera*, which is very similar to the indigo plant from which dye is obtained.

After we got back in our boat the wind freshened considerably. It was accompanied by violent squalls from the south-west, which forced us to put in at little Green Island. These squalls are all the more dangerous and destructive to small craft as they strike down at an angle, deflected in this direction by the steep slope of the hills along the channel. As soon as we arrived back on board ship, we got under way. That evening we anchored in North-West Port. We saw two canoes, each with three men, who took fright at our approach and paddled quickly towards land. When they got there they hurriedly took their canoes out of the water and carried them into the woods. During the night we saw several fires along the coast.

On the 29th [19 January] I landed on the southern side of the eastern entrance to the channel. We saw several natives but they ran away as we drew near. The headland that encloses the harbour here is composed of a sort of soft slate overlain with sandstone. The soil is sandy and just as poor as that which I had seen the day before. The new plants I found were one species of *Dodonaea*, one of *Bosea*, and the same *Spinifex* I had seen the previous year on the Barren Islands. This grass which grows in the sand along the shore has a very large seed head that is globular and bearded. It contains a seed of the same size and shape as wheat and is also farinaceous. I am convinced that if it could be cultivated it too could serve as food for man. I was only able to find withered samples of this grass and so could collect only a very small number of seeds. (In the large number of spikes which I tore open in order to obtain the grain I managed to find only three seeds, which I have sent with several other species of seed to Madame Bonaparte, wife of the First Consul.)[140]

On the sandy beach of this shore I found several valves of the *Solen*, commonly called the knife handle, along with the separate valves of a very beautiful shell. These valves possess delicate, raised longitudinal bands which are slightly reflected backward.

On the 30th [20 January] the longboat was sent out to Point Gicquel to collect wood. I went ashore at this spot but had no more luck than on the previous two days. The soil is a little better but all the ground cover had recently been burnt by the natives. I found only a species of *Asplenium* which grows on the old trunks of fallen, rotting trees. I also collected several specimens of a medium-sized tree belonging to the genus *Eucalyptus*. *Casuarinas* grow plentifully along this headland. I saw a giant kangaroo and observed that when this creature moves quickly it uses only its two hind legs.

On 1 Pluviôse [21 January] Citizen Hamelin received orders to explore the coast of the mainland with the aim of locating the rivers marked on the charts and finding out whether water could be easily obtained there, as both ships were in short supply. He set out in the longboat and I went with him. I initially asked to be put ashore close to our ships and I walked along the edge of the water for a considerable distance. I found only a poor soil which supported here and there a tough, unattractive fern, which is very common all along the channel. I came across several dry watercourses.

I got back on board and we made our way into a cove where a river was marked on d'Entrecasteaux's chart and on a hand-drawn

English chart. We did indeed find it but it is only a small stream, the mouth of which is clogged with mud and blocked by tree trunks carried down during the rainy season. The soil here is excellent and there is a great density of plant life. This thick vegetation, sustained by the life-giving waters, contrasts strikingly with the sterility found in some other parts of the channel. The banks of the stream are covered with ferns, among which I observed one very beautiful species of tree-fern. The other plants I found are: a species of creeper, which I believe to belong to the genus *Bignonia*, a species of *Pteris*, a lovely species of mimosa tree (*Mimosa decurrens*), which secretes a yellowish gum that is highly soluble in water, several other mimosas, a species of *Tetratheca*, a *Persoonia*, a *Basueria*, a *Styphelia*, and a lovely species of veronica with white flowers. In the marshy areas, I found great quantities of a species of *Samolus* and a species of *Sida*, a herbaceous plant with fleshy leaves and a spike of white sessile flowers on a stem around one foot tall. We noticed tree trunks that had been felled by axes and saws, along with fresh droppings that looked like horse dung and were similarly lumpy. We heard the shrill and plaintive cries of an animal which seemed to come from far away.

The water in this bay is shallow and so it is easy to collect the large oysters which are plentiful there. On the shore we saw enormous piles of shells left by the natives, who use them for food.

From there we went a short distance to a second bay where we found another freshwater stream. As in the bay we had just visited, the soil is good and the plants are similar.

As we returned on board ship that evening we saw some natives in a canoe crossing from the mainland to Bruny Island.

Citizen Ronsard had received orders to explore the far end of the harbour. On his return he reported that he had found a river where water could easily be procured. As a result, on 3 Pluviôse [23 January], the longboats of both ships set off, but only reached the watering place with much difficulty. The head of the harbour is obstructed by a mudbank that is partially exposed at low tide and only navigable at high tide through a narrow channel. In addition to this, the sailors found they had to roll the barrels a long way.

CHAPTER 5: VAN DIEMEN'S LAND AND WESTERN PORT

The river, which I followed upstream for around 5 miles, is really just a large brook that runs over a rocky bed. On either side of it spreads a broad and fertile plain. The soil is composed mainly of vegetable matter. I had occasion to admire the most splendid trees I had yet seen in these forests, which are as ancient as the soil they shade. I estimated that some of the trunks rose 60 feet or more from their base to the first branches. These superb stems are perfectly straight and appear very healthy.

The new plants I found are: two plants of the family Rubiaceae, three of the family Jasmineae, one of the family Guttiferae, several highly aromatic and very pretty species of the family Compositae. The remaining plants belonged to the genera *Rubus, Conchium, Pimelea, Billardiera, Embothrium* and *Mimosa*. The indigo tree which I had come across previously is very common here.

I saw two snakes which were about 6 feet long and coloured like burnished steel, several very large rats, and the droppings of a carnivorous animal, probably those of a dog.

As I walked back to the longboats I came across six or seven shelters on a hill not far from the left bank of the river and these were exactly the same as the ones I had seen on Partridge Island. The openings of these shelters also faced east. They could only have been vacated a short time beforehand as the ashes of a nearby fire were still warm. In great quantities all around lay the remains of crabs and lobsters which had been eaten by the natives. Several branches still bearing their leaves lay in the shelters, along with a granite cutting stone used to remove the bark with which the shelters had been built. I could see the cuts that had been made with it on the surrounding trees.

On the 5th [25 January] I returned to the watering place and walked a very long way up the river but saw nothing of interest. I merely found the same plants that I had already collected on the 3rd.

On the banks of the river I found a spear and saw two giant kangaroos. That day I left some glass beads and small knives in the shelters mentioned above; when I came back I found that the objects had been taken away by the natives, who had no doubt been hiding very close by.

On the 7th [27 January] I went ashore with Citizen Freycinet, lieutenant, abeam of the ships, on the eastern side of the harbour. We covered a distance of around 2 leagues. At first we encountered only burnt-out terrain with poor soil, until we reached a place where a small rivulet moistened the soil with a barely perceptible trickle of muddy water. Here debris deposited by the abundant plant life had covered the ground with a very substantial layer of vegetable matter.

In one *Eucalyptus* we saw a very large eagle's nest. (Several days later I went walking in this area with Captain Hamelin, who instructed his men to fell the tree containing the nest. We estimated that an equivalent of 20 faggots of wood had gone into its construction. The nest had been abandoned.)

That same day, 7 Pluviôse, the water was constantly brackish at the watering place and the barrels could not be filled. During the ebb tide, slight fluctuations in flow occur. Sometimes, after falling for just an hour, the tide suddenly rises again, or grows slack. I believe that these fluctuations are caused by the winds outside the harbour reversing the direction of the current. I walked once again along the banks of the river, which is the only area that supports any abundance of plant life, but I did not come across anything that I hadn't already collected on previous days.

Even though we had been in North-West Port for a long time, we had not managed to make contact with any of the natives. Those we had seen in the distance had fled hurriedly at our approach. When, on the [blank],[141] the commander and Citizen Hamelin went ashore together on Bruny Island at the same place I had landed on 29 Nivôse [19 January], they saw around twenty natives who behaved in a very friendly manner towards them. Several allowed Citizen Petit to draw them. One snatched away his portrait but then gave it back. They quite happily exchanged their spears for buttons and bottles. They particularly prized the bottles, not for their use as containers, but rather because they could smash them and use the shards to scrape down and sharpen their spears, something that is normally done with pieces of granite. The encounter appeared to have passed off harmoniously. However, as the commander and his companions were embarking, the natives started hurling stones at them with great force and continued to rain missiles on them for a long while after they had put out from shore. The commander was even slightly injured on the hip.

Two days later the commander and Citizen Hamelin went ashore again at the same place. I went with them. We saw the same natives who had attacked them on the previous occasion. Trusting in our benevolence or our impotence, they approached us without displaying the slightest fear or taking any precautions, for they had no weapons at all. I recognised them as the same men I had encountered that first time on Partridge Island, around 15 leagues away from our present location. The man who had given me his necklace also recognised me and was very friendly towards me. That day their behaviour gave us no cause for complaint and they even helped the men who were fishing to draw their nets onto the beach. They do not seem to like fish and refused even to try those which the sailors had cooked up for their meal.

During our stay in the channel we had several other encounters with the natives. However, for reasons which I have shared with Citizen de Jussieu, professor of natural history, in the letter I have written him,[142] I shall conclude this section with some reflections on the plant life of the channel.

While our stay in D'Entrecasteaux Channel coincided with the middle of summer, it was nevertheless a very suitable time for carrying out botanical research because plants develop more slowly in sheltered regions and the period between flowering and the fruit reaching maturity is longer than in exposed regions. However, the soil is generally sandy and barren, and there is not a great variety of plant life.

When, from the middle of the channel, one surveys the coast on all sides, one sees hills rising gently in long, undulating chains, one behind the other, their uniform coat of vegetation mottling only as the angle of the light changes, brightening or darkening in tone. Several trees, still standing though they are withered up to their crowns, attest to the vast age of these forests.

A student of nature might hope to discover a vast field for his observations behind this curtain of greenery, but going ashore finds only a sandy soil which reluctantly supports a scattering of scraggy plants. As well as being barren, this land is frequently swept by fires lit by the natives, whether to rid their forest homes of grasses and bushes that impede their movement, or to eradicate insects and especially that large species of stinging ant which, if its numbers were to swell, could create great discomfort for men who do not wear clothes and who live in open dwellings. However, from time to time one comes across spots where a regular covering of shade produces perpetually damp conditions, sustaining a mass of plants, the detritus from which fertilises the soil in which they grow. But the naturalist faces another obstacle to his enquiries here: the vegetation is so densely tangled that he cannot penetrate into the thickets, which, in any case, do not possess a great variety of plant life.

The most numerous plants along the channel are undoubtedly those of the Compositae and myrtle families: its covering of vegetation is, as it were, parcelled out between them. These plants, and especially those of the family Compositae, are highly aromatic, and now that celebrated chemists are using chemical analysis to shed light on the history of plants, I am convinced that no place is better suited for performing experiments on the *true sap* of plants, which is contained in great quantity by those found here.

A great many *Mimosa* grow here, some of which secrete a gum that could prove useful in the productive arts.

The red gum of the *Eucalyptus*, which combines a styptic and astringent taste with a slightly bitter note, could, after proper study, provide doctors with an extremely useful remedy.

The *Xanthorrhoea*, or gum plant of Phillip, is not common along the channel. I found it only on Bruny Island. (It is different from

CHAPTER 5: VAN DIEMEN'S LAND AND WESTERN PORT

those which I later saw around Sydney.) Its trunk secretes great quantities of red resin and its scape a highly soluble white gum.

I believe that D'Entrecasteaux Channel is subject to frequent and sudden fluctuations in temperature. I am of the view that the vast forests covering this region powerfully draw in cold weather and fogs, but I do not believe that the cold is quite as extreme as others have previously maintained. The temperature here in summer is cooler than in our southern departments but in winter it must be quite similar to the temperature in those departments to which this region corresponds in southern latitude. In all the branches of nature one comes across the analogues of entities that are found in warm climates. One piece of evidence for my supposition is that it takes more than a single season for the fruits of certain plants of the myrtle family to ripen, and if temperatures fell as low as has been assumed, how could the seeds survive?

After we sailed out from Port Jackson for the first time, we rounded the South Cape of Van Diemen's Land.[143] During the twelve days that we remained in the vicinity of that coast (although much further to the south) I carefully observed the thermometer. It was then the middle of the month of Prairial, corresponding in this hemisphere to the month of Brumaire[144] in the northern hemisphere. Every day terrible gales blew from the south, chilling the air even further. However, the temperature (on the Réaumur scale) stood at:

14 Prairial [3 June 1802] at 5 o'clock in the evening 9.2°	Latitude at midday 44° 55'. Estimated longitude 146° 44'. Observed longitude 147° 58'. South-easterly winds. Cloudy weather all day. We ran at 8 or 9 knots.
15 Prairial [4 June] at 5 o'clock in the evening 7.8°	Estimated latitude 45° 56'. Estimated longitude 142° 15'. Southerly winds. Cloudy weather in the morning, clear in the evening. We ran at 6 or 7 knots.

16 Prairial [5 June] at 5 o'clock in the evening 8°	Observed latitude 44° 55'. Estimated longitude 140° 3'. Westerly winds. Clear skies in the morning, cloudy in the evening. We ran at 3 knots in the morning, 5 knots in the evening.
17 Prairial [6 June] at 5 o'clock in the evening 8.6°	Observed latitude 46° 11'. Estimated longitude 139° 40'. South-westerly winds. The previous night a strong gale from the west, clear skies in the morning, cloudy in the evening.
18 Prairial [7 June] at 5 o'clock in the evening 8°	Observed latitude 46° 26'. Estimated longitude 138° 45'. North-north-westerly winds. Cloudy skies. Strong breeze.
19 Prairial [8 June] at 5 o'clock in the evening 8°	Estimated latitude 46° 84'. Estimated longitude 135° 27'. North-north-westerly winds in the morning, cloudy skies. Storm. In the evening the winds turned westerly and the weather cleared. That day the mainsail was carried away by the wind.
20 Prairial [9 June] at 5 o'clock in the evening 7.4°	Estimated latitude 45° 55'. Estimated longitude 138° 16'. North-westerly and north-north-westerly winds. We ran at 7 or 8 knots. Clear skies in the evening.
21 Prairial [10 June] at 5 o'clock in the evening 8°	Observed latitude 44° 39'. Estimated longitude 139° 14'. Variable winds, calm for part of the day. A light shower of rain in the evening.
22 Prairial [11 June] at 5 o'clock in the evening 8.4°	Observed latitude 44° 42'. Estimated longitude 140° 16'. Variable winds, almost calm.

23 Prairial [12 June] at 5 o'clock in the evening 8.8°	Observed latitude 44° 28'. Estimated longitude 140° 28'. Almost calm, clear skies.
24 Prairial [13 June] at 5 o'clock in the evening 9.8°	Observed latitude 44° 50'. Estimated longitude 140° 46'. Clear skies, moderate breeze from the north-east.
26 Prairial [15 June] at 5 o'clock in the evening 10°	Observed latitude 43° 31'. Observed longitude 143° 5'. Clear skies, moderate breeze from the south-south-east.

What I have written about D'Entrecasteaux Channel forms only a brief and incomplete account. As the government may wish to establish a settlement in this location, I consider it vital to include every observation that may shed light on the advantages and disadvantages it offers. That is why I have deferred this task. Our long stay in Port Jackson has given me material for several important notes, but the comparative study I intend to make of these two places requires longer reflection.

I offer no details either about Maria Island, which we visited after leaving the channel. The island is of little significance and more or less the same plants are found there as along the channel. We had several encounters with the natives, who appeared no different from those we had met previously: they have the same woolly hair[145] and like them blacken their skin and scar parts of their bodies.

While we were anchored off this island we had the misfortune to lose Citizen Maugé, zoologist. He died on 1 Ventôse [20 February] from the effects of dysentery, which had afflicted him since Timor.

Description of a Grave I Found on Maria Island

On 29 Pluviôse [18 February 1802] I landed on the west coast of the island. Around 100 paces from the shore, I came across two huts that were joined together. They seemed to have been built very recently and their entrances faced east. The strips of bark that served as a roof had been joined together more skilfully and the pieces of wood that formed the frame were more deeply embedded in the ground than I had seen on previous occasions. Inside the huts were several bundles of a long supple grass that grows plentifully across the whole island, several branches of *Exocarpos cupressiformis* on which the leaves were still green, and several stalks of *Mesembryanthemum edule*, from which the fruit had been removed. I placed several glass necklaces, a small knife and a mirror inside the two huts. Fifteen paces from these shelters I saw another which appeared to have been knocked down. Struck by the thickness and length of the strips of bark, I went over to examine it. I then realised that what I had taken for a shelter was in fact a collection of bark strips which had been carefully arranged over a hemispherical mound. When I turned over the strips I saw that they were covered in lines which had been made deliberately and formed patterns resembling the tattoos of these people.

The mound was covered with a layer of grass held in place by eight sticks that had been bent into bows and their ends driven into the ground at equal intervals. Beneath the grass lay a heap of ashes. I have no doubt that these ashes were mixed with the remains of a corpse, for the second surgeon[146] on the *Naturaliste*, who went with me, recognised part of a femur and an ankle bone, but these bones had been so thoroughly burnt that they crumbled to dust when touched. This tomb appeared to have been erected quite recently.

On the same island, Citizen Péron, zoologist, came across another tomb similar to the one I have described.

★

After we left Maria Island, we headed for Banks Strait. During this passage we became separated from the *Géographe*.

On 18 Ventôse [9 March], the sky had a stormy appearance: large black clouds stood motionless and the sun shone a lurid red, its spreading rays very distinct on the horizon. In the curtain of cloud which hung above it I made out a well-defined tail which I took to be a marine waterspout in the process of forming. After watching it for half an hour and observing that it did not alter in shape, I went down between decks. But I had scarcely reached my cabin when I heard Captain Hamelin cry out: 'A waterspout! A waterspout!' I dashed back up. It was 6 o'clock in the evening. On the horizon I could see a black column stretching down vertically from the great curtain of clouds I mentioned. This column was touching the sea; it was a long way away from us. It was regular in width along its lower two-thirds, but the section touching the cloud widened into a funnel-shape. After three minutes it tilted over, fractured, and vanished completely.

Some time before the waterspout appeared the wind had veered from west-north-west to south-east.

Accompanying the waterspout: a moderate breeze; thermometer 13.8° (Réaumur scale).

On the morning of the 19th [10 March], we entered Banks Strait, which lies between Van Diemen's Land and the Furneaux Islands. The tip of Van Diemen's Land, which forms the southern side of the entrance to the strait, is low-lying, rocky and barren. From a distance the sharp, scattered rocks look like rubble and this spit of land resembles the ruins of an ancient city. Further along, the coast is wooded but still low-lying and foamy seas roll onto beaches of white sand. Inland a few isolated rocks can be seen, which fancy lends the form of ancient monuments. Smoke rising through the trees from native fires, clear skies and calm weather create a scene that is both charming and sublime.

During our stay in the strait I went ashore on Swan Island, Preservation Island and Clarke Island in turn. I was stranded for four days on the two latter islands by a fierce gale in which the *Naturaliste* lost two anchors and was forced to get under way in a hurry. On these two islands we found a great deal of wreckage from various ships which had foundered there. On Clarke Island we came across a transom, among other pieces, which the sailors thought must have come from a ship the same size as our own. (We later learnt in Port Jackson that some of this wreckage was from the *Sydney Town*,[147] an English ship that had been wrecked on Preservation Island with the loss of a great many of its crew.)[148]

I also went ashore on Waterhouse Island and at several points along the north coast of Van Diemen's Land. All of the islands I have mentioned are small and uninhabited. They are of interest, however, due to the large number of seals found on them. On Waterhouse Island I saw herds of several hundred, but they did not flee when I approached, no doubt because they have never been hunted. I observed several individuals which were the size of oxen. In spite of their daunting appearance, these amphibious quadrupeds are not to be feared, nor are they difficult to kill. Nature has denied them the means both of defending themselves and of attacking their enemies. When they are surprised on land they have great difficulty in fleeing. As a result the English, who relentlessly hunt the creatures for their fur and oil on these coasts, use just heavy lead clubs to beat them to death. This unceasing slaughter will soon lead to a considerable reduction in the numbers of these animals.

We also came across an extraordinary number of penguins on these islands. These birds live in a location where nothing disturbs their peace, their pairing or their breeding, and from which they can never migrate since they are physically incapable of flight. They multiply endlessly and, having no enemies, experience no fear and were quite at ease among us. On Preservation Island especially, where I stayed for three days, these birds would often peck at us in an attempt to dislodge us from our place beside the fires we lit to dry our clothes, which were continually soaked by heavy rains. The sailors, who often behaved with needless and senseless cruelty towards these animals, abused their trust and slaughtered a large number of them.

CHAPTER 5: VAN DIEMEN'S LAND AND WESTERN PORT

Western Port

Across its breadth, Western Port has a pleasant appearance and a strong and vigorous covering of vegetation. The ground is generally low-lying and, as much of it is not usually inhabited, the lovely tangles of greenery in which it is covered have been much less scarred by fire than the vegetation we observed in D'Entrecasteaux Channel.

Along the shoreline there are white sandy beaches and stretches of red clay soil overlaying ferruginous rock, which evidently contains a large amount of ore.

I went ashore several times and shall present my observations in order.

On the evening of 20 Germinal, Year X [10 April 1802], we landed on the western shore of the second channel. Commander Milius recognised that this portion of land, which is marked on the English chart as forming part of the mainland, is in fact an island.[149] It appears to be inhabited only at rare intervals, as we found just a few very old traces of fire; the vegetation, growing in a rich soil that remains damp in the perpetual shade, had made a strong recovery from the flames. We had difficulty finding even a small area free of bushes and creepers where we could spend the night. It was a rather unpleasant night as we were attacked by swarms of mosquitoes. We slept around a large fire, which kept them at bay to some extent.

Along this section of coast, a hill slopes gently down to the seashore. I ventured inland on three separate occasions and, after endless struggles with the dense plant growth, reached the summit of the hill, which appeared to form a fairly large, level plateau. It was covered all over in a thick layer of rich compost, which was made up of large amounts of vegetable debris and a clay soil containing a great deal of iron oxide.

As we were leaving the channel on the 21st [11 April], we saw thick smoke rising up from the headland on the eastern side of the entrance and heard the cries of several natives. Citizen Milius steered towards them. As we drew near we could see only a single native, who was completely naked and unarmed and who waved at us to come ashore on the other side of the headland. This headland, which has been named the Cape of Fires in the survey done by Citizens Milius and Faure, has a remarkably strange shape. It looks exactly like a square bastion with walls that slope outwards towards the base. The tip of the headland appears so regular that it might have been built by engineers. On the northern side of the large basin, a smooth sheer cliff runs along the coast for about a mile and looks just like a castle wall. This cliff is 50 to 60 feet high and is made up of layers of reddish soil which contain varying amounts of iron oxide and overlie rocks of the kind already mentioned above. A few bushes grow out of the jutting base and help support the soil. When the tide is high, the sea washes against the foot of the cliff, but when it goes out it exposes the shoreline for around 150 paces.

After we rounded the Cape of Fires we saw about a dozen natives on the cliff top who uttered loud cries as they ran forward to meet our boats. They were unarmed. We were eager to meet them but, thinking that they might be frightened by a large group, Captain Milius ordered everybody to remain in the boats. He and I alone went ashore.

The ebb tide was beginning to slacken. Unarmed, we approached the natives, who sat down at the top of the cliff and spoke excitedly among themselves. We too sat down on a rock and made friendly gestures towards them. I cried out *gougloua medi* several times, words which, in the language of the inhabitants of D'Entrecasteaux Channel, mean 'Come and sit down'. They did not appear to understand me, as they kept repeating these words and looking at one another as though seeking an explanation. (I later learnt that these peoples do not share the same language; each region has its own.) Citizen Milius held up pieces of white paper and necklaces of glass beads but our invitations were unsuccessful. We went up to the foot of the cliff. We invited them once more to come down but they again refused, signalling to us to climb up once we had removed our clothes. Citizen Milius agreed to show them this mark of trust. After partially undressing, he started to climb up but found it very difficult as he only had a few bushes and tufts of grass to grasp on to. He nearly tumbled down when the stem of tree snapped beneath him and fell away. When he reached the halfway point he signalled to one of the savages to come down and give him a hand up. The savage refused, gesturing instead that he should hold onto the grass, and pointing out the easiest places. Eventually Citizen Milius reached the top of the cliff.

The first emotion the natives displayed was one of fear. They drew back twenty paces. Citizen Milius thought that the natives might still be unsettled by the few remaining pieces of clothing he had on. He removed all of these and threw them to the natives, who picked them up and folded them carefully. Less mistrustful after this, the natives invited him to follow them inland, indicating that he could warm himself there and have something to eat. He explained with gestures that the ground would hurt his feet as he was not wearing shoes. They understood this very clearly. However, they were not willing to return his shoes and conveyed to him that he would be walking only on soft grass, which would not hurt him.

I remained at the foot of the cliff all this time. Citizen Milius called down to me to climb up with the box containing glass beads and other trinkets. When I reached the top of the cliff though and held out the box to Citizen Milius containing the gifts for them, the natives were seized with sudden terror and fled, uttering cries that might have been calls to their compatriots for help. We tried in vain to calm their fears with gestures and shouts. Fortunately they dropped Citizen Milius's clothes as they ran away; he followed after them for some time but was unable to regain their trust.

The natives seemed even more timid than the inhabitants of D'Entrecasteaux Channel and Maria Island. Have they had reason to regret previous encounters with Europeans? There were around twenty of them and only two of us – and we had placed ourselves entirely in their hands, unarmed and with no line of retreat. And yet it was they who fled in sheer terror, which seemed entirely at odds with the welcoming cries they had uttered when they first saw us.[150]

These savages are somewhat different from those of D'Entrecasteaux Channel. They are much more like the inhabitants of New South Wales,[151] whom Monsieur Cook describes in volume 4 of his first voyage.[152] They have pleasant features and are well-proportioned; they are of the same colour as those savages I had previously seen blackening themselves with ground charcoal.[153] Their bodies are covered with fewer scars and are painted instead with strange markings. (They paint themselves like this when they are at war.) Several had white rings around their eyes and red or white stripes and crosses on their faces and other parts of their bodies. Several had threaded a thin piece of wood around 6 or 7 inches long through the cartilage of the nose. Monsieur Cook observed this uncomfortable and extravagant ornament among the peoples of New Wales.[154] One of them wore a white feather in his hair and a necklace strung with small pieces of rush that had been charred at either end. All were naked apart from one who appeared more serious than the others and wore over the upper part of his body a black fur, which had perhaps taken its colour from the smoke and the charcoal which are ever-present in the lives of these people. Citizen Milius believes that this man was a chief.[155] There were no women or children with them and they were followed by several dogs of the breed that in France we call the 'fox-dog'. These ones had larger though slightly shorter heads and russet coats.

Citizen Milius was so intent on completing his mission that he refused to waste even a single moment and got back into his boat as soon as he saw that the savages had been frightened away, as the obstacle that now lay in the way of our communicating with them could only have been overcome with patience.

I found here the same type of soil that I had seen on the western side of the channel, but the ground had been cleared of creepers and shrubs by fires which the natives take care to light at frequent intervals.

That night we slept on the western headland of the first channel. Our sleeping-place was more comfortable than on the previous night because the ground was less thickly covered with vegetation. Since it looked as though it would be easy to make my way inland in this spot, I decided to stay there while Citizens Milius and Faure were exploring the channel. And so I kept some supplies and remained there by myself. Citizen Milius, who at low tide had driven a graduated pole into the shore at the tip of the headland, asked me to observe the tides.

This section of the coastline is at first sandy, dry and infertile. *Banksias*, *Casuarinas* and a species of *Leptospermum* with blue-green leaves are all that grow there. There are no *Eucalyptuses*. As you go inland, a greater amount of vegetable matter starts to appear in the sand, and after just a league, there are hills where the soil is the same as that along the coast of the second channel. The most common trees then are *Eucalyptuses*.

Before I reached the higher ground, I only saw very old traces of the natives. But in the hills I came across the ashes of fires that had only recently been put out. I saw the fresh prints of dog paws on the ground and two fires burning a short distance away.

The tide I observed on the morning of the 23rd [13 April] rose 6 feet. It was high at 7 o'clock. On the evening of the 22nd, the tide had risen around 7 feet. (The tides last six hours.)

The dinghy returned at midday on the 23rd. I got aboard and Citizen Milius set off then to explore the head of the second channel. The land here is a little higher than that surrounding the large basin. It also appeared to be covered in vegetation. We did not go ashore that night.

It was during this last survey that Citizen Milius began to suspect, due to the shape and lie of the land, that this channel was connected to the first. And so he sent out the small dinghy, which confirmed that the English chart was incorrect.

The 24th [14 April] was spent in sounding the large basin. We went ashore briefly on a small islet located in the eastern part of it. This islet is merely a low rock covered with a little compost. It offered nothing of interest. I simply observed that most of the ferruginous and foliated rocks, which compose the base of the land around this harbour, had been formed by layers of silt hardening over time. The unusual hollows they contain are due to small purple crabs that burrow into them; water fills these cavities and small waves produced by the eddying tide sculpt them further. On the shore I found rocks of this type ranging in state from the alluvial through to hardened stone. All displayed the same structure.

That night we slept in the boat once more. The next day, the 25th [15 April], Citizens Milius and Faure took a number of bearings. We noticed on that same day that the coastline where we had had our encounter with the natives on the 21st [11 April] was on fire. We tried to land there but the wind was against us. We went ashore on Western Island,[156] which forms the southern side of the harbour. This island is around 4 leagues across, from east to west, and 1½ leagues from north to south.

We landed on a sandy beach and I found only sand as far as I was able to make my way inland. The plants are very dense and vigorous, which I believe is due to the presence of moisture and to the alluvial soil which must lie beneath the sand.

That evening we returned to the headland where I had stayed alone and we spent the night there. We remained there for the whole of the 26th [16 April] while Citizens Milius and Faure plotted all the hazards that lie in the main entrance to the harbour.

Finally, on the 27th [17 April], we set off to rejoin our ship. We passed out through the narrow entrance on the eastern side of the harbour and briefly went ashore again – on the easternmost headland of Western Island, which we climbed up in order to check on the position of our ship. We found several springs there large enough to supply a ship's needs in an emergency. I went with Citizen Milius. It was with great difficulty that we made our way up to the top of the headland, as the vegetation is dense and tangled with creepers that are a great obstacle to anyone trying to make his way into these uninhabited parts. I found here a thick layer of light compost that was not mixed with iron oxide. A belt of granitic rock runs around this part of Western Island. Every time I have encountered these huge round granite boulders, piled up haphazardly and containing great quantities of feldspar crystals, I have noticed that there are always springs nearby or at least places where a considerable quantity of fresh water filters up through the ground. (I observed this on Preservation Island, Clarke Island, and on the coast of Van Diemen's Land near Waterhouse Island.) I believe that in an emergency one could obtain fresh water by digging holes where such piles of rock are found.

During this trip I found only three plants that I had not seen before. (1) A shrub of the genus *Rhizophora* which grows on muddy tidal shores. (2) A parasitic plant of the genus *Loranthus*. I was unable to procure a sample of this plant because the trunks of the *Eucalyptus* on which it grows were much too tall. (3) A small undershrub around 18 inches tall which belongs to the family Rosaceae. It grows on the western headland of the first channel. *Oxalis acetosella* also grows plentifully on this headland. This plant, which tastes exactly like sorrel, might offer some relief to those suffering from scurvy. We picked some and made a salad, which we ate with much pleasure.

I observed one *Eucalyptus* whose whole trunk was lapped by seawater but which for all that grew no less vigorously than the others.

Most of the land at Western Port is excellent and highly suited to all our European crops. It would be all the easier to cultivate as the compost forms a thick layer, there are no steep slopes, and the underlying layer of rock does not protrude above the soil. If in some places the ground consists solely of sand, I am convinced that these are no more than narrow strips and that inland the soil is substantial and fertile.

Along this coast we saw a great many black swans, gulls, teals, cormorants, storks, curlews, oyster catchers and large pelicans.

Among the land birds, I observed a superb species of red parrot. I believe that it is the variety of Tabuan parrot described by Monsieur Latham.[157] I killed two but as this was during the first few days we spent in the harbour, they were spoiled by the time I got back and were impossible to skin. On Western Island, which had the most plentiful bird life, I also saw several species of flycatcher that were remarkable for the beauty of their plumage. They were very trusting of me and I was easily able to observe them, as they came and perched fearlessly on the small bushes around me. On several occasions I thought I could catch one by darting out my hand but their nimbleness far outdid mine.

We came across plenty of crows and large numbers of quail of the same species that we had already seen in Van Diemen's Land.

Shellfish are not common on this coast. The only interesting specimen I found was a species of pullet or *Terebratula*, which is perhaps the same as that on which Monsieur Lamanon wrote a learned essay in *The Voyage of La Pérouse*.[158] I found it dead and cast up on the shore.

At the head of the first channel the sailors caught great quantities of a large red fish of the genus *Sciaena*, which the English call 'ten-pound fish'. This fish, which is remarkable for the dual bulges in its occipital bone, is excellent when eaten fresh and when salted tastes like cod.

We arrived back on the *Naturaliste* the same day we left Western Port. As soon as we were on board, the ship set sail for Port Jackson, where we arrived a few days later.

Port Jackson, 15 Fructidor, Year X [2 September 1802]

Théodore Leschenault
Chief botanist
Born in Chalon-sur-Saône on 14 November 1773.

Appendix

The two texts presented here, relating to the culture of the west African people the 'Macpas' and to the geography of Madagascar, were included by Leschenault after 'Letter 1' in Chapter 1 of his journal; they have been moved to this appendix as they do not form part of the narrative of his journey to Australia.

★

A Note on the Macpas

You will find inserted here a note about the Macpas, an African tribe previously unknown to Europeans; and a second note about Madagascar.

A Note on the Macpas,[159] *a Tribe from the Interior of Africa, who Live More than 100 Leagues from the West Coast in around Latitude 5° North*

This note is based on information from Bognam-nonen-derega,[160] a young native travelling with Citizen Michaux, naturalist, who bought him in America and prevailed on the government to appoint him (under the name 'Morlot')[161] as an assistant gardener to accompany Citizen Michaux on the scientific expedition commanded by Captain Baudin.

The Macpas have jet black skin, thick lips and very flat noses. They are generally robust and healthy. They are ruled by a chief judge who resolves their disputes. Their religion is a corrupted form of Mohammedanism. Nobody owns the soil; the harvest belongs simply to the sower. Their farming method consists simply of turning over the earth and burying the grain, a type of millet. The tool they use is a spade with a curved handle. They have iron and copper mines; they work these metals crudely.

They do not have military leaders. It seems that they gather together of their own accord to fight and the leader is the man whose ideas most appeal to the throng. Children follow the warriors and are given the job of picking up arrows.

Gentle and welcoming by nature, they only take up arms to repel raids launched by their neighbours, who come and steal their children in order to sell them to the Europeans. It was in precisely this way that the young Bognam-nonen-derega was carried off at the age of twelve and sold to the English. It seems that the raiders carry out these abductions under the cover of thick fog, which allows them to creep right up to the huts without being seen and vanish without a trace.

They poison their arrows by dipping them in the juice of a species of centipede (mixed together with several different plants) which can be found hiding under sheets of bark on the trunks of old trees. The insect is crushed and the arrows are soaked in its juice. Once the arrows have been prepared in this way, the slightest wound they inflict will bring about a painful death within a matter of minutes; there is no medicine that can halt the rapid action of the poison.

Their doctors use several medicines derived from the plant world, which they administer while performing magic rituals and spells. They bury their dead with great care, wrapping the head and feet with lengths of cotton, enfolding the body in a sheet of bark, and placing it in a grave. Friends and relatives pay their respects to the dead person as music plays; the instruments are a drum beaten with the hands and a flute with which they produce rather melodious sounds. Their clothing is a cotton sarong that they make themselves, and which covers them completely, from their shoulders to their feet. No Europeans have ever visited their lands; these people trade with their neighbours, have no words to express any number higher than ten, and have no knowledge of the art of writing.

The Macpas' huts are circular; an earth wall is raised up to a height of around 6 feet and roofed with cane or reeds. Mats are laid out to divide up the interior; women occupy one side and men the other.

The domestic animals of this country are: very large, smooth-haired sheep (no doubt the Indian brown dog),[162] goats and dogs. They have no beasts of burden. They rear a great many chickens and ducks.

They shape all their teeth into the form of canine teeth so that they can readily gnaw on bones. They eat the flesh of elephants; to catch this animal they dig a very deep pit, cover it with branches and banana leaves, and then drive the animal so that it falls into the trap, where it is bludgeoned to death.

Although I have written this note based on information provided by a very intelligent young native, I cannot guarantee its complete accuracy.

Information Provided to me by Citizen d'Aumont, a Naval Officer who has Often Travelled to Madagascar

The island of Madagascar is fertile and thickly wooded and is threaded with navigable rivers. Sugar cane grows naturally, cotton is easily cultivated, and silk can be found in the woods (the worm that produces it is different from the one we know in Europe). The indigo plant could be grown there successfully. Trees that supply dyes and timber are plentiful. Iron mines are also found there.

With all these advantages, it would be possible to establish sugar refineries, indigo factories and cotton factories. As these people are already skilful weavers, they would only require competent managers to oversee their workshops.

It is easy to grow crops everywhere.

The domestic animals are:

Cattle: these are common and attractive.

Sheep: there is a wide variety of species; those from the Cape of Good Hope and Arabia, and the brown dog from India, are found there.

Goats are common and cost next to nothing, along with all types of poultry, turkeys, geese, chickens, ducks.

The wild animals are:

Boar, guinea-fowl, partridge, snipe, many types of duck, teal, quail; all other types of game would multiply rapidly if brought there.

Everything necessary for life can be found in abundance. Wheat and rice are cultivated there. Every kind of vegetable, along with several types of European tree, would grow there, as they do in the Isle of France. Fruits native to the country are: oranges, mandarins, tamarind of the Indies, bananas, plums, potatoes and many others that would take too long to list. All these fruits are delicious and grow wild there. The rivers and the sea swarm with vast numbers of fish.

The claims made in Europe about it being an unhealthy island are not true. It could become a very healthy place if the waters in the low-lying regions were drained – which he believes could easily be done. The people are kind and welcoming. They would only turn hostile if their freedom were restricted or their beliefs were not respected.

A colony run by wise and enlightened men would soon flourish.

Although Citizen d'Aumont has visited the island on several occasions, he did not identify which harbour would be best suited for establishing a settlement.

I forgot to mention that spices grow very easily on this island and that the nut known by its inhabitants as *arabine sara* is native to it. It is a marvellous spice, which botanists call *Agathophyllum*.[163]

All these details were confirmed for me by Citizen Dupuy,[164] who was *intendant* of the Isle of France for several years.

Charles-Alexandre Lesueur, *Leschenault aboard the 'Géographe'* (detail), pencil on paper. Le Havre, Muséum d'histoire naturelle: inv. 13015.

SELECTED LETTERS

Introduction

These eleven letters offer additional perspectives on Leschenault's involvement in the Baudin expedition. Nine were written by Leschenault, one by his brother Samuel, and another is from the minister for the navy and colonies. The earliest is Leschenault's letter of application to join the voyage as a botanist; the next his letter of appointment dated 14 September 1800. Two further letters, composed by Leschenault in Paris and Le Havre in September and October 1800, discuss preparations for the voyage. Although Leschenault sent letters home from ports of call en route to Australia, these are now thought lost. Two letters written in Sydney have survived: the first, a friendly note in Latin to his new acquaintance Robert Brown; the second, a detailed report on his Australian experiences sent to Jussieu. Samuel Leschenault in Chalon also received a letter (now thought lost) from Théodore in Sydney and relayed this news to Jussieu. The final letters, dating from the years 1807 to 1814, deal with the aftermath of the voyage: Leschenault's return to France via the Dutch East Indies, French Guiana and the United States; his attempt to recover specimens of Australian wood from the Muséum; his wish to be involved in writing the official account of the expedition; and exchanges of Australian plant specimens between Paris and London.

LETTER 1

Théodore Leschenault, probably addressing Antoine-Laurent de Jussieu
Undated (before mid-September 1800), Paris

In this letter of application to join the Baudin expedition, Leschenault sets out the extent of his botanical expertise and explains why he has a suitable character for enduring its likely hardships. The letter was probably addressed to Jussieu, a leading botanist at the Muséum d'histoire naturelle, who was president of the commission set up by the Institut de France to advise the government on the scientific side of the voyage.

★

Method of collection which I believe I am capable of using and which I promise to apply with all the enthusiasm of one who is eager to learn.

I shall examine and make accurate notes on:

1. The aspect of the place in which I collect samples.
2. The nature of the soil, that is, whether it is clayey, stony, sandy or consists of plant debris.
3. Whether it is sheltered or shaded by woods and hills.
4. Whether it is exposed to the sun's heat, strong winds or streams.
5. Whether it is marshy or simply damp due to the proximity of the sea, a river or a marsh. If the plant is aquatic, I shall identify whether it is submerged or floating.

Examination of the plant

The root
1. Its position in the soil, that is, whether it is perpendicular, oblique, horizontal or creeping.
2. Its shape.
3. Whether the lateral radicles are numerous and their position in relation to the main root.
4. The consistency of the root, that is, whether it is hard or soft.
5. Whether, when it is cut, it releases a large amount of sap, or, on the contrary, whether it remains dry.

The stem
1. Whether it is herbaceous or woody, hollow, solid or spongy.
2. Its position.
3. Its shape and colour.
4. Whether it is woody or branchy; the position of the branches in relation to the stem; the nature of the bark.
5. Whether it is mono- or dicotyledonous, which I shall recognise, in the case of the first, by the fact that the outside of the stem will be denser and harder than the inside, and that there will be less medullary substance around the sap vessels. If it is dicotyledonous, there will be a medullary canal, medullary rays, and layers which will have grown excentrically in the wood and concentrically in the bark.
6. I shall cut open a piece of the stem and carefully examine whether a large amount of liquid comes from the proper vessels. I shall note whether this liquid is resinous, gummous or aqueous; whether it takes on colour or fades through contact with air and light; and whether there is a large amount of sap in the tree.

The leaves
1. Their position in relation to the stem.
2. Their shape.
3. Their colour. Whether they are solitary or accompanied by stipules, sessile or supported by petioles, thin or fleshy, downy or smooth, deciduous or evergreen. Whether the lateral veins are parallel to the central vein, or whether, on the contrary, the veins form angles; whether the intermediate fibres are dense or diffuse.

The organs of fructification and the fruit
1. The flowers. Whether they are hermaphroditic, dioecious, or monoecious. Whether a stem has a single flower, or, on the contrary, each flower supported on a pedicel is joined to several others on a common peduncle; their position.
2. Whether the calyx is monophyllous or polyphyllous, its shape and divisions. Whether it is inferior or superior to the ovary.
3. The corolla. Whether it is monopetalous or polypetalous, its divisions, relating it as far as possible to Tournefort's classes,[1] and seeking, if possible, to find points of comparison with flowers from our regions. I shall precisely record the colour and scent of the corolla, its thickness or transparency.
4. The stamens. Their number, shape and position. Whether the anthers are sessile or supported by filaments in relation to the ovary, corolla and receptacle.
5. The pistil. Its shape and position, the number of styles and stigmas. Whether they are sessile or supported by styles.
6. The ovary. Its shape; whether it is a cupule, a berry or a siliqua. Whether, on the contrary, the fruit is naked. Whether the ovary is monospermous or polyspermous, the number of seeds if possible. Whether the pellicle of the seed is rough or smooth, the stage of maturity in the fruits when I find them.

In short, I shall supply extremely detailed descriptions so that the learned men tasked with classifying my discoveries can easily assign them a suitable place. I shall take precise notes about the varieties and accidents I observe in individual plants of the same species.

Believing myself capable of accurately recording these sorts of notes, I am putting myself forward as a student and botanical collector for the planned expedition. I should inform you that, while my knowledge of botany is modest, I have much experience in drawing, which should come in useful on certain occasions, and am a skilful enough writer to be able to describe a location or relate an event with fluency.

I am twenty-seven years old and have an honest nature, the composure and courage to endure the trials of a long and difficult voyage, and a burning desire to learn.

Guided by the learned men who will lead the section I am applying to join, I believe that I will be capable of carrying out the aims of the commission in charge of recruitment for the expedition.

 Leschenault of Chalon-sur-Saône, Department of Saône-et-
  Loire, residing in Paris, rue Copeau, no. 499

LETTER 2

Pierre-Alexandre-Laurent Forfait, minister for the navy and colonies, to Théodore Leschenault
27 Fructidor, Year VIII [14 September 1800], Paris

Pierre-Alexandre-Laurent Forfait (1752–1807), a naval engineer who also served as a deputy during the Revolution, was appointed minister for the navy and colonies by Napoléon Bonaparte in November 1799, during the early days of the Consulate, and held this position until 1 October 1801. He was the government minister responsible for organising the expedition but had resigned from office by the time the first of the expedition's ships, the *Naturaliste*, returned to France in June 1803. Although Leschenault lacked experience, he was appointed to the expedition as one of its head botanists (rather than as an assistant) and was awarded the higher salary that went with that post.

---

*

Liberty, Equality
Paris, 27 Fructidor, Year VIII of the French Republic,
One and Indivisible
The Minister for the Navy and Colonies

To Citizen Lechesnau, Botanist

Paris

I am informing you, Citizen, that the First Consul has appointed you as a member of the expedition of discovery commanded by Captain Baudin in the capacity of botanist with a salary of 4200 francs.

You will embark on the corvette the *Géographe* and your salary will accrue from the first of that month.

You are advised to obtain instructions from Commander Baudin concerning the date of your departure for Le Havre and follow his directives precisely.

I have no doubt that, during the voyage you are to undertake, you will hasten to fulfil the trust that the government has placed in you. You are aware of its intentions and its proposed objectives, and I am convinced that you will make every effort to contribute to the success of the expedition.

Forfait

LETTER 3

Théodore Leschenault to Antoine-Laurent de Jussieu
5 Vendémiaire, Year IX [27 September 1800], Paris

With his departure from Paris imminent, Leschenault informs his mentor of the fact and expresses his gratitude for the support he has received from him.

★

5 Vendémiaire

Monsieur,

I leave for Le Havre on the day after tomorrow, at five o'clock in the morning. The coach passes through Magny[2] between 11 o'clock and noon, but does not stop long enough for me to have the joy of embracing you and expressing my thanks for the great surprise I had on receiving my engagement and seeing that I was to be classed as a head [botanist] rather than an assistant. The trust you have shown me places me under the great obligation of living up to it. Though I may lack the necessary abilities, I will nevertheless make every effort to fulfil the proposed objectives. In any case I will ask for your indulgence, which is no less than your merit.

The captain has informed us that we set sail on 10 Vendémiaire [2 October].

Monsieur de Candolle[3] has given me a note on the experiments to be performed on monocotyledons.

Please accept, Monsieur, along with your kind family, my humble respects, devotion and affection, and I remain always, Monsieur, your affectionate servant and disciple

Leschenault

LETTER 4

Théodore Leschenault to Antoine-Laurent de Jussieu
Undated (*c.* 16 October 1800), Le Havre

In this letter, written as the expedition awaited favourable winds for departure, Leschenault restates in a more formal manner some of the information that appears in two letters to an unnamed friend which he transcribed into his journal – see pp. 78–79.

★

Le Havre

Monsieur,

If I have put off writing to you for so long, it is because I wished to offer you an accurate picture of the expedition. I believe that the delay it has suffered has not been at all detrimental. We have had time to get to know one another. The most perfect harmony reigns among us and is cemented each day by the endless bowls of punch drained by naturalists and sailors alike.

I dare to assert that among us there will be none of those selfish ambitions that can harm an expedition; each will value his observations only to the extent that they gain the approval of all.

Monsieur Germain, a wealthy amateur botanist of this town, invited us a few days ago to lunch at his nearby country house. Messieurs Michaux, Maugé, Riedlé, Delisse and I had a look around his garden and his hothouses. He maintains everything with great care and good taste. We promised him some seeds.

All my colleagues join me in offering you their regards.

Please convey my humble respects to your kind family, and my fond wishes to Messieurs Mirbel[4] and Candolle, and I offer you also my affectionate regards.

Your devoted servant and disciple

Leschenault

LETTER 5

Théodore Leschenault to Robert Brown
Undated (c. 17 May 1802), Port Jackson, New South Wales

This note, written in Latin, was probably sent by Leschenault to Robert Brown on around 17 May 1802, that is, shortly before the *Naturaliste* sailed out of Sydney on its abortive first attempt to return to the Isle of France. The two botanists coincided in Sydney over two periods, 9–18 May and 28 June – 22 July 1802, and went plant collecting with the English botanist Peter Good. In a letter to Joseph Banks written on 30 May 1802, Brown described Leschenault as 'a pupil of Jussieu. He is a young man, and, as far as I could judge from my very short acquaintance with him, an acute observer'.[5] In 1810, Brown named the Australian plant genus *Leschenaultia* for him, commenting: 'I have named it in honour of my esteemed friend, Lechenault, a celebrated voyager and accomplished botanist whose plant illustrations, especially from the west coast of New Holland, as well as the islands of Java and Timor, are eagerly awaited'.[6] After their return to Europe, the two men exchanged plant specimens and amiable letters – see Letter 11, below.

*

Aboard the *Investigator*
Port Jackson

Sir,

The winds are favourable and we are preparing to depart – most unwillingly, as I am not able to go to your ship. My pain is the greater to the degree that your company is the sweeter. I desire your friendship and cherish it – it will always be dear to me. I will be pleased to hear news of your arrival in Europe.

Cordially, your servant

Th. Leschenault
Botanist

In France, my address in Paris is Hôtel de Genève, rue Saint-Thomas du Louvre; in Burgundy, Chalon-sur-Saône.[7]

LETTER 6

Théodore Leschenault to Antoine-Laurent de Jussieu
20 Brumaire, Year XI [11 November 1802], Sydney,
New South Wales

Leschenault wrote to Jussieu from each port of call to update him on the progress of the expedition; the letters he wrote from Tenerife, the Isle of France and Timor are apparently lost. Leschenault sent this letter, along with his journal and various collections, from Sydney to France aboard the *Naturaliste*. The three ships of the expedition, the *Géographe*, the *Naturaliste* and the newly constructed *Casuarina* sailed out of Sydney harbour on 18 November 1802. This letter would have reached Jussieu in June 1803.

★

Monsieur,

Two years into this expedition, I am sending you a part of my work. I hope that you find some value in it as your respect is what I seek most. But I can scarcely expect you to be pleased with it; every day I am conscious how much greater my expertise would need to be for me to reap all the benefits of this voyage I have undertaken.

I wrote to you in turn from Tenerife, the Isle of France and Timor; I gave you a brief account of my work. I go further today: I am sending you my private journal and the descriptions and drawings of forty plants which, I think, belong to new genera.[8]

I have avoided the systematic mentality which I believe to be detrimental to observation and have supplied only an account of phenomena.[9] Sometimes, however, I have allowed myself a few reflections. But, often, later observations made me aware that I was mistaken in my conjectures, and so you will find a great many crossings-out and added notes in my journal. There would have been a great many more if I had had the time to reread it closely and to muse on each of the sensations I felt in the act of observing. I ask you to forgive my style and spelling. An account written hastily in a ship tossed constantly by the waves and intended only for a beloved mother and forgiving friends cannot be as accurate as one written in the solitude of a study. In any case, on a voyage of this sort, events occur in such rapid succession that the mind is constantly distracted by new objects and cannot perceive them from all the perspectives they offer.

You will find there is a gap between D'Entrecasteaux Channel and Western Port. I was busy at that time classifying plants I had collected in the channel and I did not have time to put the notes I had taken on loose sheets into any sort of order. In any case, nothing of much interest happened during that period. It's true, I could have filled in this gap during my stay in Port Jackson. I even began to do so, but due to the poor state of my health, and under the impression that I would be returning to France aboard the *Naturaliste*, I put off completing this piece of work – to which I thought I could add additional interest by drawing up a table comparing all the places we had visited south of this harbour, in the belief that I should not omit any observation about the places in which the government might intend to establish a settlement. As far as my meagre talents allow, I would willingly have elaborated on the physical composition of this country and on the advantages that might result from taking active possession of it.

Neither do I discuss the English colony where we have stayed for a long time, and which, founded scarcely fifteen years ago, offers a remarkable contrast between, on the one hand, a strong and powerful nation which, in a short space of time, has managed to turn uncultivated and rather barren land to the greatest account, and, on the other, savage men who have not been civilised by the arrival among them of hardworking strangers. These savages, moving without fear among the English, who accord them the greatest freedom, have kept their old customs. They wear no clothing and their weapons, watercraft and possessions are the same as they were before the arrival of the English. This should not be attributed to a sort of national pride but to a profound and dull-witted apathy which prevents them from trying to copy others. They have, however, started to feel a need for clothing and for a more secure food supply than fishing and hunting can provide, but they beg for these things without making any effort to try and obtain them through work. They are passionately attached to tobacco and spirits, which rouse them to anger and vengeance. Their numbers are small because continual quarrels and fights between them, and their barbaric behaviour towards the weaker sex, wipe out the generations as quickly as they breed. In a century in which civilisation is pushing, as it were, into all corners of the globe, it is interesting to try and grasp everything that may shed light on natural man, but, although there are some learned and observant men in this colony, the metaphysical history of the indigenous peoples remains almost unknown. Is it really the case that these men of nature resemble a society of badly behaved children who, in all that they do, perform only a series of horrific, unreflecting actions?

I am sending you just 40 drawings and 40 descriptions with three boxes of unclassified plants. I do though have around 150 drawings and a much greater number of descriptions. I have not sent you these or my herbarium of classified plants, which includes a specimen of each species I have collected, since it is vital that I keep hold of these so that I can do my work properly. We are to travel to more or less the same places as last year. I shall often need to compare the new specimens I collect with the old ones.

So far it is only the English who have observed the plants of New Holland in the places where they grow. Banks, Solander, Dryander and Smith[10] have in turn described a great many genera, most of which were not yet known in France when I set out. My stay in Port Jackson has been very helpful as it has enabled me to learn what has been done so far by the English botanists. Colonel Paterson,[11] a member of the Royal Society of London, who is highly regarded in Europe for a journey he made to Africa, welcomed me with the utmost kindness. He did not hesitate to supply me with anything that could help my work. He was even so kind as to accompany me on trips to the Blue Mountains and the Parramatta and Hawkesbury regions. I am equally grateful to Monsieur Brown, the botanist with the English expedition, and to the botanist Caley,[12] who was sent out to this country at the expense of the famous Sir Joseph Banks, your illustrious friend.

In the places I have visited on both the east and west coasts of New Holland there are only a small number of genera, almost all of them new, but these contain a large number of species. These genera belong to a small number of natural families: the tall trees for the most part belong to the family Myrtaceae, the shrubs and undershrubs to the families Myrtaceae, Proteaceae, Leguminosae and Compositae; the grasses to the families Compositae, Campanulaceae, Orchidaceae and Liliaceae; cryptogamous plants and plants of the family Gramineae are not very common, something I attribute to a soil that is, almost everywhere, sandy and dry. I believe that this is also the reason why the leaves of all the plants I observed in this vast land are small and tough in nature.

If they were analysed chemically, these plants might supply products useful to science and medicine, for almost all contain large amounts of highly aromatic true sap. So far, however, none of the doctors working in the English colony on the east coast has carried out any experiments. They confine themselves to using medicines sent out from Europe without trying to take advantage of those that the country they live in would supply them with in great quantity. Only occasionally, in persistent cases of dysentery, do they use the red gum of the *Eucalyptus*, which is highly astringent.

I have named some of the plants I am sending you. The names I have given them are those of people I hold in high esteem or my friends. Far from home, it is a great pleasure for me to be able to offer this mark of respect to those who are so often in my thoughts or whose brilliant minds have sparked my enthusiasm. But it is possible that several of the plants I thought were new are not in fact so, and so I ask you to transfer their names to ones I have not named.

When I arrived in this port I was in very poor health and it was my intention to return to France. I put this request in writing to Monsieur Baudin, urging him to grant his consent, but several remarks he made, remarks which seemed to me to show signs of consideration and friendship, caused me to abandon this plan, which I would never have conceived if Monsieur Hamelin were to have continued the expedition with the *Naturaliste*.[13] Having travelled aboard this vessel for a year, I have had many reasons to be pleased with this officer, who diligently performs his important duties. On every occasion, he has been quick to offer any form of assistance I might require in my work and has shown towards the naturalists on his ship every consideration they are due for the honest and blameless way in which they have behaved.

I set out on this expedition with great enthusiasm and, despite the trials and privations that accompany any long voyage, and despite the poor state of my health, the same enthusiasm endures. If I have sometimes suffered, the study of nature has offered me great delights by way of compensation. It is only with difficulty that I may describe for you the sensations I felt the first time I went ashore on an unknown coast. My whole being was filled with confused pleasure, everything around me sparked my curiosity, pebbles, shells washed up on the beach, plants. I collected all with wild enthusiasm but was soon forced to abandon a portion of these riches I had so recklessly amassed.

I say again, Monsieur, that I feel that I lack vast swathes of knowledge that might allow me to reap all the benefits of this voyage, and I am forced to rely simply on my own abilities. All the artists appointed by the government disembarked at the Isle of France due to illness. Two others whom the commander brought on board to work for him are not at the naturalists' disposal. Just one of them is prepared, almost against Monsieur Baudin's will, to spend part of his time drawing the fascinating collections that my friend Péron has amassed with such enthusiasm. And now, as the expedition's sole botanist, I am forced to apply my mediocre skills to drawing the plants I collect. I have no one to assist me in collecting, drying and describing these plants. Vastly different resources have been made available on the expedition of discovery commanded by the English captain Flinders to the botanist Brown, whom I befriended during his stay in this port.

The corvette the *Géographe*, from which we had been separated for a long time, arrived here in the most dreadfully ragged state. Its crew had been greatly ravaged by disease and death. Only four men were in a fit state to perform their duties. The health of all has been restored by their long stay. The supplies we have taken on are of good quality, which gives us grounds to hope that the remainder of our voyage will be favourable. For over two more years I shall remain in regions far distant from you. I shall redouble my efforts and strive even harder. I am highly conscious of the obligation I owe you for placing your trust in me and selecting me ahead of several others. As a result of the irreparable losses which I still feel with all my heart, I have been left solely responsible for the branch of natural history concerned with botany.[14] I find that my work grows easier day by day as I become accustomed to making observations. On my return I hope to be able to present you with far more worthy findings than I have produced so far.

I am sending around 130 species of seeds to Madame Bonaparte, who had asked me to collect some for her. I sincerely hope that the plant I have named for the First Consul is a new species and may flourish in Europe.[15]

After you have read my journal and shared any information you believe may be useful to the expedition, I ask you to send it on to my good mother, to whom I have mentioned it in a letter.

Please pass on my regards to Madame de Jussieu and my friendly wishes to Messieurs Mirbel and Candolle. I remain, respectfully,
Your servant and disciple,

Th. Leschenault
Head botanist of the expedition

Sydney, 20 Brumaire, Year XI

LETTER 7

Samuel Leschenault to Antoine-Laurent de Jussieu
4 Messidor, Year XI [23 June 1803], Chalon-sur-Saône

Samuel Leschenault was Théodore's younger brother by three years and the sibling to whom he was closest throughout his life. In this letter written to Jussieu, Samuel expresses his excitement at having just received a letter from Théodore written in Sydney, a town he could not locate on any map. The letter from Théodore to Samuel is apparently lost.

---

*

Chalon-sur-Saône, 4 Messidor, Year XI

Monsieur,

I have just this moment received a letter from my brother and am writing in haste to alert you that you are to receive his journal, although I assume it will reach you before this missive.

In his letter he discusses at some length the most interesting discoveries of his voyage. He tells me how grateful he is for Captain Hamelin's support. I am very sorry not to have been able to make the acquaintance of this worthy officer. And yet I do have some hope of meeting him, as my brother informs me that his affairs may bring him to Burgundy. I shan't hesitate to take this opportunity to express my thanks to him for the kindness he has shown an adored and respected friend.

He writes that he has collected a huge number of plants that are unknown in Europe. (I know how much that will please you; he reckons the figure to be 450 so far.) He has enclosed around 130 species of seed that he is sending to Madame Bonaparte.

It seems that he has enjoyed good health until now and still feels the same enthusiasm he had when he set out on the expedition. I presume that it has been as successful as he hoped and I have no doubt that he has reaped the most valuable rewards from it. He dates his letter from Sydney on the east coast of New Holland, where an English colony has been established. Although he has provided me with a wealth of information about the natives of the region, I have nevertheless leafed in vain through maps and dictionaries: I have so far been completely unable to locate the place where he is staying. He is full of praise for the exceptionally warm and obliging manner in which Colonel Paterson, the lieutenant governor of this colony, has welcomed him. This man, whose merits are known throughout Europe, has a wife who combines the graces of her sex with a remarkable erudition.[16]

I shall never forget the kind way in which you welcomed my brother. He owes his success to you and I join him in conveying to you our deepest gratitude.

Yours very respectfully,

S. Leschenault

Rue des Cornillons
Department of Saône-et-Loire

LETTER 8

Théodore Leschenault to Antoine-Laurent de Jussieu
17 July 1807, Saint-Nazaire

After leaving the Baudin expedition at Timor in June 1803 due to ill health, Leschenault travelled on to Java. With support from Nicolaus Engelhard (1761–1831), the Dutch governor of the north-east coast of the island, Leschenault based himself at Semarang for three years and went exploring and collecting in eastern Java, Madura and Bali. In November 1806, with France still at war with Britain, he loaded his large collection of plant and animal specimens aboard a neutral vessel, the American brig *Sally and Hetty*, and sailed in steerage around Cape Horn to Cayenne and then on to Philadelphia. He spent two months in the United States before completing the final leg of his journey home. He arrived at the port of Saint-Nazaire on the west coast of France on 16 July 1807, from where he wrote to Jussieu.

★

Monsieur,

Finally, after an absence of nearly seven years, I am now back in my own country. You are aware of the reasons that forced me to leave the expedition commanded by Captain Baudin. After doing so, I travelled to Java, where I remained in poor health for nearly a year. When I had fully recovered, I initially sought passage home, but the captains of neutral vessels were extremely reluctant to accept passengers. Some even had explicit orders from their owners not to do so. The sight of the lovely island of Java kindled in me a great desire to explore it. Monsieur Engelhard, the governor of Java, who has a passion for science and takes a keen interest in its advancement, offered to provide for my needs. I accepted. I have brought back to France, Monsieur, the fruits of my travels, which lasted around two years. My collections consist of a herbarium containing around 900 species of plants; 130 species of stuffed birds (around 20 species are from Cayenne or the United States; I collected them during my passage to Philadelphia); 20 species of quadrupeds; 200 species of insects, mostly butterflies; 30 species of snakes, preserved in spirits; several fishes and molluscs; several animal skeletons; and two stone statues found in ruined temples in the interior of the island of Java, temples whose origins are completely unknown to the Javanese themselves. These collections have been in their boxes for around 10 months; I hope that they will still be in good condition. I will find out in Nantes, where I intend to open up the boxes and reorganise them so that they may be safely transported by road to Paris.

I left Batavia 8 months ago on an American vessel. After a passage of 4 months and 20 days I arrived in Philadelphia, where I stayed for 7 weeks. There, with the help of Professor Barton,[17] I obtained a passport from the English ambassador[18] to ensure that I, and my collections, would be treated with due consideration by his nation's fleet. I finally left Philadelphia in the middle of last month and, after a superb 26-day passage, arrived at the mouth of the Loire, where our ship has been at anchor since yesterday. It has to remain in quarantine for 8 days. I will stay another 8 to 10 days in Nantes to inspect and reorder my boxes and will then travel on to Paris. I cannot express how delighted I shall be to see you again. I shall feel no end of joy if you should take some measure of satisfaction in laying eyes once more on a man who feels for you all the respect, admiration and affection that you inspire in all who have the honour to know you.

Monsieur Irénée du Pont de Nemours,[19] whom I had the honour of meeting in America, has asked me to convey his respects to you.

I was deeply gratified to learn from the newspapers of Monsieur Mirbel's political advancement.[20] Please give my regards to Madame de Jussieu.

I remain respectfully, Monsieur, your very humble and obedient servant and disciple

Leschenault de la Tour

Saint-Nazaire, 17 July 1807

P. S. I would be very grateful to hear from you before I leave Nantes. If you would be so kind as to write, please address your letters to me, *poste restante*, in Nantes.

LETTER 9

Théodore Leschenault to the directors of the Muséum d'histoire naturelle
4 November 1807, Paris

Contrary to Forfait's instructions, Leschenault had some personal objects, five Australian tree trunks, transported back to France aboard the *Naturaliste*. In this letter he seeks permission from the directors of the Muséum d'histoire naturelle to reclaim the wood from the Muséum's workshop.

★

Paris, 4 November 1807
Meeting of 4 November 1807

To the Administrators of the Jardin des plantes

Messieurs,

When the corvette the *Naturaliste* left Port Jackson to return to France, Monsieur Hamelin allowed me to stow on board five tree trunks that I had bought in Port Jackson, namely three of *Casuarina* and two of *Xylomelum*. Monsieur Hamelin has written to inform me that these pieces of wood were sent to the Muséum with other similar pieces. I waited to receive this letter of confirmation, which I have passed on to Monsieur Desfontaines,[21] before requesting you, Messieurs, to allow me to collect them from your carpentry workshops, where I have ascertained they still remain.

I am honoured to be, respectfully,
Messieurs,
Your very humble and obedient servant,
Leschenault de la Tour

LETTER 10

Théodore Leschenault to Jean-Pierre Bachasson,
 comte de Montalivet, minister of the interior
7 November 1813, Paris

When François Péron died in December 1810, just two volumes of the official account of the Baudin expedition, entitled the *Voyage de découvertes aux terres australes* (Voyage of Discovery to the Southern Lands), had been published: part 1 of the *Historique* (Narrative) and part 1 of the atlas. The artist Charles-Alexandre Lesueur, who had worked closely with Péron and provided illustrations for the atlas, inherited Péron's papers and sought permission from the government to complete the second part of the narrative. He was rejected for this role. Leschenault, who had been working as an inspector of merino sheep since July 1811, an arduous job which involved long periods of travel along bad roads through France's remote departments, applied to the minister of the interior to take over from Lesueur. The letter below may be one of several he wrote on the subject. He, too, was rejected. The task was given instead to Louis Freycinet, who published the second part of the *Historique* in 1816.

★

Paris, 7 November 1813

Monseigneur,

I have the honour to inform Your Excellency that Monsieur Lesueur has now returned to Paris. I shall busy myself with the continuation of the *Voyage to the Southern Lands* as soon as I know Your Excellency's intentions and I have your permission to relieve Monsieur Lesueur of the papers and journals which are essential to me. If Your Excellency would grant me a short interview, you might convey to me your detailed instructions about the course my work should take.

I have the honour, Monseigneur, to be Your Excellency's most humble and obedient servant

Leschenault
Grand Hôtel de Richelieu, rue Neuve Saint-Augustin

LETTER 11

Théodore Leschenault to Robert Brown
11 July 1814, Paris

During the Napoleonic Wars ordinary communications between France and Britain were heavily restricted. After Napoléon's abdication on 6 April 1814, travel resumed between the two nations and Leschenault soon received a letter from his old friend Robert Brown, conveyed by two visiting English botanists, Dawson Turner and William Jackson Hooker. In his response, Leschenault promises to send Brown various Australian plant specimens, describes his recent publications, and alludes to mutual friends they knew in New South Wales.

★

Paris, 11 July 1814

Monsieur and respected friend,

I am very disappointed to have missed Messieurs Turner and Hooker.[22] I was in the countryside during their stay here. I would have been delighted to meet them and to have been of assistance to them in any way. I received your letter only four days ago. Monsieur Turner had left it with Monsieur Thouin[23] along with the parcel of specimens that you were kind enough to send me and which greatly delighted me.

Since learning of your wishes, I have hastened to fulfil your requests. Today I am sending by coach a parcel containing around 100 specimens of plants from the west and south-west coasts of New Holland. Among these are the four plants about which you have requested information. I am including two species of the plant you have seen in Dampier's *Voyage*.[24]

I have only been able to send you a very poor specimen of *Pileanthus limacis*.[25] I have taken it from Monsieur de Jussieu's herbarium. We do not have *Cephalotus follicularis*[26] in fruit. I found it only in flower in King George Sound.

As far as possible I have tried to provide you with two of every specimen. It is possible some are not held in the herbarium of the honourable Sir Joseph Banks. I ask you to present these to him as a mark of my respect for this learned patron of the natural sciences.

Among the plants I have the honour to send you are several specimens of *Fucus*. I hope that Monsieur Turner may find in them something worthy of his interest. I am sorry that while he was here he did not see the herbarium of my good friend Monsieur Benjamin Delessert,[27] the banker. He has a fine collection of *Fucus*. His herbarium contains a large number of rare plants from every corner of the globe. He also has Burman's original herbarium.[28] I very much look forward to introducing you to Monsieur Delessert when you come to Paris.

Monsieur Turner would have found some very valuable items in Monsieur Lamouroux's[29] herbarium, but unfortunately he is no longer in Paris. He has been living in Caen for several years, where he holds a post in the educational system.

I'm also including with my parcel three copies of my little 'Note on the Vegetation of New Holland'.[30] It is a very mediocre work. I ask you to judge it leniently and, if you consider it worthwhile, to offer a copy to the honourable Sir Joseph Banks and another to Monsieur Turner. I have seen Monsieur de Jussieu with a copy of the *Appendix* you sent him.[31] I am very sorry to say that I am not currently familiar enough with the English language to benefit from reading it, but I shall ask Monsieur de Jussieu to lend it to me and I shall study it carefully.

I have not seen Messieurs du Petit Thouars,[32] Bonpland[33] and Palisot de Beauvois[34] since receiving your letter, but I can assure you that they would be only too happy to help you with the exchanges you would like to make. You can rest assured that when you arrive here all portfolios and herbaria will be open to you and you will everywhere receive the welcome you deserve. I have been asked by Messieurs de Jussieu, Desfontaines and Deleuze[35] to let you know that they will be delighted to see you. You can procure in the Jardin royal at the Muséum the plants from New Holland that you lack, where these are held in the herbarium I deposited in the Cabinet of Natural History. We shall rely on your generosity for several specimens that we lack.

I have been deterred from undertaking the publications I might have done by the loss of my botanical journal which contained nearly 800 descriptions and 250 drawings. I gave the journal and drawings to Monsieur Baudin when I left the expedition at Timor. On my return to France, I heard nothing about these papers that were of such importance to me. I would have had to work solely from dried plants. In any case, your fine work left me little to do.[36]

My herbarium from Java contains many interesting plants, but so far conditions have not been very suitable for publishing and my job takes up a considerable amount of my time, which has so far prevented me from doing anything.[37]

In the *Annales du Muséum d'histoire naturelle* I have published: (1) a paper on *Antiaris toxicaria* and *Strychnos tieute*, plants which provide the famous poison known as *bohun upas*;[38] (2) a description of the volcano Mt Ijen on the island of Java;[39] (3) the note on the vegetation of New Holland that I'm sending you.

In the *Annales des voyages* I've also published a description of the mountains of Tenggar, on the island of Java,[40] and a short description of Kupang on the island of Timor.[41]

If it had not been for political events, the second volume of the *Voyage to the Southern Lands* would already have appeared. The new government has not yet had time to see to this.

Monsieur Freycinet's nautical account and the maps have been finished and are about to be published.[42] I have used some of the names that appear on the maps of our voyage to indicate the places where the plants I am sending you are found.

Now that the seas are open to France, I am very eager to visit several different regions of India. If some arrangements I am trying to make fall into place, I shall perhaps set off to undertake new researches in natural history. If this happens, I shall ask you for letters of introduction and, if I have time, will come to London and call on you, and various institutions, to request them. I should be delighted to keep you informed of what I collect.

I shall pass on your congratulations to Messieurs Lesueur and Freycinet as soon as I see them.[43]

I am asked by my friend Monsieur Langlès,[44] a member of the Institut and conservator of oriental manuscripts at the Bibliothèque du roi, to offer you his compliments and to pass on his wish of making your acquaintance.

The parcel I am sending you is a rather paltry thing. I ask you simply to take it as a mark of my friendship, and as a slight advance on all that will be placed at your disposal in my herbarium, which is held in the Cabinet of Natural History.

I very much look forward to your arrival and assure you that I shall do all that I am able to assist you.

It was with great sorrow that I received your sad news concerning Colonel Paterson, Governor King and Captain Flinders.[45]

You should have received a letter from Monsieur de Jussieu by Monsieur Roche.

Yours respectfully,
Your devoted and affectionate servant and friend

Leschenault de la Tour
Grand Hôtel de Richelieu, rue Neuve Saint-Augustin, Paris

P. S. The package I am sending will arrive in London in five or six days' time at the parcel office of the White Bear, Piccadilly. It is addressed as follows:[46]

Natural History
Dried Plants of the Western and South-Western Coasts
of New Holland
Directed to Mr Robert Brown, Naturalist
To the Care of the Honourable Sir Joseph Banks
President of the Royal Society
London

*

Archival Sources

Letter 1: Paris, Archives nationales, MUS/AJ/15/569, f. 348.
Letter 2: Paris, Archives nationales, F/17/3979.
Letters 3–4: Paris, Archives nationales, MUS/AJ/15/569, ff. 370, 344.
Letter 5: London, Natural History Museum Library and Archives. This letter could not be located in 2016. The original Latin text appears in David J. Mabberley, *Jupiter Botanicus: Robert Brown of the British Museum* (Braunschweig: Verlag von J. Cramer; London: British Museum (Natural History), 1985), pp. 94–95, and has been used with the author's kind permission.
Letters 6–8: Paris, Muséum national d'histoire naturelle, Fonds Jussieu, Fonds Phanérogamie.
Letter 9: Paris, Archives nationales, MUS/AJ/15/598.
Letter 10: Paris, Archives nationales, F/17/1023.
Letter 11: London, British Library, Add. MS 32440, ff. 35–38.

Notes

INTRODUCTION

1 Auction catalogue 3 December 2016, Geoffroy-Bequet Auctioneers, Royan, item 239.
2 See article L211–4 of the *Code du patrimoine*, www.legifrance.gouv.fr, consulted 5 March 2021.
3 Forfait to Baudin, 7 Vendémiaire, Year IX [29 September 1800], cited in Nicolas Baudin, *Mon voyage aux terres australes: journal personnel du capitaine Baudin*, ed. Jacqueline Bonnemains (Paris: Imprimerie nationale, 2000), p. 99.
4 See Théodore Leschenault to Antoine-Laurent de Jussieu, 20 Brumaire, Year XI [11 November 1802], Letter 6 of the Selected Letters, p. 253.
5 See Letter 6, p. 258, and also Samuel Leschenault to Jussieu, 4 Messidor, Year XI [23 June 1803], Letter 7, p. 259.
6 François Péron, *Voyage de découvertes aux terres australes, exécuté par ordre de sa majesté l'empereur et roi, sur les corvettes le Géographe, le Naturaliste, et la goélette le Casuarina, pendant les années 1800, 1801, 1802, 1803 et 1804, Historique*, vol. 1 (Paris: Imprimerie impériale, 1807), pp. 238–39. Leschenault's journal is also cited in François Péron and Louis Freycinet, *Historique*, vol. 2 (Paris: Imprimerie royale, 1816), p. 262.
7 The auction house declined to provide any information about the provenance of the manuscript.
8 See Letter 1, p. 245.
9 Paris, Archives nationales: MUS/AJ/15/569, f. 370; cited in Michel Jangoux, *Le Voyage aux terres australes du commandant Nicolas Baudin: genèse et préambule (1798–1800)* (Paris: Presses de l'Université Paris-Sorbonne, 2013), p. 205.
10 See p. 248 and Leschenault to Jussieu, 20 Brumaire, Year XI [11 November 1802], Letter 6, p. 258.
11 Leschenault to an unnamed recipient at the Ministry of the Interior, 27 August 1807. Paris, Archives nationales: F/1dII/L/16.
12 Jean-Joseph-Eugène Deschamps, 'Leschenault de la Tour, Jean-Baptiste-Louis-Claude-Théodore, voyageur et naturaliste français', *Nouvelle Biographie générale, depuis les temps les plus reculés jusqu'à nos jours*, ed. Ferdinand Hoefer, 46 vol. (Paris: Firmin Didot frères, fils et compagnie, 1852–1866), vol. 30, col. 923.
13 Register of marriage contracts for Chalon, 1792–1799, p. 53. Mâcon, Archives départementales de Saône-et-Loire.
14 See Edward Duyker, *François Péron, an Impetuous Life: Naturalist and Voyager* (Carlton: The Miegunyah Press, 2006), p. 50. The institution was renamed the École de médecine (School of Medicine) at the end of 1796.
15 Deschamps, 'Leschenault de la Tour', col. 923.

16 See Louis Reutter de Rosemont, *Histoire de la pharmacie à travers les âges*, 2 vol. (Paris: Peyronnet and compagnie, 1932), vol. 2, pp. 332–34.

17 Abel Jeandet, 'Notice sur la vie et les travaux de Leschenault de la Tour', *Bulletin de la Société des sciences naturelles de Saône-et-Loire* (1883), pp. 123-58 (p. 126).

18 See the decree of 20 September 1792, in André-Rémi Arnoult, ed., *Collection des décrets de l'Assemblée nationale législative* (Dijon: Causse, 1792), pp. 765–69, and Roderick Phillips, 'Women and family breakdown in eighteenth-century France: Rouen, 1780-1800', *Social History* 1/2 (1976), pp. 197–218 (p. 204).

19 See my chapter 'A scientific voyager in limbo: Théodore Leschenault's return to imperial France', in *'Roaming Freely throughout the Universe': Nicolas Baudin's Voyage to Australia and the Pursuit of Science*, ed. Jean Fornasiero and John West-Sooby (Adelaide: Wakefield Press, 2021), pp. 267–85.

20 Oddly enough, Leschenault's godfather, who is called 'Jean-Baptiste Guillemardet de la Jonchère' in the baptismal register, goes by the forenames 'Jean-Jacques' in other records. He died the following year, on 7 December 1774. Leschenault's godmother was Guillemardet's wife, Antoinette-Geneviève Renard, who contracted to remarry in 1783.

21 The concept of collective lordship is discussed in Germain Butaud, 'Remarques introductives: autour de la définition et de la typologie de la coseigneurie', *Mélanges de l'École française de Rome – Moyen Âge* 122/1 (2010), pp. 5–12.

22 *Mémoire imprimé pour Théodore Leschenault, procureur du roi au bailliage de Chalon sur le retrait féodal exercé par le comte de Montbarrey sur le fief de Rupt, dépendant de la seigneurie de Savigny-en-Revermont acquis en 1768 par Théodore Leschenault* (1770). Mâcon, Archives départementales de Saône-et-Loire: J1-1149. See also Sébastien Évrard, 'Droit et territoire: un conflit en Bresse bourguignonne à la fin de l'Ancien Régime', *Cahiers Haut-marnais* 248–51 (2007), pp. 241–68, and Claude Courtépée, *Description générale et particulière du duché de Bourgogne, précédée de l'abrégé historique de cette province*, 2nd edn, 4 vol. (Dijon: Lagier, 1847–1848), vol. 3, p. 351.

23 See Henri Beaune and Jules d'Arbaumont, *La Noblesse aux états de Bourgogne de 1350 à 1789* (Dijon: Lamarche, 1864), p. 91, and André Bourée, *La Chancellerie près le parlement de Bourgogne de 1476 à 1790* (Dijon: Bellais, 1927), p. 389.

24 See Roland Mousnier, *The Institutions of France under the Absolute Monarchy, 1598–1789*, trans. Brian Pearce and Arthur Goldhammer, 2 vol. (Chicago: University of Chicago Press, 1979–1980), vol. 2, pp. 287–96.

25 Joseph Garnier, *Inventaire sommaire des archives départementales antérieures à 1790, Côte d'or; Archives civiles, série B: parlement de Bourgogne* (Dijon: Darantière, 1894), p. 180.

26 See David D. Bien, 'Manufacturing nobles: the chancelleries in France to 1789', *Journal of Modern History* 61/3 (1989), pp. 445–86.

27 See Bourée, *La Chancellerie près le parlement de Bourgogne*, p. 50, and William Doyle, 'The price of offices in pre-revolutionary France', *The Historical Journal* 27/4 (1984), pp. 831–60.

28 'Undated memoir against the principal of the college of Chalon-sur-Saône' [1770]. Chalon-sur-Saône, Archives municipales: GG 61. The principal was dismissed later

that year but no replacement found for him until 1782 – see Henri Batault, 'Essai historique sur les écoles de Chalon-sur-Saône du quinzième à la fin du dix-huitième siècle', *Mémoires de la Société d'histoire et d'archéologie de Chalon-sur-Saône* 6/1 (1872), pp. 141–50.

29 Letter to Samuel Leschenault, Paris, 19 September 1809. Mâcon, Archives départementales de Saône-et-Loire: 1/F/225.

30 Will of Théodore Leschenault, 3 October 1825. Paris, Archives nationales: Répertoires de Pierre Eugène Cottenet, MC/RE/L/15.

31 Letter to Jean-Baptiste-Antoine Leschenault, 2 September 1807. Private collection.

32 Letter to Samuel Leschenault, 19 May 1809. Mâcon, Archives départementales de Saône-et-Loire: 1/F/225.

33 Letter to Jean-Baptiste-Antoine Leschenault, 2 September 1807. Private collection.

34 Letter to Samuel Leschenault, 19 May 1809. Mâcon, Archives départementales de Saône-et-Loire: 1/F/225. On Anne Leschenault's career, see Louis-Marie-François Bauzon, *Recherches historiques sur la persécution religieuse dans le département de Saône-et-Loire pendant la Révolution (1789–1803): l'arrondissement de Chalon* (Chalon-sur-Saône: Marceau, 1889), pp. 316–17, and Christelle Morin-Dufoix and Françoise Novarina-Raslovleff, 'L'hôpital à l'époque napoléonienne', *Bulletin de l'Association Abigaïl Mathieu* (2016), pp. 4–22, www.ch-chalon71.fr, consulted 1 June 2020.

35 On Chalon during the Revolution, see Daniel Ligou, 'La Révolution française', in *Histoire de Chalon-sur-Saône*, ed. Pierre Lévêque (Dijon: Éditions universitaires de Dijon, 2005), pp. 143–54.

36 See Adrien Arcelin, 'La noblesse du bailliage de Chalon-sur-Saône en 1789', *Mémoires de la Société d'histoire et d'archéologie de Chalon-sur-Saône* 8 (1895–1901), pp. 303–20, and Henri Beaune and Jules d'Arbaumont, *La Noblesse aux états de Bourgogne de 1350 à 1789* (Dijon: Lamarche, 1864), pp. 90–91.

37 William Doyle, *The French Revolution: A Very Short Introduction* (Oxford: Oxford University Press, 2001), p. 40; see also Peter McPhee, *The French Revolution, 1789–1799* (Oxford: Oxford University Press, 2002), p. 52.

38 See Élisabeth-François de Lacuisine, *Le Parlement de Bourgogne depuis son origine jusqu'à sa chute*, 2nd edn, 3 vol. (Dijon: Rabutot; Paris: Durand, 1864), vol. 3, pp. 398–403.

39 See Bauzon, *Recherches historiques sur la persécution religieuse*, pp. 21–36.

40 On the situation in Saône-et-Loire, see Paul Montarlot, *Les Députés de Saône-et-Loire aux assemblées de la Révolution, 1789–1799* (Autun: Dejussieu, 1905), p. 42, Roland Carraz, 'Lettres de Leschenault et Moyne, députés extraordinaires de la ville de Chalon à la Constituante, aux maires et officiers municipaux de Chalon-sur-Saône, 11 juin 1790–12 juillet 1790', *Cahiers de la Bourgogne moderne* 1 (1972–1973), pp. 2–18, and Colin Lucas, *The Structure of the Terror: The Example of Javogues and the Loire* (Oxford: Oxford University Press, 1973).

41 See Henri Huet, 'Les incarcérés de Chalon-sur-Saône pendant la Révolution française', *Mémoires de la Société d'histoire et d'archéologie de Chalon-sur-Saône* 60 (1991), pp. 55–105 (p. 70).

42 See Huet, 'Les incarcérés de Chalon-sur-Saône', pp. 125–32, and Émile Pérusson, *Festival chalonnais—1842. Première Partie: Notice historique d'introduction sur le couvent des Cordeliers de Saint-Laurent-les-Chalon* (Chalon-sur-Saône: Duchesne, 1842), pp. 66, 71.
43 Lucas, *The Structure of the Terror*, pp. 76, 359.
44 See Huet, 'Les incarcérés de Chalon-sur-Saône', p. 64. On the revolutionary festivals, see Mona Azouf, *Festivals and the French Revolution*, trans. Alan Sheridan (Cambridge, Mass.: Harvard University Press, 1988).
45 Deschamps, 'Leschenault de la Tour', col. 923.
46 Huet, 'Les incarcérés de Chalon-sur-Saône', p. 93.
47 See Courtépée, *Description générale et particulière du duché de Bourgogne*, vol. 3, p. 231, and Victor Fouque, *Histoire de Chalon-sur-Saône depuis les temps les plus reculés jusqu'à nos jours* (Chalon-sur-Saône: Chez l'auteur, 1844), pp. 553–54.
48 Reproduced in Marie-Thérèse Suhard-Maréchal, *Saint-Laurent* (Chalon-sur-Saône: Société d'histoire et d'archéologie de Chalon-sur-Saône, 1994), p. 81.
49 See Pérusson, *Festival chalonnais*, pp. 66, 71.
50 Huet, 'Les incarcérés de Chalon-sur-Saône', p. 95.
51 For this description of conditions in the prison, I have relied on Huet's 'Les incarcérés de Chalon-sur-Saône', *passim*, and Pérusson's *Festival chalonnais*, pp. 61–79.
52 See 'Registre des délibérations de l'Administration municipale', 5 Vendémiaire, Year II [26 September 1794]. Chalon-sur-Saône, Archives municipales: 1D1/8.
53 Letter to Samuel Leschenault, 19 May 1809. Mâcon, Archives départementales de Saône-et-Loire: 1/F/225.
54 Nicolas Baudin to the members of the Institut national, 16 Ventôse, Year VIII [7 March 1800], cited in Jangoux, *Le Voyage aux terres australes*, pp. 45–48.
55 See Antoine-Laurent de Jussieu, 'Plan du voyage qui doit être exécuté par le capitaine Baudin', 4 Floréal, Year VIII [24 April 1800], cited in Jangoux, *Le Voyage aux terres australes*, pp. 51–54.
56 Report signed by Pierre Forfait, minister for the navy and colonies, 8 Floréal, Year VIII [28 April 1800], cited in Jangoux, *Le Voyage aux terres australes*, p. 58.
57 John Dunmore, *French Explorers in the Pacific*, 2 vol. (Oxford: Clarendon Press, 1969), vol. 2, p. 11.
58 See, for example, Jean Fornasiero and John West-Sooby, eds, *French Designs on Colonial New South Wales: François Péron's Memoir on the English Settlements in New Holland, Van Diemen's Land and the Archipelagos of the Great Pacific Ocean* (Adelaide: Friends of the State Library of South Australia, 2014), p. 19. The French text is available in Roger Martin, ed., *Mémoire sur les établissements anglais à la Nouvelle Hollande, à la terre de Diémen, et dans les archipels du grand océan Pacifique, Revue de l'Institut Napoléon* 176/1 (1998).
59 Flinders' *A Voyage to Terra Australis* was published in 1814.
60 See Pierre Forfait, 'Mémoire pour servir d'instruction particulière au citoyen Baudin, capitaine des vaisseaux de la République, commandant les corvettes Le Géographe et Le Naturaliste dans le voyage d'observations et de recherches relatives à la géographie et

NOTES

à l'histoire naturelle, dont la conduite et la direction lui sont confiées', 6 Vendémiaire, Year IX [28 September 1800], in Jangoux, *Le Voyage aux terres australes*, p. 290.
61 'Mémoire du roi pour servir d'instruction particulière au sieur de La Pérouse', in Louis-Antoine Destouff, baron de Milet-Mureau, *Voyage de La Pérouse autour du monde*, 4 vol. and atlas (1797–1798), vol. 1, pp. 48–49.
62 'Questions d'histoire naturelle', unsigned and undated memorandum, in Baudin, *Mon voyage aux terres australes*, p. 50.
63 See Letter 3, p. 248.
64 See Jangoux, *Le Voyage aux terres australes*, p. 81.
65 See Péron, *Voyage de découvertes, Historique*, vol. 1, p. 445, n. *a*.
66 See Letter 6, p. 256, and Robert Brown, *Nature's Investigator: The Diary of Robert Brown in Australia, 1801-1805*, ed. T. G. Vallance, D. T. Moore and E. W. Groves (Canberra: Australian Biological Resources Services, 2001), p. 203.
67 See Brown to Joseph Banks, 30 May 1802, cited in Brown, *Nature's Investigator*, p. 206.
68 See Baudin to Hamelin, 15 Vendémiaire, Year X [7 October 1801], in Baudin, *Mon voyage aux terres australes*, p. 368. See also Baudin to Jussieu, 20 Brumaire, Year XI [11 November 1802], cited in Jean Fornasiero and John West-Sooby, 'Voyages et déplacements des savoirs: les expéditions de Nicolas Baudin entre Révolution et Empire', *Annales historiques de la Révolution française* 385 (2016), pp. 23–45 (p. 43).
69 Nicolas Baudin, *The Journal of Post Captain Nicolas Baudin, Commander-in-Chief of the Corvettes Géographe and Naturaliste, Assigned by Order of the Government to a Voyage of Discovery*, trans. Christine Cornell (Adelaide: Libraries Board of South Australia, 1974), p. 473, entry of 15 Pluviôse, Year XI [4 February 1803].
70 Baudin, *The Journal of Post Captain Nicolas Baudin*, pp. 490, 494, entries of 6 and 9 Ventôse, Year XI [25 and 28 February 1803].
71 Antoine-Laurent de Jussieu, 'Instructions rédigées par M. de Jussieu pour les naturalistes de l'expédition', in André-Pierre Ledru, *Voyage aux îles de Ténériffe, La Trinité, Saint-Thomas, Sainte-Croix et Porto-Ricco, exécuté par ordre du gouvernement français, depuis le 30 septembre 1796 jusqu'au 7 juin 1798, sous la direction du capitaine Baudin, pour faire des recherches et des collections relatives à l'histoire naturelle*, 2 vol. (Paris: Arthus Bertrand, 1810), vol. 1, p. xvii.
72 See Leschenault to Robert Brown, 11 July 1814, Letter 11, p. 270.
73 See Leschenault to Jussieu, 20 Brumaire, Year XI [11 November 1802], Letter 6, p. 254.
74 Leschenault to Jussieu, Letter 6, pp. 253–54.
75 See Letter 6, p. 253; see also Paul Gibbard, 'Empiricism and sensibility in the Australian journal of Théodore Leschenault de la Tour', in *Natural History in Early Modern France: The Poetics of an Epistemic Genre*, ed. Raphaële Garrod and Paul J. Smith (Leiden: Brill, 2018), pp. 263–88.
76 On this, see Peter F. Stevens, *The Development of Biological Systematics: Antoine-Laurent de Jussieu, Nature and the Natural System* (New York: Columbia University Press, 1994), pp. 23–62, and Emma C. Spary, *Utopia's Garden: French Natural History from Old Regime to Revolution* (Chicago and London: Chicago University Press, 2000), p. 201.
77 See Letter 6, p. 257.

78 Théodore Leschenault, 'Notice sur la végétation de la Nouvelle-Hollande', *Annales du Muséum d'histoire naturelle* 17 (1811), pp. 81–98 (p. 86).
79 Leschenault, 'Notice sur la végétation de la Nouvelle-Hollande', p. 87.
80 See Joseph-Marie Degérando, *Considérations sur les diverses méthodes à suivre dans l'observation des peuples sauvages* (Paris: Société des observateurs de l'homme, Year VIII [1800]), Georges Cuvier, 'Instructions sur l'anthropologie et sur les recherches à faire en faveur de cette branche de la science, dans un voyage autour du monde', in Maurice Girard, *François Péron: naturaliste, voyageur aux terres australes* (Paris: Baillière; Moulins: Enaut, 1857), pp. 264–69, and Louis-François Jauffret's untitled instructions in Baudin, *Mon voyage aux terres australes*, pp. 60–63.
81 Indigenous genetic material does persist in the modern Canary Islanders: see Stefan Halikowski Smith, 'The mid-Atlantic islands: a theatre of modern ecocide?', *International Review of Social History* 55 (2010), supplement, pp. 51–77 (p. 76).
82 Degérando, *Considérations sur les diverses méthodes à suivre*, p. 57.
83 See Jacques-Julien Houtou de Labillardière, *Relation du voyage à la recherche de La Pérouse*, 2 vol. (Paris: Jansen, 1800), vol. 2, pp. 5–80.
84 Péron, *Voyage de découvertes, Historique,* vol. 1, p. 446.
85 See Letter 6, p. 255.
86 Report by André Thouin cited in 'Extrait du registre des délibérations de l'assemblée des professeurs du Muséum d'histoire naturelle', 10 Messidor, Year XI [29 June 1803]. Paris, Archives nationales: F/17/3979. See also Paul Postiau and Michel Jangoux, 'Les récoltes botaniques de l'expédition Baudin aux terres australes (1801–1803)', in *Portés par l'air du temps: les voyages du capitaine Baudin*, ed. M. Jangoux, special number of *Études sur le dix-huitième siècle* 38 (2010), pp. 241–51.
87 See Leschenault to Jussieu, Letter 6, p. 258.
88 See S. G. M. Carr, 'The French contribution to the discovery of Australia and its flora', *Endeavour* (new series) 35 (1976), pp. 21–26.
89 See Leschenault to Brown, 11 July 1814, Letter 11, p. 270.
90 See Michel Jangoux, 'The herbarium of the *terres australes* (Baudin expedition, 1800-1804)', website of the Baudin Legacy Project, baudin.sydney.edu.au, consulted 1 April 2021. Some of these specimens can be viewed online in the digital collections of the Muséum national d'histoire naturelle (science.mnhn.fr).
91 See the comments cited by Frank Horner, *The French Reconnaissance: Baudin in Australia, 1801-1803* (Carlton: Melbourne University Press, 1987), p. 360.
92 Robert Brown, *Prodromus florae Novae Hollandiae et Insulae Van Diemen* (London: Taylor and Company, 1810), p. 581.
93 See Letter 11, p. 270.
94 Théodore Leschenault, 'Notice sur la végétation de la Nouvelle Hollande et de la terre de Diémen', in Péron and Freycinet, *Voyage de découvertes, Historique*, vol. 2, pp. 358–72.
95 Théodore Leschenault, 'Mémoire sur le *Strychnos tieute* et l'*Antiaris toxicaria*, plantes vénineuses de l'île de Java, avec le suc desquelles les indigènes empoisonnent leurs flèches', *Annales du Muséum d'histoire naturelle* 16 (1810), pp. 459–82.

NOTES

96 The letter to Montalivet of 21 January 1811, housed in the Archives nationales (série F, F/1/dII/P/5), bears a signature that is illegible. An excerpt from the letter appears in Jean-Luc Chappey, 'François Péron and the invention of the nineteenth century', in *'Roaming Freely throughout the Universe'*, pp. 60–63.
97 See Leschenault to Montalivet, 7 November 1813, Letter 10, pp. 266–67.
98 Brown, *Prodromus*, p. 581.
99 See Rachel Thorpe, 'Shire of Gingin Community Infrastructure Plan, March 2016', p. 10, gingin.wa.gov.au, consulted 15 April 2021.

JOURNAL OF THÉODORE LESCHENAULT, 1800–1802
Chapter 1: Le Havre to Tenerife

1 The opening part of the journal consists of transcriptions of various documents: four personal letters written by Leschenault, followed by his second-hand descriptions of Madagascar and the 'Macpa' people of west Africa. The letters are all probably addressed to the same person, identified as 'Citizen J' in the third letter, a male friend living in Paris. The identity of this person is not known; it is not likely to have been the other 'J' to whom Leschenault wrote, his mentor Jussieu, whom he addressed much more formally.
2 A region of Normandy occupying the chalk plateau that lies between the Seine estuary and the English Channel to the north.
3 Linnaeus divided the plant kingdom into twenty-four classes, one of which was Cryptogamia, plants with concealed reproductive organs. Nicolas Jolyclerc had recently published *Cryptogamie complète, ou description des plantes dont les étamines sont peu apparentes* (Paris: Levacher, Year VII [1798–99]), a French adaptation of part of Johann Gmelin's edition of Linnaeus's works.
4 After 'Letter 1', Leschenault copied into his journal passages relating to the Makpa people of west Africa and the geography of Madagascar; these have been moved to an appendix since they do not form part of the narrative of the voyage.
5 These guests included Jacques-Claude Beugnot (1761–1835), prefect of Seine-Inférieure, Charles-Henri Bertin (1752–1822), maritime prefect of Le Havre, and General Jacques-Léonard Muller (1749–1824), inspector of the 15th division of the French army.
6 The French-American Quasi-War of 1798–1800 was an undeclared naval war fought by France and the United States in the Caribbean Sea and the west Atlantic. The French government, accusing the US of reneging on treaty obligations through its rapprochement with Britain, authorised privateers to start seizing American merchant ships; in response the US suspended payment of debts it owed France from the American Revolutionary War, and in July 1798 authorised its newly reformed navy to attack French warships. The 'war' was concluded by a treaty signed on 30 September 1800 at the château of Mortefontaine near Paris. The USS *Portsmouth* was carrying the American negotiators Oliver Ellsworth (1745–1807) and William Vans Murray

(1760–1803) when it sailed from Le Havre. See Dudley W. Knox, ed., *Naval Documents related to the Quasi-War between the United States and France* (Washington: United States Government Printing Office, 1937), pp. 404, 539.

7   Alan Hyde Gardner (1770–1815), who later rose to the position of Admiral of the Blue, was the son of Admiral Alan Gardner (1742–1809), 1st Baron Gardner, who had fought against the French in the Seven Years' War, the American Revolutionary War and the French Revolutionary Wars.

8   Mutineers seized the Dutch frigate *Iazon* in 1796 and surrendered it to the Royal Navy at Greenock in Scotland. The British Admiralty commissioned the vessel as the 32-gun *Proselyte* and it served on the West Indies station and was later involved in the unsuccessful Anglo-Russian invasion of Holland in 1797. After a period spent blockading French ports, it returned to the Caribbean and was wrecked off Philipsburg, Sint Maarten, on 4 September 1801.

9   Widely used across continental Europe until the mid-nineteenth century, this temperature scale, named for René-Antoine Ferchault de Réaumur (1683–1757), a French entomologist and physicist who experimented with alcohol-and-water thermometers in the early 1730s, sets the mark of 0° at the freezing point of water and 80° at the boiling point of water. The conversion from the Réaumur to the Celsius scale involves multiplying by one and a quarter; 10° Réaumur is equivalent to 12.5° Celsius.

10   José Juan Perlasca y Bardela (*c.* 1740–1805) served as a cavalry officer in the Spanish army in conflicts including the Spanish-Portuguese War (1762–1763), the Invasion of Algiers (1775) and the War of the Pyrenees (1793–1795) and rose to the rank of lieutenant general. He was appointed interim commandant general of the Canary Islands in April 1798 and held that position in his own right from June 1799 to May 1803. He suffered from poor health in this period and his duties were often performed by his deputy (and eventual successor) Fernando de Cagigal de la Vega y Martínez Niño (1756–1824). See the 'Diccionario biográfico electrónico' website, dbe.rah.es, consulted 26 March 2020.

11   Leschenault is probably referring to the *Géographe*'s two unofficial artists, Charles-Alexandre Lesueur (1778–1846) and Nicolas-Martin Petit (1777–1804), rather than to its official artists, Jacques-Gérard Milbert (1766–1840) and Louis Lebrun (1769/1770–?). Milbert seems to have taken a different route that day: see Jacques-Gérard Milbert, *Voyage pittoresque à l'Île-de-France, au Cap de Bonne-Espérance et à l'Île de Ténériffe*, 2 vol. and atlas (Paris: Nepveu, 1812), vol. 1, pp. 37–86. The second lieutenant is Leschenault's friend François-André Baudin.

12   [*Author's note*] *Laguna* means 'lake'. The plain is in effect a great pool that had dried up before our stay.

13   This fungus was described and drawn under the same name by Leschenault's colleague on the expedition Jean-Baptiste Bory de Saint-Vincent in *Essais sur les Isles fortunées et l'antique Atlantide* (Paris: Badouin, Year XI [1803]), pp. 303–304 and pl. 4. The fungus has been reclassified as *Laurobasidium lauri* (Geyler) Jülich 1982. Bory de Saint-Vincent (1778–1846) had joined the expedition as a zoologist but abandoned it at the Isle

of France. In subsequent years, Bory pursued a career as an officer in the French army and continued to work as a naturalist, publishing prolifically on zoology and geography.

14   Pierre-Marie-Auguste Broussonet (1761–1807) was a naturalist with interests in ichthyology, agronomy and botany, and a politician. After studying medicine in Montpellier, he moved to London where he worked on classifying fish in the Linnaean style, met Banks, Solander and others, and was admitted to the Royal Society in 1781. On relocating to Paris, he was appointed secretary of the Société d'agriculture, joined the Académie des sciences in 1785, and founded the Société linnéenne de Paris. During the revolutionary period, he was elected as a deputy in the French Assembly but was forced to flee abroad after the fall of the Girondin party in 1793. Under the Directory, he was appointed to a consular post in Mogador (modern-day Essaouira), Morocco, in 1797. With plague threatening the city, he decamped to the Canary Islands in 1799 and worked there as the French consul for trade. He returned to France in 1803 and took up the post of professor of botany at Montpellier, where he oversaw the renovation of the botanical gardens.

15   The Vidogne, Vidogna or Videuño grape variety was used in making the light dry white wine called Vidonia; Malvasia was a fortified white wine.

16   The unsuccessful amphibious assault on Santa Cruz by the Royal Navy took place between 22 and 25 July 1797. Its leader, Admiral Horatio Nelson (1758–1805), was hit in the right arm by a musket ball as he tried to land. He was taken back to his flagship, HMS *Theseus*, where a surgeon amputated the arm. The wound to Nelson's right eye was in fact inflicted several years earlier, on 12 July 1794, during an attack on the Corsican town of Calvi.

17   According to a late sixteenth-century history of Tenerife, two Guanche herdsmen found a statue of a dark-faced woman holding a child and the stub of a green candle in around 1400 at the place now known as Candelaria (south of Santa Cruz) – see Alonso de Espinosa, *Del origen y milagros de la Santa Imagen de Nuestra Señora de Candelaria* (Seville: J. de León, 1594), pp. 30–36, 55. The statue was removed by a Guanche leader and venerated by the people as the goddess Chaxiraxi (the sun mother), but later Christian invaders insisted that the image represented the Virgin Mary. A cult quickly sprang up around the Virgin of Candelaria and she was adopted as a patron saint of the Canary Islands in 1559.

18   Miguel de la Grúa Talamanca y Branciforte, 1st marquis of Branciforte (*c.* 1750–1812), Italian-Spanish army officer, commandant general of the Canary Islands from 1784 to 1789, built the esplanade in 1787. He was appointed viceroy of New Spain in 1794 but was removed from the position in 1798 after accusations of corruption. See the 'Diccionario biográfico electrónico', dbe.rah.es, consulted 26 March 2020, and Juan Tous Meliá, *Santa Cruz de Tenerife a través de la cartografía, 1588–1899* (Santa Cruz: Museo Militar Regional de Canarias, 1994), p. 66.

19   In fact, two commandants held office between Branciforte and Perlasca: José Joaquín Avellaneda Sandoval y Rojas (*c.* 1715–1794), from 1789 to 1791, and Antonio Gutiérrez de Otero y Santallana (1729–1799), from 1791 to 1799. See the 'Diccionario

biográfico electrónico', dbe.rah.es, consulted 26 March 2020, and José Desiré Dugour, *Apuntes para la historia de Santa Cruz de Tenerife* (Santa Cruz: J. Benitez y compañía, 1875), pp. 143–75.

20 Luis de la Cerda (1291–1348), great-grandson of King Alfonso X of Castile and son of the exile Alfonso de la Cerda, was born in France and lived both there and in Spain. While serving as the French ambassador to the Holy See at Avignon, he developed a plan to convert the Guanches of the Canary Islands to Christianity. Pope Clement VI granted him the islands in perpetuity in 1344, along with the title 'Prince of Fortuna'. The proposed crusade was abandoned when Luis died several years later.

21 Jean de Béthencourt (1362–1425) led an expedition to the Canary Islands in 1402 together with fellow French nobleman Gadifer de la Salle (*fl. c.* 1340–1415). With support from Enrique III, king of Castile (1379–1406, r. 1390–1406), he conquered Lanzarote, Fuerteventura and Hierro. Enrique granted Béthencourt lordship of the islands; it was Béthencourt himself who seems to have adopted the title 'King of the Canaries'. See Joseph F. O'Callaghan, 'Castile, Portugal, and the Canary Islands: claims and counterclaims, 1344–1479', *Viator* 24 (1993), pp. 287–309.

22 Known as Prince Henry the Navigator, Infante Dom Henrique of Portugal (1394–1460), the fourth son of Portuguese King João I, played a key role in the expansion of the Portuguese empire. In 1448, Henry bought the lordship of Lanzarote from Maciot de Béthencourt (nephew of Jean), but this sale was not recognised by the Guanches or Castilians. The competing claims of Portugal and Castile over the islands during the mid-fifteenth century were resolved in favour of Castile by the Treaty of Alcáçovas in 1479.

23 The quintal was a unit of measurement equivalent to 100 pounds.

24 Pico Viejo (3135 metres), part of the Teide volcano complex, erupted for three months from 9 June to 8 September 1798. It adjoins Pico del Teide (3718 metres), the highest peak on the island.

Chapter 2: Tenerife to the Isle of France

25 There were in fact three men named Baudin on the expedition: this is François-André Baudin (1774–1842), who was a constant source of irritation to the commander Nicolas Baudin. François-André left the *Géographe* at the Isle of France on 25 April 1801 – see 'Leschenault's Shipmates Mentioned in the Journal'.

26 Between June and September 1795, the British mounted an amphibious assault that resulted in the capture of the Cape Colony from the Batavian Republic, a client state of France.

27 Bartolomeu Dias (*c.* 1450–1500), Portuguese explorer, was appointed by João II, king of Portugal (1455–1495, r. 1481–1495), to sail around the southern tip of Africa in the hope of discovering a sea route to India. The expedition set out in 1487 and sailed around the cape without sighting land; the cape was only sighted in May 1488 on the return journey.

NOTES

28 Vasco da Gama (c. 1469–1524) set out from Lisbon with a fleet of four ships in July 1497, rounded the cape in late November, sailed up the eastern coast of Africa, and crossed over to Calicut (Kozhikode), India, where he arrived in May 1498.

29 Rather than Manuel I, king of Portugal (1469–1521, r. 1495–1521), it was the previous king, Manuel's elder cousin, João II, who changed the name given by Dias in order to encourage investment in the Indian Ocean trade. See Glenn J. Ames, ed., *Em nome de Deus: The Journal of the First Voyage of Vasco da Gama to India, 1497–1499* (Leiden: Brill, 2009), pp. 2–3.

30 A general term used by sailors for dolphins, porpoises and whales. Bory de Saint-Vincent, travelling on the *Naturaliste*, identified these particular animals as fin whales, Linnaeus's *Balaena physalus* (now *Balaenoptera physalus*) – see *Voyage dans les quatre principales îles des mers d'Afrique, fait par ordre du gouvernement, pendant les années neuf et dix de la République (1801 et 1802): avec l'histoire de la traversée du capitaine Baudin jusqu'au Port-Louis de l'île Maurice*, 3 vol. and atlas (Paris: Buisson, Year XIII [1804]), vol. 1, p. 145.

31 A marine league, or sea league, was equivalent to 3 nautical miles, or one-twentieth of a degree of latitude, and measured roughly 5.6 kilometres.

32 The colonists of the Isle of France feared that Baudin had been sent out by the Consulate to compel them to comply with the French government decree of 1794 abolishing slavery. Two commissioners, René-Gaston Baco de la Chapelle (1751–1800) and Étienne-Laurent-Pierre Burnel (1762–1835), had arrived on the island on just such a mission in 1796 and had been expelled by Governor Malartic; see n. 48. Wealthy French sugar-producing colonies in the Caribbean had been thrown into turmoil by the Revolution. In Saint-Domingue (modern-day Haiti), slaves led by François-Dominique Toussaint Louverture (1743–1803) rebelled in 1791; French commissioners sent out to restore order abolished slavery in the colony in an effort to gain the allegiance of slaves and people of colour. Various factions fought for control of the island for a further decade. In Guadeloupe, the British took advantage of the prevailing chaos to invade in 1794; Jean-Baptiste Victor Hugues (1762–1826), sent out as a commissioner by the Convention to emancipate slaves on the island, repelled the invaders and executed colonists who had supported them. See William S. Cormack, 'Victor Hugues and the reign of terror on Guadeloupe, 1794–1798', *Proceedings of the Meeting of the French Colonial Historical Society* 21 (1997), pp. 31–41.

33 That is, members of the Intermediary Commission of the island, a small body that attended to matters of governance when the Colonial Assembly was not in session.

34 Jacques-Henri Bernardin de Saint-Pierre (1737–1814), author and naturalist, published *Voyage à l'Isle de France, à l'Isle de Bourbon, au Cap de Bonne-Espérance*, 2 vol. (Amsterdam; Paris: Merlin, 1773), based on a journey he made in 1768–1771. In Letter 12, 'Des noirs', vol. 1, pp. 188–204, he condemns the brutal treatment of slaves on the Isle of France, describing their harsh working conditions, the punishments they suffered, and their evident emotional distress. He was horrified to witness the hunt for escaped slaves treated as a form of sport. Bernardin later achieved fame with his *Études de la nature*

(1784) and his novel *Paul et Virginie* (1788), which was set on the island. In 1797 he was appointed *intendant* of the Jardin des plantes in Paris.

35 See Pliny, *Natural History*, trans. H. Rackham, W. H. S. Jones and D. E. Eichholz, 10 vol. (London: Heinemann; Cambridge, Mass.: Harvard University Press, 1938–1962), vol. 2, pp. 485–87, book 6, ch. 36, 'Islands off Africa'.

36 Louis-Marie Aubert du Petit Thouars (1758–1831), the orphan child of a noble family, developed an interest in botany while in the French army. He was stranded on the Isle of France in 1793 after a plan to initiate a private search for the missing navigator La Pérouse went awry. He remained on the Mascarene Islands for ten years, studying their plants and compiling a herbarium of some 2000 specimens. He returned to France in 1802, where he published his *Histoire des végétaux recueillis sur les îles de France, La Réunion (Bourbon) et Madagascar* (Paris: Huzard, Year XII [1804]). See 'Aubert Aubert du Petit Thouars', *Biographie universelle et portative des contemporains, ou dictionnaire des hommes vivants, et des hommes morts depuis 1788 jusqu'à nos jours*, ed. François-Georges de Sainte-Preuve, Alphonse Rabbe and Claude Vieilh de Boisjoslin, 5 vol. (Paris: Levrault, 1834), vol. 5, pp. 363–64, and Jean-Pierre Flourens, 'Éloge historique d'Aubert-Aubert Du-Petit-Thouars', *Mémoires de l'Académie des sciences de l'Institut de France* 20 (1849), pp. i–xxxi.

37 Jean-Marthe-Adrien Lhermite (1766–1826) joined the navy in 1780 and saw action in the American Revolutionary War. As a frigate commander he took part in the Glorious First of June and raided British shipping in the Channel and along the Irish and Norwegian coasts. While captain of the frigate *Preneuse* on the Indian Ocean station in 1798–1799, Lhermite captured numerous merchantmen and fought many battles with British warships. In December 1799, as the *Preneuse* was returning from the southern African coast to the Isle of France, it was intercepted by HMS *Tremendous* and HMS *Adamant* and Lhermite was forced to beach his ship in Tombeau Bay, where it was burnt by a boarding party. Lhermite was captured but immediately released on parole, and he remained on the Isle of France until late 1801. During the Napoleonic Wars he was promoted to rear admiral and appointed maritime prefect of Toulon. He remained a celebrated figure on the island: decades later, according to Adrien d'Épinay, 'the generation of 1810 still loved to recount the great exploits of this illustrious sailor to their families' – see *Renseignements pour server à l'histoire de l'Île de France jusqu'à l'année 1810, inclusivement; précédés de notes sur la découverte de l'île, sur l'occupation hollandaise, etc.* (Mauritius: Nouvelle Imprimerie Dupuy, 1890), p. 403.

38 In Torquato Tasso's epic poem *Jerusalem Delivered* (*La Gerusalemme liberata*, 1581), set during the First Crusade (1096–1099), the Saracen sorceress Armida is ordered to murder the Christian knight Rinaldo but instead falls in love with him and holds him captive in an enchanted garden (cantos 14–16). When Rinaldo's friends Carlo and Ubaldo come to look for him, they encounter a charming sight: 'a garden opens in a blithe expanse. / Still ponds and crystal fountains, mossy cells, / bright varied blooms and sundry trees, green plants / of all kinds, sunlit hillocks, shady dells, / forests and caves it offers at one glance' (*The Liberation of Jerusalem*, trans. Max Wickert, ed. Mark Davie (Oxford: Oxford University Press, 2009), p. 287, canto 16, stanza 9). Armida's

garden was a standard point of literary reference – Bory de Saint-Vincent compared the forests near Laguna on Tenerife to it in his *Voyage dans les quatre principales îles* (vol. 1, pp. 60–61).

39 Jean-Nicolas Céré (1738–1810), botanist, was born on the Isle of France, studied at Vannes and Paris, and served as an officer with French naval forces in India from 1757 to 1759 during the Third Carnatic War. After returning to his native island, he worked with Pierre Poivre at the latter's private botanical garden in Pamplemousses. The garden was bought by the Crown in 1772 and Céré was appointed its director in 1775. He devoted much of his energy to acclimatising exotic spice trees, vegetables and fruit trees.

40 Du Petit Thouars refers to this plant as *Cycas circinalis*, the '*samble* of Madagascar', in his *Histoire des végétaux recueillis*, p. 2; it now bears the name *Cycas thouarsii* R.Br. 1810.

41 Secret expeditions were sent out from the Isle of France to bring back spice trees from the Dutch East Indies. Pierre Poivre (1719–1786), *intendant* of the Isle of France from 1767 to 1773, organised several such missions from the 1750s to the 1770s. On this Franco-Dutch rivalry, see, for example, Charles Corn, *The Scents of Eden: A Narrative of the Spice Trade* (New York: Kodansha International, 1998), pp. 223–24, and Dorit Brixius, 'A hard nut to crack: nutmeg cultivation and the application of natural history between the Maluku islands and Isle de France (1750s–1780s)', *British Journal for the History of Science* 51/4 (2018), pp. 585–606. Leschenault himself was later involved in the spice trade and in 1821 transported cinnamon trees he had collected in Ceylon to the Isle of Bourbon.

42 Nicolas Baudin was the fifth of at least ten siblings. His brother Augustin was also a mariner and apparently brought out an *Ayapana* plant from Rio de Janeiro to the Isle of France in 1797 – see Louis Bouton, *Plantes médicinales de Maurice*, 2nd edn (Port Louis: Dupuy and Dubois, 1864), pp. 84–85.

43 This plant has borne several different scientific names over the years, including *Eupatorium triplinerve* Vahl 1794 and *Eupatorium ayapana* Vent. 1803; its accepted name is *Ayapana triplinervis* (Vahl) R. M. King & H. Rob 1970.

44 These figures are the yield per seed, a measure of soil fertility used by Continental agronomists in this period.

45 In Cochinchina (now southern Vietnam), 'dry rice' was grown in newly cleared jungle, watered only by rainfall. It was highly valued: according to Thomas Jefferson, who tried to obtain samples from Cochinchina, it had 'the reputation of being the whitest to the eye, best flavoured to the taste, and most productive' (letter to William Drayton, 30 July 1787, *Founders Online*, US National Archives, founders.archives.gov, consulted 30 November 2020).

46 The name used on Mauritius to refer to the common myna.

47 The name 'bengali', as Anthony Cheke explains, was a 'catch-all name for weaver finches in the eighteenth century, though by the 1760s in the Mascarenes it became attached to the red avadavat *Amandava amandava*, before transferring, in Mauritius, to the common waxbill *Estrilda astrild* – from Africa, not Bengal'. See Anthony Cheke

and Julian Hume, *Lost Land of the Dodo: An Ecological History of Mauritius, Réunion and Rodrigues* (London: Poyser, 2008), p. 315, n. 270.

48 Anne-Joseph-Hippolyte de Maurès, comte de Malartic (1730–1800), was a French army officer who served in the European and Canadian theatres of the Seven Years' War and later commanded a regiment in the Antilles. Having risen to the rank of lieutenant general, he was appointed governor general of the Mascarene Islands in 1792 and set about calming the revolutionary turmoil there and reorganising the islands' defences against the British. When in June 1796 two agents of the Directory, Baco and Burnel, arrived on the Isle of France to enforce the decree abolishing slavery, they met with public hostility and Malartic expelled the two men from the island. The colonists are said to have carried the governor through the streets on their shoulders. Malartic died on 28 July 1800, and his body lay in state for several weeks until he was buried in a provisional tomb. On 29 July 1801, just over three months after the Baudin expedition left the Isle of France, Malartic's remains were transferred to their new resting place. The monument, topped with an obelisk, was only completed in 1847; it bore the legend: 'To the saviour of the colony'. See 'Malartic, Anne-Joseph-Hippolyte, comte de', *Biographie universelle*, vol. 3, p. 418, Allister Macmillan, ed., *Mauritius Illustrated: Historical and Descriptive, Commercial and Industrial* (London: Collingridge, 1914), p. 26, and Claude Wanquet, 'L'Île de France à l'arrivée de Baudin (mars 1801), une île malade du syndrome de Saint-Domingue', in *Baudin-Flinders dans l'océan Indien: voyages, découvertes, rencontre*, eds Serge M. Rivière and Kumari R. Issur (Paris: L'Harmattan, 2006), pp. 19–42.

49 François-Louis Magallon, comte de la Morlière (1754–1825), entered the army in 1769, took part in the French conquest of Corsica, and rose steadily through the ranks. He served in the Revolutionary Wars and in 1795 was promoted to the position of major general. The government charged him with the task of organising the defence of the Mascarene Islands and he arrived on the Isle of France in June 1796, accompanied by a detachment of troops and the commissioners Baco and Burnel. When the commissioners received a hostile reception from the colonists and were expelled by Malartic, Magallon fell in line with the governor's decision. Magallon subsequently served as governor general of the Mascarene Islands from 1800 to 1803 and as interim governor of the Isle of Bourbon from 1803 to 1805. See Claude Wanquet, *La France et la première abolition de l'esclavage, 1794–1802: le cas des colonies orientales, Île-de-France (Maurice) et la Réunion* (Paris: Karthala, 1998), pp. 342–51.

50 Riedlé died in Timor on 21 October 1801.

51 Horace Bénédict de Saussure (1740–1799), Swiss physicist, geologist and alpinist, in 1783 devised a hygrometer that used human hair to measure atmospheric humidity, relying on the characteristic of hair to elongate or contract as the proportion of moisture in the air changed. François Péron claimed that Baudin's was the first voyage of exploration to carry hygrometers but Alexander von Humboldt pointed out that La Pérouse had used them earlier – see Alexander von Humboldt, *Voyage aux régions équinoxiales du nouveau continent, fait en 1799, 1800, 1801, 1802, 1803 et 1804*, 6 vol. (Paris: Schœll, 1814–1820), vol. 1, p. 242.

52 [*Author's note*] Year IX of the Republic.
53 [*Author's note*] Interruption during our stay on Tenerife.
54 A fuller version of Péron's table of data was published, with various modifications, by Louis Freycinet in the volume *Navigation et géographie* (Paris: Imprimerie royale, 1815), pp. 475–81, as part of the official account of the voyage.
55 This complex device, consisting of a mercury thermometer encased successively within glass, wooden and metal receptacles, with insulating layers of ground charcoal and wax, along with a mechanism for letting in water, is described in Péron and Freycinet, *Voyage de découvertes, Historique*, vol. 2, pp. 323–46, ch. 36, 'Mémoire sur la température de la mer, soit à sa surface, soit à de grandes profondeurs'.
56 Péron also discusses this subject in the official account, *Voyage de découvertes, Historique*, vol. 1, pp. 38–41.
57 [*Author's note*] Almost all molluscs are phosphorescent.
58 [*Author's note*] Should we attribute these sudden changes to the spontaneous movement of myriads of the animalcules that cause phosphorescence? But given how small these microscopic creatures are, can we assume that they should be able to move so quickly?
59 Bertrand Bajon (*fl.* 1751–1801), military surgeon, travelled to French Guiana in 1764 with the newly appointed governor Étienne-François Turgot (1721–1789). After leaving the colonial service, Bajon remained in Guiana for a period, working as a doctor in private practice and collecting tropical plants for the Jardin du roi in Paris. His description of phosphorescence in the Atlantic appears in his *Mémoires pour servir à l'histoire de Cayenne, et de la Guyane française*, 2 vol. (Paris: Grangé, Duchesne and L'Esprit, 1777–1778), vol. 2, pp. 402–414, 'Observations sur les corps lumineux qui brillent dans l'obscurité, dans la mer'.
60 Henri Peyroux de la Coudrenière (*c.* 1743 – *c.* 1811) was a French businessman, naturalist and colonial administrator. In an article entitled 'Observations sur la lumière de l'eau de la mer', published in *Observations sur la physique, sur l'histoire naturelle et sur les arts* 5 (1775), pp. 451–52, he rejected the idea that luminescence in sea water was caused by microscopic animals and attributed it instead to phosphorescent material. Coudrenière was acquainted with Nicolas Baudin and his brother Alexandre: all three had been involved in a scheme to bring Acadian refugees from France to Spanish Louisiana in 1785. Coudrenière devised the venture as a way of ingratiating himself with the Spanish authorities and Nicolas and Alexandre captained vessels carrying Acadians to New Orleans. At around the same time, Coudrenière sent documents to the Spanish and French governments outlining his ideas for colonising Van Diemen's Land. He later served as the Spanish commandant at the posts of Sainte-Genevieve (1787–1794) and New Madrid (1798–1803), located in what is now Missouri. Alexandre's business connections with Nicolas continued: he accompanied Nicolas on a voyage transporting provisions from New Orleans to the Isle of France in 1786–1787 and later bought a plantation 4 miles outside New Orleans where, by 1807, he owned 19 slaves and had 135 acres of sugar cane, corn and rice under cultivation (see Henry C. Bezou, *Metairie: A Tongue of Land to Pasture* (Gretna, La.: Pelican Publishing, 1973), p. 60, and Carl A. Brasseaux and Glenn R. Conrad, *The Road to Louisiana:*

The Saint-Domingue Refugees, 1792–1809 (Lafayette, La.: University of Southwestern Louisiana, 1992), pp. 149, 229.

61 [*Author's note*] After making other observations, I realised that a very large number of molluscs are phosphorescent.

62 Zoophytes were considered to be a form of life midway between animals and plants, as the Greek meaning of the name (animal-plant) indicates.

63 A line was one-twelfth of a French inch, that is, around 2.3 millimetres.

64 The generic name is confusing: Leschenault may be offering an abbreviation of Linnaeus's name for the pilot fish *Gasterosteus ductor* or may have intended to write *Gadus* (a genus that includes the Atlantic cod). The current name for the pilot fish is *Naucrates ductor*.

65 Leschenault is apparently contesting an idea put forward by Étienne Geoffroy Saint-Hilaire (1772–1844), professor of zoology at the Muséum d'histoire naturelle. When sailing between Tunisia and Malta in 1798 as part of Napoléon Bonaparte's expedition to Egypt, Geoffroy witnessed pilot fish investigate, seemingly on a shark's behalf, a piece of bacon thrown into the water as bait by a sailor. Geoffroy later published an account of this incident in 'Note sur quelques habitudes communes au requin et au pilote', *Bulletin des sciences, par la Société philomathique* 63 (1802), pp. 113–14. Leschenault must have learnt of Geoffroy's observation prior to the article's publication.

66 As reported by Nicolas Villault, *Relation des côtes d'Afrique, appellées Guinée* (Paris: Denys Thierry, 1669), p. 378.

67 [*Author's note*] Is this the epiploon?

68 Péron named this species of sea butterfly *Hyalaea australis* and included Lesueur's painting of it in the atlas of the *Voyage de découvertes* published in 1807 (pl. 31, fig. 5), but the species had in fact already been described by Peter Forsskål under the name *Cavolinia tridentata* in 1775.

69 See Georges Cuvier, *Tableau élémentaire de l'histoire naturelle des animaux* (Paris: Baudouin, Year VI [1797]), pp. 378–83.

70 Joseph Hugues Boissieu de la Martinière, also known as Joseph La Martinière (1758–1788), medical doctor and naturalist, travelled as a botanist on La Pérouse's expedition and perished with other members of the expedition at Vanikoro. Some of his writings and specimens survived as they were sent back to France from prior ports of call. For his description of the medusa, see his 'Mémoire sur quelques insectes' in Milet-Mureau, *Voyage de La Pérouse autour du monde*, vol. 4, pp. 87–88; and for his drawings, *Atlas*, pl. 20, fig. 13, 14.

71 Péron and Lesueur named this pelagic sea slug *Glaucus eucharis*; see the *Voyage de découvertes, Historique*, vol. 1, p. 46, and *Atlas*, pl. 29, fig. 2. Its accepted name is *Glaucus atlanticus* Forster, 1777.

72 See Milet-Mureau, *Voyage de La Pérouse autour du monde*, vol. 4, p. 89, and *Atlas*, pl. 20, fig. 15, 16. The Bashee or Bashi Islands are now part of the province of Batanes in the northern Philippines.

73 John Hawkesworth (*c.* 1715–1773), literary critic and editor, was commissioned by the British Admiralty to edit the journals of James Cook and Joseph Banks from Cook's

first voyage to the Pacific, along with papers from other captains' voyages. It was Joseph Banks (rather than Hawkesworth) who made a tentative link between the shell and the Ancients: 'It dyes linen cloth, and it may perhaps be worth enquiry, as the shell is certainly found in the Mediterranean, whether it be or not the *purpura* of the Ancients' – see John Hawkesworth, ed., *An Account of the Voyages Undertaken by the Order of His Present Majesty, for Making Discoveries in the Southern Hemisphere, and Successively Performed by Commodore Byron, Captain Wallis, Captain Carteret, and Captain Cook, in the Dolphin, the Swallow, and the Endeavour*, 3 vol. (London: Strahan and Cadell, 1773), vol. 2, p. 14. Georg Forster (1754–1794), a German naturalist who accompanied Cook on his second voyage to the Pacific, pointed out that the Ancients obtained purple dye not from (pelagic) sea snails but from rock snails – see Forster's *A Voyage around the World, in His Britannic Majesty's Sloop, Resolution, Commanded by Capt. James Cook, During the Years 1772, 3, 4, and 5*, 2 vol. (London: White, Robson and Elmsly, 1777), vol. 1, p. 52, note. French translations of these works appeared in 1774 and 1778 respectively.

74 [Author's note] Nota. Since that time Citizen Péron, zoologist, has collected a large number of zoophytes and molluscs. His descriptions and the drawings done under his watchful eye provide all the information necessary for a complete understanding of these animals.

Chapter 3: South-west New Holland to Timor

75 [Author's note] Vancouver found beds of marl in King George Sound (near the Leeuwin coast).

76 This is Louis Freycinet of the *Naturaliste*, rather than his brother Henri of the *Géographe*: see 'Leschenault's Shipmates'.

77 The months of the republican calendar lasted 30 days; Prairial began on the equivalent of 20 or 21 May, while Frimaire began on 21, 22 or 23 November.

78 Arthur Phillip (1738–1814), naval officer and first governor of New South Wales (1788–1792), describes the 'yellow gum plant' (a grass tree or species of *Xanthorrhoea*) in *The Voyage of Governor Phillip to Botany Bay: With an Account of the Establishment of the Colonies of Port Jackson and Norfolk Island* (London: Stockdale, 1789), p. 60, with illustration pl. 3. George Vancouver (1757–1798) commanded a Royal Navy expedition that circumnavigated the globe between 1791 and 1795, exploring the north-west coast of North America, the Hawaiian Islands and the south-west coast of Australia. In King George Sound he observed a 'gum plant' that matched Phillip's description – see *A Voyage of Discovery to the North Pacific Ocean, and Round the World*, 3 vol. and atlas (London: G. G. and J. Robinson, 1798), vol. 1, p. 51. Leschenault would have consulted the French translation of Vancouver's account: *Voyage de découvertes à l'Océan Pacifique du Nord, et autour du monde*, 3 vol. and atlas (Paris: Imprimerie de la République, Year VIII), vol. 1, pp. 79–80.

79 The botanist Jacques-Julien Houtou de Labillardière (1755–1834) visited Australia in 1792–1793 with d'Entrecasteaux's expedition in search of La Pérouse. In his *Relation du voyage à la recherche de La Pérouse*, 2 vol. (Paris: Jansen, 1800), vol. 1, pp. 185–86, he suggests that Phillip's 'yellow gum plant' is in fact a species of *Dracaena*.

80 The genus was named (from the Greek words for 'yellow' and 'flow') by the English botanist James Edward Smith (1759–1828) in the *Transactions of the Linnaean Society* in May 1798, relying on an incomplete specimen and description sent to London from Port Jackson by the surgeon-general John White. See E. Charles Nelson and D. J. Bedford, 'The names of the Australian grass-tree: *Xanthorrhoea* Sm. and *Acoroides* C. Kite (Xanthorrhoeaceae)', *Botanical Journal of the Linnean Society* 112/2 (1993), pp. 95–105.

81 In his botanical notebooks, Leschenault describes this plant more fully and names it *Baudinia coccinea*. Labillardière was the first to publish a description of this plant in 1806 in *Novae Hollandiae plantarum specimen*, 2 vol. (Paris: Huzard, 1804–1806), vol. 2, pp. 25–26 and pl. 164, in which he named it *Calothamnus sanguinea*. Leschenault adopts Labillardière's new name when discussing the plant in his 'Note on the vegetation of New Holland' published in the *Annales du Muséum d'histoire naturelle* 17 (1811), p. 89. Augustin Pyramus de Candolle, in *Prodromus systematis naturalis regni vegetabilis*, 22 vol. (Paris: Treuttel and Würtz, 1824–1873), vol. 3 (1828), p. 211, alludes to Leschenault's unpublished description of the plant.

82 The Vasse-Wonnerup Estuary, north-east of modern Busselton.

83 Louis Freycinet rather than his brother Henri.

84 If Leschenault has accurately recorded the sound, the Noongar word in question may possibly be *balayi*, a term of warning meaning 'look out!', according to Brenda Larsen. See Rose Whitehurst, *Noongar Dictionary: Noongar to English and English to Noongar*, 2nd edn (Perth: Noongar Language and Culture Centre, 1997), p. 1, and George Fletcher Moore, *A Descriptive Vocabulary of the Language in Common Use amongst the Aborigines of Western Australia; with Copious Meanings, Embodying Much Interesting Information Regarding the Habits, Manners and Customs of the Natives, and the Natural History of the Country* (London: Orr, 1842), p. 145, where it is spelt *wola*.

85 Depuch writes the word *mouye* (Péron, *Voyage de découvertes, Historique*, vol. 1, pp. 85, 87). The Noongar word in question may possibly be *moorli-moorli* (devil), or, if indicating a type of land, *moyootj* (swamp country). See Whitehurst, *Noongar Dictionary*, p. 19.

86 Probably the bulbs from a species of *Haemodorum*, or bloodroot, which are bright red when alive and turn black when dead; the bloodroots are related to the kangaroo paws *Anigozanthos* and *Macropidia*. The species whose spicy-tasting roots the Noongar of Geographe Bay preferred to eat was *Haemodorum spicatum*, known in local dialects as *borana* or *bohn* – see Stephen D. Hopper and Hans Lambers, 'Human relationships with and use of kwongkan plants and lands', in *Plant Life on the Sandplains in Southwest Australia: A Global Biodiversity Hotspot*, ed. Hans Lambers (Crawley: University of Western Australia Publishing, 2014), pp. 290–94.

87 [*Author's note*] I was later told that larger ones had been seen, though these were scarcely constructed any better.

88 [*Author's note*] Citizen Bailly, mineralogist on the *Naturaliste*, told me that he found several fish-traps at the edge of the river. These are semi-circular recesses. Several are placed side by side, separated only by a small, narrow space through which the fish can

enter, but from which they cannot escape once they have done so. He maintained that these fish-traps, made with sticks driven into the ground, were skilfully constructed. Dampier also records seeing fish-traps in Shark Bay, on the western coast of New Holland.

89 [*Author's note*] Having had the opportunity to study these people more closely, I have learnt that they draw their small boats up into the woods. Such is the skill with which they wield their spears, these become fearsome weapons in their hands and are as deadly as the arrows used by other savage peoples.

90 According to Péron, during this walk Leschenault 'felt so unwell due to the wretched effects of the food we had eaten that he could not keep up; he fell down repeatedly, uttering profound sighs, and appeared to be in great agony' (*Voyage de découvertes, Historique*, vol. 1, p. 94).

91 A dead sea otter was purchased by Cook's crew in Nootka Sound in the Pacific Northwest in April 1788 and was drawn by the expedition's artist John Webber (1751–1793) – see James Cook and James King, *A Voyage to the Pacific Ocean; Undertaken by Command of His Majesty, for Making Discoveries in the Northern Hemisphere: Performed under the Direction of Captains Cook, Clerke, and Gore, in the Years 1776, 1777, 1778, 1779, and 1780*, 4 vol. (London: Stockdale, Scatcherd, Whitaker, Fielding and Hardy, 1784), vol. 2, pp. 234–35, and plate (between those pages). Leschenault used the French translation, which Baudin had in his shipboard library: *Troisième Voyage de Cook, ou Voyage à l'Océan Pacifique, ordonné par le Roi d'Angleterre, pour faire des découvertes dans l'Hémisphère Nord*, trans. J. N. Demeunier, 4 vol. (Paris: Hôtel de Thou, 1785), *Cartes et figures*, pl. 43.

92 The Dutch explorers Dirk Hartog and Willem de Vlamingh had previously encountered these islands. The smaller of the northern islands was renamed Bernier Island by Louis Freycinet, after the expedition's astronomer Pierre-François Bernier (1779–1803), who died at sea on the night of 5 June 1803.

93 The plant which Dampier collected at Shark Bay and called *Dammara* (comparing it to plants collected by Georg Eberhard Rumphius (1627–1702) on Ambon Island in the Moluccas) is now known as *Beaufortia sprengelioides* de Candolle (Craven). Like *Melaleuca*, it belongs to the family Myrtaceae. See William Dampier, *A Voyage to New Holland, etc. in the Year 1699* (London: Knapton, 1703), p. 158, and tab. 3 (French translation: *Voyage aux terres australes, à la Nouvelle Hollande, etc., fait en 1699*, 4 vol. (Paris: Machuel, 1722), vol. 4, p. 142 and plate), and George Seddon, *The Old Country: Australian Landscapes, Plants and People* (Cambridge: Cambridge University Press, 2005), p. 33.

94 Robert Brown, after visiting the Sherardian Herbarium in Oxford to examine the specimen drawn in tab. 3, fig. 3, of Dampier's *Voyage*, and having also studied specimens brought back from Shark Bay by the Baudin expedition, placed this plant in a new genus *Diplolaena*; it was subsequently classified as *Diplolaena grandiflora* by René Desfontaines in 1817, who consulted Leschenault's specimens from Shark Bay. See Robert Brown, 'General remarks, geographical and systematical, on the botany of *Terra Australis*', in Matthew Flinders, *A Voyage to Terra Australis: Undertaken for the*

Purpose of Completing the Discovery of that Vast Country, and Prosecuted in the Years 1801, 1802 and 1803, 2 vol. and atlas (London: Nicol, 1814), vol. 2, p. 546, and Seddon, *The Old Country*, p. 33.

95 The banded hare-wallaby, *Lagostrophus fasciatus* (Péron and Lesueur, 1807); see Péron, *Voyage de découvertes, Historique*, vol. 1, pp. 114–18, and *Atlas*, pl. 27.

96 [*Author's note*] The belly of the kangaroo is very large in proportion to the rest of its body; the intestinal canal is extremely long and very broad.

97 This is a species of spiny-tailed gecko, *Strophurus spinigerus spinigerus* (Gray, 1842), *Strophurus rankini* (Storr, 1979) or *Strophurus strophurus* (Duméril and Bibron, 1836); all excrete a black liquid from their tails as a defence mechanism.

98 This lizard was named *Scincus tropisurus* by Péron; it is now known as the northern bobtail (*Tiliqua rugosa palarra*, Shea, 2000). Dampier found the same type of lizard on Dirk Hartog Island in 1699 and referred to it as the 'guano' (a variant spelling of 'iguana'), comparing it to a lizard he had found in 1682 on Blanquilla Island in the Caribbean Sea. See Dampier, *A Voyage to New Holland*, pp. 123-24, Péron, *Voyage de découvertes, Historique*, vol. 1, p. 118, and Alex S. George, *William Dampier in New Holland: Australia's First Natural Historian* (Melbourne: Bloomings Books, 1999), p. 132.

99 Leschenault may be referring to the 'beautiful' lizard, '4 to 5 feet long', that Péron recorded finding on Bernier Island and named *Tupinambis endrachtensis* (Péron, *Voyage de découvertes, Historique*, vol. 1, p. 118). This is the sand goanna *Varanus gouldii* (Gray, 1838). Leschenault appears to have added the sentence containing the genus name '*Gouanaea*' at a later date, perhaps after discussion with British naturalists in Sydney. Dampier's 'guano', along with 'guana', 'gohanna' and 'goanna', are all variant spellings of 'iguana'. On the lizards of Bernier Island, see G. M. Storr and G. Harold, 'Herpetofauna of the Shark Bay region, Western Australia', *Records of the Western Australian Museum* 6/4 (1978), pp. 449–67.

100 The date is missing in the manuscript. The *Géographe* weighed anchor on 23 Messidor [12 July 1801].

101 In the copy he made of his brother's manuscript, Samuel Leschenault also left the date blank – but later inserted '3 Thermidor, Year IX' [22 July 1801].

102 After rounding North West Cape, Baudin sighted what he believed to be Willem's River south of the Cape Range. A river had been placed there on a seventeenth-century Dutch chart but did not in fact exist in that location.

103 Péron gave it the name Depuch Island in his published account. Called Warmalana by the Ngarluma people, it is home to thousands of rock engravings. When Ronsard went ashore, he saw no sign of human habitation apart from two burnt tree trunks and some recently broken rocks.

104 [*Author's note*] Since then we have learnt that the natives of New Holland deliberately set fire to the great forests in which they live in order to clear away bushes and grasses that impede them.

105 1 Fructidor [19 August 1801].

Chapter 4: Timor

106 Hans Andries Lofsteth, *commissaris* (commissioner), temporary commander of Dutch Timor from 1800 until his death in office on 10 October 1802. Under the Dutch East India Company (*Vereenigde Oostindische Compagnie* or VOC), the permanent commander or chief agent usually went by the title of *opperhoofd* (commander); after the dissolution of the VOC in 1799–1800, the term *resident* was used instead.

107 Willem Adriaan van Este (1735–1789) had served as acting *opperhoofd* of Dutch Timor from 1766 to 1767 and then as *opperhoofd* proper from 1777 to 1789. The mutiny aboard HMS *Bounty* took place on 28 April 1789 near the Pacific island of Tofua; its commander William Bligh (1754–1817) was set adrift in a small boat with 18 crew and they sailed some 6700 kilometres west to Kupang, which they reached on 14 June. Bligh describes his meeting with van Este in his *A Narrative of the Mutiny, on Board His Majesty's Ship Bounty, and the Subsequent Voyage of Part of the Crew, in the Ship's Boat, from Tofoa, One of the Friendly Islands, to Timor, a Dutch Settlement in the East Indies* (Dublin: White, Byrne, Moore, Jones, Dornin and Grueber, 1790), pp. 131–33.

108 Threatened by Royal Navy warships that had arrived from the Moluccas, the Dutch *opperhoofd* Timotheus Wanjon surrendered Kupang on 10 June 1797. The town was then occupied by a small garrison of sepoys, who came under attack the following day from Timorese fighters. A number of soldiers were killed and their severed heads were reportedly carried off into the interior. After the British retreated to their ships, they bombarded the town, damaging the fort and many houses, and the Timorese plundered the ruins. See Steve Farram, 'Jacobus Arnoldus Hazaart and the British interregnum in Netherlands Timor, 1812–1816', *Bijdragen tot de taal-, land- en volkenkunde* 163/4 (2008), pp. 458–60.

109 Leschenault uses 'latanier' as a general term for palm trees.

110 The French naturalist Jacques-Christophe Valmont de Bomare (1731–1807) published several works on mineralogy and natural history in the 1750s and 1760s. On what he calls the roussette, that is, the large flying fox *Pteropus vampyrus* (Linnaeus, 1758), see his *Dictionnaire raisonné universel d'histoire naturelle*, 4th edn, 15 vol. (Lyon: Bruyset frères, 1791), vol. 3, p. 316.

111 The 40-gun frigate the *Virginie*, laid down in Brest in 1794, was captured by Sir Edward Pellew in HMS *Indefatigable* in April 1796 after a 15-hour chase from the Lizard, Cornwall, to Ushant, and a lengthy night-time action. The vessel was recommissioned by the Royal Navy as HMS *Virginie* and served in the East Indies, West Indies and western Europe before being converted to a receiving ship in 1811.

112 The piastre was the name given to the Spanish *peso duro*, piece of eight, or dollar. One pound *poids de marc* was equivalent to around 490 grams. The picul was an Asian measure of weight, deriving from the weight a person could carry on a shoulder-pole; the picul varied from region to region, but was roughly equivalent to 60 kilograms.

113 Leschenault cites the French translation; for the English original, see Cook and King, *A Voyage to the Pacific Ocean*, vol. 3, p. 312.

114 [*Author's note*] *Nota*. It seems that the Malays have had some dealings with the inhabitants of New Holland, for they are quite familiar with them and call them *orang talandian*, naked men.

115 On page 80 of the manuscript, there are two red marks indicating where a piece of paper containing this note had been stuck in; this piece of paper is now missing. The text of the note was preserved in the copy of the journal made by Samuel Leschenault and in Péron and Freycinet, *Voyage de découvertes, Historique*, vol. 2, p. 262.

116 A Malay word also spelt *coracora*, *kora kora*, etc.

117 [*Author's note*] I possess one of these gold crescents from Timor.

118 The last two lines of this paragraph were a later addition by Leschenault. In various Indonesian languages the word *kuni* and similar forms refer to turmeric rather than the spice saffron. In Malay, 'turmeric' is *kunyit*; *negri* (also *negeri*) means 'village', *hutan* 'forest'. Turmeric was also known to Euopeans as 'Indian saffron'. False saffron, or safflower, is *Carthamus tinctorius*. See Waruno Mahdi, *Malay Words and Malay Things: Lexical Souvenirs from an Exotic Archipelago in German Publications before 1700* (Wiesbaden: Harrassowitz Verlag, 2007), pp. 159-63, and Ritsuko Kikusawa and Lawrence A. Reid, 'Proto who utilised turmeric, and how?', in *Language Description, History and Development: Linguistic Indulgence in Memory of Terry Crowley*, ed. Jeff Siegel, John Lynch and Diana Eades (Amsterdam: John Benjamins Publishing, 2007), pp. 341–54.

119 Leschenault uses the French term *sou* (one-twentieth of a franc) as an equivalent for the Dutch term *stuiver* (one-twentieth of a guilder in the Netherlands, but one-sixteenth of a guilder in the Indies). The Dutch rix-dollar (*rijksdaalder*), equivalent to 48 *stuivers* or 3 guilders, was similar in value to the Spanish piastre, mentioned in note 112.

120 See Valmont de Bomare, *Dictionnaire raisonné d'histoire naturelle*, vol. 2, pp. 871–72. Ernst Christoph Barchewitz (1687–1758), a tanner from near Erfurt in central Germany, joined the Dutch East India Company as a soldier and sailed for Batavia in April 1711. He was posted in 1714 to the island of Leti, to the north-east of Timor, as its administrator and remained there until 1720. He published a detailed account of his travels in 1730 under the title *Allerneueste und wahrhaffte Ost-Indianische Reise-Beschreibung* (Most Recent and Reliable East Indian Travel Account), which he expanded and republished in new editions in later years. For his observations on the cuscus, see *Neu-vermehrte Ost-Indianische Reise-Beschreibung* (Erfurt: Jungnicol, 1751), p. 532.

121 The Swedish naturalist Carl Peter Thunberg (1743–1828), one of Linnaeus's disciples, joined the Dutch East India Company and travelled to South Africa and Asia to make collections of natural history. He encountered the insect which he named *Lampyris japonica* during his stay in Japan in 1775–1776 – see his *Dissertatio entomologica: novas insectorum species*, part 4 (Uppsala: Edman, 1784), pp. 79–80.

122 For the 'Malay vocabulary' compiled by Labillardière in Ambon and Java, see his *Relation du voyage à la recherche de La Pérouse*, vol. 2, 'Vocabulaires', pp. 5–43.

123 [*Author's note*] *Nota*. As the list I have compiled could be useful if we visit the Moluccas or other parts of the Indies, I have not included it with the journal I am sending back to France.

NOTES

124　Baudin may have had a copy of a report written by the naval officer François Étienne de Rosily-Mesros (1748–1832), who visited north-eastern Timor in 1772 aboard the *Gros Ventre*, commanded by Saint-Allouarn. Rosily's account of his stay and his 417-word vocabulary, which contains words from a variety of languages including Makasai, Galoli, Tetum, Portuguese and Malay, were copied into the registers of the Académie royale de marine in 1773 or 1774. Baudin possessed a copy of Rosily's map of Timor – see *The Journal of Post Captain Nicolas Baudin*, p. 573, Anne Lombard-Jordan, 'Un mémoire inédit de F. E. de Rosily sur l'île de Timor (1772)', *Archipel* 23 (1982), pp. 75–104, and Luis Thomaz, 'Note sur le « Dictionnaire françois et timorien » de F. E. de Rosily', *Archipel* 23 (1982), pp. 105–108.

125　These Chinese characters are written by Leschenault in a rather shaky hand. The name is likely to have been, in modern romanisation, Zhang Yangnan (Mandarin) or Dijong Yangnam (Cantonese), but Leschenault appears to have inserted a faulty version of the character 'ken'(肯), with the hook in the base incorrectly turned outward, in place of the more likely third character 'nan' (南).

126　This copy of Leschenault's letter to Baudin appears on a separate sheet of paper that has been stuck into the journal.

127　The text of this letter, with minor variants, can also be found in Baudin's edited journal – see Baudin, *Mon voyage aux terres australes*, p. 368.

128　Henri Freycinet rather than his brother Louis.

129　Having travelled with Cook's third expedition to the Pacific, David Nelson was selected by Joseph Banks to serve as the botanist on Bligh's voyage on the *Bounty* to collect breadfruit trees from Tahiti. After suffering illness during the long journey in an open boat from Tofua to Timor, Nelson died in Kupang on 20 July 1789. Nelson's funeral was well attended and Bligh recorded that 'the body was interred behind the chapel, in the burying-ground appropriated to the Europeans of the town. I was sorry I could get no tombstone to place over his remains' (Bligh, *A Narrative of the Mutiny*, p. 140).

Chapter 5: Van Diemen's Land and Western Port

130　The chapter heading in the manuscript contains the crossed-out words 'Port Jackson; description of [*illegible words*] private citizens'. Some details of this visit are discussed in Letter 6.

131　[*Author's note*] The steep contours of this coast suggest that the swell coming from the *south* breaks against it with great force.

132　Captain James Cook (1728–1779) was stabbed to death on 14 February 1779 in a dispute with local inhabitants at Kealakekua Bay on Hawaii Island. The ships commanded by Jean-François de Galaup, comte de La Pérouse (1741–1788?), sank off Vanikoro, one of the Solomon Islands, after leaving Port Jackson in March 1788; his fate was not learnt until 1826. Paul Antoine Fleuriot de Langle (1744–1787) was the second-in-command on La Pérouse's expedition; he died in an encounter with a group of Samoans on the island of Tutuila. Antoine Bruni d'Entrecasteaux (1737–1793), leader of the expedition sent in search of La Pérouse, died of scurvy in the Bismarck Archipelago off New Guinea. Marc-Joseph Marion du Fresne (1724–1772) led an expedition from the Isle of France to explore the south Pacific and was killed by Maori in the Bay of Islands, New Zealand. Robert de Lamanon (1752–1787), a naturalist on La Pérouse's expedition, died in the same confrontation as Fleuriot de Langle.

133 On these genera, see James Edward Smith, *A Specimen of the Botany of New Holland*, 4 parts (London: Sowerby, 1793–1795), part 1, pp. 15–16, 45–49.

134 Leschenault probably drew this word from the vocabulary list compiled by Labillardière, where it is, however, spelt *quangloua* – see Labillardière, *Relation du voyage à la recherche de La Pérouse*, vol. 2, 'Vocabularies', p. 46 (Vocabulary of the savages of Cape Diemen).

135 Petit's portrait of this man, called Ouriaga, appeared in the first volume of the *Atlas*, published in 1807, fig. 9.

136 [*Author's note*] They may have had contact with the crews of the ships commanded by Monsieur d'Entrecasteaux; in any case the English have often visited this passage.

137 See Labillardière, *Relation du voyage à la recherche de La Pérouse*, vol. 1, pp. 127 and 167, and *Atlas*, pl. 5, 'Savages of Cape Diemen preparing their meal', and pl. 9, fig. 3 and 4.

138 Labillardière published his description of *Mazeutoxeron rufum* in 1800 in his *Relation du voyage à la recherche de La Pérouse,* vol. 2, pp. 11–12, with an illustration in the *Atlas*, pl. 17; the English botanist Henry Cranke Andrews had previously described *Correa alba* in volume 1 of *The Botanist's Repository, for New, and Rare Plants* (London: Bensley, 1797), pl. 18.

139 Péron quotes this paragraph and the following one in the *Voyage de découvertes, Historique*, vol. 1, pp. 238–39.

140 On the seeds sent to Joséphine Bonaparte, see Letters 6 and 7.

141 10 Pluviôse [30 January] – see *The Journal of Post Captain Nicolas Baudin*, pp. 319–23.

142 This letter was perhaps an early draft of the one dated 20 Brumaire, Year XI [11 November 1802] which Leschenault sent to Jussieu from Sydney with the journal – see Letter 6.

143 After only three weeks in Sydney, and without waiting for Baudin to arrive there in the *Géographe*, Hamelin, captain of the *Naturaliste*, set off for the Isle of France on 17 May 1802. The vessel ran into foul weather and contrary winds off Van Diemen's Land and, low on supplies, Hamelin was forced to turn around. The *Naturaliste* arrived back in Sydney on 28 June.

144 Leschenault pointed out in Chapter 1 that the weather conditions during Prairial in the southern hemisphere corresponded rather with those of Frimaire in the northern.

145 [*Author's note*] There is a remarkable difference between the hair of the inhabitants of New Holland and that of the inhabitants of Van Diemen's Land. The former have long hair like the people of the Moluccas, while the latter have woolly hair like the blacks of the African coast. This difference is all the more extraordinary as Van Diemen's Land is separated from the coast of New Holland only by Bass Strait and there is no other land nearby.

146 François Collas, whose position was also described as that of 'pharmacist'; he transferred to the *Géographe* in Port Jackson on 3 November 1802.

NOTES

147 The vessel was in fact called the *Sydney Cove*. It began to founder in stormy weather en route from Calcutta to Sydney and was grounded by its captain on Preservation Island on 9 February 1797. The 17 men who set out for Sydney in the ship's longboat were wrecked on what is now known as Ninety Mile Beach in Victoria, and were forced to try and make their way on foot from there to Sydney. They were generally helped by local Indigenous peoples but also had some hostile encounters. Just three men survived the 11-week journey. Eight of the other survivors who had remained behind on Preservation Island perished when the sloop *Eliza*, one of the rescue vessels sent out from Sydney, was wrecked on its return leg. The schooner the *Entreprise*, mentioned by Leschenault in the following note, was captained by Alexandre Josselin Lecorre (1766–1802) and sank near the Sister Islands on 27 October 1802. Leschenault must have added this note after the date he records completing the manuscript (2 September 1802) and not long before the manuscript was put aboard the *Naturaliste* for the return trip to France.

148 [*Author's note*] Shipwrecks are already common in Bass Strait. In addition to our discoveries, the English captain, Flinders, said that he found several pieces of wreckage around King Island, and we have just learnt that the French schooner the *Entreprise*, which left Port Jackson around a month before us to hunt seals in the strait, was wrecked on the Two Sisters, small islands to the north-east of the Furneaux Islands. Captain Lecorre, whom I had met in Port Jackson, perished with five other men. The rest of the crew managed to reach the island and some were picked up by a small English schooner.

149 The French named this island Île des Français, or French Island.

150 [*Author's note*] Having gained a greater understanding of the customs of these people, I have reason to believe that when they invited us to accompany them unarmed and unclothed into the depths of the forest they were instigating some piece of treachery, and fled when I appeared because they thought that we had discovered their aim and I was giving Citizen Milius a box containing weapons.

151 [*Author's note*] I wrote these observations before I arrived in Port Jackson.

152 In this volume Cook describes encounters with the Gweagal people at Botany Bay and the Guugu Yimithirr people at Endeavour River between April and July 1770. Leschenault used the French translation: John Hawkesworth, ed., *Relation des voyages entrepris par ordre de Sa Majesté britannique, actuellement régnante, pour faire des découvertes dans l'hémisphère méridional*, 4 vol. (Paris: Saillant and Nyon, 1774), vol. 4, pp. 18–59, 116–36. For the English original, see *An Account of the Voyages Undertaken by the Order of His Present Majesty*, vol. 3, pp. 153–84, 227–42.

153 [*Author's note*] Unlike the inhabitants of D'Entrecasteaux Channel, they have long hair; a very remarkable characteristic, as I have said before.

154 See Hawkesworth, ed., *Relation des voyages entrepris par ordre de Sa Majesté britannique*, vol. 4, p. 43; *An Account of the Voyages Undertaken by the Order of His Present Majesty*, vol. 3, pp. 172–73.

155 [*Author's note*] I now consider this observation to be wrong because the natives who live around Port Jackson, and who must be very similar to these people, do not have

chiefs. They show respect only for their doctors, whom they view as sorcerers, and for the most renowned warriors, but this homage derives from fear and terror and not from a sense of loyalty.

156 This island, known as Corriong or Millowl in the Boonwurrung language, was named Snapper Island, then Grant Island, and finally Phillip Island by the British. It appears on Freycinet's map of Western Port under the name Île des Anglais, or English Island.

157 The English naturalist John Latham (1740–1837) described the Tabuan parrot, named for the island of Tongatapu (or 'Tonga-Tabu'), in *A General Synopsis of Birds*, 3 vol. (London: White, 1781–1785), vol. 1, p. 214, and pl. 7. It was thought that the same species of parrot occurred in New South Wales, as indicated in *The Voyage of Governor Phillip to Botany Bay*, p. 153, and plate; the Australian bird was later called the king parrot (*Alisterus scapularis*).

158 See Robert de Lamanon's essay, 'Mémoire sur les térébratules ou poulettes, et description d'une espèce trouvée dans les mers de la Tartarie orientale', in Milet-Mureau, *Voyage de La Pérouse autour du monde*, vol. 4, pp. 116–33.

Appendix: A Note on the Macpas; Information about Madagascar

159 Perhaps the Makpa people of what is now eastern Nigeria, who, as C. K. Meek records, were said to have occupied 'the hill country round Kentu' (near Bissaula) at the beginning of the nineteenth century (*Tribal Studies in Northern Nigeria*, 2 vol., London: Kegan Paul, 1931, vol. 2, p. 606).

160 [*Author's note*] This name means 'complete and lasting happiness'.

161 The Makpa boy dubbed not 'Morlot' but 'Merlot' by the botanist André Michaux, in what must have been intended as a reference to his skin colour (*merlot* referring to the young blackbird rather than the grape), left the Baudin expedition at the Isle of France on 20 April 1801. Michaux and he travelled to Madagascar, probably in mid-1802, where they established a garden near Toamasina in the north-east of the island. Michaux intended to start exporting tropical plants to France but contracted a fever and died on 11 October 1802. Bognam-nonen-derega sought to leave Madagascar after Michaux's death, but was refused permission by Zakavolo (ruler of the Betsimisaraka people from 1791 to 1803) on the grounds that a black man could leave the island only when he was sold. He seems to have continued working as a gardener for the nobility at Foulpointe (Mahavelona) until the fall of Zakavolo in 1803, when he was sold as a slave – to the dismay of Michaux's son (see Charlie Williams, Eliane M. Norman and Walter Kingsley Taylor, eds, *André Michaux in North America: Journal and Letters, 1785–1797* (Tuscaloosa: University of Alabama Press, 2020), pp. 340–44). Leschenault refers to Bognam-nonen-derega again in an article published in 1810, 'Mémoire sur le *Strychnos tieute* et l'*Antiaris toxicaria*', *Annales du Muséum d'histoire naturelle* 16 (1810), pp. 459–82 (pp. 463–65), in which he alludes to the Makpa youth's knowledge of poisons.

162 The astronomer and traveller Guillaume Le Gentil (1725–1792) had recorded eating *chien marron* (brown dog) on the Coromandel Coast during his stay in India

in 1768–1769, observing: 'I am not sure whether this animal, which I have eaten myself, is a dog or a sheep [...]. Brown dog is not a very refined dish; it is however the ordinary mutton of the region, or it at least takes the place of this; and I have sometimes eaten some very good examples of it. When brown dog has been nicely fattened, it is very tender and I would have it in preference to three-quarters of the mutton eaten in Paris. It has exactly the same taste' (*Voyage dans les mers de l'Inde, fait par ordre du roi à l'occasion du passage de Vénus sur le disque du soleil le 6 juin 1761 et le 3 du même mois 1769*, 2 vol. (Paris: Imprimerie royale, 1779–1781), vol. 1, p. 315). Le Gentil suggests that this is the same species of animal as the dog which James Cook observed the Tahitians eating; whether it was in fact a type of dog or sheep Le Gentil left up to naturalists to resolve.

163 The nut, sometimes called clove nutmeg, is from the plant named *Ravensara aromatica* by Pierre Sonnerat and now known as *Cryptocarya agathophylla* van der Werff. The genus *Agathophyllum* appears in Jussieu's *Genera plantarum* of 1789.

164 André-Julien, Comte Dupuy (1753–1832), *intendant* of the Isle of France from 1789 to 1798. The *intendant* was an administrator who oversaw the finances and the legal system on the island; he worked alongside the governor general of the Mascarene Islands, who was the military chief in the region. Dupuy was recalled to France in late 1800 and was involved in negotiations for the Treaty of Amiens in 1802. He was later civil governor of the French colonies in India from 1816 to 1825, where Leschenault encountered him once more.

SELECTED LETTERS

1 Joseph Pitton de Tournefort (1656–1708), a professor of botany at the Jardin des plantes in Paris from 1683, published his book *Éléments de botanique ou méthode pour connaître les plantes* (Elements of Botany or Method for Understanding Plants) in 1694. In it he divided plants into 22 classes based on the form of their corollas; it remained an influential work for many decades.

2 Magny-en-Vexin lay some 60 kilometres to the north-west of Paris along the main coach road to Rouen.

3 Augustin Pyramus de Candolle (1778–1841), a Swiss botanist, had moved in 1798 from Geneva to Paris, where he published his *Plantarum historia succulentum* in 1799 and made the acquaintance of leading French botanists. He was appointed professor of botany at the University of Montpellier in 1807 and devoted much of his career to developing a natural method of plant classification.

4 Charles-François Brisseau de Mirbel (1776–1854), after several quarrels with the revolutionary authorities, fled Paris for the south of France, where he studied botany under Louis Ramond, baron de Carbonnières, and conducted field work in the Pyrenees. On his return to Paris in 1798, Mirbel worked as assistant naturalist at the Muséum d'histoire naturelle. In 1803 he was appointed director of the gardens of the Château de Malmaison and in 1806 took up the position of secretary to King Louis Napoléon of Holland. He later worked at the Ministry of the Interior under

the Restoration and as a director of the Muséum d'histoire naturelle. He published numerous articles and books on the classification and anatomy of plants and made important observations about the membranes of plant cells. See Anselme Payen, *Éloge historique de M. de Mirbel* (Paris: Imprimerie et librairie d'agriculture et d'horticulture Mme Veuve Bouchard-Huzard, 1858), and Peter F. Stevens, *The Development of Biological Systematics: Antoine-Laurent de Jussieu, Nature and the Natural System* (New York: Columbia University Press, 1994), pp. 72–79.

5   Brown to Banks, 3 May 1802, cited in Brown, *Nature's Investigator*, p. 206.
6   Brown, *Prodromus*, p. 581.
7   I am grateful to Yasmin Haskell for translating the Latin text into English.
8   The four notebooks are now in the Muséum national d'histoire naturelle, Paris. For the images, Latin descriptions and translations into French, see Théodore Leschenault, *Les Carnets botaniques*, ed. Michel Jangoux, Viviane Desmet and Claude Lefebvre, the Baudin Legacy Project, https://baudin.sydney.edu.au, consulted 1 June 2020.
9   By rejecting the *esprit systématique* (systematic mentality), Leschenault endorses empiricism over rationalism, observation over *a priori* systems, Jussieu's 'natural method' of classification over Linnaeus's 'artificial system'. See the Introduction, pp. 33–34.
10 The Swedish naturalist Daniel Solander (1733–1782) studied botany under Linnaeus at Uppsala University and afterwards took up a position at the library of the British Museum cataloguing its natural history collections. He accompanied Banks on Cook's first voyage to the Pacific and, although he published little, left many plant descriptions in manuscript form. Jonas Carlsson Dryander (1748–1810), a Swedish botanist, also studied under Linnaeus, and served as librarian to Banks and to the Royal Society. He published a paper on Australian plants in 1806. Leschenault makes reference in his journal to the new genera described by James Edward Smith in *A Specimen of the Botany of New Holland* of 1793–1795. Dryander and Smith never visited Australia.
11 William Paterson (1755–1810), army officer and lieutenant governor of New South Wales, was a keen naturalist. He had explored the interior of southern Africa between 1777 and 1779, published *A Narrative of Four Journeys into the Country of the Hottentots, and Caffraria* in 1789, and been elected to the Royal Society in 1798. He was sent to Van Diemen's Land in 1804 to found a settlement there, with the aim of obstructing rumoured French plans for the island, but was obliged to return to New South Wales in 1809 after the rebellious army corps deposed Governor Bligh. After ordering Bligh's departure, he administered New South Wales for eight months until the new governor, Lachlan Macquarie, arrived with his own regiment. Paterson left New South Wales, accompanied by the army corps, in May 1810 and died at sea off Cape Horn on 21 June.
12 After initially teaching himself about botany, George Caley (1770–1829) received training in various botanical gardens before being sent out to New South Wales as a plant collector by Banks. He arrived in the colony in April 1800, where his salary was paid by Banks and he received provisions and a cottage in Parramatta from

the government. Caley collected plants with the help of local Indigenous people, collaborated with Robert Brown and explored Western Port and the Blue Mountains; he never published the results of his work. Caley returned to England in 1810 and held the position of curator of the Saint Vincent botanic gardens in the West Indies between 1815 and 1822.

13   Baudin had decided that the *Naturaliste* would sail from Sydney back to France with exhausted expedition members and various collections rather than continue with the exploration of the Australian coast. Leschenault emphasises the point that, had the *Naturaliste* remained in Australian waters, he would have preferred to sail with its captain, Hamelin, rather than on the *Géographe* with Baudin, whom he found less congenial.

14   Two of the botanical staff from the *Géographe* had died: the gardener Anselme Riedlé in Timor on 21 October 1801 and the assistant gardener Antoine Sautier at sea, en route from Timor to Van Diemen's Land, on 15 November 1801. Those from the *Naturaliste* had all abandoned the expedition at the Isle of France in April 1801: the botanist André Michaux, along with his assistant Jacques Delisse, and the assistant gardeners François Cagnet and Merlot (Bognam-nonen-derega). Only the teenage assistant gardener Antoine Guichenot remained with Leschenault on the expedition.

15   This is a tree which Leschenault found near D'Entrecasteaux Channel and named *Bonapartea laureata* (see Leschenault, *Les Carnets botaniques*, p. 20). He described its leaves as having a laurel-like smell (hence the specific name) and its seeds as being acrid with a smell between cardamom and cloves. It is now known as the mountain pepper tree, *Tasmannia lanceolata* (Poir.) A.C.Sm.

16   Elizabeth Paterson (1770–1839), née Driver, was born in Montrose, Scotland, where her parents ran a tavern. She married Captain William Paterson, also a native of Montrose, in 1789 and sailed with him for Sydney in 1791 with the third fleet of convicts. She was admired for her intelligence and sociability. In 1800, she was involved in founding a school in Sydney for orphan girls and from 1805 to 1808 lived at the new settlement of Port Dalrymple in northern Van Diemen's Land. She left New South Wales in 1810 with her husband, who died on the voyage back to England. She remarried in 1814 but was widowed again six weeks later.

17   Benjamin Smith Barton (1766–1815), botanist and professor of *materia medica* at the University of Pennsylvania, author of the first American textbook on botany.

18   David Erskine, 2nd Baron Erskine (1776–1855), British minister to the United States from 1806 to 1809.

19   Éleuthère Irénée du Pont de Nemours (1771–1834), after troubles with the revolutionary authorities in France, decided to move with his family to the United States, where he arrived in 1800. In 1802 he set up a gunpowder factory near Wilmington, Delaware, drawing on expertise in chemistry he had gained while working under Antoine-Laurent de Lavoisier at the Arsenal in Paris and at the government gunpowder works at Essonne. His company (a forerunner of E. I. du Pont de Nemours and Co.) became highly profitable, especially when demand for gunpowder rose during the War of 1812.

20 The botanist Mirbel, whom Leschenault had met at the Muséum d'histoire naturelle (see Letter 4, n. 4), was appointed first secretary to King Louis of Holland on 2 October 1806. Louis Bonaparte, younger brother of the emperor Napoléon, had been installed on the throne in June 1806 when the Batavian Commonwealth was reorganised as the Kingdom of Holland.

21 René Louiche Desfontaines (1750–1833) developed an interest in botany while studying medicine in Paris and was admitted to the Académie des sciences at a young age. In 1783, he left for north Africa and spent two years collecting plants and animals in Tunisia and Algeria. He was appointed professor of botany at the Jardin du roi in 1786 and he retained his position as the institution was remoulded as the Muséum d'histoire naturelle during the Revolution. His publications include *Flora Atlantica* (1798–1799), a paper on the structure of monocotyledons, several catalogues of the botanic garden in Paris, and a history of tree cultivation in France; he also published a book on ornithology. See Jean-Marc Drouin, 'Collecte, observation et classification chez René Desfontaines (1750–1833)', in *Le Muséum au premier siècle de son histoire*, ed. Claude Blanckaert, Claudine Cohen, Pietro Corsi and Jean-Louis Fischer (Paris: Éditions du Muséum national d'histoire naturelle, 1997), pp. 263–76.

22 William Jackson Hooker (1785–1865), an English botanist, visited Paris with his friend and employer Dawson Turner (1775–1858), banker and botanist, and Turner's family; there the two men met Jussieu, Desfontaines and Lamarck. The following year Hooker married Turner's eldest daughter Maria. With the support of Banks, Hooker was appointed professor of botany at the University of Glasgow in 1820; he became the first full-time director of Kew Gardens in 1841 and oversaw its development as the national botanic garden. Turner was an expert on algae, mosses and lichens, and published *A Synopsis of British Fuci* in 1802; in later years he turned his attentions to antiquities, pictures and manuscripts. See Joseph Dalton Hooker, *A Sketch of the Life and Labours of Sir William Jackson Hooker, Late Director of the Royal Gardens of Kew* (Cambridge: Cambridge University Press, 1903), p. xxii, and Sylvia FitzGerald, 'Hooker, Sir William Jackson', and Angus Fraser, 'Turner, Dawson', *Oxford Dictionary of National Biography*, www.oxforddnb.com, consulted 20 April 2020.

23 André Thouin (1747–1824) was born at the Jardin du roi, son of the head gardener Gabriel, whose position he took over in 1764. Thouin greatly expanded the garden, published a range of works on agronomy, grafting, and the cultivation of exotic plants – and also composed the instructions on acclimatising plants for La Pérouse's expedition. During the Revolution he held various political positions and was appointed professor at the Muséum in 1793.

24 In his account, Dampier provided illustrations of eight plants from north-western Australia (and an additional two incorrectly identified as coming from that region) – see Dampier, *Voyage to New Holland*, pp. 156–60 and tab. 2–4, George, *William Dampier in New Holland*, p. 26, and note 93 to the journal, above.

25 Common name: coastal coppercups; first described by Labillardière in *Novae Hollandiae plantarum specimen*, 2 vol. (Paris: Huzard, 1804–1806), vol. 2, p. 11 and tab. 149.

26 Common name: Albany pitcher plant; first described by Labillardière in *Novae Hollandiae plantarum specimen*, vol. 2, p. 7 and tab. 145.
27 Jules Paul Benjamin Delessert (1773–1847), son of the banker Étienne Delessert (1735–1816), served as an artillery officer in the French army before taking up a position at his father's bank in 1795. He pursued a wide range of commercial ventures, establishing a cotton factory, a sugar refinery and the savings bank Caisse d'Épargne. He served nine terms in the French parliament between 1815 and 1842 and was an advocate for humane causes such as the abolition of the death penalty and the amelioration of foundling hospitals and prisons. A keen naturalist, he used his wealth to amass some of the largest collections of plants and shells in Europe, along with a library of 30,000 books. On his herbarium, see Thierry Hoquet, 'Botanical authority: Benjamin Delessert's collections between travellers and Candolle's natural method', *Isis* 105/3 (2014), pp. 508–39.
28 Following the death of Nicolaas Burman (1734–1793), who was professor of botany at the University of Amsterdam, Delessert acquired his herbarium of 29,000 specimens in 1800. The collection had been begun by Nicolaas's father, Johannes Burman (1707–1780), who had preceded Nicolaas as professor of botany. See Mary Gunn and L. E. Codd, *Botanical Exploration of Southern Africa* (Cape Town: Balkema, 1981), p. 266.
29 Jean-Vincent-Félix Lamouroux (1779–1825) studied the natural sciences at the École centrale in Agen, south-east of Bordeaux, and, while employed as a designer and commercial traveller for his father's calico printworks, published papers on aloes and seaweeds. He moved to Paris in 1808 to study medicine and made the acquaintance of leading naturalists. In 1809 he was appointed adjunct professor of natural history at the newly established Faculty of Caen. There he published numerous works on marine organisms, focusing on algae and hydrozoa, and amassed large collections that were acquired after his death by the town of Caen. When Leschenault visited Lamouroux in spring 1813, he reported to Delessert that his friend seemed 'very bored' in Caen, missed the resources available in Paris and was frustrated that he remained 'merely an adjunct professor' despite having been promised the vacant professorship (Leschenault to Delessert, 1 May 1813, Paris, Bibliothèque de l'Institut de France, MS 2450/31/777-78). See also J. P. Lamouroux, *Notice biographique sur J. V. F. Lamouroux* (Paris: Fournier, 1829), and Philippe Lauzun, *Une famille agenaise: les Lamouroux* (Agen: Veuve Lamy, 1893).
30 First published in the *Annales du Muséum d'histoire naturelle* 17 (1811), pp. 81–98.
31 Robert Brown's 'General remarks, geographical and systematical, on the botany of *Terra Australis*' were included as Appendix 3 in Flinders' *A Voyage to Terra Australis*, vol. 2, pp. 533–613. As this work was only published on 18 July 1814, Brown must have distributed his article as a preprint.
32 Du Petit Thouars, whom Leschenault had met on the Isle of France in 1801 (see the journal, n. 36), had returned to France in 1802.
33 Aimé Bonpland (1773–1858) was a celebrated botanist who had travelled in southern and central America and the United States with Alexander von Humboldt between 1799 and 1804. On his return, he deposited his plant collections with the Muséum

d'histoire naturelle and took over from Mirbel as director of Joséphine's gardens at Malmaison in 1805. He went back to South America after the fall of Napoléon and lived in Paraguay and Argentina. In his book *Description des plantes rares cultivées à Malmaison et à Navarre* (Paris: Didot l'aîné, 1813), illustrated by Pierre-Joseph Redouté, he describes a number of Australian plants that were brought back by the Baudin expedition and grown at Malmaison.

34 Ambroise-Marie-François-Joseph Palisot, baron de Beauvois (1752–1820), abandoned his career as a lawyer and financial administrator in 1777 to pursue his interest in botany. In 1786 he set off for Benin, where he made collections of plants and insects, and in 1788 travelled on to Saint-Domingue (modern-day Haiti) to recover his health. There he became involved in the administration's battle to preserve slavery, but after five years fled the strife-torn island for Philadelphia, where, despite his poverty, he continued to make collections of natural history. He returned to France only in 1798, where he was appointed to the Académie des sciences in 1806. He published notable works on the plants of Benin and on the insects of Africa and America, along with numerous studies of mosses.

35 Joseph-Philippe-François Deleuze (1753–1835) served as an officer in the French army before devoting himself to the natural sciences. He joined the Muséum d'histoire naturelle in 1795 as an assistant naturalist and in 1802 was appointed secretary of its journal, the *Annales du Muséum d'histoire naturelle*. He supplemented his income with work as a censor for the Restoration government in 1814. In 1828 he was appointed librarian of the Muséum. He published translations of nature poems by Erasmus Darwin and James Thomson, along with several books on animal magnetism (for which he was attacked in the press), a history of the Muséum and other works of natural history.

36 Robert Brown published his *Prodromus florae Novae Hollandiae et Insulae Van Diemen* in London in 1810.

37 Having worked for several years as an inspector of merino sheep under the Empire, Leschenault obtained a job in June 1814 with the Restoration government writing letters and reports at the Bureau of Agriculture.

38 'Mémoire sur le *Strychnos tieute* et l'*Antiaris toxicaria*, plantes vénineuses de l'île de Java, avec le suc desquelles les indigènes empoisonnent leurs flèches', *Annales du Muséum d'histoire naturelle* 16 (1810), pp. 459–82.

39 'Notice sur un lac d'acide sulfurique qui se trouve au fond d'un volcan du mont Idienne, situé dans la province de Bagnia-Vangni, côte orientale de l'île de Java', *Annales du Muséum d'histoire naturelle* 18 (1811), pp. 425–46.

40 'Description des montagnes de Tingar, district de Passourouang dans l'île de Java par M. Leschenault de la Tour, naturaliste de l'expédition de découvertes, correspondant de la Société de l'émulation de l'Île-de-France, et membre de plusieurs sociétés savantes. A Monsieur N. Engelhard, gouverneur de Java, 15 février, 1806', *Annales des voyages, de la géographie, de l'histoire et de l'archéologie* 14/40–42 (1811), pp. 314–34.

41 'Description de la ville de Coupang et de ses environs, sur la côte sud-ouest de l'île de Timor; extrait d'un voyage inédit aux Indes orientales', *Annales des voyages, de la géographie, de l'histoire et de l'archéologie* 16/46–48 (1811), pp. 279–306.

42 These maps of Louis Freycinet's were published in December 1814 in the volume *Atlas (Navigation et géographie)* (bearing a publication date of 1812) and supplemented or updated those that had appeared in part 2 of the *Atlas (Historique)* in 1811; his nautical account was published in 1815 under the title *Navigation et géographie*.

43 That is, for their work on various published volumes of the *Voyage de découvertes aux terres australes*.

44 Louis-Mathieu Langlès (1763–1824), linguist and librarian, studied Arabic and Persian while also serving as a constable responsible for preventing duels in the French army. He obtained a position at the Bibliothèque royale in 1792 and was appointed conservator of manuscripts the following year. In response to his lobbying, the National Convention established a school for contemporary eastern languages; Langlès was appointed its administrator and professor of Persian. He published numerous translations from languages including Persian, Arabic and English, and also wrote a two-volume work on the monuments of India. Langlès worked with Leschenault on his project to publish a Malay grammar and dictionary but the project foundered with the fall of Napoléon.

45 Paterson, lieutenant governor of New South Wales when Leschenault visited (see n. 11, above), and Philip Gidley King (1758–1808), its then governor, had died in recent years. Flinders was gravely ill in London with kidney disease and died a short time later, on 19 July 1814.

46 The details of the address are given in English.

Bibliography

PRIMARY SOURCES

Manuscripts
Journal of Théodore Leschenault, 1800-1802
    Paris, Archives nationales: MAR/5JJ/56/B
Journal of Théodore Leschenault, 1801-1802 (copy by Samuel Leschenault)
    Paris, Archives nationales: MAR/5JJ/56
Letters of Théodore Leschenault
    London, British Library
    Mâcon, Archives départementales de Saône-et-Loire
    Paris, Archives nationales
    Paris, Bibliothèque de l'Institut de France
    Paris, Muséum national d'histoire naturelle
    Private collection
Family documents
    Chalon-sur-Saône, Archives municipales
    Mâcon, Archives départementales de Saône-et-Loire
    Paris, Archives nationales
    Private collection

Published Works
Andrews, Henry Cranke, *The Botanist's Repository, for New, and Rare Plants, Containing Coloured Figures of Such Plants Botanically Arranged After the Sexual System of Linnaeus, in English and Latin. To Each Description is Added, a Short History of the Plant, etc.*, 10 vol. (London: Bensley, 1797–1814).
Arnoult, André-Rémi, ed., *Collection des décrets de l'Assemblée nationale législative* (Dijon: Causse, 1792).
Bajon, Bertrand, *Mémoires pour servir à l'histoire de Cayenne, et de la Guyane française*, 2 vol. (Paris: Grangé, Duchesne and L'Esprit, 1777–1778).
Barchewitz, Ernst Christoph, *Neu-vermehrte Ost-Indianische Reise-Beschreibung* (Erfurt: Jungnicol, 1751).
Baudin, Nicolas, *Journal du voyage aux Antilles de 'La Belle Angélique' (1796–1798)*, ed. Michel Jangoux (Paris: Presses de l'Université de Paris-Sorbonne; Brussels: Académie royale de Belgique, 2009).

——, *The Journal of Post Captain Nicolas Baudin, Commander-in-Chief of the Corvettes Géographe and Naturaliste, Assigned by Order of the Government to a Voyage of Discovery*, trans. Christine Cornell (Adelaide: Libraries Board of South Australia, 1974).

——, *Mon voyage aux terres australes: journal personnel du commandant Baudin*, ed. Jacqueline Bonnemains (Paris: Imprimerie nationale, 2000).

Bernardin de Saint-Pierre, Jacques-Henri, *Voyage à l'Isle de France, à l'Isle de Bourbon, au Cap de Bonne-Espérance*, 2 vol. (Amsterdam; Paris: Merlin, 1773).

Bligh, William, *A Narrative of the Mutiny, on Board His Majesty's Ship Bounty, and the Subsequent Voyage of Part of the Crew, in the Ship's Boat, from Tofoa, One of the Friendly Islands, to Timor, a Dutch Settlement in the East Indies* (Dublin: White, Byrne, Moore, Jones, Dornin and Grueber, 1790).

Bonpland, Aimé, *Description des plantes rares cultivées à Malmaison et à Navarre* (Paris: Didot l'aîné, 1813).

Bory de Saint-Vincent, Jean-Baptiste, *Essais sur les Isles fortunées et l'antique Atlantide* (Paris: Badouin, Year XI [1803]).

——, *Voyage dans les quatre principales îles des mers d'Afrique, fait par ordre du gouvernement, pendant les années neuf et dix de la République (1801 et 1802): avec l'histoire de la traversée du capitaine Baudin jusqu'au Port-Louis de l'île Maurice* 3 vol. and atlas (Paris: Buisson, Year XIII [1804]).

Brown, Robert, 'General remarks, geographical and systematical, on the botany of *Terra Australis*', in Matthew Flinders, *A Voyage to Terra Australis: Undertaken for the Purpose of Completing the Discovery of that Vast Country, and Prosecuted in the Years 1801, 1802 and 1803*, 2 vol. and atlas (London: Nicol, 1814), vol. 2, pp. 533–618.

——, *Nature's Investigator: The Diary of Robert Brown in Australia, 1801–1805*, ed. T. G. Vallance, D. T. Moore and E. W. Groves (Canberra: Australian Biological Resources Services, 2001).

——, *Prodromus florae Novae Hollandiae et Insulae Van Diemen* (London: Taylor and Company, 1810).

Candolle, Augustin Pyramus de, *Prodromus systematis naturalis regni vegetabilis*, 22 vol. (Paris: Treuttel and Würtz, 1824–1873).

Cook, James, and James King, *A Voyage to the Pacific Ocean; Undertaken by Command of His Majesty, for Making Discoveries in the Northern Hemisphere: Performed under the Direction of Captains Cook, Clerke, and Gore, in the Years 1776, 1777, 1778, 1779, and 1780*, 4 vol. (London: Stockdale, Scatcherd, Whitaker, Fielding and Hardy, 1784); French translation: *Troisième Voyage de Cook, ou Voyage à l'Océan Pacifique, ordonné par le Roi d'Angleterre, pour faire des découvertes dans l'Hémisphère Nord, pour déterminer la position et l'étendue de la Côte Ouest de l'Amérique Septentrionale, sa distance de l'Asie, et résoudre la question du passage au Nord. Exécuté sous la direction des Capitaines Cook,*

Clerke et Gore, sur les vaisseaux la Résolution et la Découverte, en 1776, 1777, 1778, 1779 et 1780, trans. J. N. Demeunier, 4 vol. (Paris: Hôtel de Thou, 1785).

Coudrenière, Henri Peyroux de la, 'Observations sur la lumière de l'eau de la mer', *Observations sur la physique, sur l'histoire naturelle et sur les arts* 5 (1775), pp. 451–52.

Cuvier, Georges, 'Instructions sur l'anthropologie et sur les recherches à faire en faveur de cette branche de la science, dans un voyage autour du monde', in Maurice Girard, *François Péron: naturaliste, voyageur aux terres* australes (Paris: Baillière; Moulins: Enaut, 1857), pp. 264–69.

——, *Tableau élémentaire de l'histoire naturelle des animaux* (Paris: Baudouin, Year VI [1797]).

Dampier, William, *A Voyage to New Holland, etc. in the Year 1699* (London: Knapton, 1703); French translation: *Voyage aux terres australes, à la Nouvelle Hollande, etc., fait en 1699*, 4 vol. (Paris: Machuel, 1722).

Degérando, Joseph-Marie, *Considérations sur les diverses méthodes à suivre dans l'observation des peuples sauvages* (Paris: Société des observateurs de l'homme, Year VIII [1800]); English translation: *The Observation of Savage Peoples*, trans. F. C. T. Moore (London: Routledge and Kegan Paul, 1969).

Du Petit Thouars, Aubert Aubert, *Histoire des végétaux recueillis sur les îles de France, La Réunion (Bourbon) et Madagascar* (Paris: Huzard, Year XII [1804]).

Espinosa, Alonso de, *Del origen y milagros de la Santa Imagen de Nuestra Señora de Candelaria* (Seville: J. de León, 1594).

Flinders, Matthew, *A Voyage to Terra Australis: Undertaken for the Purpose of Completing the Discovery of that Vast Country, and Prosecuted in the Years 1801, 1802 and 1803*, 2 vol. and atlas (London: Nicol, 1814).

Fornasiero, Jean, and John West-Sooby, eds, *French Designs on Colonial New South Wales: François Péron's Memoir on the English Settlements in New Holland, Van Diemen's Land and the Archipelagos of the Great Pacific Ocean* (Adelaide: Friends of the State Library of South Australia, 2014).

Forster, Georg, *A Voyage around the World, in His Britannic Majesty's Sloop, Resolution, Commanded by Capt. James Cook, During the Years 1772, 3, 4, and 5*, 2 vol. (London: White, Robson and Elmsly, 1777).

Geoffroy Saint-Hilaire, Étienne, 'Note sur quelques habitudes communes au requin et au pilote', *Bulletin des sciences, par la Société philomathique* 63 (1802), pp. 113–14.

Hawkesworth, John, ed., *An Account of the Voyages Undertaken by the Order of His Present Majesty, for Making Discoveries in the Southern Hemisphere, and Successively Performed by Commodore Byron, Captain Wallis, Captain Carteret, and Captain Cook, in the Dolphin, the Swallow, and the Endeavour*, 3 vol. (London: Strahan and Cadell, 1773); French translation: *Relation des voyages entrepris par ordre de Sa Majesté britannique, actuellement régnante, pour faire des découvertes dans l'hémisphère méridional*, 4 vol. (Paris: Saillant and Nyon, 1774).

Humboldt, Alexander von, *Voyage aux régions équinoxiales du nouveau continent, fait en 1799, 1800, 1801, 1802, 1803 et 1804*, 6 vol. (Paris: Schœll, 1814–1820).

Jussieu, Antoine-Laurent de, *Genera plantarum secundum ordines naturales disposita juxta methodum in Horto regio Parisiensi exaratam* (Paris: Hérissant, 1789).

Labillardière, Jacques-Julien Houtou de, *Novae Hollandiae plantarum specimen*, 2 vol. (Paris: Huzard, 1804–1806).

——, *Relation du voyage à la recherche de La Pérouse*, 2 vol. (Paris: Jansen, 1800).

Lamanon, Robert de, 'Mémoire sur les térébratules ou poulettes, et description d'une espèce trouvée dans les mers de la Tartarie orientale', in Milet-Mureau, *Voyage de La Pérouse autour du monde*, vol. 4, pp. 116–33.

Latham, John, *A General Synopsis of Birds*, 3 vol. (London: White, 1781–1785).

Ledru, André-Pierre, *Voyage aux îles de Ténériffe, La Trinité, Saint-Thomas, Sainte-Croix et Porto-Ricco, exécuté par ordre du gouvernement français, depuis le 30 septembre 1796 jusqu'au 7 juin 1798, sous la direction du capitaine Baudin, pour faire des recherches et des collections relatives à l'histoire naturelle*, 2 vol. (Paris: Arthus Bertrand, 1810).

Le Gentil, Guillaume, *Voyage dans les mers de l'Inde, fait par ordre du roi à l'occasion du passage de Vénus sur le disque du soleil le 6 juin 1761 et le 3 du même mois 1769*, 2 vol. (Paris: Imprimerie royale, 1779–1781).

Leschenault, Théodore, *Les Carnets botaniques*, ed. Michel Jangoux, Viviane Desmet and Claude Lefebvre, the Baudin Legacy Project, baudin.sydney.edu.au.

——, 'Description de la ville de Coupang et de ses environs, sur la côte sud-ouest de l'île de Timor; extrait d'un voyage inédit aux Indes orientales', *Annales des voyages, de la géographie, de l'histoire et de l'archéologie* 16/46–48 (1811), pp. 279–306.

——, 'Description des montagnes de Tingar, district de Passourouang dans l'île de Java par M. Leschenault de la Tour, naturaliste de l'expédition de découvertes, correspondant de la Société de l'émulation de l'Île-de-France, et membre de plusieurs sociétés savantes. A Monsieur N. Engelhard, gouverneur de Java, 15 février, 1806', *Annales des voyages, de la géographie, de l'histoire et de l'archéologie* 14/40–42 (1811), pp. 314–34.

——, 'Mémoire sur le *Strychnos tieute* et l'*Antiaris toxicaria*, plantes vénineuses de l'île de Java, avec le suc desquelles les indigènes empoisonnent leurs flèches', *Annales du Muséum d'histoire naturelle* 16 (1810), pp. 459–82.

——, 'Notice sur un lac d'acide sulfurique qui se trouve au fond d'un volcan du mont Idienne, situé dans la province de Bagnia-Vangni, côte orientale de l'île de Java', *Annales du Muséum d'histoire naturelle* 18 (1811), pp. 425–46.

Milbert, Jacques-Gérard, *Voyage pittoresque à l'Île-de-France, au Cap de Bonne-Espérance et à l'Île de Ténériffe*, 2 vol. and atlas (Paris: Nepveu, 1812).

Milet-Mureau, Louis-Antoine Destouff, baron de, *Voyage de La Pérouse autour du monde*, 4 vol. and atlas (Paris: Imprimerie de la République, 1797–1798).

Milius, Pierre Bernard, *Pierre Bernard Milius, Last Commander of the Baudin Expedition: The Journal, 1800–1804*, trans. Kate Pratt, ed. Peter Hambly, with an introduction by Anthony Brown (Canberra: National Library of Australia, 2013).

Paterson, William, *A Narrative of Four Journeys into the Country of the Hottentots, and Caffraria. In the Years One Thousand Seven Hundred and Seventy-Seven, Eight and Nine* (London: Johnson, 1789).

Péron, François, and Louis Freycinet, *Voyage de découvertes aux terres australes, exécuté par ordre de sa majesté l'empereur et roi, sur les corvettes le Géographe, le Naturaliste, et la goélette le Casuarina, pendant les années 1800, 1801, 1802, 1803 et 1804*, 3 vol. and atlas (in two parts) (Paris: Imprimerie impériale [subsequently Imprimerie royale], 1807–1816).

——, *Voyage de découvertes aux terres australes, exécuté par ordre du gouvernement, sur les corvettes le Géographe, le Naturaliste, et la goélette le Casuarina, pendant les années 1800, 1801, 1802, 1803 et 1804*, 2nd edn, 4 vol. and atlas (Paris: Arthus Bertrand, 1824).

Phillip, Arthur, *The Voyage of Governor Phillip to Botany Bay: With an Account of the Establishment of the Colonies of Port Jackson and Norfolk Island* (London: Stockdale, 1789).

Pliny, *Natural History*, trans. H. Rackham, W. H. S. Jones and D. E. Eichholz, 10 vol. (London: Heinemann; Cambridge, Mass.: Harvard University Press, 1938–1962).

Smith, James Edward, *A Specimen of the Botany of New Holland*, 4 parts (London: Sowerby, 1793–1795).

Tasso, Torquato, *The Liberation of Jerusalem*, trans. Max Wickert, ed. Mark Davie (Oxford: Oxford University Press, 2009).

Thunberg, Carl Peter, *Dissertatio entomologica: novas insectorum species*, part 4 (Uppsala: Edman, 1784).

Valmont de Bomare, Jacques-Christophe, *Dictionnaire raisonné universel d'histoire naturelle*, 4th edn, 15 vol. (Lyon: Bruyset frères, 1791).

Vancouver, George, *A Voyage of Discovery to the North Pacific Ocean, and Round the World; In which the Coast of North-west America Has Been Carefully Examined and Accurately Surveyed. Undertaken by His Majesty's Command, Principally with a View to Ascertain the Existence of Any Navigable Communication Between the North Pacific and North Atlantic Oceans; and Performed in the Years 1790, 1791, 1792, 1793, 1794, and 1795, in the Discovery Sloop of War, and Armed Tender Chatham, Under the Command of Captain George Vancouver*, 3 vol. and atlas

(London: G. G. and J. Robinson, 1798); French translation: *Voyages de découvertes à l'Océan Pacifique du Nord et autour du monde, dans lequel la côte Nord-Ouest de l'Amérique a été soigneusement reconnue et exactement relevée: ordonné par le roi d'Angleterre, principalement dans la vue de constater s'il existe, à travers le continent de l'Amérique, un passage pour les vaisseaux, de l'Océan Pacifique du Nord à l'Océan Atlantique septentrional; et exécuté en 1790, 1791, 1792, 1793, 1794 et 1795 par le Capitaine George Vancouver*, 3 vol. and atlas (Paris: Imprimerie de la République, Year VIII).

Villault, Nicolas, *Relation des côtes d'Afrique, appellées Guinée* (Paris: Denys Thierry, 1669).

Williams, Charlie, Eliane M. Norman and Walter Kingsley Taylor, eds, *André Michaux in North America: Journal and Letters, 1785–1797* (Tuscaloosa: University of Alabama Press, 2020).

SECONDARY SOURCES

Ageorges, Roger, *Île de Ré, terres australes: les voyages du capitaine Baudin, marin et naturaliste* (Sainte-Marie de Ré: Groupement d'études rétaises, 1994).

Ames, Glenn J., ed., *Em nome de Deus: The Journal of the First Voyage of Vasco da Gama to India, 1497–1499* (Leiden: Brill, 2009).

Arcelin, Adrien, 'La noblesse du bailliage de Chalon-sur-Saône en 1789', *Mémoires de la Société d'histoire et d'archéologie de Chalon-sur-Saône* 8 (1895–1901), pp. 303–320.

Azouf, Mona, *Festivals and the French Revolution*, trans. Alan Sheridan (Cambridge, Mass.: Harvard University Press, 1988).

Baigent, Elizabeth, 'Solander, Daniel (1733–1782), botanist', *Oxford Dictionary of National Biography*, www.oxforddnb.com.

Barker, Robyn M., 'The botanical legacy of 1802: South Australian plants collected by Robert Brown and Peter Good on Matthew Flinders' *Investigator* and by the French scientists on Baudin's *Géographe* and *Naturaliste*', *Journal of the Adelaide Botanic Gardens* 21 (2007), pp. 5–44.

Batault, Henri, 'Essai historique sur les écoles de Chalon-sur-Saône du quinzième à la fin du dix-huitième siècle', *Mémoires de la Société d'histoire et d'archéologie de Chalon-sur-Saône* 6/1 (1872), pp. 141–50.

Bauzon, Louis-Marie-François, *Recherches historiques sur la persécution religieuse dans le département de Saône-et-Loire pendant la Révolution (1789–1803): l'arrondissement de Chalon* (Chalon-sur-Saône: Marceau, 1889).

Beaune, Henri, and Jules d'Arbaumont, *La Noblesse aux états de Bourgogne de 1350 à 1789* (Dijon: Lamarche, 1864).

Bezou, Henry C., *Metairie: A Tongue of Land to Pasture* (Gretna, La.: Pelican Publishing, 1973).

Bien, David D., 'Manufacturing nobles: the chancelleries in France to 1789', *Journal of Modern History* 61/3 (1989), pp. 445–86.

Blight, Mary, 'The story of Vasse and the Wardandi Noongar: a new perspective', Honours thesis, University of Western Australia, 2021.

Bonnemains, Jacqueline, 'Biography of Charles-Alexandre Lesueur', in *Baudin in Australian Waters: The Artwork of the French Voyage of Discovery to the Southern Lands, 1800–1804*, ed. Jacqueline Bonnemains, Elliott Forsyth and Bernard Smith (Melbourne: Oxford University Press in association with the Australian Academy of the Humanities, 1988), pp. 19–26.

——, 'Biography of Nicolas-Martin Petit', in *Baudin in Australian Waters: The Artwork of the French Voyage of Discovery to the Southern Lands, 1800–1804*, ed. Jacqueline Bonnemains, Elliott Forsyth and Bernard Smith (Melbourne: Oxford University Press in association with the Australian Academy of the Humanities, 1988), pp. 27–30.

Bourée, André, *La Chancellerie près le parlement de Bourgogne de 1476 à 1790* (Dijon: Bellais, 1927).

Bouton, Louis, *Plantes médicinales de Maurice*, 2nd edn (Port Louis: Dupuy and Dubois, 1864).

Brasseaux, Carl A., and Glenn R. Conrad, *The Road to Louisiana: The Saint-Domingue Refugees, 1792–1809* (Lafayette, La.: University of Southwestern Louisiana, 1992).

Brixius, Dorit, 'A hard nut to crack: nutmeg cultivation and the application of natural history between the Maluku islands and Isle de France (1750s-1780s)', *British Journal for the History of Science* 51/4 (2018), pp. 585–606.

Butaud, Germain, 'Remarques introductives: autour de la définition et de la typologie de la coseigneurie', *Mélanges de l'École française de Rome – Moyen Âge* 122/1 (2010), pp. 5–12.

Cap, Paul-Antoine, *Le Muséum d'histoire naturelle*, 2 vol. (Paris: Curmer, 1854).

Carr, D. J., and S. G. M. Carr, *People and Plants in Australia* (Sydney: Academic Press, 1981).

Carr, S. G. M., 'The French contribution to the discovery of Australia and its flora', *Endeavour* (new series) 35 (1976), pp. 21–26.

Carraz, Roland, 'Lettres de Leschenault et Moyne, députés extraordinaires de la ville de Chalon à la Constituante, aux maires et officiers municipaux de Chalon-sur-Saône, 11 juin 1790–12 juillet 1790', *Cahiers de la Bourgogne moderne* 1 (1972–1973), pp. 2–18.

Cheke, Anthony, and Julian Hume, *Lost Land of the Dodo: An Ecological History of Mauritius, Réunion and Rodrigues* (London: Poyser, 2008).

Copans, Jean, and Jean Jamin, eds, *Aux origines de l'anthropologie française: les mémoires de la Société des observateurs de l'homme en l'an VIII* (Paris: Le Sycomore, 1978).

Cormack, William S., 'Victor Hugues and the reign of terror on Guadeloupe, 1794–1798', *Proceedings of the Meeting of the French Colonial Historical Society* 21 (1997), pp. 31–41.

Corn, Charles, *The Scents of Eden: A Narrative of the Spice Trade* (New York: Kodansha International, 1998).

Courtépée, Claude, *Description générale et particulière du duché de Bourgogne, précédée de l'abrégé historique de cette province*, 2nd edn, 4 vol. (Dijon: Lagier, 1847–1848).

Deschamps, Jean-Joseph-Eugène, 'Leschenault de la Tour, Jean-Baptiste-Louis-Claude-Théodore, voyageur et naturaliste français', *Nouvelle Biographie générale, depuis les temps les plus reculés jusqu'à nos jours*, ed. Ferdinand Hoefer, 46 vol. (Paris: Firmin Didot frères, fils et compagnie, 1852–1866), vol. 30, col. 923–27.

Desmet, Viviane, and Michel Jangoux, 'Un naturaliste aux terres australes: Jean-Baptiste Leschenault de la Tour (1773–1826)', in *Portés par l'air du temps: les voyages du capitaine Baudin*, ed. M. Jangoux, special number of *Études sur le dix-huitième siècle* 38 (2010), pp. 225–32.

Douglas, Bronwen, 'Philosophers, naturalists, and Antipodean encounters, 1748–1803', *Intellectual History Review* 23/3 (2013), pp. 387–409.

——, Fanny Wonu Veys and Billie Lythberg, eds, *Collecting in the South Seas: The Voyage of Bruni d'Entrecasteaux, 1791–1794* (Leiden: Sidestone Press, 2018).

Doyle, William, *The French Revolution: A Very Short Introduction* (Oxford: Oxford University Press, 2001).

——, 'The price of offices in pre-revolutionary France', *The Historical Journal* 27/4 (1984), pp. 831–60.

Drouin, Jean-Marc, 'Collecte, observation et classification chez René Desfontaines (1750–1833)', in *Le Muséum au premier siècle de son histoire*, ed. Claude Blanckaert, Claudine Cohen, Pietro Corsi and Jean-Louis Fischer (Paris: Editions du Muséum national d'histoire naturelle, 1997), pp. 263–76.

Dubois, Laurent, '"The price of liberty": Victor Hugues and the administration of freedom in Guadeloupe, 1794–1798', *The William and Mary Quarterly* 56/2 (1999), pp. 363–92.

Dugour, José Desiré, *Apuntes para la historia de Santa Cruz de Tenerife* (Santa Cruz: J. Benitez y compañía, 1875).

Dunmore, John, *French Explorers in the Pacific*, 2 vol. (Oxford: Clarendon Press, 1969).

Duyker, Edward, *François Péron, an Impetuous Life: Naturalist and Voyager* (Carlton: The Miegunyah Press, 2006).

——, and R. d'Unienville, 'Faure, Pierre Ange François Xavier (1776–1855)', *Dictionnaire de Biographie mauricienne* 54 (2000), pp. 1744–45.

Épinay, Adrien d', *Renseignements pour servir à l'histoire de l'Île de France jusqu'à l'année 1810, inclusivement; précédés de notes sur la découverte de l'île, sur l'occupation hollandaise, etc.* (Mauritius: Nouvelle Imprimerie Dupuy, 1890).

Évrard, Sébastien, 'Droit et territoire: un conflit en Bresse bourguignonne à la fin de l'Ancien Régime', *Cahiers Haut-marnais* 248–251 (2007), pp. 241–68.

Farram, Steve, 'Jacobus Arnoldus Hazaart and the British interregnum in Netherlands Timor, 1812–1816', *Bijdragen tot de taal-, land- en volkenkunde* 163/4 (2008), pp. 458–60.

FitzGerald, Sylvia, 'Hooker, Sir William Jackson', *Oxford Dictionary of National Biography*, www.oxforddnb.com.

Flourens, Jean-Pierre, 'Éloge historique d'Aubert-Aubert Du-Petit-Thouars', *Mémoires de l'Académie des sciences de l'Institut de France* 20 (1849), pp. i–xxxi.

Fornasiero, Jean, and John West-Sooby, 'Baudin's books', *Australian Journal of French Studies* 39/3 (2002), pp. 215–49.

——, and John West-Sooby, 'Voyages et déplacements des savoirs: les expéditions de Nicolas Baudin entre Révolution et Empire', *Annales historiques de la Révolution française* 385 (2016), pp. 23–45.

——, Lindl Lawton and John West-Sooby, eds, *The Art of Science: Nicolas Baudin's Voyagers, 1800–1804* (Adelaide: Wakefield Press, 2016).

——, Peter Monteath and John West-Sooby, *Encountering Terra Australis: The Australian Voyages of Nicolas Baudin and Matthew Flinders*, 2nd edn (Adelaide: Wakefield Press, 2010).

Fouque, Victor, *Histoire de Chalon-sur-Saône depuis les temps les plus reculés jusqu'à nos jours* (Chalon-sur-Saône: Chez l'auteur, 1844).

Fraser, Angus, 'Turner, Dawson', *Oxford Dictionary of National Biography*, www.oxforddnb.com.

Garnier, Joseph, *Inventaire sommaire des archives départementales antérieures à 1790, Côte d'or; Archives civiles, série B: parlement de Bourgogne* (Dijon: Darantière, 1894).

Gauvin, Jean-François, 'The instrument that never was: inventing, manufacturing, and branding Réaumur's thermometer during the Enlightenment', *Annals of Science* 69/4 (2012), pp. 515–49.

George, Alex S., *William Dampier in New Holland: Australia's First Natural Historian* (Melbourne: Bloomings Books, 1999).

Gibbard, Paul, 'A scientific traveller in limbo: Théodore Leschenault's return to imperial France', in *'Roaming Freely throughout the Universe': Nicolas Baudin's Voyage to Australia and the Pursuit of Science*, ed. Jean Fornasiero and John West-Sooby (Adelaide: Wakefield Press, 2021), pp. 267–85.

———, 'Empiricism and sensibility in the Australian journal of Théodore Leschenault de la Tour', in *Natural History in Early Modern France: The Poetics of an Epistemic Genre*, ed. Raphaële Garrod and Paul J. Smith (Leiden: Brill, 2018), pp. 263–88.

———, 'Théodore Leschenault de la Tour: the affable botanist', in *The Art of Science: Nicolas Baudin's Voyagers, 1800–1804*, ed. Jean Fornasiero, Lindl Lawton and John West-Sooby (Adelaide: Wakefield Press, 2016), p. 76.

———, 'Théodore Leschenault de la Tour: botanist of the Baudin expedition', website of the Western Australian Museum, museum.wa.gov.au.

Girard, Maurice, *François Péron: naturaliste, voyageur aux terres australes* (Paris: Baillière; Moulins: Enaut, 1857).

———, 'Notice nécrologique sur la vie et les travaux scientifiques d'Adolphe Doumerc', *Annales de la Société entomologique de France* 8 (1868), pp. 885–96.

Gunn, Mary, and L. E. Codd, *Botanical Exploration of Southern Africa* (Cape Town: Balkema, 1981).

Harrison, Carol E., 'Projections of the revolutionary nation: French expeditions in the Pacific, 1791–1803', *Osiris* 24/1 (2009), pp. 33–52.

Hooker, Joseph Dalton, *A Sketch of the Life and Labours of Sir William Jackson Hooker, Late Director of the Royal Gardens of Kew* (Cambridge: Cambridge University Press, 1903).

———, *On the Flora of Australia, its Origin, Affinities, and Distribution; Being an Introductory Essay to the Flora of Tasmania* (London: Lovell Reeve, 1859).

Hopper, Stephen D., and Hans Lambers, 'Human relationships with and use of kwongkan plants and lands', in *Plant Life on the Sandplains in Southwest Australia: A Global Biodiversity Hotspot*, ed. Hans Lambers (Crawley: University of Western Australia Publishing, 2014), pp. 290–94.

Hoquet, Thierry, 'Botanical authority: Benjamin Delessert's collections between travellers and Candolle's natural method', *Isis* 105/3 (2014), pp. 508–39.

Horner, Frank, *The French Reconnaissance: Baudin in Australia, 1801–1803* (Melbourne: Melbourne University Press, 1987).

Huet, Henri, 'Les incarcérés de Chalon-sur-Saône pendant la Révolution française', *Mémoires de la Société d'histoire et d'archéologie de Chalon-sur-Saône* 60 (1991), pp. 55–105.

Jangoux, Michel, 'The herbarium of the *terres australes* (Baudin expedition, 1800–1804)', the Baudin Legacy Project, baudin.sydney.edu.au.

———, *Le Voyage aux terres australes du commandant Nicolas Baudin: genèse et préambule (1798–1800)* (Paris: Presses de l'Université Paris-Sorbonne, 2013).

———, 'Les zoologistes et botanistes qui accompagnèrent le capitaine Baudin aux terres australes', *Australian Journal of French Studies* 41/2 (2004), p. 55–78.

Jeandet, Abel, 'Notice sur la vie et les travaux de Leschenault de la Tour', *Bulletins de la Société des sciences naturelles de Saône-et-Loire* 2 (1883), pp. 123–58.

Jones, Rhys, 'Natural images of man', in *Baudin in Australian Waters: The Artwork of the French Voyage of Discovery to the Southern Lands, 1800–1804*, ed. Jacqueline Bonnemains, Elliott Forsyth and Bernard Smith (Melbourne: Oxford University Press in association with the Australian Academy of the Humanities, 1988), pp. 35–64.

Kikusawa, Ritsuko, and Lawrence A. Reid, 'Proto who utilised turmeric, and how?', in *Language Description, History and Development: Linguistic Indulgence in Memory of Terry Crowley*, ed. Jeff Siegel, John Lynch and Diana Eades (Amsterdam: John Benjamins Publishing, 2007), pp. 341–54.

Knox, Dudley W., ed., *Naval Documents related to the Quasi-War between the United States and France* (Washington, D.C.: United States Government Printing Office, 1937).

Konishi, Shino, *The Aboriginal Male in the Enlightenment World* (London: Pickering and Chatto, 2012).

Lacuisine, Elisabeth-François de, *Le Parlement de Bourgogne depuis son origine jusqu'à sa chute*, 2nd edn, 3 vol. (Dijon: Rabutot; Paris: Durand, 1864).

Lamouroux, J. P., *Notice biographique sur J. V. F. Lamouroux* (Paris: Fournier, 1829).

Lauzun, Philippe, *Une famille agenaise: les Lamouroux* (Agen: Veuve Lamy, 1893).

Lévêque, Pierre, ed., *Histoire de Chalon-sur-Saône* (Dijon: Éditions universitaires de Dijon, 2005).

Ligou, Daniel, 'La Révolution française', in *Histoire de Chalon-sur-Saône*, ed. Pierre Lévêque (Dijon: Éditions universitaires de Dijon, 2005), pp. 143–54.

Lombard-Jordan, Anne, 'Un mémoire inédit de F. E. de Rosily sur l'île de Timor (1772)', *Archipel* 23 (1982), pp. 75–104.

Lucas, Colin, *The Structure of the Terror: The Example of Javogues and the Loire* (Oxford: Oxford University Press, 1973).

Ly-Tio-Fane, Madeleine, *Joseph Hubert and the Société des sciences et arts de l'Isle de France, 1801–1802* (Port Louis: Royal Society of Arts and Sciences of Mauritius, 1961–1962).

——, *Le Géographe et le Naturaliste à l'Île de France, 1801, 1803: ultime escale du capitaine Baudin* (Port Louis: Presse MSM, 2003).

Mabberley, David J., *Jupiter Botanicus: Robert Brown of the British Museum* (Braunschweig: Verlag von J. Cramer; London: British Museum (Natural History), 1985).

Macmillan, Allister, ed., *Mauritius Illustrated: Historical and Descriptive, Commercial and Industrial* (London: Collingridge, 1914).

Macquet, Adolphe, *L'Instruction à l'Île Maurice, ancienne Île de France: à l'origine de sa colonisation* (Mauritius: Engelbrecht, 1890).

Mahdi, Waruno, *Malay Words and Malay Things: Lexical Souvenirs from an Exotic Archipelago in German Publications before 1700* (Wiesbaden: Harrassowitz Verlag, 2007).

Marchant, Leslie, *France australe* (Perth: Scott Four Colour Print, 1998).

Mayer, Wolf, 'The geological work of the Baudin expedition in Australia (1801–1803): the mineralogists, the discoveries and the legacy', *Earth Sciences History* 28 (2009), pp. 293–324.

McPhee, Peter, *The French Revolution, 1789–1799* (Oxford: Oxford University Press, 2002).

Meek, Charles K., *Tribal Studies in Northern Nigeria*, 2 vol. (London: Kegan Paul, 1931).

Meliá, Juan Tous, *Santa Cruz de Tenerife a través de la cartografía, 1588–1899* (Santa Cruz: Museo militar regional de Canarias, 1994).

Montarlot, Paul, *Les Députés de Saône-et-Loire aux assemblées de la Révolution, 1789–1799* (Autun: Dejussieu, 1905).

Moore, George Fletcher, *A Descriptive Vocabulary of the Language in Common Use amongst the Aborigines of Western Australia; with Copious Meanings, Embodying Much Interesting Information Regarding the Habits, Manners and Customs of the Natives, and the Natural History of the Country* (London: Orr, 1842).

Mousnier, Roland, *The Institutions of France under the Absolute Monarchy, 1598–1789*, trans. Brian Pearce and Arthur Goldhammer, 2 vol. (Chicago: University of Chicago Press, 1979–1980).

Nelson, E. Charles, and D. J. Bedford, 'The names of the Australian grass-tree: *Xanthorrhoea* Sm. and *Acoroides* C. Kite (Xanthorrhoeaceae)', *Botanical Journal of the Linnean Society* 112/2 (1993), pp. 95–105.

O'Callaghan, Joseph F., 'Castile, Portugal, and the Canary Islands: claims and counterclaims, 1344–1479', *Viator* 24 (1993), pp. 287–309.

Payen, Anselme, *Éloge historique de M. de Mirbel* (Paris: Imprimerie et librairie d'agriculture et d'horticulture Mme Veuve Bouchard-Huzard, 1858).

Pérusson, Émile, *Festival chalonnais–1842. Première Partie: Notice historique d'introduction sur le couvent des Cordeliers de Saint-Laurent-les-Chalon* (Chalon-sur-Saône: Duchesne, 1842).

Phillips, Roderick, 'Women and family breakdown in eighteenth-century France: Rouen, 1780–1800', *Social History* 1/2 (1976), pp. 197–218.

Plomley, N. J. B., *The Baudin Expedition and the Tasmanian Aborigines 1802* (Hobart: Blubber Head Press, 1983).

Pluchet, Régis, 'En marge de l'expédition vers les terres australes: un portrait du botaniste André Michaux', in *Portés par l'air du temps: les voyages du capitaine Baudin*, ed. Michel Jangoux, special number of *Études sur le dix-huitième siècle*, 38 (2010), pp. 205–11.

Postiau, Paul, and Michel Jangoux, 'Les récoltes botaniques de l'expédition Baudin aux terres australes (1801–1803)', in *Portés par l'air du temps: les voyages du capitaine Baudin*, ed. M. Jangoux, special number of *Études sur le dix-huitième siècle* 38 (2010), pp. 241–51.

Précis sur la colonisation des bords de la Mana, à la Guyane française (Paris: Imprimerie royale, 1835).

Robert, Adolphe, and Edgar Bourloton, eds, *Dictionnaire des parlementaires français, depuis le 1er mai 1789 jusqu'au 1er mai 1889*, 5 vol. (Paris: Bourlon, 1889–1891).

Rosemont, Louis Reutter de, *Histoire de la pharmacie à travers les âges*, 2 vol. (Paris: Peyronnet et compagnie, 1932).

Sainte-Preuve, François-Georges de, Alphonse Rabbe and Claude Vieilh de Boisjoslin, ed., *Biographie universelle et portative des contemporains, ou dictionnaire des hommes vivants, et des hommes morts depuis 1788 jusqu'à nos jours*, 5 vol. (Paris: Levrault, 1834).

Sankey, Margaret, 'Writing the voyage of scientific exploration: the logbooks, journals and notes of the Baudin expedition (1800–1804)', *Intellectual History Review* 20/3 (2010), pp. 401–13.

Secord, Anne, 'Caley, George (1770–1829), naturalist and farrier', *Oxford Dictionary of National Biography*, www.oxforddnb.com.

Seddon, George, *The Old Country: Australian Landscapes, Plants and People* (Cambridge: Cambridge University Press, 2005).

Smith, Stefan Halikowski, 'The mid-Atlantic islands: a theatre of modern ecocide?', *International Review of Social History* 55 (2010), supplement, pp. 51–77.

Southwood, Jane, and Donald Simpson, 'Baudin's doctors: French medical scientists in Australian waters, 1801–1803', *Australian Journal of French Studies* 41/2 (2004), pp. 152–64.

Spary, Emma C., *Utopia's Garden: French Natural History from Old Regime to Revolution* (Chicago and London: Chicago University Press, 2000).

Stevens, Peter F., *The Development of Biological Systematics: Antoine-Laurent de Jussieu, Nature and the Natural System* (New York: Columbia University Press, 1994).

Storr, G. M., and G. Harold, 'Herpetofauna of the Shark Bay region, Western Australia', *Records of the Western Australian Museum* 6/4 (1978), pp. 449–67.

Suhard-Maréchal, Marie-Thérèse, *Saint-Laurent* (Chalon-sur-Saône: Société d'histoire et d'archéologie de Chalon-sur-Saône, 1994).

Thomaz, Luis, 'Note sur le « Dictionnaire françois et timorien » de F. E. de Rosily', *Archipel* 23 (1982), pp. 105–108.

Thompson, Mack, 'The origins of E. I. Du Pont de Nemours and Company, 1801–1805', *Papers of the Annual Meeting of the Business History Conference* 15 (1968), pp. 16–34.

Violot, Raoul, *Histoire des maisons de Chalon*, 2 vol. (Paris: Éditions F. E. R. N., 1969).
Wanquet, Claude, *La France et la première abolition de l'esclavage, 1794–1802: le cas des colonies orientales, Île-de-France (Maurice) et la Réunion* (Paris: Karthala, 1998).
——, 'L'Île de France à l'arrivée de Baudin (mars 1801), une île malade du syndrome de Saint-Domingue', in *Baudin-Flinders dans l'océan Indien: voyages, découvertes, rencontre*, ed. Serge M. Rivière and Kumari R. Issur (Paris: L'Harmattan, 2006), pp. 19–42.
Watts, Iain P., 'Philosophical intelligence: letters, print, and experiment during Napoleon's Continental blockade', *Isis* 106/4 (2015), pp. 749–70.
West-Sooby, John, 'An artist in the making: the early drawings of Charles-Alexandre Lesueur during the Baudin expedition to Australia', in *Framing French Culture*, ed. Natalie Edwards, Ben McCann and Peter Poiana (Adelaide: University of Adelaide Press, 2015), pp. 53–80.
Whitehurst, Rose, *Noongar Dictionary: Noongar to English and English to Noongar*, 2nd edn (Perth: Noongar Language and Culture Centre, 1997).

Index of Scientific Names

Abrus precatorius: 182
Achyranthes aspera: 90
Agathophyllum: 235, 299n
Agave: 86
Agave americana: 90
Aletris: 202
Alisterus scapularis: 298n
Aloe dichotoma: 181
Amandava amandava: 285n
Anigozanthus: 290n
Antiaris toxicaria: 270
Apocynaceae: 177, 179
Arum esculentum: 87, 90
Asclepius: 180
Asplenium: 90, 211
Atriplex: 137
Ayapana: 109, 285n
Ayapana triplinervis: 285n

Balaena physalus: 283n
Balaenoptera physalus: 283n
Banksia: 202, 227
Banksia nivea: 136
Basueria (?): 212
Baudinia coccinea: 136, 290n
Beaufortia sprengelioides: 291n
Bignonia: 212
Billardiera: 213
Bonapartea laureata: 301n
Bosea: 211

Cacalia: 84, 86
Cacalia ficoides: 90
Cactus opuntia: 90
Calothamnus sanguinea: 290n
Campanulaceae: 256
Canna indica: 179
Carthamus tinctorius: 294n
Casuarina: 211, 227, 264

Casuarina equisetifolia: 202, 207
Cavolinia tridentata: 288n
Cephalotus follicularis: 269
Cineraria populifolia: 90
Clavaria: 90
Clavaria lauri: 90, 280n
Clematis: 202
Clitoria: 182
Compositae: 36, 202, 213, 216, 256
Convolvulus canariensis: 90
Convolvulus floridus: 90
Corispermum: 182
Correa: 207
Correa alba: 296n
Cryptocarya agathophylla: 299n
Cryptogamia: 279n
Cycas circinalis: 285n
Cycas thouarsii: 285n
Cynometra cauliflora: 178
Cyperus: 149

Dammara: 149, 291n
Datura stramonium: 88, 90
Delphinus phocoena: 127
Dianella: 210
Diodon: 128-29
Diomedea exulans: 100, 125–26
Diplolaena: 291n
Diplolaena grandiflora: 291n
Dodartia: 180
Dodonaea: 211
Dolichos catianus: 179
Dolichos curiformis: 182
Dolichos pruriens: 182
Dracaena: 136, 289n

Echeneis naucrates: 127
Echeneis remora: 127
Embothrium: 213

INDEX OF SCIENTIFIC NAMES

Epilobium: 210
Eranthemum salsoloides: 90
Erica arborea: 89
Erythrina corallodendron: 182
Eschara: 133
Estrilda astrild: 285n
Eucalyptus: 36, 137, 202, 211, 214, 216, 227, 229, 256
Eucalyptus globulus: 207
Eucalyptus resinifera: 202, 207
Eupatorium: 109
Eupatorium ayapana: 285n
Eupatorium triplinerve: 285n
Euphorbia: 84, 86, 87
Euphorbia canariensis: 90
Euphorbia quadrangularis: 90
Exocarpos cupressiformis: 209, 220

Ficus indica: 157, 177, 182
Fucus: 78, 269
Fucus granulatus: 101
Fucus natans: 97
Fucus palmatus: 205, 206
Fucus pyriferus: 100, 205
Fungus: 90

Gardenia: 181
Gasterosteus ductor: 127, 288n
Genista: 137
Geranium: 202
Glaucus atlanticus: 288n
Glaucus eucharis: 288n
Glycine ilicifolia: 136
Gnaphalium: 137
Goodenia: 202
Goodeniaceae: 44
Gossypium rubrum: 180
Gramineae: 256
Guttiferae: 213

Haemodorum: 290n
Haemodorum spicatum: 290n
Helix janthina: 131
Hibiscus: 182
Hirundo esculenta: 160
Hyalaea australis: 288n

Hydatis hydatigena: 127
Hypericum androsaemum: 89

Illecebrum paronychia: 90
Indigofera: 210

Jasmineae: 209, 213
Jatropha globosa: 181
Justicia: 181
Justicia betonica: 109

Labiatae: 209
Lagostrophus fasciatus: 292n
Lampyris japonica: 185, 294n
Lathyrus amphicarpos: 179
Laurobasidium lauri: 280n
Laurus indica: 89, 92
Laurus nobilis: 89
Leguminosae: 36, 256
Leptospermum: 137, 202, 227
Leschenaultia: 44, 251
Leschenaultia biloba: 44
Leschenaultia formosa: 44
Leschenaultia macrantha: 44
Lichen roccella: 92
Liliaceae: 256
Lonchitis: 207
Loranthus: 229

Macropidia: 290n
Malva: 182
Mazeutoxeron: 48, 207
Mazeutoxeron rufum: 207, 296n
Melaleuca: 138, 144, 150, 176, 202, 291n
Mentula: 160
Mesembryanthemum edule: 137, 220
Mimosa: 107, 150, 213, 216
Mimosa decurrens: 212
Myrtaceae: 36, 256, 291n

Naucrates ductor: 288n
Nyctanthes sambac: 181

Orchidaceae: 256
Ornithogalum longibracteatum: 90

Oxalis acetosella: 229
Oxalis minuta: 90

Pandanus: 169
Parietaria arborea: 89
Pavetta: 210
Pergularia glabra: 164, 181
Periploca: 86, 88, 90, 179
Persoonia: 212
Philadelphus: 202, 207
Phyllanthus: 182
Pileanthus limacis: 269
Pimelea: 213
Plumeria alba: 182
Procellaria pelagica: 83, 125
Proteaceae: 36, 256
Pteris: 212
Pteropus vampyrus: 293n

Ravensara aromatica: 299n
Rhizophora: 229
Rosaceae: 229
Rubiaceae: 210, 213

Salpa: 129-30
Samolus: 212
Sciaena: 230
Scincus tropisurus: 292n
Scirpus: 136
Scrophularia: 180

Sida: 182, 212
Sida indica: 88, 90
Simia aygula: 183
Solen: 211
Spinifex: 149, 211
Squalus carcharias: 126
Strophurus rankini: 292n
Strophurus spinigerus spinigerus: 292n
Strophurus strophurus: 292n
Strychnos tieute: 270
Styphelia: 202, 212

Tasmannia lanceolata: 301n
Terebratula: 230
Tetratheca: 212
Tiliqua rugosa palarra: 292n
Tournefortia argentea: 181
Tupinambis endrachtensis: 292n

Ulva: 78
Uvaria cananga: 164, 168, 181

Varanus gouldii: 292n
Veronica: 212
Visnea mocanera: 89

Xanthorrhoea: 33, 136, 216, 289n, 290n
Xylomelum: 264
Xyris: 202

General Index

NOTE: Théodore Leschenault is designated by the initials 'TL'. A page number in italics refers to a biographical note in the section 'Leschenault's Shipmates Mentioned in the Journal'.

Académie des sciences (Academy of Science): 281n, 302n, 304n
Académie royale de marine (Royal Naval Academy): 295n
Adamant, fourth-rate ship: 284n
Adeje (Canary Islands): 89
Admiral Island (Western Australia): *see* Depuch Island
Adventure Bay (Tasmania): 209
Africa: 48, 63, 65, 91, 94, 100, 111, 118, 119, 174, 231–33, 255, 279n, 282n, 284n, 285n, 296n, 301n, 302n, 304n
Agen (France): 303n
Albany (Western Australia): 45
Alderney (Channel Islands): 82
Alfonso X (1221–1284), king of Castile, Léon and Galicia: 282n
Alfonso de la Cerda (1270–1333), grandson of Alfonso X: 282n
Algeria: 302n
Algiers, Invasion of (1775): 280n
Amadima, raja of Savu: 191
Amanuban (Indonesia): 191
Amarasi, Timorese emperor: 158
Amari, raja: 158, 182, 191
Ambon (Indonesia): 291n, 294n
American Revolutionary War (1775–1783): 279n, 280n
Americas, the: 91, 92, 109, 115, 195, 199
Andrews, Henry Cranke (1758/1759–1835), English botanist: 296n
Antilles: 286n
Apollo: 88
Arabia: 234

Argentina: 304n
Armida, Saracen sorceress: 108, 284n
Arsenal de Paris: 301n
Asia: 63, 294n
Atlantic Ocean: 1, 31, 41, 63, 66, 69, 279n, 287n, 288n
Augsburg (Germany): 70
Aumont, Citizen d', naval officer: 233, 234
Australia: 1, 4, 7, 23, 34, 36, 38, 42, 43, 44, 45, 46, 48, 65, 231, 241, 289n, 300n, 302n; *see also* New Holland
Auvergne (France): 69
Avellaneda Sandoval y Rojas, José Joaquín (*c.* 1715–1794), Spanish colonial administrator: 281n
Avignon (France): 282n

Baco de la Chapelle, René-Gaston (1751–1800), politician: 283n, 286n
Bailly, Charles-Joseph (1777–1844), mineralogist: *63*, 290n
Bajon, Bertrand (*fl.* 1751–1801), surgeon: 124, 287n
Bali (Indonesia): 28, 173, 261
Banks, Sir Joseph (1743–1820), English botanist: 27, 251, 255, 256, 269, 272, 277n, 281n, 289n, 295n, 300n, 302n
Banks Strait (Tasmania): 220, 221–22
Banque de Maurice (Bank of Mauritius): 64
Barchewitz, Ernst Christoph (1687–1758), officer of the Dutch East India Company: 184, 294n

GENERAL INDEX

Barren Island (Western Australia): *see* Bernier Island
Barren Islands (Western Australia), *also known as* Dorre Islands: 149, 211
Barton, Benjamin Smith (1766–1815), American botanist: 262
Bashee Islands (Philippines): 130, 288n
Bass Strait: 26, 27, 221–22, 230, 296n, 297n
Bastille fortress, storming of: *see* French Revolution
Batanes (Philippines): 288n
Batavia (Java), *now known as* Jakarta: 28, 41, 157, 159, 161, 162, 163, 164, 166, 186, 188, 262, 294n
Batavian Commonwealth: 302n
Batavian Republic: 282n
Baudin, Alexandre (b. 1755, d. in or after 1825), captain in merchant marine, brother of Nicolas: 287n
Baudin, François-André (1774–1842), naval officer: 31, 63, 98, 280n, 282n
Baudin, Louis-Augustin (1745–1821), captain in merchant marine, brother of Nicolas: 109, 285n
Baudin, Thomas-Nicolas (1754–1803), commander of expedition to Australia, captain of *Géographe*: 63–64, 102, 133, 153, 246–47, 261, 282n, 283n, 285n, 286n; attacked by Bruny Islanders, 40; butterfly collection, 185; clash with Le Bas de Saint-Croix in Kupang, 67; confronts privateer, 83; criticised by TL, 32, 195–96; death, 43; delayed on Isle of France, 25; delayed on Tenerife, 24; in D'Entrecasteaux Channel, 201, 204–205, 214–15; employs artists, 67, 70, 124, 131, 257, 280n; encounters Royal Navy frigate in English Channel, 82; expedition to West Indies, 4, 64, 68, 70, 115, 195, 199; at Geographe Bay, 134, 137, 138, 145; hosts lunch aboard *Géographe* at Le Havre, 79–80; illness, 66, 192, 197; at Kupang, 155, 156, 192–93, 195, 197; looks after kangaroo, 151; loses TL's papers, 30, 42–43, 270; misses rendezvous with *Naturaliste*, 148; mourns Riedlé's death, 195; names Admiral Island, 152; permits TL to transfer from *Géographe* to *Naturaliste*, 26, 192–93; persuades TL to remain with expedition, 27–28, 257; plans expedition to Australia, 21, 276n; quarrels with TL, 27–28; receives instructions for expedition to Australia, 23–24, 272n, 277n; at Shark Bay, 149; shipboard library, 23, 189, 291n; sights New Holland, 25; studies marine animals, 131; TL names plant for, 136; writings, 29
Bay of Bengal: 66
Bay of Islands (New Zealand): 296n
Bays, estate of (France): 9
Belle Angélique, ship: *see* West Indies, voyage of *Belle Angélique* to
Bellefin, Jérôme-Jean-Claude (1764–1835), surgeon: 64, 180
Benin: 304n
Berber people: 37
Bernardin de Saint-Pierre, Jacques-Henri (1737–1814), naturalist: 104–105, 283–84n
Bernier Island (Western Australia), *also known as* smaller Dorre Island *and* Barren Island: 25, 148, 149–51, 152, 191, 291n, 292n
Bernier, Pierre-François (1779–1803), astronomer: 93, 291n
Bertin, Louis-Charles-Henri (1752–1822), government administrator: 279n
Besnard, Citizen: 104, 109, 112
Béthencourt, Jean de (1362–1425), adventurer: 93, 282n
Béthencourt, Maciot de, ruler of Canary Islands: 282n
Beugnot, Jacques-Claude, Comte (1761–1835), politician: 279n
Bibliothèque du roi (King's Library), Paris: 271, 305n
Biche, schooner: 65, 66

Binzoa: *see* Raijua
Bismarck Archipelago (Papua New Guinea): 295n
Bissaula (Nigeria): 298n
Bizouard, Nicolas, school principal: 12, 274–75n
Black River (Mauritius): 102
Blanquilla Island (Venezuela): 292n
Bligh, William (1754–1817), officer of the Royal Navy: 156, 195, 293n, 295n, 300n
Blue Mountains (New South Wales): 26, 256, 301n
Bognam-nonen-derega, *also known as* Merlot (b. *c.* 1784, d. after 1803), Makpa botanist: 32, 37, 68–69, 231–32, 298n, 301n
Bois de Boulogne, Paris: 7
Bonaparte, Joséphine *née* Marie Josèphe Rose Tascher de la Pagerie, *1st married name* de Beauharnais (1763–1814), empress of the French (1804–1810): 42, 211, 258, 259, 296n, 304n
Bonaparte, Louis Napoléon (1778–1846), king of Holland (1806–1810): 299n, 302n
Bonaparte, Napoléon (1769–1821), first consul (1799–1804), emperor of the French (1804–1814/1815): 246, 302n; abdicates, 268, 304n, 305n; approves Baudin expedition, 22; coronation, 20; expedition to Egypt, 288; plan to invade England, 66
Bonin, Marguerite (1779–?), wife of TL: divorce, 7; marriage, 6
Bonnefoi de Montbazin, Louis-Charles-Gaspard (1778–?), naval officer: 64, 207–208
Bonpland, Aimé (1773–1858), botanist: 42, 269, 303–304n
Boonwurrung people: language of, 298n
Bordeaux (France): 17, 147, 194, 303n
Bory de Saint-Vincent, Jean-Baptiste-Geneviève-Marcellin (1778–1846), naturalist: 280–81n, 283n, 285n

Botany Bay (New South Wales): 297n
Bougainville, Hyacinthe-Yves-Philippe-Florentin de (1781–1846), naval officer, son of Louis-Antoine: 64, 98, 194
Bougainville, Louis-Antoine de (1729–1811), navigator: 23, 64, 98
Boullanger, Charles–Pierre (1772–1813), geographer: 68
Boulogne (France): 66
Bounty, ship: 156, 195, 293n, 295n
Branciforte, Miguel de la Grúa Talamanca y, 1st marquis of Branciforte (*c.* 1750–1812), Spanish colonial administrator: 93, 281n
Brazil: 8, 65
Brest (France): 66, 293n
British Museum, London: 300n
Brittany (France): 68, 147
Broussonet, Pierre-Marie-Auguste (1761–1807), botanist: 90, 281n
Brown, Robert (1773–1858), Scottish botanist: 26–27, 42, 44, 241, 256, 258, 277n, 291n, 300n, 301n, 303n, 304n; 'General remarks, geographical and systematical, on the botany of *Terra Australis*', 269, 291n, 303n; *Prodromus florae Novae Hollandiae et Insulae Van Diemen*, 42, 43, 270, 304n; TL's letters to, 251–52, 268–72, 278n
Bruny Island (Tasmania): 201, 202, 203–208, 209, 210–11, 212, 214–215, 216
Bruny Islanders: 26, 39–40, 202–208, 210, 211, 212, 214–15, 216, 226
Bunbury (Western Australia): 45
Burgundy (France): 13, 252, 259
Burman, Johannes (1707–1780), Dutch botanist: 303n
Burman, Nicolaas (1734–1793), Dutch botanist, son of Johannes: 269, 303n
Burnel, Étienne-Laurent-Pierre (1762–1835), colonial administrator: 283n, 286n
Busselton (Western Australia): 290n

Cagigal de la Vega y Martínez Niño, Fernando de, marquis of Casa Cagigal (1756–1824), Spanish colonial administrator: 280n

Cagnet, Jean-François (1756–?), assistant gardener: 301n

cahiers de doléances (lists of grievances): *see* French Revolution

Calcutta (India), *now known as* Kolkata: 297n

Caley, George (1770–1829), English botanist: 26, 256, 300–301n

Calvi (Corsica): 281n

Cameroon: 298n

Canary Islands: 37, 38, 85, 90, 91, 92, 93, 280n, 281n, 282n; history, 93–94; *see also* Guanche people *and* Tenerife

Candelaria (Canary Islands): 281n

Candolle, Augustin Pyramus de (1778–1841), Swiss botanist: 24, 248, 250, 258, 290n, 291n, 299n, 303n

Cannonier Point (Mauritius): 102

Canton (China), *now known as* Guangzhou: 69, 160

Cape Colony: 282n

Cape Finisterre (Spain): 83

Cape Horn (Chile): 300n

Cape of Fires (Victoria): 224

Cape of Good Hope (South Africa): 22, 25, 100–101, 105–106, 131, 147, 234, 282–83n

Cape Leeuwin (Western Australia): 25, 133, 134

Cape Leschenault (Western Australia): 44, 45

Cape Range (Western Australia): 292n

Caribbean Sea: 63, 279n, 280n, 283n, 292n

Casquets (Channel Islands): 82

Castile, kingdom of: 93, 282n

Casuarina, schooner: 27, 28, 65, 253

Cayenne (French Guiana): 41, 124, 261, 262

Central America: 303n

Céré, Jean-Nicolas (1738–1810), botanist: 107–108, 285n

Cérès, frigate: 64

Cerne: 105

Ceylon, *now known as* Sri Lanka: 285n

Chalon-sur-Saône (France): 3–4, 230, 241, 245, 252, 259, 275n; commemorated in Western Australia, 45; TL commemorated in, 44; TL's early years in, 6, 8–21

Chaxiraxi, Guanche sun goddess: 281n

Cheke, Anthony (1945–), British ecologist: 285n

Chile: 21

Choteau, Citizen, notary: 104, 108

Clarke Island (Tasmania): 221–22, 229

Clement VI, Pope, *born* Pierre Roger (1291–1352): 282n

Clorinde, frigate: 71

Cochinchina (southern Vietnam): 110, 285n

Code du patrimoine (Heritage Law): 1

Collas, François (1776–1826), pharmacist: 220, 296n

Committees, of General Safety, Public Safety and Surveillance: *see* French Revolution

Concordia Fort, Kupang: 155, 157, 158, 159, 161, 194, 293n

Congo River: 68

Consulate (1799–1804): 247, 283n

Convent of the Cordeliers, Chalon-sur-Saône: 6, 18–20, 276n

Cook, James (1728–1779), English navigator: 22–23, 39, 131, 199, 226, 288n, 291n, 297n, 298n, 300n; *A Voyage to the Pacific Ocean*, 148, 166; death, 201, 295n

Coromandel Coast (India): 298n

Corsica (France): 286n

Coudery, Marie-Pierrette, sister-in-law of TL: 14

Coudrenière, Henri Peyroux de la (*c.* 1743–*c.* 1811), colonial administrator: 124, 287n

Crétet, Emmanuel (1747–1809), politician: 29

Cumberland, Monsieur de: 94

Cuvier, Jean-Léopold-Nicolas-Frédéric, *known as* Georges (1769–1832), zoologist: 37, 129

Dampier, William (1651–1715), English navigator: 143, 291n, 292n; *A Voyage to New Holland*, 150, 269, 291n, 302n
Darwin, Erasmus Robert (1731–1802), English poet: 304n
David, Jacques-Louis (1748–1825), painter: 70
Decrès, Denis (1761–1820), statesman: 29
Degérando, Joseph-Marie (1772–1842), anthropologist: 36, 38, 39
Delessert, Étienne (1735–1816), banker: 303n
Delessert, Jules Paul Benjamin (1773–1847), banker, son of Étienne: 269, 303n
Deleuze, Joseph-Philippe-François (1753–1835), naturalist: 269, 304n
Delisse, Jacques (1773–1856), botanist: 4–5, 64, 114, 191, 249, 301n
Denham, Sir Henry Mangles (1800–1887), officer of the Royal Navy: 45
D'Entrecasteaux Channel (Tasmania): 23, 26, 30, 35–36, 201, 301n; plants of, 201–202, 205, 207, 209–10, 212–13, 215–17, 223, 301n; stay in, 200–219; temperature chart at sea off, 217–19; weather, 217; *see also* Bruny Islanders
Dépôt général de la Marine: 65, 66
Depuch de Monbreton, Alexandre-Jean (1744–?), politician, father of Louis-Alexandre: 65
Depuch de Monbreton, Louis-Alexandre (1774–1803), mineralogist: 65, 98, 118, 123, 134, 135, 140, 142, 145, 163, 194, 201, 290n
Depuch Island (Western Australia), *also known as* Admiral Island *and* Warmalana: 152, 292n
Deschamps, Jacques-Charles (1778–?), ironmaster, brother-in-law of TL: 13

Deschamps, Jean-Joseph-Eugène (1811–?), nephew of TL: 6–7, 18, 44
Desfontaines, René Louiche (1750–1833), botanist: 4–5, 42, 264, 270, 302n
Dias, Bartolomeu (c. 1450–1500), Portuguese navigator: 100, 282n, 283n
Didon, frigate: 69
Dieppe (France): 71
Dijon (France): 10, 11, 12
Dili (East Timor): 288
Directory (1795–1799): 21, 281n, 286n, 303n
Dirk Hartog Island (Western Australia): 149, 292n
Dorre Islands (Western Australia), *also known as* Barren Islands: 149; *see also* Bernier Island
Doyle, William (1942–), English historian: 15
Dryander, Jonas Carlsson (1748–1810), Swedish botanist: 255, 300n
Du Chilleau, Jean-Baptiste (1735–1824), bishop of Chalon-sur-Saône: 16
Dunmore, John (1923–), New Zealand historian: 22
Du Petit Thouars, Louis-Marie-Aubert (1758–1831), botanist: 107, 109, 269, 284n, 285n, 303n
Du Pont de Nemours, Éleuthère Irénée (1771–1834), industrialist: 262, 301–302n
Dupuy, André-Julien, Comte (1753–1832), colonial administrator: 235, 299n
Dutch East India Company: 155, 158, 159, 160, 161, 173, 185, 293n, 294n
Dutch East Indies: 28, 41, 43, 100, 241, 285n, 293n, 294n; *see also* Batavia, Java, Kupang *and* Timor

Eastern Cove, Kangaroo Island (South Australia): 27
École centrale (Central School), Agen: 303n
École centrale de santé (Central School of Health), Paris, *later known as* École de médicine (School of Medicine): 6, 273n

École des mines (School of Mines), Paris: 65
École polytechnique, Paris: 63, 64, 65, 68
Egypt and Syria, French Campaign in (1798–1801): 14, 288n
Eliza, sloop: 297n
Ellsworth, Oliver (1745–1807), American diplomat: 279n
Endeavour River (Queensland): 297n
Endeavour Strait (Queensland): 161
Engelhard, Nicolaus (1761–1831), Dutch colonial administrator: 28
English Channel: 64, 66, 82, 123, 279n, 284n
Enrique III (1379–1406), king of Castile: 282n
Entrecasteaux, Antoine-Raymond-Joseph de Bruni d' (1737–1793), navigator: 23, 201, 211, 289n, 295n, 296n
Entreprise, schooner: 47, 297n
Eora people: 27, 39, 40–41, 254–55, 260, 297–98n, 301n
Épinay, Prosper-Adrien-Félix-Charles d' (1830–1897), author: 284n
Erskine, David Montagu, 2nd Baron Erskine (1776–1855), English diplomat: 262, 301n
Essonne (France): 301n
Estates General: *see* French Revolution
Este, Sara van, *née* Tielman, *1st married name* de Witt, wife of Willem Adriaan van Este: 156, 166, 189–90
Este, Willem Adriaan van (1735–1789), commander of Dutch Timor: 156
Europe: 2, 21, 27, 48, 84, 88, 89, 90, 92, 100, 103, 107, 109, 110, 134, 161, 167, 189, 233, 234, 251, 252, 255, 256, 258, 259, 260, 280n, 293n, 303n

Falkland Islands: 65
Faure, Pierre-Ange-François-Xavier (1777–1855), geographer: 65, 68, 224, 227, 228
First Coalition, War of (1792–1797): 6
First Crusade (1096–1099): 283n

First French Empire (1804–1814/1815): 64, 304n
Flat Island (Mauritius): 102
Fleuriot, Paul Antoine Marie, vicomte de Langle (1744–1787), naval officer: 201, 295n, 296n
Flinders, Matthew (1774–1814), English navigator: 23, 26, 258, 271, 276n, 297n, 305n
Fluted Cape (Tasmania): 209
Forfait, Pierre-Alexandre-Laurent (1752–1807), statesman: 1, 2, 3, 23, 264; letter from, 246–47
Forster, Georg (1754–1794), German naturalist: 131, 289n
Fortunate Isles: *see* Canary Islands
Foulpointe (Madagascar), *also known as* Mahavelona: 69, 298n
Fourcroy, Antoine-François de (1755–1809), chemist: 5
France: 1, 2, 3, 6, 8, 11, 12, 13, 14, 15, 16, 17, 21, 26, 27, 28, 34, 36, 41, 43, 44, 48, 63, 64, 65, 66, 67, 68, 69, 70, 77, 79, 82, 91, 103, 104, 106, 107, 124, 147, 184, 185, 226, 241, 246, 252, 253, 254, 255, 257, 261, 262, 264, 266, 268, 270, 271, 279n, 281n, 282n, 284n, 287n, 288n, 294n, 297n, 298n, 299n, 301n, 302n, 303n, 304n
French-American Quasi-War (1798–1800): 279–80n
French Guiana: 8, 66, 70, 241, 287n
French Revolution (1789–1799): 246, 302n; Anne Leschenault's experience of, 14; arrest of Leschenaults, 17–18; *cahiers de doléances* (lists of grievances), 15; Chalon during, 16, 275n; Committee of General Safety, 18; Committee of Public Safety, 17; Committee of Surveillance, 6, 17, 18; *départements* created, 16; divorce legalised, 7; emigration, 16; Estates General, 15, 65; executions, 17; feudalism abolished, 16; French Revolutionary Wars (1792–1802), 69, 280n, 284n, 286n; Girondins, 19;

GENERAL INDEX

Great Fear (1789), 16; imprisonment of Leschenaults, 15–20; lasting effect on TL, 21; Law of Suspects, 17, 19; Montagnards, 17, 20; National Assembly (1789), 15–16, 281n; National Constituent Assembly (1789–1791), 18; National Convention (1792–1795), 17, 283n, 305n; outbreak of, 15; *parlements* abolished, 16; property holdings of Leschenault family during, 6; religious orders abolished, 18; storming of Bastille fortress, 15; Terror (1793–1794), 6, 17–20; War in the Vendée (1793–1796), 17

Freycinet, Louis-Claude de Saulces de (1779–1842), *known as* Louis Freycinet, naval officer: 43, 65, 67, 135, 140, 266, 270, 271, 287n, 289n, 290n, 291n, 295n, 298n; *Voyage autour du monde*, 65; *Voyage de découvertes aux terres australes*, 266, 270, 287n, 298n, 305n

Freycinet, Louis-Henri de Saulces de (1777–1840), *known as* Henri Freycinet, brother of Louis-Claude, naval officer: 65, 66, 194, 214, 289n, 290n, 295n

Freycinet, Rose de, *née* Rose Pinon (1794–1832), traveller, wife of Louis Freycinet: 65

Friendly Islands: 144

Fuerteventura (Canary Islands): 94, 282n

Furneaux Islands (Tasmania): 26, 221–22, 297n

Gallet, Citizen, naval officer: 104, 107

Gama, Vasco da (*c.* 1469–1524), Portuguese navigator: 100, 283n

Gardner, Alan, 1st Baron Gardner (1742–1809), officer of the Royal Navy: 82, 280n

Gardner, Alan Hyde, 2nd Baron Gardner (1770–1815), officer of the Royal Navy, son of Alan Gardner: 82, 280n

Gauthier, Louis-François-Anne, uncle of TL: 19

Gauthier, Marguerite (*c.* 1744–1809), mother of TL: 3, 9, 12–13, 31, 32, 33, 78, 189, 254, 258

Gauthier, Pierre, grandfather of TL: 9

Gauthier de la Tournelle, Gabriel, nobleman: 15, 19

Genise, branch of river Saône: 18

Genoa (Italy): 65

Geoffroy Saint-Hilaire, Étienne (1772–1844), naturalist: 288n

Géographe, corvette: 7, 8, 24–28, 31–32, 62, 81; air and sea temperatures measured from, 115–17, 287n; artists attached to, 86, 280n; in the Atlantic Ocean, 31, 82–84, 95–100, 115–31; biographical notes about TL's shipmates on *Naturaliste* and, 63–71; death of Maugé aboard, 219; at D'Entrecasteaux Channel, 200–216; departure from Isle of France, 133; departure from Le Havre, 80–81; departure from Port Jackson, 253; encounters Royal Navy frigate in English Channel, 81–82; at Geographe Bay, 25, 133–48; Geographe Bay named for, 25, 134; at Isle of France, 102–104, 282n; at Kangaroo Island, 27; at King George Sound, 28; at Kupang, 25, 28, 155–56; at Le Havre, 78–81; live plants transported on, 41; at Maria Island, 219–20; missed rendezvous with *Naturaliste*, 25, 27, 148, 191; passage from Geographe Bay to Shark Bay, 148; passage from Isle of France to New Holland, 133; passage from Shark Bay to Kupang, 152–55; at Port Jackson, 26, 258; return to France, 28, 41; separation from *Naturaliste*, 25, 26, 83, 148, 220, 258; at Shark Bay, 25, 28, 149–50, 152; at Tenerife, 24, 83–84, 95–96, 123; TL appointed to, 5–6, 246–47; TL evicted from cabin on, 27–28; TL's cabin on, 24; TL's closest friends on, 193–94; TL's papers lost on, 30, 270; TL transfers from, 26,

191–93; TL transfers from *Naturaliste* back to, 27; TL travels on, 7, 79–104, 115–56; TL visits friends on, 201; visited by Royal Navy frigate in Kupang roads, 157–58
Geographe Bay (Western Australia), *also* Géographe Bay: 25, 33, 35, 39, 71, 133–48, 149, 191, 194, 200, 290n; naming of, 25, 134
Germain, Citizen: 78, 249
Germany: 294n
Girondins: *see* French Revolution
Glorious First of June (1794): 284n
Gomera (Canary Islands): 94
Gonneville, Binot Paulmier de (*fl.* early sixteenth century), navigator: 22
Good, Peter (?–1803), British assistant gardener: 26, 251
Gran Canaria (Canary Islands): 86, 94
Grand Hôtel de Richelieu, Paris: 267, 271
Great Bay (Tasmania): 201
Great Britain: 29, 261, 268, 279n
Great Fear (1789): *see* French Revolution
Green Island (Tasmania): 209–10
Greenland: 64
Greenock (Scotland): 280n
Groix, Battle of (1795): 69
Gros Ventre, fluyt: 295n
Guadeloupe: 71, 104, 283n
Guanche people (of the Canary Islands): 37–38, 93, 94–95, 96, 278n, 281n, 282n
Guichenot, Antoine (1783–1867), assistant gardener: 28, 41, 301n
Guillemardet, Antoinette-Geneviève, *née* Renard, godmother of TL: 274n
Guillemardet de la Jonchère, Jean-Jacques (?–1774), tax official, godfather of TL: 9, 274n
Gunners' Quoin (Mauritius): 102, 103
Gutiérrez de Otero y Santallana, Antonio (1729–1799), Spanish colonial administrator: 281n
Guugu Yimithirr people: 297n
Gweagal people: 297n

Hamelin, Jacques-Félix-Emmanuel (1768–1839), captain of *Naturaliste*: 26, 66, 139, 141–42, 145–46, 182, 189, 193, 208, 209, 211, 214, 215, 221, 257, 259, 264, 277n, 296n, 301n
Hartog, Dirk (1580–1621), Dutch navigator: 291n
Haskell, Yasmin: 300n
Havana (Cuba): 92
Hawaiian Islands (USA): 289n, 295n
Hawkesbury River (New South Wales): 26, 256
Hawkesworth, John (*c.* 1715–1773), editor: 131, 288–89n
Heirisson, François-Antoine-Boniface (1776–1834), naval officer: 67, 140
Henri III (1551–1589), king of France: 9
Henrique, Dom, *known as* Prince Henry the Navigator (1394–1460), Portuguese prince: 93–94, 282n
Hierro (Canary Islands): 94, 282n
Holland: 89, 280n, 302n
Hooker, Maria Sarah, *née* Turner, Lady Hooker (1797–1872), wife of Sir William Jackson Hooker: 302n
Hooker, Sir William Jackson (1785–1865), English botanist: 268, 302n
Hôtel de Genève, Paris: 252
Humboldt, Friedrich Wilhelm Heinrich Alexander von (1769–1859), German naturalist: 286n, 303n
Hyères Islands (France): 65

Iazon, frigate: 280n
Île Saint-Laurent, Chalon-sur-Saône (France): 14
Indé (Indonesia): 171
Indefatigable, ship of the line: 293n
India: 44, 63, 100, 104, 106, 234, 271, 182, 282–83n, 285n, 298n, 305n
Indian Ocean: 66, 283n, 284n
Indigenous peoples (of Australia): 23, 24, 36, 38–41, 48, 144, 153, 190, 221, 226, 292n, 297n; in D'Entrecasteaux Channel, 26, 39–40, 201, 202–208, 210, 211, 212, 213, 214–15, 216, 224,

225, 226; at Geographe Bay, 25, 38, 135, 137, 138, 140–45, 147; on Maria Island, 38, 219, graves, 219–20; in Sydney, 39, 40–41, 254–55, 260, 297–98n, 301n; in Western Port, 40, 223–26, 227, 228; *see also* Boonwurrung people, Bruny Islanders, Eora people, Guugu Yimithirr people, Gweagal people, Ngarluma people, Noongar people *and* Wardandi people
Ingouville (France): 78
Institut de France (Institute of France), Paris: 5, 21, 114, 242, 271
Investigator, sloop: 26, 251
Ireland: 284n
Irish Rebellion (1798): 69
Isle of Bourbon, *now known as* Réunion: 66, 69, 103, 106, 107, 285n, 286n
Isle of France, *also known as* Mauritius: 4, 21, 25, 26, 31, 32, 34, 35, 41, 43, 63, 64, 65, 66, 67, 68, 69, 70, 80, 234, 235, 251, 253, 281–82n, 284n, 285n, 287n, 296n, 299n, 303n; animals, 112–14; animals observed during passage to, 125–32; arrival at, 101–104; Baudin's death on, 41; delays, defections and desertions on, 25, 31, 67, 70, 257, 282n, 298n, 301n; history, 105–106; passage to, 97–104; plants, 108–110; plants transported to, 110–11; slaves and slavery, 21, 37, 40, 103–105, 111–12, 283n, 286n; stay on, 104–114
Isthmus Bay (Tasmania): 209

Jangoux, Michel (1946–), Belgian marine biologist: 42
Japan: 294n
Jardin des plantes (Botanical Gardens), Paris: 195, 264, 284n, 299n; *see also* Jardin du roi *and* Muséum d'histoire naturelle, Paris
Jardin du roi (King's Garden), Paris: 287n, 302n; *see also* Jardin des plantes *and* Muséum d'histoire naturelle, Paris

Jauffret, Louis-François (1770–1840), anthropologist: 37, 278n
Java (Indonesia): 28, 42, 161, 190, 251, 261–62, 270, 294n
Jeandet, Jean-Pierre-Abel (1816–1899), archivist: 7, 44
Jefferson, Thomas (1743–1826), American statesman: 285n
Joannis, Monsieur, Timorese trader: 166, 167, 182, 189, 190, 193, 194
João II (1455–1495), king of Portugal: 283n
John the Baptist, saint: 9
Junon, frigate: 71
Jussieu, Antoine-Laurent de (1748–1836), botanist: 3, 5, 7, 24, 29–31, 32, 33–34, 35, 36, 39, 69, 215, 241, 269, 270, 271, 272, 279n, 296n, 300n, 302n; letters to, 242–46, 248–50, 253–65; recommends TL for expedition, 5
Jussieu, Bernard de (1699–1777), botanist, uncle of Antoine-Laurent de Jussieu: 69
Jussieu, Thérèse-Adrienne de, *née* du Boisneuf (1767–1857), wife of Antoine-Laurent de Jussieu: 258, 262

Kaiserslautern (Germany): 70
Kangaroo Island (South Australia): 27
Kealakekua Bay (USA): 295n
Kentu (Nigeria): 298n
Kera (Indonesia): 156, 199
Kew Gardens, London: 302n
King, James (1750–1784), officer of the Royal Navy: 165
King, Philip Gidley (1758–1808), English colonial administrator: 27, 271, 305n
King George Sound (Western Australia): 28, 269, 289n
King Island (Tasmania): 27, 297n
Kozhikode (India): 283n
Kupang (Timor): 26, 28, 32, 41, 270, 293n, 295n; stay in, 155–200

Labillardière, Jacques-Julien Houtou de (1755–1834), botanist: 23, 39, 42, 136, 186, 202, 207, 209, 289n, 290n, 294n,

296n, 302n, 303n; *Novae Hollandiae plantarum specimen*, 42, 290n, 303n; *Relation du voyage à la recherche de La Pérouse*, 39, 186, 206, 289n, 294n, 296n
La Clayette (France): 13
La Laguna (Canary Islands), *also known as* San Cristóbal de la Laguna: 86–88, 89, 90, 91, 280n, 285n
Lamanon, Jean Honoré Robert de Paul de (1752–1787), naturalist: 201, 230, 296n, 298n
Lamarck, Jean-Baptiste-Pierre-Antoine de Monet, chevalier de (1744–1829), naturalist: 302n
Lamouroux, Claude (1741–1820), merchant, father of Félix: 303n
Lamouroux, Jean-Vincent-Félix (1779–1825), botanist: 269, 303n
Lancelin (Western Australia): 45
Langlès, Louis-Mathieu (1763–1824), linguist: 271, 305n
Lanzarote (Canary Islands): 94, 282n
La Orotava (Canary Islands): 89, 91
La Pérouse, Jean-François de Galaup, comte de (1741–1788), navigator: 23, 201, 284n, 286n, 288n, 289n, 295n, 296n, 302n
Larsen, Brenda: 290n
Latham, John (1740–1837), English ornithologist: 229
Lavoisier, Antoine-Laurent de (1743–1794), chemist: 301n
Law of Suspects: *see* French Revolution
Le Bas de Sainte-Croix, Alexandre (1759–1828), naval officer: 67, 98, 141, 144, 194
Leblanc, Citizen: 104
Lebrun, Louis (1769/1770–?), artist: 280n
Lecorre, Alexandre Josselin (1766–1802), ship's captain: 297n
Ledru, André-Pierre (1761–1825), botanist: 4–5
Leeuwin's Land (Western Australia): 134, 137, 148, 149, 289n
Le Gentil, Guillaume (1725–1792), astronomer: 298–99n

Le Havre (France): 2, 4, 7, 24, 37, 41, 67, 77–81, 82, 83, 98, 125, 196, 241, 247, 248, 249, 279n, 280n
Le Monnier, Louis-Guillaume (1717–1799), botanist: 69
Le Pouce, mountain (Mauritius): 102, 107
Leschenault, Anne (1736–1822), nun, aunt of TL: 14, 16
Leschenault, Claude (*fl.* 1690–1711), lawyer: 10
Leschenault, Claude-Théodore (1730–1797), lawyer, father of TL: 6–7, 9–12; imprisonment during French Revolution, 15–20
Leschenault, Henriette-Eugénie-Marguerite (1785–?), sister of TL: 11, 13; beneficiary of TL's will, 13; marriage, 13
Leschenault, Jacques (*c.* 1696–1782), surgeon, lawyer, grandfather of TL: 10
Leschenault, Louis-François-Théodore (1768–?), lay canon, brother of TL: 13–14, imprisonment during French Revolution, 17–20
Leschenault, Théodore-César (1779–?), soldier, brother of TL: 13–14
Leschenault (de la Tour), Jean-Baptiste-Louis-Claude-Théodore (1773–1826), botanist: appointed to Baudin expedition, 4–8, 246–47; in D'Entrecasteaux Channel, 200–217, 219, encounters Bruny Islanders, 202–205, 205–207, 210, 215, plants, 207, 210–11, 215–17, reports attacks on French sailors, 207–208, 214–15, visits Green Island, 209–210, visits North West Bay, 209, 211–12, 212–14, visits Partridge Island, 201–205; divorce, 7–8; early life, 8–14; education, 12; on Furneaux Islands, 221–22; at Geographe Bay, 134–48, encounter with Noongar people, 140–44, reflections on, 146–47, stranded ashore, 144–46; forebears, 9–11;

imprisonment during Revolution, 6, 15–21; on Isle of France, 103–110, 111–15, albino woman, 111, animals, 112–14, botanical gardens, 108–109, defections at, 114–15, history, 106, meets Céré, 108–109, meets Du Petit Thouars, 107, meets Lhermite, 107–108, plants, 109–110, Port Louis, 107, Port Louis harbour, 103, slavery, 104–105, 112, trade 106; journal, form of, 29–32, method of observation, 33–41, rediscovery of, 1–4, tone of, 32–33; legacy, in France, 41–44, in Australia, 44–45; in Le Havre, 78–81, departs from, 80–81; on Maria Island, 219, graves, 219–20; marriage, 6; 'Note on the Vegetation of New Holland', 3, 36, 43, 269, 270, 290n; passage from Geographe Bay to Shark Bay, 148; passage from Isle of France to New Holland, 133; passage from Le Havre to Tenerife, 80–83; passage from Shark Bay to Timor, 152–55; passage from Tenerife to Isle of France, 95–103, 110–11, 115–17, animals observed during, 125–32, crossing of Equator, 99–100, sighting of Cape of Good Hope, 100, study of air and sea temperatures, 115–19, 122–23, study of humidity, 120–22; passage from Timor to D'Entrecasteaux Channel, 199–201; in Port Jackson and Sydney, 2, 5, 26–27, 30, 33, 39, 40, 47–48, 136, 216, 219, 222, 230, 241, 251–52, 253, 254–58, 259–60, 264, 292n, 295n, 296n, 297n, 298n, botanises, 26, 256, British colony, 22, 254, Indigenous people, 27, 38, 40, 254–55, 260; professional ambitions, 8; relations with Baudin, 26, 27–28, 30, 32, 42–43, 131, 136, 192–93, 195–96, 270; relations with Brown, 26, 42–43, 44, 241, 251–52, 256, 258, 268–72; relations with family, 11–14; renames himself 'Leschenault de la Tour', 20; in Shark Bay, 149–53, animals of Bernier Island, 149–51; study of phosphorescence, 123; on Tenerife, 84–95, animals, 91–92, geology, 95, Guanche people, 94–95, 96, the 'hermit of the rocks', 87, inhabitants, 93, La Laguna, 86, 87–88, plants, 88–90, Santa Cruz, 84–86, 87–88, 92–93, Santa Cruz harbour, 91, trade, 92, visits commandant general, 85; in Timor, 155–97, amulets and necklaces, 174–75, animals, 183–85, Baudin's illness, 193, 197, dance, 172, 173, death of Riedlé, 194, friendships with Timorese people, 189–91, graves of Riedlé and Nelson, 294–95, inhabitants, ordinary, 168–77, inhabitants, wealthy, 162–68, Kupang, 156–57, Malay language, 186–89, mineral deposits, 185–86, music, 171–72, plants, 177–83, provisioning for voyage, 196, rajas, 158–59, 172–73, slaves, 166, Timorese weapons, 175, TL's transfer to *Naturaliste*, 191–94, trade, 159–61, visit of *Virginie*, 157–58; travels from Paris to Le Havre, 77–78; views on ecological degradation, 146–47, 222; in Western Port, 223–30, encounter with Indigenous people, 224–26, geology, 223–24, 227–28, 228–29, plants, 227, 229

Leschenault (de Rupt), Jean-Baptiste-Claude-Samuel (1776–1854), banker, brother of TL: beneficiary of TL's will, 3, 13; copy of journal, 3–4, 47, 292n, 294n; letter to Jussieu, 241, 259–60; relations with TL, 3, 12–13, 21

Leschenault (de Rupt), Louise-Étiennette-Stéphanie (1811–1830), daughter of Samuel: 3

Leschenault (du Villard), Henry-Joseph-Gabriel (1915–2017), preservationist, great-grandson of Jean-Baptiste-Antoine: 4

Leschenault (du Villard), Jean-Baptiste-Antoine (1775–1859), cavalry officer, son of Marc-Antoine-Joseph Leschenault du Villard (1745–1801): 3–4

Leschenault (du Villard), Marc-Antoine-Joseph (1745–1801), landowner: 16

Leschenault (du Villard), Marc-Antoine-Joseph (1776–1840), doctor, son of Marc-Antoine-Joseph Leschenault (du Villard) (1745–1801): 7

Leschenault (du Villard), Pierre-Jacques (1777–1809), doctor, son of Marc-Antoine-Joseph Leschenault (du Villard) (1745–1801): 7

Leschenault Conservation Park (Western Australia): 45

Leschenault Estuary (Western Australia): 44, 45

Lesueur, Charles-Alexandre (1778–1846), artist: 67, 70, 86, 184, 266, 271, 280n, 288n

Leti (Indonesia): 294n

Levillain, Stanislas (1774–1801), zoologist: *68*, 147; death, 199

Le Villard, château: 4

Lharidon de Créménec, François-Étienne (1768–1807), medical officer: 32, *68*, 95, 98, 140, 180

Lhermite, Jean-Marthe-Adrien (1766–1826), naval officer: 107–108, 284n

Linnaeus, Carl (1707–1778), Swedish botanist: 34, 78, 83, 92, 97, 100, 101, 125, 126, 127, 129, 279n, 283n, 288n, 293n, 294n, 300n

Lisbon (Portugal): 283n

Lizard Point (England): 82, 293n

Lofsteth, Hans Andries (?–1802), interim commander of Dutch Timor: 156, 157, 158, 159, 161, 174, 194, 293n

Loire, river (France): 262

London (England): 241, 255, 271, 272, 281n, 290n, 304n, 305n

Louis XVI (1754–1793), king of France: 15, 16

Louis XVIII (1755–1824), king of France: 8, 9, 54

Luis de la Cerda (1291–1348), expatriate prince of Castile: 93, 282n

Lycée colonial, Port Louis (Mauritius): 65

Lyon (France): 6, 12, 13, 17

Mabberley, David John (1948–), botanist: 272

Maclure, William (1763–1840), Scottish geologist: 67

Mâcon (France): 44

Macpa people: *see* Makpa people

Macquarie, Lachlan (1762–1824), Scottish colonial administrator: 300n

Madagascar: 68, 69, 71, 105, 106, 107, 108, 113, 231, 279n, 285n, 298n; description, 32, 48, 233–35

Madura (Indonesia): 28, 261

Magallon, François-Louis, comte de la Morlière (1754–1825), colonial administrator: 114, 286n

Magnien, Joseph, lawyer, uncle of TL: 19

Magny (France): 248, 299n

Maillard, Citizen: 111

Makpa people (of west Africa): 37, 48, 68, 279n, 298n; description, 231–33; *see also* Bognam-nonen-derega

Malartic, Anne-Joseph-Hippolyte de Maurès, comte de (1730–1800), colonial administrator: 114, 283n, 286n

Malay language: 26, 32, 186–89, 294n, 295n

Malmaison, château: 42, 299n, 304n

Malta: 288n

Malvasia wine: 92, 281n

Manuel I (1469–1521), king of Portugal: 100, 283n, 286n

Maria Island (Tasmania): 26, 39, 68, 225; graves, 219–220

Marion du Fresne, Marc-Joseph (1724–1772), navigator: 23, 201

Marseille (France): 17
Martha, Congregation of the Hospitaller Sisters of Saint: 14
Martinière, Joseph Hugues Boissieu de la, *known as* Joseph La Martinière (1758–1788), botanist: 130, 288n
Martinique: 66
Mary, mother of Jesus: 93, 281n
Mascarene Islands: 284n, 285n, 286n, 299n
Maugé, René (b. between 1756 and 1758, d. 1802), zoologist: 68, 125, 132, 151, 201, 249; death, 68, 219
Mauritius: 4, 105, 285n; *see also* Isle of France
Maurouard, Jean-Marie-Toussaint (1772–?), naval officer: 68, 207–208
Mediterranean Sea: 63, 66, 289n
Meek, Charles Kingsley (1885–1965), British anthropologist: 298n
Merlot: *see* Bognam-nonen-derega
Michaux (*also* Michaud), André (1746–1802), botanist: 4–5, 24, 25, 31, 68, 69, 114–15, 191, 231, 249, 298n, 301n
Michaux, François-André (1770–1855), botanist, son of André: 298n
Middle Island (Western Australia): 149
Miguel Albertus, raja of Amanuban: 191
Milbert, Jacques-Gérard (1766–1840), artist: 280n
Milius, Pierre-Bernard (1773–1829), naval officer: 29, 40, 66, 69–70, 200; at Western Port, 223–28, 297n
Ministry for the Navy and Colonies (France): 1, 2, 3, 5, 32, 70
Ministry of the Interior (France): 273n, 300n
Mirbel, Charles-François Brisseau de (1776–1854), botanist: 250, 258, 262, 299–300n, 302n, 304n
Missouri (USA): 287n
Mogador (Morocco), *now known as* Essaouira: 281n
Moluccas (Indonesia), *now known as* Maluku Islands: 109, 144, 162, 166, 182, 186, 291n, 293n, 294n, 296n

Montagnards: *see* French Revolution
Montalivet, Jean-Pierre Bachasson, comte de (1766–1823), statesman: 43, 279n; TL's letter to, 266–67
Montpellier (France): 281n
Montrose (Scotland): 301n
Moore, George Fletcher (1798–1886), Irish colonist in Western Australia: 71
Mortefontaine, château: 279n
Mount Ijen (Java): 270
Muller, Jacques-Léonard (1749–1824), army officer: 279n
Murray, William Vans (1760–1803), American diplomat: 279–80n
Muséum d'histoire naturelle (Museum of Natural History), Le Havre: 67
Muséum d'histoire naturelle (Museum of Natural History), Paris: 3, 5, 7, 21, 29, 30, 33, 34, 41, 42, 44, 63, 68, 70, 241, 242, 264, 270, 288n, 299n, 300n, 302n, 303–304n

Nantes (France): 262, 263
Napoleon I: *see* Bonaparte, Napoléon
Napoleonic Wars (1803–1815): 64, 71, 268, 284n
National Assembly (1789): *see* French Revolution
National Constituent Assembly (1789–1791): *see* French Revolution
National Convention (1792–1795): *see* French Revolution
Naturaliste, corvette: 2, 24, 25–28, 30, 41, 63, 64, 65, 66, 67, 68, 69, 71, 83, 114, 146, 147, 149, 180, 190, 220, 230, 254, 257, 296n, 297n; absence of botanists on, 191; air temperature measured aboard, 217–19; in Banks Strait, 220–22; biographical notes about TL's shipmates on *Géographe* and, 63–71; death of Levillain aboard, 200; delayed arrival in Kupang, 25, 191; in D'Entrecasteaux Channel, 200–16; departure from Le Havre, 80–81; departures from Port Jackson, 26, 27, 217, 251, 253; at Geographe

Bay, 138–39; at Isle of France, 102, 301n; live plants transported on, 41; at Maria Island, 219–20; missed rendezvous with *Géographe*, 25, 27, 148, 191; at Port Jackson, 251–52; return to France, 41, 246, 253, 301n; at Rottnest Island, 25; separation from *Géographe*, 25, 26, 83, 148, 220, 246, 258; at Shark Bay, 149; slow speed of, 24, 101; TL's collections and papers transported on, 29–30; TL's wood samples transported on, 264–65; TL transfers to, 26, 191–93; TL travels on, 201–230; waterspout seen from, 220–21; off Western Port, 230

Nelson, David (?–1789), English botanist: 92, 295n

Nelson, Horatio, 1st Viscount Nelson (1758–1805), officer of the Royal Navy: 92, 281n

Netherlands: 294n

New Guinea: 22, 144, 296n

New Harmony (USA): 67

New Holland: 3, 13, 21–23, 25–26, 27, 28, 36, 42, 43, 63, 81, 133–34, 136, 144, 147, 149, 152–53, 155, 161, 176, 190, 200, 251, 255–56, 260, 268–70, 272, 291n, 292n, 294n, 296n

New Madrid (USA): 287n

New Orleans (USA): 287n

New Savu (Indonesia): 199

New South Wales: 2, 4, 22, 24, 26, 27, 40, 226, 251, 253, 268, 289n, 298n, 300n, 301n, 305n

New Spain: 281n

New Zealand: 144, 296n

Ngarluma people: 292n

Niépce, Joseph Nicéphore (1765–1833), inventor: 12

Nigeria: 68, 298n

Ninety Mile Beach (Victoria): 297n

Noongar people: 25, 38, 71, 135, 137, 138, 140–45, 147

Nootka Sound (Canada): 285n

Normandy (France): 33, 279n

North Sea: 63

North West Cape (Western Australia): 292n

North-West Port (Tasmania), *now known as* North West Bay: 209, 210, 211–12, 213, 214

Norway: 284

Nouvelle Biographie générale: 13, 44

Nuyts Archipelago (South Australia): 26, 27, 28

Ouriaga, Indigenous Tasmanian man: 296n

Owen, Robert (1771–1858), Welsh social reformer: 67

Oxford (England): 291n

Pacific Ocean: 22, 23, 64, 65, 288n, 289n, 291n, 293n, 295n, 296n, 300n

Palisot, Ambroise-Marie-François-Joseph, baron de Beauvois (1752–1820), naturalist: 269, 304n

Palma (Canary Islands): 94

Pamplemousses (Mauritius): 102, 285n

Paraguay: 304n

Paris (France): 2, 3, 4, 5, 6–7, 9, 12, 13, 15, 16, 17, 18, 20, 21, 24, 30, 37, 41, 44, 63, 65, 70, 85, 98, 103, 109, 166, 194, 195, 241, 242, 245, 246, 248, 252, 262, 264, 266, 268, 269, 271, 275n, 279n, 281n, 284n, 285n, 299n, 301n, 302n, 303n

Parramatta (New South Wales): 27, 256, 300n

Parramatta River (New South Wales): 26

Partridge Island (Tasmania): 201–205, 207, 213

Paterson, Elizabeth, *née* Driver (1770–1839), Scottish philanthropist, wife of William Paterson: 260, 301n

Paterson, William (1755–1810), Scottish colonial administrator: 26, 255–56, 260, 271, 300n, 301n, 305n

Pays de Caux (France): 77

Pellew, Sir Edward (1757–1833), officer of the Royal Navy: 293n

GENERAL INDEX

Perlasca y Bardela, José Juan (*c.* 1740–1805), Spanish colonial administrator: 85, 280n, 281n

Péron, François (1775–1810), naturalist: 3, 67, *70*, 117, 118, 124, 125, 257, 288n, 289n, 292n; discovers tomb on Maria Island, 220; at Geographe Bay, 137–38, 145–46, 291n; hydrometer, 122–23, 287n; hygrometer, 286n; in King George Sound, 28; on King Island, 27; opinions about Bruny Islanders, 39; relations with TL, 32, 43, 98, 194; *Voyage de découvertes aux terres australes*, 22, 43, 65, 67, 266

Perth (Western Australia): 45

Petiot, Jean-Joseph (1751–1833), lawyer, politician: 15

Petit, Nicolas-Martin (1777–1804), artist: *70*, 86, 132, 214, 280n, 296n

Phaéton, brig: 66

Philadelphia (USA): 41, 67, 261, 262, 304n

Philipsburg (Sint Maarten): 280n

Phillip, Arthur (1738–1814), English colonial administrator: 136, 216, 289n

Phillip Island (Victoria), *also known as* Western Island: 228, 229, 298n

Pico del Teide (Canary Islands): 83, 282n

Pico Viejo (Canary Islands): 282n

Pieter Both, mountain (Mauritius): 102, 107

Pliny the Elder, Gaius Plinius Secundus, known as (23/24–79 CE), writer: 105

Point Gicquel (Tasmania): 48, 211

Poivre, Pierre (1719–1786), botanist: 285n

Pondicherry (India), *now known as* Puducherry: 8, 44

Portaiaia, Castor ans: 191

Port Cygnet (Tasmania): 208–209

Port Dalrymple (Tasmania): 301n

Port Jackson (New South Wales): 2, 23, 26, 27, 30, 47, 48, 63, 64, 65, 68, 69, 136, 217, 219, 222, 230, 251, 264, 290n, 295n, 296n, 297n; letter describing, 253–58; *see also* Sydney

Port Louis (Mauritius): 25, 65, 69, 102–104, 106–107

Portsmouth, corvette: 81, 299n

Portugal: 100, 282n, 283n

Poudre d'Or (Mauritius): 102

Pouilly de la Tour, Jean-Louis (?–1794), engineer: 20

Preneuse, frigate: 284n

Preservation Island (Tasmania): 221, 222, 229, 297n

Proselyte, frigate: 82, 280n

Pyrenees, mountains: 299n

Pyrenees, War of the (1793–1795): 280n

Raijua (Indonesia): 199

Ramond, Louis-François-Élisabeth, baron de Carbonnières (1755–1827), naturalist: 299n

Réaumur, René-Antoine Ferchault de (1683–1757), physicist: 115, 280n

Recherche Bay (Tasmania): 201

Redouté, Pierre-Joseph (1759–1840), artist: 42, 304n

Republican calendar: 2, 48, 289n

Restoration, Bourbon (1814/1815–1830): 8, 64, 66, 69, 300n, 304n

Rhine, river: 70

Richard, Louis-Claude-Marie (1754–1821), botanist: 69

Riedlé, Anselme (1768–1801), German gardener: *70*, 78, 135–36, 191, 249; death, 26, 115, 194–95, 286n, 301n

Rio de Janeiro (Brazil): 64, 285n

Rivière du Rempart (Mauritius): 102

Roaring Forties, winds: 22

Robespierre, Maximilien-Marie-Isidore de (1758–1794), lawyer: 20

Roche, Monsieur: 271

Rochefort (France): 66

Ronsard, François-Michel (1769–1836), naval officer: 71, 143–44, 152, 153, 212, 292n; duel with Le Bas de Sainte-Croix, 26, 67

Rosily-Mesros, François Étienne de (1748–1832), naval officer: 295n

Roti (Indonesia): 160, 171, 173, 188

Rottnest Island (Western Australia): 26, 148, 191
Round Island (Mauritius): 102
Rousseau, Jean-Jacques (1712–1778), Genevan philosopher: 39
Royal Society, London: 255, 272, 281n, 300n
Royan (France): 1, 3, 47
Rumphius, Georg Eberhard (1627–1702), German botanist: 291n
Rupt, fief of (France): 9, 20

Sahul Bank: 160
Saint-Allouarn, Louis-François-Marie Aleno de (1738–1772), navigator: 23, 295n
Saint-Cricq, Jacques de (1781–1819), naval officer: 29, 71, 133, 134, 197
Saint-Domingue, *now known as* Haiti: 68, 304n
Sainte-Geneviève (USA): 287n
Saint-Jean-de-Vaux (France): 10
Saint-Léger-sur-Dheune (France): 6
Saint-Nazaire (France): 261, 263
Saint-Vallerin (France): 13
Saint Vincent (Antilles): 301n
Saint-Vincent, parish of, Chalon-sur-Saône: 9, 13
Salle, Gadifer de la (*fl. c.* 1340–1415), adventurer: 282n
Salutation Island (Western Australia): 45
Santa Cruz de Tenerife (Canary Islands): 24, 84–96, 123, 281n
Saône, river (France): 12, 15, 18
Saône-et-Loire, department of: 17, 245, 260, 275n
Satory (France): 69
Saussure, Horace Bénédicte de (1740–1799), Swiss physicist: 115, 286n
Sautier, Antoine (?–1801), assistant gardener: 301n
Savigny-en-Revermont (France): 9
Savu (Indonesia): 158, 161, 171, 188, 191
Seabird (Western Australia): 45
Seine, river (France): 99, 279n

Semarang (Java): 28, 261
Semau (Indonesia): 155, 156, 158, 188, 199
Serpent Island (Mauritius): 102
Seven Years' War (1756–1763): 280n, 286n
Seychelles: 106
Shark Bay (Western Australia): 23, 26, 28, 35 45, 48, 133, 148–52, 191, 291n, 292n
Sherardian Herbarium, Oxford: 291n
Silva, Hendrik de: 191
Sister Islands (Tasmania): 297n
Slavery: Alexandre Baudin's slave plantation in New Orleans, 287n; Bernardin de Saint-Pierre on, 104, 283n; Bognam-nonen-derega's experience of, 68–69; Hamelin and slave ships, 66; on the Isle of France, 21, 104–105, 111–12, 283n, 286n; in Kupang and environs, 40, 158–63, 165–68, 173, 189–91; on Roti, 173; in west Africa, 37, 232
Smith, Sir James Edward (1759–1828), English botanist: 202, 255, 290n, 300n
Société d'agriculture (Society of Agriculture), Paris: 70, 281n
Société des observateurs de l'homme (Society of the Observers of Man), Paris: 37
Société linnéenne de Paris (Linnaean Society of Paris): 281n
Solander, Daniel Carlsson (1733–1782), Swedish botanist: 255, 281n, 300n
Solor (Indonesia): 158, 173, 186, 188
Sonnerat, Pierre (1748–1814), naturalist: 299n
South Africa: 294n, 300n
South America: 44, 304n
South Cape (Tasmania): 200, 217
Southern Lands: 22, 23, 64
South Seas: 38, 96, 201
Spain: 69, 91, 94, 282n
Spanish Louisiana: 287n
Spanish-Portuguese War (1762–1763): 280n

Spencer Gulf (South Australia): 27
Streets: Chalon Street, Seabird, 45; rue Copeau, Paris, 245; rue des Cornillons, Chalon-sur-Saône, 260; Grande-Rue, Chalon-sur-Saône, 11, 13; rue Leschenault de la Tour, Chalon-sur-Saône, 44; rue Neuve Saint-Augustin, Paris, 267, 271; rue Saint-Thomas du Louvre, Paris, 252
Sumatra (Indonesia): 66
Sumba (Indonesia): 171
Surinam: 8
Surville, Jean-François-Marie de (1717–1770), navigator: 23
Swan Island (Tasmania): 221
Swan River (Western Australia): 148
Sydney (New South Wales): 2, 5, 22, 26–27, 30, 33, 36, 39–40, 217, 241, 251, 259, 260, 296n, 297n, 301n; letter describing, 253–58; *see also* Port Jackson
Sydney Cove, ship: 222, 297n

Tahiti: 21, 39, 195, 295n, 299n
Tamatave, Battle of (1811): 71
Tarbes (France): 4
Tasman, Abel (1603–1659), Dutch navigator: 22
Tasso, Torquato (1544–1595), Italian poet: 284n
Tenerife (Canary Islands): 4, 24–25, 34, 37–38, 80, 83, 97, 98, 100, 115, 121, 124, 125, 132, 195, 253, 281n, 285n, 287n; stay on, 84–96
Tenggar mountains (Java): 270
Terra australis incognita: 22–23
Terror (1793–1794): *see* French Revolution
Theseus, ship of the line: 281n
Thétis, frigate: 64
Third Carnatic War (1756–1763): 285n
Thomson, James (1700–1748), Scottish poet: 304n
Thouin, André (1747–1824), botanist: 41, 69, 268, 278n, 302n

Thunberg, Carl Peter (1743–1828), Swedish naturalist: 185, 294n
Tielman, Hendrik, civil captain of Kupang: 166, 170, 176, 189, 190, 191
Timor: 3, 4, 12, 26, 28, 30, 32, 34, 37, 43, 64, 66, 67, 68, 69, 70, 71, 114, 148, 151, 152, 219, 251, 253, 261, 270, 286n, 293–95n; stay on, 155–98; *see also* Kupang
Toamasina (Madagascar): 69, 298n
Tofua (Tonga): 293n, 295n
Tombeau Bay (Mauritius): 103, 284n
Tongatapu (Samoa): 298n
Tonneliers Island (Mauritius): 106
Topaze, frigate: 64
Torres Strait: 161
Toulon (France): 66, 284n
Toulouse (France): 17
Tournefort, Joseph Pitton de (1656–1708), botanist: 244, 299n
Tournelle, estate of (France): 9, 20
Toussaint Louverture, François-Dominique (1743–1803), leader of Haitian Revolution: 283n
Treaty of Alcáçovas (1479): 282n
Treaty of Amiens (1802): 299n
Tremendous, ship of the line: 284n
Trianon Palace, Versailles: 69
Tropic of Cancer: 97, 99
Tunisia: 288n, 302n
Turgot, Étienne-François, marquis de Soumont (1721–1789), colonial administrator: 287n
Turner, Dawson (1775–1858), English botanist: 268, 269, 302n
Tutuila (American Samoa): 295n

United States of America: 4, 63, 67, 68, 69, 81, 231, 241, 261, 262, 279n, 289n, 301n, 303n
Universities: Amsterdam, 303n; Caen, 303n; Glasgow, 302n; Montpellier, 281n, 299n; Oxford, 291n; Pennsylvania, 301n; Uppsala, 300n
Uranie, corvette: 65
Ushant (France): 293n

Valmont de Bomare, Jacques-Christophe (1731–1807), naturalist: 157, 184, 293n, 294n
Vancouver, George (1757–1798), English navigator: 136, 289n
Van Diemen's Land: 4, 22, 23, 25, 26, 27, 30, 42, 199–219, 222, 229, 230, 287n, 296n, 300n, 301n
Vanikoro (Solomon Islands): 288n, 295n
Vannes (France): 285n
Vasse, Timothée-Thomas-Joseph-Ambroise (1774 – c. 1801), sailor: 71, 146
Vasse-Wonnerup Estuary (Western Australia): 39, 290n
Vendée, War in the (1793–1796): see French Revolution
Venezuela: 92
Vénus, frigate: 66
Versailles (France): 69
Victor Hugues, Jean-Baptiste (1762–1826), colonial administrator: 283n
Vidonia wine: 92, 281n
Violet, André, surveyor: 19
Virginie, frigate: 157–58, 293n
Vivant, Dominique, Baron Denon (1747–1825), *known as* Vivant-Denon, director of the Musée Napoléon (Louvre Museum): 12

Vlamingh, Willem de (1640–c. 1698), Dutch navigator: 291n

Wanjon, Timotheus (*fl.* 1789–1797), commander of Dutch Timor, son-in-law of Willem Adriaan van Este: 293n
Wardandi people: 71; *see also* Noongar people
War of 1812 (1812–1815): 301n
Waterhouse Island (Tasmania): 222, 229
Wentz, Gabriel, civil lieutenant of Kupang: 156, 191
Western Australia: 44, 45
Western Island: *see* Phillip Island
Western Port (Victoria): 26, 35, 39, 40, 223–30, 254, 298n, 301n
West Indies: 67, 280n, 293n, 301n; voyage of *Belle Angélique* to, 4, 21, 29, 63–64, 68
White, John (c. 1756–1832), Irish surgeon: 290n
White Bear Inn, London: 271
Willem's River (Western Australia): 152, 292n
Wilmington (USA): 301n

Yangnan, Tion: 191

Zakavolo (*fl.* 1791–1803), Madagascan ruler: 298n

www.ingramcontent.com/pod-product-compliance
Lightning Source LLC
Chambersburg PA
CBHW031420150426
43191CB00006B/335